Soldiers

Soldiers
A History of Men in Battle

JOHN KEEGAN and
RICHARD HOLMES

with John Gau

FOREWORD BY FREDERICK FORSYTH

KONECKY&KONECKY

Konecky & Konecky
150 Fifth Ave.
New York, NY 10011

Reprinted by arrangement with Viking Penguin, a division of Penguin Books USA, Inc.

ISBN: 1-56852-110-3

Printed in the United States of America by RR Donnelley & Sons.

Foreword

A strange thing, war. With its bloodshed and cruelty, its pain, grief and tears, it ought to fill every civilized person with the utmost and unwavering revulsion. It ought to and often does. And yet, and yet . . .

Yet there is a strange and timeless fascination about warfare and the warrior that has exercised minds and emotions since time began. Entire libraries could be filled only by books written about it; warehouses crammed with films of its depiction; archives stuffed with the talks and lectures given about it. Hardly an evening goes by but warfare is not evoked in fictional or documentary terms on television screens.

Limitless sums are expended and always have been to wage it, seek to avert it or prepare for it. Warrior civilizations have destroyed empires and created their own on the basis of it. Students have studied it, demagogues extolled it, pacifists denounced it and soldiers, willing or unwilling, taken part in it. Entire institutes have been and still are today founded and funded to probe it, dissect it and describe it. All this would not and could not have been possible but for one simple and no doubt deplorable fact – it interests us. The process of human beings making war against each other simply fascinates other human beings, and that includes *us*.

Exactly why it does must be a matter for moralists and philosophers, and none over the centuries has really come up with the ultimate answer. We know only that we do applaud our victorious fighters, we do thrill to a marching band, and we do pay authors and film-makers to describe for us or show us acts of warfare. There must be something deep inside the human psyche that lusts for and thrills to the clash of arms while enabling itself to blot out the shrieks of the maimed and dying – though the intimacy and immediacy of television may be changing that. However, a moral tract or even an explanation of the 'why' of warfare this book is thankfully not.

The 'when' of warfare is a simpler matter, an affair of historical study, and this is only touched upon in this book to explain and clarify.

It is the 'how' of warfare that concerns us here and makes this book a new addition to our understanding. Although originally devised to accompany a television series of the same name, *Soldiers* stands as a remarkable book in its own right.

In these pages the authors have undertaken to explain how warfare has been and is conducted. They have avoided the straight chronological approach, for under this method the great bulk of the work must have described warfare before the present age; wisely they have chosen to describe in sequence each arm of warfare and how these arms have developed down the years.

So here we meet the infantryman, from the great empires of the ancient world to the Roman legionary tramping with sword, shield and spear, pack and bedroll, complaints and blisters, along the dusty roads of Europe; we follow him down the centuries to the oh-so-similar Marine trudging across the bleak moors of the Falklands with his rifle and rain-cape, his blisters and his identical complaints about the sergeant, the food and the asterisking weather.

In other chapters we see far more dramatic changes, as technology caused not simply alterations of pace or style but complete transformations in all warfare. In these pages we can comprehend how the first horsemen, sweeping out of the East, became the cavalry that dominated the field until the musket hurled them back and the machine-gun finished them off. We see the arrival and the development of the tank; at first unreliable, then invincible and finally so vulnerable.

We come here to understand how the engineers make warfare possible and are locked in eternal rivalry, some charged to create the defensive fortifications, their opponents to sap and blast those redoubts away and open the road for their colleagues to sweep through.

There are the gunners, from the first powder-blackened servants of the bombards to men able to lay down such a carpet of explosive and terror that nothing could stand against them. We follow the appearance and progress of the irregulars from those three hundred who ran into the sleeping camp of the Midianites screaming 'For the sword of the Lord and of Gideon' to the SAS slipping unseen far behind the lines to wreck and sabotage the supply lines.

With the chapter on 'Air Power' there is yet another flick of the kaleidoscope and that which was invincible last year becomes as putty under the hammer of bomb and rocket delivered from the sky.

Further chapters show us how Man has handled the casualties of war – the prisoner, the wounded and the dead – from the savage penalties paid by these unfortunates until so recently to rights enshrined in the Geneva Convention. In 'Commander' are described those men who have to command armies; what they do, how they do it and sometimes what they think as they do what has to be done. In 'Sinews of War' is shown the huge administrative operation without which an army cannot move, feed or fight. 'Fighting Spirit' describes how, down the years, young men have been taken from civilian life and, by the inculcation of a sense of discipline, drill, uniformity, obedience and *esprit de corps*, transformed into fighting men.

If *Soldiers* were simply narrative it would be interesting but unremarkable. It is more; it is explanatory. Not only are the great technological, tactical and strategic innovations described to us as they appear in history, but what they did and the effect they had is explained so lucidly that what was once, to us who are not military historians, well known as fact but puzzling in origin becomes at once clear.

We learn in the clearest terms just how it was that the English longbow dominated European warfare. We see just why the musket – heavy, cumbersome, slow and ugly – nevertheless brought to an end centuries of feudal chivalry and the Middle Ages; fired in volley it could blow away the flower of chivalry, the knight-in-armour, and thus end the apparently endless domination of war and society by the man-on-the-horse.

And why were the casualties in the American Civil War so horrendously high? Here we learn why; the generals on both sides were simply fighting the wars of fifty years earlier, using the tactics of the age of the smooth-bore musket in a war in which most soldiers carried rifled weapons.

But, if they were to blame, how much more the generals of the First World War! *Soldiers* explains just why the fields of Flanders became a charnel house for millions of young men. Three technical inventions: the barbed wire entanglement, the huge howitzers whose shells could slaughter not only men but terrain itself, turning green meadows into impassable quagmires, and the magazine-fed rifle, which, along with the even more deadly machine-gun, could decuple a company's firepower – all had joined to make mass infantry charges suicidal. And yet that was exactly the tactic the generals on both sides used for four long years – massed charges of infantry over open ground, so that Flanders became the scene of the most horrific battlefield slaughter. It was an exercise in obscurantism and blindness to make the mind numb.

No potential reader should think *Soldiers* is another glorification-of-war book, even with a serious slant to it. The chapter on casualties shows that other face of war, the face that hides behind the victory parades, the glories and the triumphs, the exultations, the camaraderie, the courage, the heroism and the cheering. It is the face of pain, tears, grief, despair and death.

When we were filming the television sequences for that chapter in the TV series, we walked through those cemeteries in northern France and southern Belgium where lie in ranks, mile upon mile, the young Germans, French, British, Canadians, Australians, New Zealanders and Americans of World War I. There was an awful silence there; seven decades later no birds sang.

At Tyne Cot we saw nearly forty-seven thousand names enclosed in this one single plot. Almost thirty-five thousand carved on the walls, men who died but whose bodies were never recovered for burial; nearly twelve thousand headstones, some with names and units, many here, as elsewhere, bearing only the words 'A Soldier of the Great War: Known unto God.'

At the Washington Vietnam memorial it was the same; names, tens of thousands of names. Each a young man, and they stretch through every nation in the world. One cannot look upon all these names and not experience a sense of frisson that, despite it all, the subject of warfare should still hold this strange fascination.

This then for the history and the wounded and the dead. What of the living survivors of it all?

Perhaps the most extraordinary chapter deals with that dimension that cannot be measured in space or time but only within the human mind. In 'Experience of War' men who have been there and come back describe the journey and what it did to them. Men who have not gone into battle, risking their lives to cause another man to lose his, can never wholly understand what it is like; and men who have gone are never quite the same again.

War changes men and it changes Man; it alters our world and our history, our political systems, our social attitudes, our perceptions and our moralities. By showing how men go into it, pass through it and emerge from it, *Soldiers* tells us something we need to know.

Frederick Forsyth
London, May 1985

Acknowledgements

The illustrations are reproduced by kind permission of the following: By Gracious Permission of Her Majesty the Queen, page 99; Alte Pinakothek, Munich/Bridgeman Art Library, page 100; Associated Press, pages 160, 197, 237 (bottom), 247 (bottom), 253, 275; Kunstsammlung Basel, page 62; BBC Hulton Picture Library, pages 21, 25, 33, 40, 58, 59, 64, 78 (top), 81 (bottom), 84, 86, 87, 92, 111, 158 (top), 167, 172, 184, 208, 210 (top & middle), 215, 222, 228 (top), 232 (top), 245; Bell Helicopters/MARS, Lincs., page 191; Print Room, Berlin-Dahlem, page 254; Bibliothèque Nationale, page 85; British Aerospace/MARS, Lincs., page 194; British Library, page 20; British Museum, page 78 (bottom); British Tourist Authority, pages 45, 169; Bundesarchiv/Robert Hunt Library, pages 43, 179 (bottom); Canadian War Museum, National Museum of Man, National Museums of Canada, page 116; Cornell Capa/John Hillelson Agency, page 193; Robert Capa/John Hillelson Agency, page 269 (bottom); Cliché Musées Nationaux/Robert Harding Associates, page 173; Commonwealth Graves Commission, page 161; Dept. of Defense/MARS, Lincs., page 195; Druène Collection, Paris, page 44; Ermine Street Guard, page 60; Mary Evans Picture Library, pages 55, 209, 210 (bottom); Fairchild Corp./MARS, Lincs., page 196; the Fotomas Index, pages 28, 65, 68 (top), 213, 228 (bottom), 243, 272 (top); The Hague, page 226; Historical Research Unit, pages 49, 74, 237 (top); Hughes Helicopters/MARS, Lincs., page 140; Robert Hunt Library, pages 36 (bottom), 37, 68 (bottom), 96, 128, 142 (top), 143, 177, 179 (top), 188 (bottom), 199, 202, 205, 218, 220, 260, 263, 264, 265, 266, 272 (bottom), 274 (top); Imperial War Museum, pages 51, 71, 72, 73, 76 (bottom), 95 (bottom), 120, 121, 123, 124, 125, 127, 131, 133, 135, 136, 142 (bottom), 150, 151, 156, 189, 203, 234, 235, 238, 250, 255, 269 (top); Imperial War Museum/Robert Hunt Library, pages 34, 36 (top), 93, 162 (right), 181, 268; Israeli Press Office, page 164; Leeds City Art Gallery/Bridgeman Art Library, page 89; Lockheed California/MARS, Lincs., page 188 (top); Don McCullin/John Hillelson Agency, page 76 (top); His Grace the Duke of Marlborough, page 225; Military Archive & Research Services, page 117; Musée des Deux Guerres Mondiales, Paris, page 233; National Army Museum, London, pages 54, 109, 110, 112, 148, 212 (bottom); National Gallery, London, page 88; National Gallery of Canada, Ottawa, page 212 (top); Novosti Press Agency, pages 95 (top), 158 (bottom); The Photo Source, pages 50, 152, 162 (left), 239, 246, 247, (top), 248, 249, 252; Popperfoto, page 154; Regimental Headquarters, The Queen's Regiment, page 48; R.A.F. Museum, Hendon, pages 185, 187; R.A.M.C. Historical Museum, pages 144, 145; Sir John Soane Museum/Robert Harding Associates, page 168; Print Room,-Strasbourg, page 67; Topham, pages 138, 139; Ullstein Bilderdienst, pages 32, 70; USAF/MARS, Lincs., page 192; US Army/MARS, Lincs., page 153; US Marine Corps/MARS, Lincs., page 240; Martin von Wagner-Museum der Universität Würzburg, page 81 (top).

The publishers also wish to thank The National Trust for Places of Historic Interest or Natural Beauty and Methuen & Co. for permission to quote from Rudyard Kipling, and Chatto & Windus for permission to quote from Wilfred Owen.

Contents

Foreword   *5*

Acknowledgements   *8*

Introduction   *11*

1 The Face of Battle   *19*

2 Fighting Spirit   *39*

3 Infantry   *57*

4 Cavalry   *77*

5 Gunner   *97*

6 Tank   *119*

7 Casualty   *141*

8 Sapper   *163*

9 Air Power   *183*

10 Commander   *205*

11 Sinews of War   *221*

12 Irregular   *241*

13 Experience of War   *259*

Conclusion   *277*

Index   *284*

Introduction

Soldiers are warriors who fight for pay and, as such, are comparative latecomers to the field of human conflict. The warrior may be as old as human society itself, born of its need to protect family, territory and possessions against the greed and envy of neighbours. This book, a companion to the BBC's major television series *Soldiers,* is an attempt to trace how warriors became soldiers, and how that social process has helped to shape the character of the world in which we live.

When it was that men first learnt to turn their tools and weapons of the chase against each other we cannot now guess. Warfare of an endemic sort is a feature of tribal relations among the most primitive peoples surviving into our own age. But the purpose of such warfare is obscure and its conduct marked by little loss of life. About five thousand years ago, however, in those fertile areas of the world where men were simultaneously learning to fashion their implements from metal, to communicate in written symbols and to farm their land by co-operative effort, the nature of warfare underwent a functional change. Uniformly armed bodies of men obeying a common leadership came into being and began to fight in an organized and purposive manner.

These earliest warrior types were foot soldiers – infantrymen, as we would call them today – armed with clubs, spears and daggers, but also with close-range missile weapons, javelins, slings and the short bow. It was with such weapons that the peasant and city militias of early Egypt, Sumeria and Assyria protected and extended their irrigated lands. Such armies were temporary, however, called together only when need arose, and narrow in their campaigning range, since means neither of transport nor supply were well enough developed to permit extensive expeditions of conquest.

About 2000 B.C., however, warfare underwent a second revolution, as important as and more dramatic than the metallurgical revolution which had given man effective weapons. Somewhere on the southern fringes of the great steppe of Central Asia the horse was tamed for domestic use. Initially the driven horse – it was not yet robust enough to be ridden – fulfilled a merely auxiliary military role. But intense technological experimentation provided its masters, at some time around 1700 B.C., with the chariot. Light enough to be drawn across country, strong enough to withstand the stress and strain of a charge over rough ground, and stable enough to allow its passenger to handle missile weapons from its platform, it empowered its owner with almost irresistible force against pedestrian opponents. Charioteers literally carried all before them, so that soon after 1700 B.C. they had established 'chariot empires' around the whole temperate periphery of the steppe heartland – in the Nile Valley, Mesopotamia, Persia, northern India, northern China and Western Europe.

But the chariot empires were to prove short-lived. The technology on which they were based consumed too large a proportion of the rare metals and skills available for their warrior classes to be anything but an aristocratic minority imposed on the subordinate populations they ruled. The dissemination of iron tools and weapons, which became available in abundance about 1000 B.C., returned military power to the peasantry and townspeople of the world's fertile regions. Out of the warrior masses that this iron revolution brought into being the traditional agricultural empires – in Egypt, Assyria and China – were restored. At first their military strength rested on the armies of foot soldiers that they deployed. But about 900 B.C. a new sort of warrior made his appearance. He was a man who derived his power from a fourth military revolution, that of the adaptation of the horse to riding.

Selective breeding from chosen stallions out of prized mares probably underlay this 'cavalry revolution'. But the first ridden horses, bred by the nomad peoples of the steppe, were still not strong enough in the back to endow their rider with the capacity for shock action that would make them masters of the battlefield. The steppe pony, though it would carry its master on a thousand raiding expeditions into the civilized world from 600 B.C. to 1500 A.D., was essentially no more than a mobile platform for the archery at which the nomad peoples became so adept. Of far wider military significance was the appearance of the 'great horse' which the warriors of the Persian empire developed from 600 B.C. onwards. Large and strong enough to bear an armoured man in the line of battle, its strength underpinned the power of the Persian empire throughout its heyday, endowed Alexander the Great and his Companions with the means by which they conquered the Persian emperor's dominions, and assured the empire's survival in its long years of struggle against Rome.

The great horse and his armoured rider would dominate wide sectors of the civilized world until the application of effective firearms to warfare in the sixteenth century A.D. Between them they helped to preserve the Byzantine half of the Roman empire into the fifteenth century and to found the Christian successor states of its western regions on a secure basis. The Teutonic warriors who overran the West in the fifth century A.D. were foot soldiers in the old tradition. By the eighth century they had acquired the stirrup – instrument of a minor technical revolution in its own right – from the steppe nomads and were commonly riding to battle, armoured, on great horses. Out of that military development a whole social order was born in Western Europe, an order based on the social dominance of the peasantry by the armoured warriors who protected them. 'Feudalism' is the word historians have adopted to describe it, a word derived from the dual relationship sustained by the mounted warrior with those above and below him. From his overlord he held his land in 'feu', a contract which obliged him to come armed and mounted for war when called upon to do so. To his underlings he offered security against the depredations of other feudal warriors and defence from the attack of hostile outsiders – Vikings, Muslim invaders, steppe raiders – who sought to penetrate the boundaries of Christendom.

As Christendom waxed in strength and self-confidence, its warriors heeded the call to carry their military prowess beyond its frontiers and against the enemies whom hitherto they had always met on the defensive. In the crusading era, from the eleventh to the fourteenth centuries, Christian knights rode against the Muslim rulers of the Holy Land and the pagan Slavs of Europe's eastern boundary. During the thirteenth century the easternmost defenders of Christendom had a close call with the most formidable of the steppe nomad armies ever to threaten Europe, when Genghis Khan's horde approached its southern gateway in Hungary. Already the rulers of the largest empire the world had yet known, the Mongols might have

12

succeeded in extending its frontiers into the lands dominated by the riders of the great horse, had it not been for the death in 1241 of their king, Ogotai, at the critical moment.

Armoured horsemen and steppe nomads alike were, however, approaching the term of their power precisely at the moment when it seemed at its most extensive. Within three hundred years of the fall of the Crusader Kingdoms in Palestine and the withdrawal of the Mongols from Central Europe, a fifth military revolution brought the long dominance of the horseman in warfare to an end. Gunpowder, which allowed the warrior to substitute chemical for muscular energy in the management of his weapons, had been discovered in China in the twelfth century and, independently, in Europe in the fourteenth. By the beginning of the sixteenth century, the development of both handguns and artillery had reached a stage which robbed horse and rider of their freedom to move unchallenged about the battlefield, and returned military dominance to the infantryman.

Not only to the infantryman; it had long been a major element in the armoured horseman's control of his fellow men that his tactical prowess allowed him to build and occupy fortified strong places. Artillery brought such knights' castles crashing down by the hundred in the sixteenth century, subordinating their occupants to the will of the few dynastic rulers rich enough to own guns in quantity. In the place of these ruins, which now dotted the landscape of feudal Europe, the new rulers built frontier and civic fortresses which protected their domains against invasion and their richest urban centres against domestic rebellion.

These fortifications were the handiwork of a new breed of military engineers, who built not by rule of thumb but on mathematical principles. Geometrical calculation made their 'bastion forts' death traps for infantry to attack unsupported; when artillery joined the assault, the strength of the defences and the scientific siting of their gun positions ensured that sieges, even if successfully concluded, were long and costly. The development of a step-by-step technique of offensive siege engineering gradually empowered assaulting armies with means to overcome such fortification systems. But, extended as that development was over nearly two centuries, the overall effect of scientific fortification engineering was to consolidate the territories of the successful dynastic states and entrench the power of the monarchies that ruled them.

The spread of such fortification systems did not, however, prevent those monarchies from waging war. On the contrary; though fortifications reduced the room for manoeuvre in the border regions, their indirect enhancement of state power, particularly for the raising of revenue, allowed kings to finance armies which were bigger and better equipped than any seen in the West since the collapse of the Roman empire. Campaigns, in consequence, actually increased in duration and reach, and battles in scale and intensity, during the sixteenth and seventeenth centuries.

The principal medium of such military effort, outside the fortified zones, was supplied, as we have seen, by infantry. Gunpowder had made the infantryman sovereign in warfare, so that infantry now became, in a commonly used chess analogy, 'the Queen of the battlefield'. In the early half of the gunpowder period, pikemen continued to complement the handgunner's function. By the late seventeenth century, when the musketeer had acquired the bayonet, which made his firearm also an effective edged weapon, he took the field unsupported. Artillery was not yet mobile enough to keep pace on the field with the infantry's movements; cavalry, though effective when opposing infantry already broken by fire, and indispensable in the pursuit, was too fragile an arm to risk against massed musketry.

From the mid-sixteenth century onwards, therefore, European campaigning was dominated by the foot soldier. And, increasingly, he was the permanently employed servant of one royal master – a 'regular' soldier, armed and clothed in a uniform manner. The first such soldiers had appeared in numbers in the employ of the Spanish kings at the end of the fifteenth century. France and the Habsburg lands had been the next monarchies to establish large regular armies. By the end of the seventeenth century they were the distinctive mark of all kingdoms which aspired to great power status. The populations of regions too small, remote or poor to maintain armies of their own – Switzerland, Scotland, the Balkan borderlands – contributed to the new military labour market by furnishing mercenary regiments which were hired and maintained by the rich states on a regular basis.

The model on which the bodies of regular infantry were based was still that of the old mercenary companies of the late Middle Ages, in that the tactical unit remained the company, commanded by a Captain, with a lieutenant and sergeant-major as his principal assistants. Under the new dispensation, however, the rule or 'regiment' of a Colonel, appointed by the King, was imposed on groups of companies for administrative purposes. These regiments, about a thousand men strong, became the principal instrument through which the European states settled their religious, dynastic and political differences from the seventeenth to the nineteenth century. Clad in white by the French and Habsburg Kings, red by the English, blue by the Prussian – an important newcomer to the European military scene – their long columns, swinging forward ten or fifteen miles a day in cadenced step to the rhythm of their regimental drums and fifes, emerged each campaigning season from winter quarters to manoeuvre against each other around Europe's campaigning grounds and, when advantage promised or escape was denied, to form against each other in serried ranks and put the issue to the test of volley and bayonet charge.

The primacy of the regular infantryman was somewhat diminished by the appearance of mobile battlefield artillery at the end of the eighteenth century. In the battles of the French Revolution and Empire, such artillery was frequently pushed forward to ranges at which massed infantry suffered grievously from its fire, allowing cavalry to exploit the damage done. Resolute infantry which kept its ranks closed nevertheless remained impervious to successful attack by any save its own kind. And when drilled infantry, transported by seapower to the world beyond Europe, met armies not yet schooled to its standards of discipline, the outcome of such exchanges was even more arresting. Quite tiny armies of Europeans proved able to devastate, for example, vast hosts of soldiers deployed by the Mogul emperors of India, with results that would transform the world balance of power.

In the middle of the nineteenth century, however, the technological equilibrium which had endowed the European infantryman with his battle-winning capacity was suddenly upset. New firearms, rifled to enhance accuracy at unprecedented ranges and then furnished with a magazine to decuple firepower, rendered close-order infantry tactics not merely ineffective but dangerous and self-defeating. The character of the battles of the American Civil War, 1861–65, had issued that warning in stark terms. Those fought in Europe and in its dependencies during 1866–1913 repeated it in even more threatening form. By the end of the first decade of the twentieth century it was clear to any dispassionate observer that the era of the primacy of man in warfare was drawing to a close and that the era of the primacy of the machine was at hand.

Most professional observers were, however, not dispassionate. Despite the appearance of the machine-gun, which multiplied the firepower of an infantry regiment tenfold, of quick-firing artillery, which made mass tactics suicidal, and of the aeroplane, which immediately extended an army's daily scouting range beyond that which cavalry could reach in a week, and promised an offensive effect of which

14

only visionaries had hitherto dreamt, the traditional military mind clung to traditional military methods. Cavalrymen, recruited from descendants of or aspirants to the old feudal class, continued to insist that the mounted warrior was ultimately the deciding instrument of battle. Infantrymen argued that mass tactics provided the most rapid, and therefore the best, means of bringing issues in combat to a conclusion. Even gunners, whom their new weapons, if employed from a distance, endowed with battle-winning power, sought opportunities to engage the enemy at point-blank range, where their gun crews and teams were exposed to disabling counter-fire. In the teeth of a technological revolution, as it were, Europe's professional soldiers sought to wage future war by the methods of the past rather than of the age to come.

They, and those who obeyed their orders, were to pay a terrible price for this obscurantism. When war enfolded Europe in its grasp in August 1914, the huge regular armies of the combatant states – France, Germany, Russia and Austria each fielded armies several million strong and Britain promised to do so – beat each other into bloody immobility within three months of the outbreak. Overnight the military engineer, expert in the design and construction of fortified positions, resumed the place of importance he had held in his heyday; traditional fortresses had been overwhelmed in the opening moves of the war, but field entrenchments on a scale never before seen had appeared on all fronts and were to determine the nature of the fighting across them. The gunner, too, found his role enormously enhanced. The artilleries of all the armies began a vast expansion, particularly with howitzers of heavy calibres. Within two years of the war's outbreak, it would be common practice to prepare infantry attacks with bombardments that consumed a million shells in a few days of fighting.

Yet neither field engineering nor large-scale gunnery sufficed to solve the problem of the First World War; the former could not fully protect defending infantry from the latter, which in turn generally failed to break a way through for the attacker. Two years of heartbreaking trench fighting established those facts beyond doubt. New means and methods were needed to open the front. In the third year of the war they appeared, when the British army unveiled the tank and committed it to action with infantry trained to exploit the effect it created.

From the outset, the tank aroused the strongest loyalties among tank men and excited revolutionary ideas about how it should be employed. Twice during the First World War, at Cambrai in 1917 and Amiens in 1918, sufficient numbers of tanks were made available for a mass armoured breakthrough to be essayed. In neither case was it wholly successful. The machine itself had not yet reached the stage of development at which it could achieve what was hoped for it. By 1939, however, its technical imperfections had been overcome and the German army in particular had reorganized its order of battle and rewritten its fighting doctrine to profit fully from the tank's potentiality. The resulting strategy, to be hailed as 'Blitzkrieg' – lightning war – brought the Germans a whirlwind triumph in the West in 1940 and the Russian army to its knees in 1941. The machine age in warfare did indeed seem to promise victory almost without cost to the attacker who made the right technical choice and backed his judgement with deeds.

The Germans reinforced their success on land with a brilliant and convergent effort from the air. The aeroplane had played a minor role in the First World War as an observation platform, protected by specialized fighting machines which occasionally flew ground attack missions in the later trench offensives. By 1939 the German air force was equipped with three thousand fighters and bombers of advanced performance, all designed to support the army's tank units in offensive operations. Additionally, it deployed a large force of tactical transport aircraft, some dedicated to fly and drop its newly raised units of parachute assault infantry behind enemy lines. These parachutists, supplemented by glider-borne infantry, were to intervene in the 1940 campaign with spectacular effect against strongpoints in Belgium and Holland.

Tanks, tactical aircraft, self-propelled artillery, motorized infantry; these elements of machine-age warfare were to invest its operations with the rapidity and reach not seen since the irruptions of Genghis Khan in the thirteenth century. And while the steppe horsemen merely slew and plundered, the behemoth armies of Blitzkrieg crushed all opposition they encountered, devastating the countryside over which they passed and laying waste the towns and cities that stood in their path. For the opening years of the Second World War, it seemed that armies organized on the Blitzkrieg principle were unstoppable and invincible, and that a total German victory was inevitable.

But the pendulum swing of technical riposte then came into play. During the two years in which Germany's tank and air forces had rampaged across the battlefields, the governments and industries of its surviving opponents had bent all efforts to replicating the armouries and organizations deployed against them. By 1942 Russia and Britain had raised large armoured and tactical air forces of their own, to which were then joined those furnished by the mighty and swelling industrial power of the United States. By 1943, the military balance of force in the world stood in equilibrium. Rapidly thereafter it swung the way of Germany's enemies, whose output exceeded hers some six times. By 1945 British, American and Russian tank armies had broached her frontiers and stood on her soil, while her cities and industry crumbled under the weight of their strategic air attack. Germany, the inventor of Blitzkrieg, had in her turn been blitzkrieged, and, through the iron laws of attrition that the technique had been supposed to evade, reduced to humiliating and agonized defeat.

Warfare had proved too crude and brutal a medium of human relationship to be revolutionized by mere technical ingenuity. Yet that did not mean that, in the post-war world, the search would not continue for military success without proportionate military outlay. The renaissance of irregular forces had been a noted feature of the Second World War – commandos, parachutists, long-range penetration units, subversive teams, guerrilla liaison units. The Western allies had suffused German-occupied Europe with irregulars of all sorts, while the Soviet Union had maintained large partisan units in the German rear in Russia. Both had encouraged and sustained guerrilla forces inside areas they could not immediately reach with their own regular units, as the British and Americans had also done in Japanese-occupied Asia. The rise of nationalist guerrilla movements in the remnants of the European colonial empires after 1945 – in Palestine, Indo-China, Malaysia, Algeria, Arabia, Southern Africa – prompted the states which had, as they believed, acquired expertise in irregular warfare against the Germans to mobilize the same technique against these revolutionary nationalists.

The impulse to fight fire with fire was almost uniformly unsuccessful. The British Special Air Service achieved limited dominance over the weak Malayan guerrillas in remote areas, later to be repeated against Indonesian infiltrators in Borneo. The French founded and ran anti-nationalist guerrilla groups in Algeria and Indo-China, in the latter territory later to be reformed by the Americans. The Rhodesian army conducted deep penetration operations against African guerrilla bases lying beyond the country's borders. But all, with allowance for some British success, eventually failed in staving off the inevitable. Elite forces, however dedicated and well-trained, lack the capacity to defeat guerrillas fighting on their own ground with the support, however obtained and sustained, of the local population.

16

That is not to say that guerrilla warfare is what Clausewitz would have called 'a stronger form' than conventional war. On the contrary; despite much political propaganda and ill-informed journalism lauding the cunning and skill of guerrilla fighters in the 'wars of national liberation' which have been so widely fought since 1945, they have had success only when heavily supported by conventional forces, or when established authority was ripe for defeat, and then always through methods that inflicted appalling hardship and suffering on the civilian population caught between the millstones of rebellion and repression.

Hardship and suffering are inseparable from the human experience of war; it is, indeed, war's purpose that humanity should suffer, to the point when one side is unwilling or unable to sustain the strain. That strain is frequently offset by material and spiritual alleviations. War generates a sense of unity, of pride, of identity, of excitement. Its material demands often generate prosperity, at least in the short term, by mobilizing the resources of the combatants to the full, by stimulating state expenditure and by absorbing labour previously unemployed. But, in wars fought to a decisive conclusion, costs almost always outweigh benefits, and such costs are measured in death, wounds and profound personal suffering.

Families and localities experience such suffering through the loss of those who do not return from the fighting. Soldiers experience that suffering directly. The fear of death is the soldier's universal lot. So, too, is the fear of wounding, which, for soldiers of the 'teeth arms', is all too often realized; in the British infantry of the First World War, four out of every nine soldiers who reached the front became casualties. How he may be wounded and how he will be treated have, therefore, always preoccupied the soldier, for whom the quality of his army's medical service has consequently been as important as that of his weapons or of his leadership. In some of the earliest military contracts that have come down to us, sworn between Greek mercenaries of the third century B.C. and their employers, the provision of adequate medical care ranked among the principal terms.

Yet medical care, almost until our own century, could not be adequate. Surgery, advances in which were always stimulated by warfare, could repair simple, clean wounds. But battle wounds are frequently deep and complex and easily infected by contact with clothing and the soil; gangrene, for example, a common outcome of wounds suffered in the First World War, is the consequence of falling with an open wound on to tilled ground that has been fertilized with animal manure. Fatalities in a unit that had been in action were therefore often higher on the days following a battle than on the day of fighting itself, as those who had suffered wounds not immediately fatal succumbed to their after-effects. Not until disinfectants came into common use after 1850 did this pattern begin to reverse itself; while the real improvement in the prognosis of wound treatment had to await the introduction of antibiotics, blood transfusion and intensive resuscitation during the Second World War. And by then refinements in the nature of wounding agents, particularly those producing intense blast, burn and high fragmentation effect, were causing wounds graver than any with which military medical services had yet had to deal. 'A Blighty One' – the sort of simple, disabling wound which soldiers of the First World War had welcomed as an honourable passport off the battlefield – was becoming ever more elusive.

How does the soldier, beset by the danger of death, fear of wounds and the greatly increased risk of succumbing to disease which membership of an army has entailed for most of military history, sustain his will to combat? Fighting spirit is the mood a commander strives most earnestly to generate and sustain in his army. Proper concern for his troops' welfare, by provision of good and regular food, pay and comforts – what are called the 'sinews of war' – is one means to it. Exhortation is another; many great commanders have been noted orators, skilled in appealing to the pride, patriotism and loyalty of their men and calculating, too, in their promises of fame and material reward. Punishment, of course, always threatens the soldier who will not yield to such appeals; 'pay well, command well, hang well' was Sir Ralph Hopton's summary of the seventeenth-century general's art and hangmen or their equivalents have found their place in all the armies of history.

But no general can afford to hang too extravagantly in the face of disobedience or cowardice; that will transform a bad army into a mutinous one. The wise general seeks, on the contrary, to make his men obey not because he makes them but because they so wish. And the most effective means of attaining that state of consent is by fostering among them bonds of loyalty and regard for each other too strong for the strains of battle to break. 'Small group cohesion' is what modern armies call this relationship. Whatever it is called, it has existed in good armies since the beginning of time. The hoplites of the Greek city-state militias took their place in the phalanx at the side of neighbours whose good opinion counted more strongly with them than fear of the enemy. The Roman legions made their smallest tactical unit the tentful of men who messed together throughout their service. In the mediaeval 'lance', neither knight, squire nor servant could flinch before the enemy without being damned for good in the eyes of the others. Regular armies made the platoon or company the unit of both of comradeship and firepower. And in the great conscript armies of our century, drafts of reservists have been trained together from the start of their service to foster that comradeship between them they will need to see them through the fires of combat.

This 'buddy system', based, in the words of the American military theorist S. L. A. Marshall, on a man's fear of losing 'what he holds more dear than life itself, his reputation as a man among other men', seems ultimately to be what armours the individual against the terrible experience of war. It is felt most strongly by those soldiers whose duty brings them closest to the point of danger – the infantryman, the cavalryman, in our own age the tank man. It sustains the gunner, the engineer, the airman when their missions bring them within the orbit of the enemy's firepower. It motivates the humbler servants of the fighting soldier, who work the sinews of war, and are often as much in danger as those at the front. It is life blood to the irregular, whose isolation and exposure put him more permanently at risk than any other sort of soldier.

Perhaps only the commander stands outside its influence, since for him there can be no comradeship, no shared danger, no dependence upon others when risk threatens and disaster must be braved out and stared down. His is sometimes the most extreme because the loneliest of all predicaments that a soldier undergoes and his the most total obloquy should he be proved unequal to bearing it. But he is one, nevertheless, with his soldiers in undergoing a predicament. The exact nature of that experience, and of its many variants – as known by infantryman, cavalryman, tank man, gunner, sapper, aircrew, irregular – is the subject of this book.

The Face of Battle 1

It is a joyous thing, a war. You love your comrade so much in war. When you see that your quarrel is just, and your blood is fighting well, tears rise to your eyes. A great sweet feeling of loyalty and of pity fills your heart on seeing your friend so valiantly exposing his body. And then you are prepared to go and die or live with him, and for love not to abandon him. And out of that there arises such a delight, that he who has not experienced it is not fit to say what delight is. Do you think that a man who does that fears death? Not at all, for he feels so strengthened, so elated, that he does not know where he is. Truly he is afraid of nothing.

In those words – written by the knight Jean de Beuil in the fourteenth century – rings the authentic voice of the warrior, the man who lives for battle and is fulfilled and enlarged by the experience. It is not a modern voice. Modern man is terrorized by the clash of arms, is repelled by the shedding of blood and is conditioned to mistrust the emotions which sustain the warrior in combat. Or is he?

There are times when fear drops below the threshold of the mind; never beyond recall, but far enough from the instant to become a background. Moments of great exaltation, of tremendous physical exertion, when activity can dominate over all rivals in the mind, the times of exhaustion that follow these great moments; there are occasions of release from the governance of fear. As I hurried along the lane in this nightmare wood, stepping round the bodies clustered about the shell-holes, here and there helping a wounded man to clamber over a fallen tree-trunk, falling flat on my face when the whistle of an approaching shell grew into a shrieking 'YOU', aimed at my ear, to paralyse before it killed, then stumbling on again through a cloud of bitter smoke, I learned that there was another way of making fear a thing of small account.

Wyn Griffith of the Royal Welch Fusiliers, is describing the emotional response of a twentieth-century man to a form of warfare of which Jean de Beuil could have had no premonition. The face of battle known to the knight was one seen at close hand, often at arm's length, a face larger than life, stark and menacing in feature, blood-suffused, grimacing, contorted by the rictus of a war cry thrown into the teeth of the enemy. The face shown to the fusilier is veiled by smoke and distance, an impersonal face, impressing its features upon its victims by indirect and insubstantial means – noise, shock wave, psychological sensation. The mediaeval man-at-arms confronts danger in the person of a man like himself, armed and caparisoned for combat hand-to-hand. The soldier of the industrial world apprehends danger through his nerve endings, guessing at the risks he runs and sustaining his courage not by seeking to fill his enemy with a fear greater than his own – since the enemy is unseen – but by denying his own fear to himself through an act of will.

Yet, utterly different though the experience of these two soldiers was, they are

Overleaf: Foot soldier slaughtering unhorsed man-at-arms, fifteenth century

19

The unromantic side of chivalry: a fifteenth-century depiction of crusading warfare

united by a common discovery; that man may remain captain of his soul, if not master of his fate, despite the worst of all ordeals with which life can confront him. Battle is that experience. Much also in life is terrible and terrifying – fire, flood, tempest, avalanche, earthquake and plague. But in no other circumstances than the battlefield does man confront the knowledge that he is present in that place for the purpose of suffering death at the hands of fellow man, and that he must kill if he is not to be killed himself. The battlefield, in short, is a place almost without mercy and utterly without pity, where the emotions which humanity cultivates and admires elsewhere – gentleness, compassion, tolerance, amity – have neither room to operate nor place to exist.

And yet it is clear that the knight and the fusilier are not merely men of blood and iron. Warm, generous and unselfish emotions are at play within them, emotions of friendship, concern for others, loyalty, responsibility. It is not hatred for the enemy or even a blind urge to personal survival that animates either of them, but a sense of involvement in the strange masculine society that battle calls into being, and a commitment to the ends for which battle is fought.

Battle enlarges both of them, making each in a curious fashion not less but more human. Their testimony, whose mood psychologists would call 'existential', in effect describes how the perception of intense and circumambient danger, which would normally compel a human being to flight or paralyzed inactivity, actually seems to heighten energy and function, driving those who feel its effect to overcome its source not by passive surrender to their anxieties – 'taking counsel of their fears' – but by positive and physical reaction.

This extraordinary reversal of normal psychic and nervous response to danger is of the greatest possible importance in human affairs because of the central role that battle plays in warfare. Warfare is a complex activity. In a modern society it changes the direction and heightens the tempo of almost all corporate activity,

21

economic, political, social and cultural. Even in simpler societies, the onset of war will upset the rhythms and patterns of everyday existence, taking men from their homes, casting upon women responsibilities for the livelihood and management of families they do not usually bear, creating urgent demands for foodstuffs, raw materials and means of transport far beyond those normally known in times of peace. But such changes are essentially of degree rather than kind. Life goes on. It is when the organization of death confronts that society, in particular the chosen group within it which must kill or be killed, that everything is suddenly changed. Battle is an exercise in that organization, through which the future of the participating societies is decided and by which the nature of their combatant members is tested and changed, perhaps for ever.

How do the combatants bear the experience? First of all, perhaps, and certainly in the earliest age of military history, by the individual's relationship with and trust in his personal weapons. The age is one we call heroic, because its central figures were individual warriors whose personalities were expressed by the battle gear they chose and wore and the weapons they wielded against their individual enemies.

> Achilles with wild fury in his heart,
> Pulled in upon his chest his beautiful shield –
> His helmet with four burnished metal ridges
> Nodding above it, and the golden crest
> Hephaestus locked there nodding in the wind.
> Conspicuous as the evening star that comes,
> Amid the first in heaven, at fall of night,
> And stands most lovely in the west, so shone
> In sunlight that fine-pointed spear
> Achilles poised in his right hand, with deadly
> Aim at Hector, at the skin where most
> It lay exposed.

Homer's hero Achilles, about to do single combat with his enemy, Hector, outside the walls of Troy, finds his courage in the beauty of his armour and the deadliness of his weapons. For him these weapons and trappings have personalities of their own, recognized by the name, Hephaestus, he gives his helmet crest. The naming of weapons seems a universal practice among primitive peoples, and denotes to us the rarity of the material from which they were forged and the cost of the skills which went into their making. Stone Age man did not perhaps name his clubs and axes in that way. But then battle, as far as we can tell, was not a Stone Age activity. The emergence of battle as an activity is related to the abandonment of a hunting-gathering existence for one based on pastoralism or agriculture. Such an evolution requires the possession of capital goods, which will be made of metal if that material is available. Bronze, the first effective tool material, was discovered in the Near East about 3500 B.C. and seems to have been applied to weapon manufacture at the earliest possible date.

Indeed, it was natural that it should be, for its scarcity required that it be used to win the largest possible return upon its possession. And what larger return was there to be won than by fashioning it into implements which gave the individual power over others? Whether that power was wielded against fellow members of the owner's tribe or against the tribe's enemies was immaterial. Weapon ownership conferred superior status, enjoined the acquisition of the highest skill in weapon management, tended to nurture a psychic relationship between owner and object and ultimately resolved itself in the warrior endowing his prized possessions with personalities of their own; hence ultimately, such myths as that of Excalibur, King

Arthur's magic sword, which he won the right to use by finding the strength no one else possessed to pluck it from its birthstone.

Pride in rare and precious weapons and individual skill at arms remained the basis of success in battle until very late in history. The successors of the barbarians who overthrew the Roman empire – though their weapons were by then fashioned of iron – continued to depend for victory upon skill and courage in single combat almost until the end of the Middle Ages. The personal relationship between archer and his composite bow, a miracle of technology which may have appeared as early as 1500 B.C., remained a key element in the steppe horsemen's mastery of their form of warfare until even later. And it remains, of course, the case that soldiers of the present age rely heavily upon a belief in the superiority of their weapons over those of the enemy, even though arms are now issued from mass-produced stocks rather than fashioned individually by a craftsman for his warrior-customer.

But the onset of mass-produced weapons, something approaching which was made possible by the introduction of iron about 1200 B.C., confronted the champion of single combat with a threat he had not previously had to face. It was that of a body of enemies who, because they could match him both in quantity and quality of weapons, did not need to equal him in skill in order to beat him. Not, at least, if they were prepared to undergo collective training and to conform vigorously to drill and to orders during the course of action.

We hold our flat shields, we wear our jerkins of hide. The axles of our chariots touch, our short swords meet. Standards darken the sun, the foe roll on like clouds; arrows fall thick, the warriors press forward.

They have overrun our ranks, they have crossed our line; the trace-horse on the left is dead, the one on the right is wounded.

The fallen horses block our wheels, our chariot is held fast; we grasp our jade drum sticks, we beat the rolling drums.

The words are those of a Chinese warrior of the fourth century B.C., but they might have been spoken by any soldier of an organized army from the period when such bodies began to appear, in the Near East, about 1000 B.C. And the difference between this warrior's experience of battle and that of Homer's heroes is immediately apparent. Hector and Achilles fight as individuals, indeed, as the poet tells us, almost as performers under the eye of their assembled supporters. The object of each is to outwit the other in the skill with which he handles sword and shield; their encounter is certainly a duel, even a variation on a sporting contest, despite the grim and bloody outcome it will have for whoever proves the loser. There is nothing duel-like about the Chinese battle. It is a conflict of masses, armed and dressed in a uniform fashion, ordered in ranks behind banners that mark where they must take and keep station and manoeuvred against the enemy by drumbeat. Their activity is not one enhanced or furthered by individual initiative. On the contrary, success depends upon the subordination of self to the will of the group, upon obedience to orders, in short, upon discipline.

Discipline can be imposed in a variety of ways. It can be evoked through the religious duty that a worshipper owes to a god-king; perhaps it was thus that Pharaoh Thutmose III commanded his Egyptian subjects in the first recorded battle of history, Megiddo, fought in northern Palestine in 1469 B.C. It can be translated into military society through the social duty that free men owe each other as fellow citizens, as it was by the Greeks in the militias of their city-states of antiquity's golden age. It can sometimes be bought, as it was through the mercenary system to which the Greek cities resorted when the golden age was over, and as did other rich societies in later times and different places. Finally, it can be instilled by system, organization and tradition, the practice which underlay the prolonged military success of the Roman army during the rise and dominance of the Roman empire in the West in the first three centuries of our era.

The instrument of Roman conquest was the legion, which was to change little in organization from about 300 B.C. until the later empire, seven hundred years forward in time. Recruited by conscription of all free men, ranked by class, it numbered six thousand, divided into a hundred 'centuries', each under a dependable officer known as a centurion. It was an almost entirely infantry force, the 'auxiliary' troops – archers, slingers and light cavalry – operating only on the flanks or as a skirmishing screen. The weapons of the heavy infantry, who were armoured on chest and head and carried a square shield, were sword and spear. Originally the spear was used as a thrusting weapon. By the first century B.C. it had become a throwing javelin, the *pilum*, of which each legionary carried two.

The legion's battle tactics had a deadly simplicity. Before action the officers addressed the men, calling on them to display courage and, if the enemy were barbarians, stiffening their resolution with warnings of the penalties of falling into the hands of cruel, uncivilized people. The legionaries then advanced in line, threw their javelins when they had the enemy within range, and closed immediately to handstroke distance. Caesar, describing his battle in Gaul against the Nervii in 57 B.C., gives us an eyewitness account of the nature of the action.

The soldiers of the Ninth and Tenth Legions were on the left of our line, with the Atrebates facing them. They hurled their javelins and wounded many of the enemy, who were already breathless and exhausted with running, and rapidly drove them downhill into the river. My men pursued them as they tried to get across and with their swords killed great numbers of them as they struggled in the water. The legionaries did not hesitate to cross the river themselves, and, once across, they moved forward up the difficult ground. They met with resistance, the battle was renewed and they put the enemy to flight.

In fact the legionaries were to undergo a crisis, solved only by Caesar's personal intervention, before the battle was won. But its essential character, similar to that of all edged weapon warfare, is laid bare in the passage. The fight, once joined, was short, because the muscular effort it required could not be sustained for more than a few minutes. Keeping formation was essential; each man protected his neighbour, partly with his shield, partly with his sword. Should gaps open in the ranks, a local crisis might swiftly spread into general disaster. Should it do so, it was during the flight of those who broke that the heavy casualties were inflicted, as the pursuers ran down their victims with a pitiless blood-lust that seems to overtake soldiers when they themselves are suddenly released from the danger of death in close-ordered ranks. The vanquished who survived this physical experience, and the attendant '*panique terreur*', as French professional soldiers would later characterize the emotional shock, were usually quite incapacitated from further action for a considerable time afterwards.

This pattern of conflict was to be varied in only two ways until edged weapons were displaced from the battlefield by firearms sixteen hundred years after Caesar fought. The first was the degradation of discipline brought about by the collapse of Rome at the hands of the barbarians in the fifth century A.D. The second, closely connected with the first, was the resurgence of cavalry from the seventh century A.D. onwards. Against disciplined infantry, cavalry is rarely effective. The eclipse of the legions therefore greatly enhanced its importance. The appearance of the stirrup, whose use became general by the eighth century, and of light and pliable armour for the mounted warrior, then transformed it into a decisive arm. Segmented armour, as worn by the legionaries, hampered the arm and body movements a cavalryman must make if he is to use sword or spear effectively in the saddle; and it could not be fashioned to protect his legs in any way that allowed him to grip his steed. Chain mail, which appeared in the eighth century, solved these difficulties. It was pliable enough to permit its wearer to fight and, if extended as a skirted shirt, it protected his thighs against sword or lance strokes.

The 'iron people', as the Turks were to call the western cavalrymen when they began to encounter them in the eleventh century, represented a revolutionary and usually overwhelming instrument of military force. They also composed a social and economic class which, through the demands it levied on Western Europe's agriculture, commerce and artisanship, was to determine the structure of its society from the eighth to the fifteenth century. The knight was extortionately expensive to support; his horses, equipment and followers could only be financed by allotting to his maintenance a considerable land holding, which he enjoyed and administered in return for fulfilling a military obligation to his overlord. The non-military classes, unless churchmen or townspeople, were thereby reduced to a status entirely subordinate to the warriors, which progressively partook of the character of serfdom. The justification for this social counter-revolution was the unique prowess of the knights in battle against the invaders and marauders who disturbed the security and prosperity of Europe from the eighth to the thirteenth centuries – Magyars, Moslems, Vikings and Mongol nomads.

Much of the energy of the knights was, however, expended not against alien interlopers, but against each other, either in dynastic or 'private' war. Such warfare did not always or often culminate in conflict in the open field; raids and sieges were the more commonplace military transactions. But battle was, nevertheless, the purpose for which the knights trained and grew to manhood. As the twelfth-century chivalric poet Bertrand de Born put it:

I love to see a lord when he is the first to advance on horseback, armed and fearless, thus encouraging his men to valiant service; then, when the fray has begun, each must be ready to follow him willingly, because no one is held in esteem until he has given and received blows. We shall see clubs and swords, gaily coloured helmets and shields shattered and

Thirteenth-century armoured warriors at close quarters under the walls of a castle; catapult and sappers (right)

A fourteenth-century battle; the scene in the foreground may depict the 'heaps of dead' described by mediaeval chroniclers

spoiled, at the beginning of the battle, and many vassals all together receiving great blows, by reason of which many horses will wander riderless, belonging to the killed and wounded. Once he has started fighting, no noble knight thinks of anything but breaking heads and arms – better a dead man than a live one who is useless. I tell you, neither in eating, drinking nor sleeping do I find what I feel when I hear the shout 'At Them' from both sides, and the neighing of riderless horses in the confusion, or the call 'Help! Help!', or when I see great and small fall on the grass of the ditches, or when I espy dead men who still have pennoned lances in their ribs.

Bertrand de Born's poem conveys the most vivid sense of what a knightly battle was like. But from the twelfth century onwards, knightly warfare would be infiltrated by actors whose weapons, tactics and social origins lay outside the knightly canon – crossbowmen, archers and the foot soldiers of the free cities and cantons of Flanders, northern Italy and Switzerland. All would succeed to some degree in deflecting the mounted warriors from their chosen and appointed task, which indeed was 'to advance on horseback, armed and fearless' against each other. But, though knightly equipment and behaviour altered considerably over the period, as plate armour was developed to replace chain mail, as horsemen learnt to charge with their lances 'couched', and as knights became increasingly committed to a code of manners – 'chivalry' – which set the polite against the most efficient use of arms, nevertheless the war of the knights retained a remarkable consistency from the beginning to the end of the Middle Ages. The battles of Soissons in 923, of Bouvines in 1214 and of Agincourt in 1415 resembled each other in being head-on contests between knights in linear formation, some dismounted, some mounted, who won or lost the day largely by individual courage and skill-at-arms. Mass tactics and manoeuvres played some part, but a lesser one than sheer knightly prowess.

If there was one enemy against whom knightly prowess did not automatically prevail, it was the Turkic and Mongol light horsemen whom the 'iron people' met when they went as Crusaders to the Holy Land or stood to defend Christendom's eastern frontier against invasion from the steppe. The ultimate argument of the knight was the armoured charge with couched lance, against which no infantry and only the best armoured cavalry could stand. Asian light cavalry tactics denied the

26

knights the chance to deliver it except in rare circumstances, since Turks and Mongols slipped away when the knights advanced, returning when the knights' horses were blown to harry them with showers of arrows and cut them to pieces with their curved swords when their ranks dissolved. Genghis Khan, greatest of the light cavalry leaders, who succeeded in uniting a medley of nomadic tribes into a vast migratory state, made these methods invincible. He penetrated the elaborate defences of the Chinese empire, conquered much of the Middle East and Eastern Europe and left to his successors at his death in 1227 the greatest empire the world had yet known.

Overleaf: A square of Highlanders standing to receive a charge of French cuirassiers, mid-afternoon, the battle of Waterloo, 18 June 1815

But nomadic rule, though it was to exert its sway over the embryo Russian kingdom for two hundred years, was too improvised in character to prevail against the solidly organized kingdoms of the West. There feudalism and the knights held on, to fall in the end not to external attack but to a technical revolution from within. Western warfare had, in the last two hundred years of feudalism, been undergoing marked change. The foot soldiers of the towns, and of regions where cavalry could not easily operate, like Wales and Switzerland, had been gaining remarkably in self-confidence and hence tactical effectiveness since the thirteenth century. The crossbow and the longbow were each making the battlefield a more risky place even for the most headstrong armoured horsemen. But ultimately it was the introduction of handguns and artillery at the beginning of the sixteenth century that brought him low.

Artillery was, at the outset, of less battlefield importance than handguns. At the start of the gunpowder period, cavalry occasionally made the mistake, as at Ravenna in 1512, of attacking entrenched artillery positions. There the Spanish cavalry was slaughtered by the French guns. The lesson of avoiding such death rides was easily learnt. But cavalry could not avoid arquebusiers and, later, musketeers, since these infantrymen were mobile and could shift their firepower from place to place as circumstances required. And to that firepower the cavalry could oppose no answer. The arquebus or musket ball could disable a horse; worse, it infallibly penetrated even the best and most expensive plate armour. As a result the knight's *raison d'être*, his ability as an individual to ride down any footman in his path, was instantly abolished.

Two results flowed from this technical revolution. The first was the eclipse of cavalry, which would be somewhat abated at a later stage but never reversed. The other was a resurgence of infantry to an importance it had not held since the early Roman empire. Like the legions, moreover, this reborn European infantry drew its power above all from its disciplined character and mastery of battlefield drill. The Dutchman Maurice of Nassau and the Swedish King Gustavus Adolphus perfected at the turn of the sixteenth to seventeenth centuries a tactical combination of musketeers and pikemen, trained and drilled to support each other on the battlefield, against which armies less well organized could not stand.

By the end of the eighteenth century, the pikeman had disappeared from the infantry ranks, since the musketeer, furnished with a bayonet for his firearm, could perform a double role. Cavalry, rehearsed in the tactics of the massed charge delivered at a carefully calculated moment from just beyond musket range, had somewhat regained its battlefield role; it retained its importance, never lost, in the pursuit. The most significant technical development was the enhanced function of artillery, derived from improved mobility and rate of fire. Guns, by 1800, could be moved rapidly about a battlefield, stationed at points of crisis and massed to achieve a decisive tactical effect.

This perfected form of gunpowder warfare owed much to the innovations of the Prussian Frederick the Great and to Napoleon, the military genius of the French

Revolution. It was also very much the product of the regularization of European armies which, beginning in the seventeenth century, had reached its height at the end of the eighteenth and which deeply affected the character of the revolutionary armies Napoleon had led to lightning victory in Italy and Central Europe between 1796 and 1800. But by no army was it to be practised more tellingly than the British, which, under command of Wellington, achieved unmatched levels of tactical efficiency in the Peninsula and Flanders between 1809 and 1815. Wellington's greatest victory, at Waterloo, in 1815, demonstrates in detail his army's expertise.

The battle fell into five phases, of which one was dominated by artillery, one by cavalry and three by infantry. During the second phase of the battle on 18 June 1815, the British infantry defending the ridge that Wellington had chosen as his position was subjected to prolonged artillery bombardment by Napoleon's *grande batterie* some seven hundred yards distant. Many of the British battalions managed to shelter in the dead ground behind the crest of the ridge. Some could not. Their ordeal is graphically described by an officer of the 40th Regiment. 'We had three companies [out of ten] almost shot to pieces, one shot killed and wounded twenty-five of the 4th Company, another of the same kind killed poor Fisher, our captain, and eighteen of our company, and another took the 8th and killed or wounded twenty-three. At the same time poor Fisher was hit I was speaking to him, and I got all over his brains, his head was blown to atoms.'

Some regiments suffered worse. The 27th Inniskillings, who stood for four hours under direct artillery fire, left 450 out of 750 dead or dying on the spot when they eventually moved off. The dead and dying they left behind lay in the shape of the square they had formed while suffering that torment.

The French cavalry, whose attacks filled the third phase of the battle, then replaced the British infantry as artillery targets. The British gunners, sticking to their pieces which were sited in advance of their line, continued firing until the French were almost on top of them, charging their guns with case shot, a projectile loaded with musket balls packed into a tin cylinder. The captain of a British battery describes the effect:

The [French] Cuirassiers and Cavalry might have charged through the Battery as often as six or seven times, driving us into the squares under our guns. In general a squadron or two came up the slope on our immediate front, and on their moving off at the appearance of our Cavalry charging, we took advantage to send destruction after them, and when advancing on our fire I have seen four or five men and horses piled up on each other like cards, the men not even having been displaced from the saddle, the effect of canister.

When the cavalry got within charging distance of the British infantry, the effect produced by musketry was much the same. An officer of the 95th Regiment related how his battalion dealt with the cavalry that attacked them: 'The Cuirassiers approached within thirty or forty yards of the square, when I fired a volley from my company which had the effect of bringing so many horses to the ground that it became quite impossible for the enemy to continue the charge. Half of the enemy were at that instant on the ground; some four horses and men were killed, more wounded, but by far the greater part were thrown down over the dying and wounded.'

When infantry met infantry in the climactic phase of the battle, British superiority in musketry decided the issue. An officer of the 1st Foot Guards describes how the two Guards, French and British, encountered each other:

The Grenadiers were ascending the rise shouting, 'Vive l'Empereur!'. They continued to advance until within fifty or sixty paces of our front, when the Brigade was ordered to stand up. Whether it was from our sudden and unexpected appearance, which must have seemed as if starting out of the ground, or the tremendously heavy fire we threw into them, *la Garde*, who had never before failed in an attack, *suddenly* stopped. Those who from a distance and more on the flank could see the affair, tell us that the effect of the fire seemed to force the head of the column bodily back!

Waterloo epitomized the workings of a military establishment which had been three hundred years in the making. That establishment provided states with the opportunity of deciding international quarrels with more rapidity and conclusiveness than had been possible before or since. But it did so because the human means of which it disposed varied little from country to country, while the technical means underwent change only at a very gradual rate. As a result, victory went to the side which most nearly perfected its exploitation of the potentialities inherent in the system. Unless able to achieve a marked superiority in numbers, an army won because its discipline on the battlefield and skill in weapon-handling exceeded those of its opponent.

This state of equilibrium was quickly and severely upset after Waterloo. Improvements in public health and a rise in the administrative efficiency of state were to make for a sharp increase in the size of armies. Industrialization enormously enhanced material power to wage long wars, fuelled by the output of factories and mechanized farms. And technological revolution threatened armies which did not buy weapons wisely – and extravagantly – with defeat at the hands of a better equipped foe.

During the American Civil War it was the second factor that counted most weightily. The South had courage and skill, while its equipment at least matched in quality that of the North. But it was deficient both in industry and in infrastructure – railways, all-weather roads – as well as in men. Over the course of four years its courageous armies were beaten down by weight of Northern arms and numbers. In the mid-century European wars between the Prussians and their Austrian and French enemies, superior administrative capacity decided the issue. Austria and France both lacked Prussia's efficiency in conscripting its male population and in mobilizing its reserves. Neither could in consequence bring armies to the field that matched Prussia's in size or level of training. But during the last third of the nineteenth century it was increasingly the technological factor that came to the fore. Those years were ones of rapid innovation, which saw the introduction of magazine rifles, breech-loading artillery and machine-guns. In wars between the Europeans and the technically backward peoples of Africa and Asia among whom they were scrambling for colonies, these new weapons made resistance by the ill-equipped almost completely hopeless. Perhaps no war more dramatically demonstrated the power of these new weapons than that between China and Japan in 1894–5. China, which had so successfully held at bay the steppe nomads during the centuries when they had terrorized the lands to the west, fell helpless to Japan, which, though one-tenth its size in population, had bought the best weapons European industry could manufacture and had learnt to employ them to effect.

The Sino-Japanese and, to an even greater degree, the Russo-Japanese War portended the future nature of battle in a yet more ominous way. Modern weapons, they demonstrated, had a potentiality for the infliction of death far greater than those of any previous age. A battlefield is, in a sense, a marketplace dedicated to the exchange of casualties. As long as battle depended upon the expenditure of muscular effort, that exchange was limited in duration and scale by the physical strength of the opposing sides, so that casualties remained, unless in exceptional circumstances, low. The introduction of gunpowder greatly reduced the muscular limitation on the infliction of casualties; but, because of the low rates of fire of muzzle-loading weapons and the fairly meagre stock of munitions that contemporary armies could acquire and transport, casualty figures did not greatly rise. The industrialization of warfare revolutionized the battlefield exchange; casualty rates climbed to hitherto unimaginable levels, because munitions multiplied in availability and weapons in output of firepower. An infantry battalion of a thousand men expended, for example's sake, about two thousand rounds per minute at the beginning of the nineteenth century; by the end it expended fifteen thousand rounds per minute and, if the firepower of its machine-guns is added, about 20,000. The effective range of such firepower was at the same time extended from a hundred to a thousand yards. The effects, enhanced by the power of breech-loading, quick-firing artillery, were demonstrated at the battle of Mukden, February to March 1905, where the Japanese and Russians lost respectively 70,000 and 100,000 men out of opposed armies each 300,000 strong.

Such warnings of the virtual uninhabitability of future battlefields were, however, ignored by European armies before 1914. The generals believed that with the numbers and firepower at their disposal, their attacks were guaranteed success. The contrary was, of course, the case. It was the defensive, not the offensive, which had benefited from the enhancement of weapon power, against which infantry could do little but offer up their lives in heroic sacrifice. The battles of the First World War became indeed simply sacrificial in character. A British officer, waiting to attack on the Somme on 1 July 1916, described the bombardment which rained down on the German trenches:

Russian infantry attacking a German or Austrian position on the Eastern Front in the autumn of 1914; men are already falling

The artillery suddenly blazed out in one colossal roar. The dull booms of the heavy guns in the rear could just be discerned amidst the sharper and incessant cracks of the 18-pounders and 4.7s that were closer to the line. There seemed to be a continual stream of shells rumbling and whining overhead on their way to the enemy positions, where the succession of explosion added to the general noise. Fifteen-inch howitzers and 9.2 shells were falling in Gommecourt Wood, whose trees were uprooted and flung into the air, and eventually the Wood was in flames. The landscape seemed to be blotted out by drifting smoke.

Despite this awesome preparation, the German defenders, sheltering in deep dugouts beneath their trenches, were scarcely affected. As the British artillery fire slackened at the moment of attack, they raced to man their parapet and bring the assaulting British infantry under rifle and machine-gun fire. A Northumberland Fusilier experienced the consequences: 'I could see away to my left and right, long lines of men. Then I heard the "patter, patter" of machine guns in the distance. By the time I'd gone another ten yards there seemed to be only a few men left around me; by the time I had gone twenty yards, I seemed to be on my own. Then I was hit myself.'

Sixty thousand British soldiers were hit on 1 July 1916, out of some 240,000 who crossed the front line. Twenty thousand died. It is unlikely that all suffered wounds that were immediately fatal – gross injuries of the head or vital organs. Far more probable was it that they died of shock or dehydration during the course of that day or the next. For the scale of the wounding inflicted by the Germans wholly overwhelmed the British medical services. Battalions had allotted only thirty-two

The leading wave of a French infantry assault on German trenches, Western Front, 1916

German casualties of trench warfare, Ypres, 1917

men to act as stretcher bearers. As it took four men to carry each casualty, and his evacuation might require an hour's work, it was unavoidable that battalions which had suffered three, four or five hundred casualties were obliged to allow a high proportion of their wounded to linger in no-man's-land beyond the time when they might have been saved. Two young British officers, crossing the battlefield three weeks later, stumbled upon evidence of the consequences of that delay: 'The wounded, who could not be brought in had crawled into shell holes, wrapped their waterproof sheets round them, taken out their Bibles, and died like that.'

A battle, it has been said, produces 'an epidemic of casualties', which may indeed be regarded as its object. In an earlier age, warfare itself had frequently produced epidemics of organic disease in the armies assembled to proceed on campaign. Such epidemics were the outcome of the poor hygiene and medical ignorance which prevailed before the scientific developments of the nineteenth century. The First World War was the first in which deaths from wounds exceeded those from disease, so that the conflict itself may be viewed as a competition in the infliction of wound epidemics by one side or the other. The common soldiers quickly came so to regard it. The 'wrong' wound, which disabled for life, was feared almost more than death itself; the 'right' wound, which conferred on the victim an honourable discharge from duty, was highly prized, and those who suffered one were congratulated and envied by their less fortunate comrades.

No battle of the First World War, not even those in which the newly invented tank was employed, escapes characterization as a 'wound epidemic' transaction; hence the blanket concept of 'attrition' retrospectively applied to its conduct by strategists and historians. But hindsight also allows us to see it as a transitional conflict, interposed between the warfare preceding and succeeding the scientific revolution which helped to determine its character. By 1939, when the Second World War broke out, two technical and scientific developments had matured to a stage which demoted the 'wound epidemic' phenomenon to a secondary status.

34

The first was medical. The rapid evacuation of casualties from the battlefield, by mechanical transport, and their speedy treatment with blood transfusion, analgesic and eventually antibiotic techniques combined to blur, even abolish, the distinction between the 'wrong' and the 'right' wound, at least in the armies of advanced countries. The second was technical. The perfection of the tank, and the successful adaptation of the aircraft to a ground attack role, meant that the offensive, so consistently frustrated on the battlefields of the First World War, might henceforth be implemented with swift and dramatic effect; more important, in human terms, with comparatively trifling loss of life. 'Blitzkrieg', as the German style of rapid armoured breakthrough came to be called, induced exhilaration, even euphoria among the troops committed to practise it, so shattering were the results and so cheap the attendant costs. One hundred and forty German divisions attacked the Western armies in May 1940, a force of some 1,200,000 fighting soldiers. At the end of the campaign, six weeks later, their fatal casualties were fewer than 30,000, or about two per cent of those engaged. If the wounded are included, German casualties in a campaign that overwhelmed Belgium, Holland and France, were less than half of those the Kaiser's army had suffered at the battle of Verdun in 1916. Verdun had ended in stalemate; the 1940 campaign had made Germany master of the West.

This tide of lightning victory was to persist. In the spring of 1941 the German armies overran the Balkans and Greece. In the summer they drove into European Russia to reach by December the outskirts of its three western metropolises – Leningrad, Kiev and Moscow. In the course of their advance they had devastated the Russian armies opposing them, encircling in three great manoeuvres nearly two million Soviet soldiers.

Winston Churchill, reflecting on the character of the First World War, had written that 'Victory was to be bought so dear as to be almost indistinguishable from defeat.' At the end of 1941 it seemed that victory could be bought by the new methods of warfare at a price scarcely higher than that incurred by participating in an arms race. Given the right choice of investment in weapons and military organization a country might apparently emerge victorious from the most risky of military enterprises at a human cost which, whatever the pain to the families directly affected, scarcely afflicted the feelings of the nation as a whole.

The appearance of cheap victory was, however, to prove illusory. War always engages human passions – hatred, recalcitrance, vindictiveness – and never more so than when one side is made to feel that it has been beaten in a less than fair fight. It was thus that Hitler's enemies felt at the end of 1941, and Japan's too. Revolutionary technical means, allied to surprise attack, were judged to be the explanation of the lightning victories won between 1939 and 1942. Surprise attack was thereafter an exhausted option; while technical means could be duplicated. And so they were. By what was to prove the mid-point of the war, the Soviet Union, the United States and Britain were equipping their armies and air forces with material as good as or better than that with which their opponents were provided, and from an industrial base some six times as large.

Strategically, such disparity left the outcome in no doubt. The Axis powers were doomed to defeat, once the era of Blitzkrieg was past, a certainty that the development of nuclear weapons only confirmed. But in human terms the war remained fraught with terrible and tragic consequences. Blitzkrieg had seemed to promise decisive results without proportionate cost. The equalization of weapon power between the two sides made the achievement of decision on the battlefield slow and laborious, and its price cruelly high. From no matter what theatre of the war – Russia, North Africa, Italy, Normandy, Burma, the Pacific – fighting soldiers

A German casualty of the battle of Normandy, 1944

American infantry taking cover behind animal victims of the battle of Normandy, 1944

reported their experience, the gist of their stories was identical. It was one of terror, pain and wounds, against which neither new weapons nor modern military medicine provided any certain protection. 'Inside each wrecked tank,' an observer of the Desert War recalled, 'a putrid blackening paste on the walls was what an armour-piercing shell had left of the men who manned it. These were the details of the scene repeated again and again in every corner of the desert landscape; a great rubbish heap of metal and human flesh. So the victors sat, gazing across the gigantic desolation.'

At Stalingrad, a German soldier beheld a similar sight:

The country for miles around was strewn with smaller equipment – tin hats, gas masks, ground sheets, entrenching tools, even rifles and grenades. All of this stuff had been thrown away because it had become a mere hindrance, or because the men who carried it had become the wounded in their endless columns, with blood-soaked bandages and tattered uniforms, summoning the last vestiges of their strength merely to drag themselves on through the snow. Or else the equipment had belonged to the countless men now rigid and dead, of whom no one took any more notice than we did of all that abandoned material.

A New Zealand officer found his Italian battlefield, save for a difference of climate, an almost identical sight: 'It bore that chill, suspended, deadened atmosphere of ground which is being fought for. The shell-pitted fields, grass torn and trampled, or else lush and arid, covering unseen minefields, and over all the marks of shelling – smashed and splintered trees, like plants broken off half-way up their stems, shallow craters, with their dead, dried sterile earth, their burnt black edges and littered jagged shrapnel covering the fields of some ugly disease, all were there.'

A Japanese officer, escaping from defeat at the hands of the Americans in the Philippines in 1944, looked back across the battlefield from which he had fled.

There was the sound of heavy firing. It was almost daylight. By the river in the West, the air was full of noise and smoke. The mighty concatenation of explosions approached our forest and seemed to fuse the whole surrounding sky into a narrow strip. The roar of guns grew terrifyingly close, and with it came a bellowing rumble as of distant thunder. Beyond the hills, which I had crossed the day before, I could see a single reconnaissance plane flying round in small circles, like a bird of prey watching for its victim. I looked round and counted my companions-in-despair. We were eight soldiers in all. Only one of us was completely immobile. The others were suffering from diarrhoea, beri-beri, tropical ulcers, bullet wounds or a combination of these complaints. Like me they were the rejects, the debris of a defeated army.

A French casualty of the battle of France, 1940

American medics treating a child victim of the Normandy battle, 1944

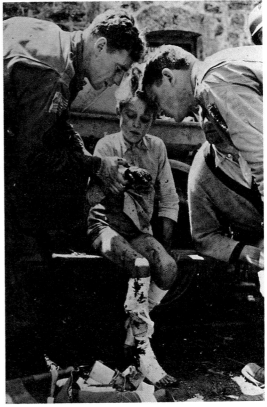

Japanese soldiers were reduced to such a state only by extremes of violence. General Bill Slim, commanding the British-Indian army in Burma, recalls how they fought at Mandalay:

Mandalay Hill is a great Rock rising abruptly from the plain to nearly eight hundred feet. Its steep sides are covered with temples and pagodas, now honey-combed for machine-guns, well-supplied and heavily garrisoned. Throughout the day and night, of March 9, 1944, the fiercest hand-to-hand fighting went on, as a Gurkha battalion stormed up the slopes and bombed and tommy-gunned their way into the concrete buildings. Next day two companies of a British battalion joined them, and the bitter fighting went on. The Japanese stood to the end, until the last defenders holding out in cellars were destroyed by petrol rolled down in drums and ignited by tracer bullets. When shortly afterwards I visited it, the blackened masks of fire and the sights and stench of carnage were only too obvious.

Such terrible events are never forgotten even by those who survive them physically unscathed. An American survivor of Normandy, a battle fought between armies of the same race and culture, by the same conventions of war and allegedly with mutual respect, remembers how his comrades slept out the aftermath of battle on the ground they had wrested from the enemy:

You could not see the sleeping men, but you could hear them. There was much whimpering and moaning, as in a hospital ward. Occasionally one would cry out or mumble a few incoherent words. But the worst sounds were of men grinding their teeth as they slept. They had fallen out here about five o'clock and they had got out their wounded and got in ammunition and cold rations. But they weren't digging trenches or doing all the book prescribed, because they had had three days of hard fighting and they were exhausted. They pitched down in the places the Germans had left and they slept, for tomorrow they had to go ahead again.

And not only they – the young, pupil, conscript soldiers of a great democracy learning the trade of war far from home at the hands of an enemy who had recently bestridden two continents. Millions of other young men, many not born when the great peace of 1945 descended on an exhausted world, would face tomorrows in which they would have to 'go ahead again'. The residues of world war and the collapse of empires it brought in its train would compel young Jews, Arabs, Indians, Pakistanis, Algerians, Africans – black or white – Vietnamese, Afghans and once again Frenchmen, Britons, Russians and Americans to gaze, as their fathers and grandfathers had done, on the face of battle. Four hundred generations of human beings had suffered the touch of its Gorgon stare. A few of the bravest and strongest among them had stared it down. Of the rest, those who had survived to find their way home took with them the burning hope and desire that they might never have to meet it again.

Fighting Spirit 2

Battle is a harrowing business. In addition to the physical risks of death or injury, the soldier is subjected to the intense psychological pressures generated by exhaustion, privation, noise, worries about family and friends, and the sight of comrades being killed and wounded. Yet, as Field-Marshal Haig admitted: 'Men are not brave by nature.' The fighting spirit that enables the soldier to meet the stress of battle must be built and sustained: training, comradeship, leadership and discipline all play their parts in its creation.

Military thinkers have for centuries recognized the importance of morale. 'You know, I am sure,' declared the Greek soldier and writer Xenophon, 'that no numbers or strength bring victory in war; but whichever army goes into battle stronger in soul, their enemies generally cannot withstand them.' Clausewitz compared the physical and moral components of war to the parts of a sword. 'One might say that the physical seems little more than the wooden hilt,' he wrote, 'while the moral factors are the precious metal, the real weapon, the finely-honed blade.' Napoleon maintained that the moral is to the physical as three is to one, and Field-Marshal Montgomery believed that: 'The morale of the soldier is the greatest single factor in war.'

It is less easy to quantify fighting spirit than a material resource like tanks, guns or aircraft, but its presence can be identified readily. There are moments in battle when logic suggests that embarking upon a particular course of action – attacking against heavy odds, or defending an untenable position – is fruitless to the point of being suicidal. But fighting spirit, with all its complex chemistry of individual and collective needs, loyalties and pressures, can urge men to go forward or stand firm even in the face of certain death.

There are striking instances where the fighting spirit of a small number of soldiers has had far greater consequences than any of them could ever have imagined. On 2 July 1863, the second day of the battle of Gettysburg, the vital hill of Little Round Top, on the left of the Union line, lay undefended before the advancing Confederates. Had it fallen, the flank of the Union position, rolling away along Cemetery Ridge, would have been turned: the battle would be lost, and with it the campaign and even the war.

A Union brigade reached the hill just in time, and on its left flank, bent at a ninety-degree angle by the pressure of the Confederate assault, was the three hundred and fifty-strong 20th Maine. It was commanded by Colonel Joshua Chamberlain, minister of the gospel, college professor and one of the outstanding amateur soldiers that both North and South produced in such abundance. There was a desperate short-range battle between the Maine regiment and its opponents, who outnumbered it by three to one. After an hour's fighting half Chamberlain's

Gettysburg, July 1863: the aftermath of fighting at Little Round Top

men were down and the rest were almost out of ammunition. A fresh Confederate attack must overwhelm the survivors and take the hill. Chamberlain then gave an almost impossible order: the 20th would fix bayonets and charge. As the men hesitated, a young lieutenant – history records his unmartial name as Holman S. Melcher – waved his sword, shouted 'Come on! Come on boys!' and ran forward. The colour party followed him, and the whole regiment lurched into a charge. Although the Confederates were numerically superior, they were unnerved by this sudden counter-attack. Their first line collapsed, and then the second: the 20th took over four hundred prisoners. There was a great deal more hard fighting to be done before Gettysburg was won. But there is widespread recognition that 'the key to the battle on the second day was the cohesiveness, willpower and courageous fighting of the 20th Maine soldiers and Chamberlain's leadership.'

The fighting spirit of small units could produce a tangible result even on the Western Front during the First World War. On 31 October 1914, a massive German attack, pushed in along the axis of the Menin road to the east of Ypres, broke the British line at Gheluvelt. There was almost nothing in reserve, and, to make matters worse, German shells hit Hooge Château, only three kilometres behind Gheluvelt, killing one divisional commander, temporarily stunning another, and killing or wounding several staff officers. The British commander-in-chief, Field-Marshal Sir John French, drove up to visit Sir Douglas Haig's I Corps headquarters at the White Château, on the Menin road between Hooge and Ypres. He made his way forward against such a strong tide of fugitives that he had to finish his journey on foot, and was disturbed to see some of Haig's howitzers coming out of action at the trot, a sure sign, he thought that all was not well. French found Haig 'very white but quite calm.' 'They have broken us right in,' he said, 'and are pouring through the gap.' Haig later recalled that French 'had no reinforcements to send me, and viewed the situation with the utmost gravity.'

Brigadier-General C. Fitzclarence, in command of the threatened sector, had already thrown in his last reserve, three companies of 2nd Battalion, The Worcestershire Regiment, under Major E. B. Hankey. The Worcesters, seven officers and 350 men strong, set off from the south-west corner of Polygon Wood, about one and a half kilometres from Gheluvelt. They marched in column of fours to a small belt of trees just west of Polderhoek Château, where they shook out into two lines fifty yards apart, with two companies in the first line and one in the second. Hankey then gave the order: 'Advance at the double. Advance.' The normally staid prose of the British Official History rises nobly to the occasion:

There were still a thousand yards to traverse, and the scene that confronted the Worcestershire was sufficient to demoralize the strongest nerves and shake the finest courage. The stretch of country which they saw in front of them was devoid of cover of any kind; beyond it lay the fences and enclosures of Gheluvelt Château and village, in which many houses were in flames. Wounded and stragglers in considerable numbers were making their way back to the shelter of the woods, some of whom cried as the advancing troops passed through them, that to go on was certain death, whilst the enemy's high explosive and shrapnel bursting overhead gave point and substance to the warning ... The first two hundred yards were crossed in one long rush; nevertheless, the Worcestershire were observed by the enemy's artillery directly they appeared in sight, and its fire was redoubled. Over a hundred men fell, but the rest still pressed on. The wire fences of the enclosures near the village and the wall and railing of the château grounds were reached and passed, and contact with the enemy's infantry gained. [The Germans] were enjoying the repose of victory, searching for water and looting, and in no expectation of such an onslaught. They offered no organized resistance, and were soon fleeing back in confusion through the village.

Gheluvelt was recaptured and the gap in the British line was sealed. Hankey's 350 men had defeated the best part of a German infantry regiment, in circumstances where the ground favoured the defender. It is no exaggeration to say that they had preserved the integrity of I Corps, and in so doing had averted the collapse of the BEF and the loss of the Channel ports, with incalculable consequences for the war as a whole. French certainly had no doubts about the value of their achievement. 'The Worcesters,' he told Lord Selborne, 'saved the Empire.'

If the presence of fighting spirit is easily visible, so too is its absence. Sometimes gloom and defeatism pervade whole armies. In 1939 France mobilized without enthusiasm for a war which few wanted and most dreaded. Haunted by the butcher's bill of 1914–18, weakened by the political dissensions of the 1930s, and, above all, convinced that the Maginot Line made a German invasion impossible, most French soldiers were unable to sustain the impact – psychological as much as physical – of the Blitzkrieg that unrolled across northern France in May 1940. Materially, the balance of forces for the campaign was by no means unfavourable to the Allies: it was only in aircraft that the Germans enjoyed a quantitative advantage. But, morally, there was no comparison between the French and their opponents. Although some French units fought, with praiseworthy determination, right up until the Armistice, in all too many cases fighting spirit evaporated into panic and despair.

At other times, the disappearance of fighting spirit has more tangible and immediate causes. Often a panic is produced by a misunderstood order, the sudden appearance of an unfamiliar enemy weapon, or the sharp jab of a sudden reverse. In the Spanish Civil War, Tom Wintringham saw one-third of a company of the British Battalion of the International Brigades bolt when its commander yelled 'liquid fire' and ran. A British regular battalion was badly shaken at Gallabat in Eritrea in November 1940 when it was unexpectedly dive-bombed. Not only did the bombs cause alarm and casualties, but a truck carrying ammunition was hit, and the sound of the rounds exploding suggested that the battalion was being attacked in the rear. When a reserve platoon moved off to deal with the supposed threat, its retirement was misinterpreted. As the brigade commander, the future Field-Marshal Slim, recorded: 'The panic spread and was not checked until a number of men had broken away, seized first-line vehicles at the foot of the hill and fled in them.'

Herbert Read watched British soldiers stream away to the rear during the German March offensive of 1918. 'On the road, the straight white road leading to the Western safety, there was something like a stampede,' he wrote. 'S. and the sergeant-major went and held it with pointed revolvers. But it was all useless . . .' The war correspondent Alan Moorehead found himself swept back with the debris of retreat when Rommel broke the Gazala line in June 1942.

All day for nine hours we ran. It was the contagion of bewilderment and fear and ignorance. Rumour spread at every halt, no man had orders. Everyone had some theory and no plan beyond the frantic desire to reach his unit . . . In ourselves we did not know what to do. Had there been someone in authority to say 'Stand here. Do this and that' – then half our fear would have vanished. So I began to realize, sitting in the swaying car, how important the thousand dreary things in an army are. The drill, the saluting, the uniform, the very badges on your arm all tend to identify you with a solid machine and build up a feeling of security and order. In the moment of danger the soldier turns to his mechanical habits and draws strength from them.

Moorehead's analysis is brilliantly perceptive. The process of military training is designed as much to inculcate the group cohesion and solidarity upon which fighting spirit depends as it is to produce an adequate level of technical or tactical expertise. The bonding process begins early. Most armies administer an oath to their recruits, a ritual which goes back at least to the *sacramentum*, the Roman military oath. Stephen Westman describes taking the oath in the German army before the First World War: 'In front of the battalion, drawn up in a square, we had to take the oath of loyalty to the Kaiser. The regimental colours were ceremoniously unfurled and about ten of us, I amongst them, had to step forward. We had to hold up our right hands, had to touch with our left the richly embroidered silken flag and repeat the words of the oath spoken by the adjutant.'

This form of oath predates the reign of Frederick the Great, and exists today in the German and Russian armies. Even the less dramatic oath used in the United States army made a profound impression on many of those who took it during the Vietnam era. 'The officer told us to step right foot forward, raise our right hand and take the oath,' remembered David Parks. 'It was all over in about a minute. I felt trapped.'

The oath-taking over, the recruit's individuality is usually assailed by a haircut which is at best short and at worst – like the Foreign Legion's *boule à zéro* – totally comprehensive. Although such *coiffures* are often defended on the grounds that they promote hygiene, their prime justification is that they create a uniformity of appearance. Indeed, the fashion for establishing this identity by cutting hair short is comparatively recent. For many years long hair, elaborately arranged, was the hallmark of the soldier. Eighteenth-century soldiers squinted under the strain of having their hair caught back into pigtails. Grenadiers sported moustaches, or painted them on if nature proved unhelpful, and light cavalrymen sprouted love-locks. When young Charles Parquin joined the 20th *Chasseurs-à-Cheval* in 1803, he found that it took a year to grow the pigtail and tresses which his regiment demanded.

Next comes the issue of uniform, a dress with symbolism all of its own. The identity of appearance that it helps to create assists the bonding process. The badges of rank which accompany it emphasize the hierarchical structure of armies and encourage deference. For centuries it also included features designed to make its wearer look broader or taller, and to promote the soldier's status in the eyes of comrades, civilians and the enemy. The anthropologist Irenäus Eibl-Eibesfeldt pointed out that: 'One threatens by making oneself bigger – whether by raising one's hackles, wearing combs in one's hair or putting on a bearskin . . .'

The recruit's successful completion of training is usually marked by the issue of an item of uniform – like a distinctive beret, arm patch or lanyard – that marks his change of status. It will also be accompanied by a parade, the culmination of long hours on the drill-square. Drill has often been attacked by military reformers and liberal politicians alike. But there is far more to it than might appear at first sight. Much present-day drill is a survival of the drill carried out as training for battle in the age of blackpowder. Constant repetition of the basic drill movements was designed to ensure that the soldier could load and fire his weapon and master a number of tactical formations. Proficiency in drill gave soldiers a real advantage on the battlefield: they could fire faster and move more efficiently than their opponents and, because many drill movements would have been repeated till they had become conditioned reflexes, the well-drilled soldier had every chance of withstanding the traumatic shock of battle.

Part of the traditional function of drill survives in present-day weapon- and low-level tactical training. In the former, men repeatedly practice loading, carrying out stoppage drills and field-stripping their weapons so that these processes are

The corporate spirit: French Grenadiers of the Imperial Guard march past, 1854

literally engraved upon their minds. Much modern battle drill involves the repetition of a particular formula until it too becomes almost second nature. As the American J. Glenn Gray observed from his own Second World War experience:

In mortal danger, numerous soldiers enter into a dazed condition in which all sharpness of consciousness is lost. When in this stage ... they can function like cells in a military organism, doing what is expected of them because it has become automatic. It is astonishing how much of the business of war can still be carried on by men who act as automatons, behaving almost as mechanically as the machines they operate.

Drill is also concerned with welding men together under circumstances of shared adversity, and with instilling into them the habit of obedience. Herbert Sulzbach, who had the unusual distinction of serving as a German officer in the First World War and a British officer in the Second, had no doubt that: 'Drill as a means to an end is indispensable to every army. It cannot be replaced entirely by individual training nor by sporting instinct. A man, unless his inherent worth is beyond all doubt, must have obedience drilled into him, so that his natural instincts can be curbed by the spiritual compulsion of his commander even in the most awful moments.' Yet drill can be overemphasized, to form a mind-dulling ingredient of that 'bull' which can so easily submerge initiative and extinguish rational thought. The Prussian army lost the battle of Jena in 1806 despite the excellence of its drill, and the Israeli army, one of the most consistently successful fighting forces of this century, is not noted for its zeal for presenting arms.

British Footguards trooping the colour, 1969

The aim of much military training is the creation of *esprit de corps*, a soldier's

44

confidence and pride in his unit. The Comte de Guibert, a distinguished eighteenth-century French theorist, argued that *esprit de corps* lay at the very heart of success in action:

Personal bravery of a single individual does not decide on the day of battle, but the bravery of the unit, and the latter rests on the good opinion and the confidence that each individual places in the unit to which he belongs. The exterior splendour, the regularity of movements, the adroitness and at the same time firmness of the mass – all this gives the individual soldier the safe and calming conviction that nothing can withstand his particular regiment or battalion.

For most of the past two centuries the regimental system flourished in the armies of Europe. Regiments were named after their colonel or the area whence their recruits came, or were simply given a number. Their uniforms bore a variety of distinguishing marks. Facing colours on collar and cuffs taxed the ingenuity of military tailors: the nine Prussian cuirassier regiments which existed in 1914 wore facings ranging from the cornflower blue of the *Garde-Kürassier Regiment*, through black, crimson red, light blue, red, rose red, Russian blue and lemon yellow to the light green of *Kürassier-Regiment* No. 8. So elaborate were the colour-codings in the Austro-Hungarian army that it was nicknamed 'the Royal and Imperial paintbox'.

These distinctions all helped to foster a unit's identity and to strengthen the bonds between its members. When Field-Marshal Slim was a young officer on the Western Front during the First World War, his battalion faltered during an attack. 'As we wavered,' wrote Slim, 'a private soldier beside me, whom one would have thought untouched by imagination, ran forward. In a voice of brass he roared "Heads up the Warwicks! Show the blighters your cap badges!" Above the din, half a dozen men each side of him heard. Their heads came up. They had no cap badges – they were wearing steel helmets – but they had remembered their Regiment.' Regimental ideology uses the achievements of one generation to encourage the next. At the battle of Alexandria in 1801 the British 28th Regiment (later The Gloucestershire Regiment) found itself attacked in both front and rear by French grenadiers. The 28th's rear rank faced about, and each rank won its own battle. Since then the Gloucesters have worn a small 'back badge' in memory of the action. Fourteen years later, at Waterloo, the regiment was badly shaken, with three sides of its square under heavy attack. It was rallied by a shout of 'Twenty-Eighth, remember Egypt!' Few of the men present had been at Alexandria, but the appeal to the regiment's ancient virtue was understood: the square braced itself and held fast.

A regiment's colours are the embodiment of its traditions and pride. They are embroidered with battle honours, hung with battle streamers, or decorated with medals, and are given an almost religious reverence. They were traditionally blessed when presented, and are accorded dignified treatment even when their useful life is over. Colours were once an important rallying-point in action, and the custom of trooping the colour dates from the time when they were marched along the ranks to ensure that soldiers would recognize them in battle.

Colours have long inspired soldiers. In 55 B.C. a Roman invasion force under the command of Julius Caesar approached the coast of England between Walmer and Deal. British tribesmen thronged the beach ready to oppose the landing, and the legionaries blenched at the prospect of wading ashore to meet them. At this crucial moment, the *aquilifer* who carried the legion's eagle, the equivalent of its colours, took decisive action, as Caesar tells us:

And then, while our troops hung back, chiefly on account of the depth of the sea, the eagle-bearer of the Tenth Legion, after a prayer to heaven to bless the legion by his act, cried: 'Jump down, soldiers, unless you wish to betray your eagle to the enemy. It shall be told that I at any rate did my duty to my country and my general.' When he had said this with a loud voice, he cast himself from the ship and began to bear the eagle against the enemy. Then our troops exhorted one another not to allow so dire a disgrace, and leapt down from the ship with one accord. When the troops on the nearest ships saw them, they likewise followed in, and drew near to the enemy.

It was reckoned a great shame for a regiment to allow its colours to be captured. On 16 May 1811 the 3rd Foot – known, from the hue of its facings, as the Buffs – formed part of a mixed English, Spanish and Portuguese force drawn up on the ridge of Albuera. As a French attack crumpled the Allied right a sudden hailstorm swept the field, reducing visibility almost to nil and drenching the locks of the defenders' muskets. French and Polish horsemen smashed into the Buffs, catching the regiment before it had time to form square. Ensign Thomas, a youth of sixteen, was bidden to surrender the Regimental colour. 'Only with my life,' he replied: he was promptly sabred and his colour was taken. Ensign Walsh, carrying the King's colour, was also cut down, but the colour was grabbed as it fell by Lieutenant Latham. A sword-cut took off half his face, and another severed his arm. He ripped the colour from its pike and stuffed it into his tunic before falling face down in the mud amongst the trampling hooves.

A fresh British brigade then came up and forced the French back until stopped by a huge mass of infantry and guns. There followed a sustained close-range firefight, as grape, roundshot and musket balls scythed through the British ranks. Men loaded and fired as in a wet and smoky nightmare, and closed to the centre as their comrades fell. Colonel Inglis, commanding officer of the 57th Regiment, lay on the ground with a grapeshot through his lung, repeating 'Die hard, 57th, Die hard.' The arrival of the Fusilier Brigade, marching on steadily though all officers above the rank of major had been hit, at last tilted the balance of the battle, and the French began to retire.

Casualties amongst the indomitable British infantry were heavy. The Buffs ended the day with only eighty-five of the 728 officers and men who had gone into action, and the 57th, with 160 left out of 600, deserved their new nickname 'The Diehards'. The 31st, who had been brigaded with the Buffs but had just managed to form square in time, had 263 survivors out of 418. Latham was picked up after the battle and, astonishingly, recovered from his wounds to soldier on one-armed and disfigured, but renowned for his bravery. Marshal Soult, the French commander, blamed his defeat on the desperate valour of men like this. 'There is no beating these troops,' he complained. 'They were completely beaten, the day was mine, but they did not know it and would not run.'

Although the Buffs, the 31st and the 57th have fallen victim to amalgamation, their traditions are preserved by the Queen's Regiment. Latham's gallantry is commemorated in the Regiment's massive silver centrepiece. And, each year, on the anniversary of Albuera, the officers and senior NCOs of each battalion of the Regiment meet to follow a custom instituted by the survivors of the 57th, and drink the health of their fallen comrades. As an officer of the regiment writes:

We are all mindful that the magnificent behaviour of our predecessors on that day, has served in the past and will always serve, as an example of bravery and discipline which we in The Queen's Regiment are proud to inherit for ourselves in the future. It also serves as a symbol of the friendship and mutual respect that the officers and Senior NCOs have for one another in our Regiment and how important it is to maintain these bonds between us.

There can be few better examples of the fighting spirit shown by one generation being used to stiffen the resolve of another.

The Queen's Regiment's Latham centrepiece commemorates the Buffs' stand at Albuera on 16 May 1811

Yet even that fluent advocate of the regimental system Brigadier Sir Martin Lindsay 'often wondered where the latter-day private soldier drew his strength to stick it, and never really found a satisfactory answer: the youth who typically was conscripted into the Army, posted overseas after a few months training, drafted to an unfamiliar regiment and only a few days later found himself in battle.' The British army is, moreover, unique in the strength of its regimental system: in many other armies the soldier risks being posted from one regiment to another almost at whim. Many of the American soldiers in the north-west Europe campaign of 1944–5 did not know the names of their regimental commanders, while their German opponents were often fighting as members of an improvised battle group whose organization cut sharply across regimental identities. Useful though regimental ideology may be, especially to regular officers and NCOs, it is clear that there must be other objects of soldiers' affection and other causes of their bravery.

48

Before narrowing the focus to look at the bonds of loyalty that link the members of small groups within the regiment, we must consider wider motivations, and examine the roles of patriotism and ideology. Both are useful aids to recruiting, especially in the early stages of a war. As General Sir Richard Gale wrote of August 1914: 'The spirit of patriotism of that age had to be experienced to be realised. The whole nation rallied behind the colours.' But patriotism and ideology become less important as the war goes on. 'Patriotism, in the trenches, was too remote a sentiment, and at once rejected as fit only for civilians, or prisoners,' thought Captain Robert Graves. A German sergeant, captured towards the end of the Second World War, laughed when his interrogators questioned him on the political opinions of his men. 'When you ask such a question,' he said, 'I realise well that you have no idea of what makes a soldier fight. The soldiers lie in their holes and are happy if they live through the next day. If we think at all, it's about the end of the war and then home.' John Dollard, author of a study on morale in the International Brigades in the Spanish Civil War, summed up the issue neatly when he wrote that: 'Ideology functions *before* battle, to get the man in; and *after* battle, by blocking thoughts of escape.'

Yet, before dismissing patriotism and ideology as sources of fighting spirit, we should consider their broader implications. Firstly, the flag-waving patriotism so prevalent at the beginning of a war often masks a deeper and more compelling belief in the underlying rightness of the cause for which the soldier fights. At the end of the day, German soldiers of two wars fought, not so much for patriotism in its loftier sense, but for their home – *Heimat.* Even in Vietnam, a war not noted for the patriotic fervour it aroused, Peter Bourne detected belief in 'an amorphous entity that may be labelled "Americanism"'. Ideology may also give the soldier the underlying conviction that his cause will eventually triumph. Henry Metelmann, a tank driver in the 24th Panzer Division, reflected on what motivated him and his tank crew.

There was a good comradeship. Most of us . . . believed in the righteousness of our cause. Most of us were I wouldn't say ardent Nazis. I never could say about myself that I was an ardent Nazi. I didn't know enough about it. But I believed that it was my right to enforce our way onto others and for that reason I was doing a God-given job to go into other countries: and how can you do it better than with a *Panzer?*

Secondly, it is clear that cultural norms, reflecting habits and values which are far more deep-seated than those springing from short-term political ideology, play an important part in determining the soldier's behaviour. The army occupied a pre-eminent position in the Germany of Kaiser Wilhelm, and rose again to enjoy similar status in the 1930s. Professional standards and soldierly honour were key motivating factors, especially as far as officers and NCOs were concerned, and helped them not only to maintain the Second World War German army at what was, man for man and division for division, a remarkably high level of combat effectiveness, but also to fight on when all hope was gone and defeat seemed imminent and inevitable. This soldierly pride could keep men faithful unto death, as Brigadier-General Jack Seely discovered when he led his Canadian cavalrymen into a wood near Moreuil in 1918, and saw 'a handsome young Bavarian' miss an approaching Canadian,

Soldierly pride radiates from these German infantrymen of the Grossdeutschland *Division*

and, as a consequence, receive a bayonet thrust right through his neck. He sank down with his back against a tree, the blood pouring from his throat. As I came close up to him I shouted in German, 'Lie still, a stretcher-bearer will look after you.' His eyes in his ashen-grey face seemed to blaze fire as he snatched up his rifle and fired his last shot at me saying loudly: 'No, no. I will not die a prisoner.' Then he collapsed in a heap.

Second World War Japanese soldiers had an even more firmly rooted culture to sustain them. For centuries the samurai, the martial caste of Japan, had lived by the precepts of *bushido*, the way of the warrior, which emphasized the primacy of honour and loyalty, the transient nature of life and the triviality of death. The attack on the values of the samurai which followed the Meiji restoration of 1868 did not, however, result in their disappearance; rather, in their extension across society so that Japanese could say to themselves: 'We are all samurai now.' During the Second World War the Japanese welded samurai ethics to a modern army, with terrible results. Prisoners who, by the harsh standards of *bushido*, should never have allowed themselves to be taken alive, were mistreated, and acts of the most revolting cruelty marked the passage of Japanese armies. Cultural conditioning largely explains, though it can never justify, this behaviour.

The same set of values which produced rape, massacre and torture also inspired a heroism which impressed many who had every reason to hate the Japanese. Relatively few British or American units in the world wars defended a position literally to the last man and the last round: usually, once a certain proportion of casualties were sustained – a proportion which depended very much upon the unit's

The ugly side of bushido: *Japanese soldiers bayonet Chinese prisoners*

morale – the survivors fled or surrendered. For the Japanese, though, defence to the last man was routine, and attacks were pressed home, time and time again, in the face of certain death. Unwounded prisoners were a rarity: only 216 of the 20,000-strong garrison of Iwo Jima were taken prisoner, and hundreds of Japanese soldiers and civilians on Okinawa killed themselves – and often their families as well – rather than face capture. Ken Harrison, who fought in Malaya as an NCO in an Australian anti-tank unit, knew the Japanese well, in battle and in a prisoner-of-war camp:

They came in all shapes and sizes and most were barbaric and sadistic . . . But there were others who were kind at a time when kindness and gentleness were the rarest of jewels . . . But good or bad, kind or sadistic, they had one supreme virtue – in the final analysis their Sun God imbued each and every one of them with a courage that I believe to be unequalled in our time. Whatever their other qualities might be, to me they are – with envy – the brave Japanese.

One ingredient of Japanese fighting morale was a religion which preached the immortality of the soul. It would be rash, even in an age when religion may seem relatively unimportant in the West, to ignore its influence upon men in battle. The function of religion as a cause of conflict remains a matter of dispute: certainly, religion has often been enlisted to legitimize attitudes and policies which are more temporal than spiritual. Similarly, the efforts of military chaplains have led to accusations that religion in wartime is used as simply another device to help buttress morale.

Closer to God: British soldiers take communion on the Western Front

Nevertheless, there is more than a little truth in the cliché that 'there are no atheists in foxholes.' A Second World War American survey discovered that soldiers with combat experience regarded prayer as a very important source of support. Furthermore, over three-quarters of those interviewed thought that their army experience had increased their faith in God. Even the most irreligious soldier may find a prayer rising to his lips as he cowers under a bombardment or listens to the squeaky rattle of tracks which heralds a tank attack. 'We all asked the help of the Lord that night,' said an American infantryman, describing an ambush in Vietnam in November 1966. And, when considering faith, we should not neglect Islam, one of the great fighting religions of history, which has long inspired Mohammedan soldiers to selfless heroism and, as the ghastly casualty figures from the Gulf War demonstrate, continues to do so today.

What is faith to the believer is superstition to the cynic. Pure superstition plays its own role in enabling men to stand the strain of war. The capricious nature of battle, where the luck of an inch here or a second there can make the difference between life and death, leads some soldiers to fatalistic indifference. It encourages others to worship at the altar of Fortune. They link their own survival to the possession of a talisman of some sort. Lieutenant E. C. Vaughan went into battle at Passchendaele with a cluster of holy medals fixed to his braces. He had been given one by a nun, and soon there was 'an ever-increasing bunch presented from various people.' In *The Great War in Modern Memory* Paul Fussell suggests that 'no front-line soldier or officer was without his amulet, and every tunic pocket became a reliquary. Lucky coins, buttons, dried flowers, hair cuttings.' John Steinbeck, serving as a war correspondent in the Mediterranean, saw the same phenomenon in the Second World War:

Whatever the cause of this reliance on magic amulets, in wartime it is so. And the practice is by no means limited to ignorant or superstitious men. It would seem that in times of great danger and emotional tumult a man has to reach outside himself for help and comfort, and has to have some supra-personal symbol to hold to. It can be anything at all, an old umbrella handle or a religious symbol, but he has to have it.

Superstition is a prop to morale, and helps to make war endurable. However, neither it, nor patriotism and ideology – even in the broadest sense – generate the sort of fighting spirit that urges men to break cover and move forward over bullet-swept ground. Even professional pride and regimental solidarity may falter at such a moment. The great American combat analyst S. L. A. Marshall argued that it was not such things that kept men going under these circumstances: it was the close bonds of comradeship forged within the infantry section or squad. 'I hold it to be one of the simplest truths of war,' he wrote, 'that the thing which enables an infantry soldier to keep going with his weapons is the near presence or presumed presence of a comrade.' His personal observations from two world wars led him to believe that, above all, men were unwilling to appear cowards in the eyes of their comrades: 'personal honour is the one thing valued more than life by the majority of men.'

Marshall was quick to note that this process depended upon a training and posting policy which encouraged the formation of well-integrated small groups of soldiers. 'The tactical unity of men working in combat,' he suggested, 'will be in the ratio of their knowledge and sympathetic understanding of one another.' The ties of comradeship that exist in a good tank crew or infantry section can attain an intensity that is, in Kipling's words, 'passing the love of women.' 'We had really worked up a close relationship,' said Henry Metelmann, describing his own panzer crew. 'I liked my comrades . . . One German soldier calls another a *kamerad* and we had a good *kameradschaft* as it's called. We were prepared to do things for each other, and not only were we comrades, we were friends. We played cards together, we knew about each other's family problems and we promised each other: "When we come home on leave I have a nice sister . . ."' The American soldier-cartoonist Bill Mauldin noticed how men often sneaked back to their units rather than spend time convalescing after their discharge from hospital. They did it:

not because their presence was going to make a lot of difference to the big scheme of the war, and not to uphold the traditions of the umpteenth regiment. A lot of guys don't know the name of their regimental commanders. They went back because they knew their companies were shorthanded, and they were sure that if someone else in their squad or section were in their shoes, and the situation were reversed, those friends would come back to make the load lighter on *them.*

The creation of robust small units, their members linked by enduring bonds of affection, is no guarantee of fighting spirit. Such groups may come to believe that their interests are best served by avoiding rather than seeking combat, and by adopting a 'live and let live' policy whenever the enemy will permit it. Modern research has shown that unofficial truces are a common feature of war: even in the First World War large sections of the Western Front relapsed into relative quiet for much of the time. During the Vietnam War, despite a policy of rotation which meant that soldiers spent only a year in-country, strong loyalties were generated in combat units. But far from promoting, say, aggressive patrol action, such loyalties often actively discouraged it: the term 'hero' became one of abuse.

Many factors help to ensure that the thousands of small groups making up an army have sets of values which promote aggression and discourage apathy. We have already identified some of them, like *esprit de corps*, professional standards, soldierly honour or belief in war aims. Leadership, as we shall see in a later chapter, has a key part in ensuring that fighting spirit is transmitted throughout an army's central nervous system down to its very fingertips.

There are two other major contributors to fighting spirit. One is the lure of reward – be it loot, money, or drink – and the other is the framework of discipline which guides the uncertain and controls the unwilling. For hundreds of years soldiers stood to profit from their efforts in battle. In the Middle Ages wealthy prisoners could be ransomed, and their horses and armour sold, by their captors. The pockets and purses of the dead were not disdained, and the systematic looting which so often followed the capture of a town gave even the humblest soldier the chance of making a fortune. In the Napoleonic Wars both prisoners and corpses were pillaged as a matter of course: even in the well-disciplined British army men might scamper from the ranks during a lull in the battle to loot nearby bodies. Despite the existence of military codes which should have prevented similar behaviour during the two world wars, it is true to say that looting was common in all armies. On some occasions it could be recognized as theft, but on others it was more easily justified as the appropriation of an item which had no obvious owner or might be termed a 'souvenir'.

Alcohol has a ready appeal for looters. It enables men to forget their plight or the horrors they have witnessed. During the Peninsular War the bloody storm of Badajoz in 1812 was followed by an orgy of drunkenness in which Wellington lost control of part of his army for almost two days. Captured stocks of drink exercised an irresistible attraction for battle-weary German soldiers in the March offensive of 1918: Stephen Westman thought that the attack was held up 'not for lack of German fighting spirit, but on account of the abundance of English drinking spirit!'

Armies have often deliberately employed drink and drugs to promote fighting spirit. The Vikings sometimes used a dried fungus whose hallucinogenic effects blurred the images of battle, and pre-combat drinking has been common for centuries. The men of the French divisions who attacked the Pratzen at Austerlitz in 1805 were fortified with a triple drink ration, nearly half a pint of brandy per man. There is some dispute over the extent to which the rum ration was deliberately used as a pre-battle stimulant in the British army of the First World War. It is, however, clear that it was the policy of many units to issue rum before an attack. The medical officer of a Black Watch battalion told the 1922 Shell Shock Committee that 'had it not been for the rum ration I do not think that we should have won the war.' In his battalion they always tried to give the men a good meal, and a double ration of rum in coffee, before they went over the top.

Just as judiciously issued alcohol has helped men cope with battle, so officially prescribed amphetamines like Benzedrine have enabled them to withstand sleep deprivation. Widely used though amphetamines are, they create problems of their own. The unpredictable nature of combat makes it hard to judge when they are likely to be needed, and their use is followed by a disabling drop-off effect. Alongside the issued drugs and drink go the privately obtained supplies. Corporal Shaw of the Life Guards, who ran amok with his sabre at Waterloo, hewing down Frenchmen until he was killed, had spent the morning of the battle drinking heavily. More often, though, illicitly obtained drink and drugs are taken, in Bill Mauldin's words, to 'dull the sharp memories of war.' Their overuse is usually an indication of poor morale, a sign that, even if men cannot escape from the war physically, they will at least blot it from their minds as best they can. In 1971 just over half the American soldiers in Vietnam had smoked marijuana, more than a quarter had experimented with heroin or opium, and almost a third had tried other psychedelic drugs.

Corporal Shaw of the Life Guards had spent the morning of Waterloo drinking heavily

This eighteenth-century German engraving shows a variety of punishments, including running the gauntlet and riding the wooden horse

Drug abuse in Vietnam became a major problem, and brought the soldier into conflict with military discipline, an apparatus without which no army can function effectively in peace or war. It was long believed that unless they were subjected to the constraint of harsh discipline, soldiers would flee from battle. Frederick the Great argued that 'the common soldier must fear his officer more than the enemy,' and his army applied a wide range of savage punishments. These ranged from 'riding the wooden horse', in which the offender sat astride a sharp-backed wooden horse, often with weights attached to his feet, to 'running the gauntlet', when the victim had to walk between two ranks of soldiers who lashed him as he passed by. A Prussian general recorded that most of those sentenced to undergo thirty-six runs, spread over three days, actually died.

Desertion, particularly if carried out in the face of the enemy, was long regarded as a capital offence. The Romans executed men who ran away in battle, and a unit which behaved badly risked being 'decimated' – having one man in ten killed. James Wolfe, who defeated the French in the battle of Quebec in 1758, had no doubts about the importance of the death penalty in preventing men from failing the test of battle. When commanding the 20th Foot at Canterbury in 1755 he ordered: 'A soldier who offers to quit his rank, or offers to flag, is to be instantly put to death by the officer who commands that platoon, or by the officer or sergeant in rear of that platoon; a soldier does not deserve to live who won't fight for his king and country.'

During the First World War the British army executed 346 soldiers, 266 of them for desertion: many of the victims would have been regarded, in a more enlightened age, as psychiatric casualties. The British abolished the death penalty for cowardice and desertion in 1930, and no British soldiers have been executed for purely military crimes since then. By contrast, the Americans shot one man – Private Eddie D. Slovik – for desertion in the Second World War. The Russian and German armies formally executed many deserters, and their officers sometimes enforced discipline with their own pistols. Such extreme measures were not unknown even amongst the Western Allies. The commanding officer of an English infantry battalion admitted that his unit was so worn out by heavy casualties in Normandy, particularly amongst its officers, that 'I have twice had to stand at the end of a track and draw my revolver on retreating men.'

Nevertheless, the discipline enforced by firing squad or pistol is inferior to that accepted, self-imposed discipline which characterizes good soldiers. Regulations designed to keep dull-witted conscripts together on the shoulder-to-shoulder battlefields of the blackpowder era are inappropriate in an age when weapons and tactics demand dispersion on the battlefield, and when initiative may be more important than blind obedience. In the last analysis, fighting spirit centres upon the morale of the individual soldier and the small group of comrades with whom he fights. S. L. A. Marshall was convinced that it was the quintessential ingredient of success in battle. 'If I learned nothing else from war,' he wrote,

it taught me the falseness of the belief that wealth, material resources, and industrial genius are the real sources of a nation's military power. These things are but the stage setting: those who manage them but the stage crew.

The play's the thing. Finally, every action large or small is decided by what happens up there on the line where men take the final chance of life or death . . . And so the final and greatest reality, that national strength lies only in the hearts and spirits of men.

Infantry 3

The foot soldier is as old as mankind itself. Although some anthropologists suggest that there was once a golden age when man was a gentle herbivore, he developed the taste for meat, the ability to make primitive weapons, which compensated for his lack of lethal teeth and claws, and the determination to use these in combat against his fellows. His weapons soon took on the characteristics which still define them: projectile weapons, like the stone, bow and arrow or throwing-spear, and shock weapons, like the stabbing-spear and club. Just as these crude arms were essentially the tools of the hunter, so too were early tactics – the ambush and the raid – little more than an extension of the hunt.

A crucial transformation, which turned the infantryman from an individual warrior into a tiny component of a complex fighting machine, took place in distant antiquity. From about 2500 B.C. the foot soldiers of Mesopotamian city-states like Ur and Lagash – in what is now Iraq – were armed and equipped alike, and went into battle in massed phalanxes, their long spears forming a bristling hedge, their bodies protected by shields and their heads by helmets. Discipline and training were important, for, if these large formations were not to fall into disorder, their members needed to master simple drills for marching and using their weapons.

Specialist infantry were the mainstay of the great empires of the ancient world. The details of dress, equipment and weaponry varied from Assyria to Egypt and from Persia to Greece, but the essential features remained the same. Some foot soldiers, such as the Cretan archers and Rhodian slingers who provided the firepower of Alexander the Great's infantry, used missile weapons: others, like the armoured spearmen who stood shoulder-to-shoulder in the Macedonian phalanx, plied spear and sword. But the most formidable infantry of the era, whose sheer fighting efficiency was not to be equalled in the West for at least a thousand years after the birth of Christ, were the Roman legions.

Rome's ascent to power was long and painful. Her ascendancy within Italy was only assured after she had defeated local adversaries and, in a struggle ending in 272 B.C., expelled the invading Greek forces of Pyrrhus, King of Epirus. Between 264 and 201 B.C. Rome fought two major wars against Carthage, her main rival for power in the central Mediterranean. During the second of these conflicts the Carthaginians invaded Italy, and won major victories on the River Trebia, at Lake Trasimene and at Cannae. Cannae was the tactical masterpiece of Hannibal, the Carthaginian commander. His army formed up with its centre deliberately weak and its flanks strong. As the attacking Romans pressed the Carthaginian centre back, Hannibal's wings swung in to trap them in a battle of encirclement in which at least 47,500 Roman infantry were killed. Hannibal may have won what was to be regarded for centuries as the perfect example of the battle of annihilation, but

57

*Assyrian infantry
besieging a city*

he could not win the war, and in 202 B.C. Publius Cornelius Scipio inflicted a decisive defeat upon the Carthaginians at Zama in North Africa.

In the legions that fought Hannibal there was an intimate connection between political privilege and military obligation, just as there had been amongst the hoplite infantry of the Greek city-states. The Roman citizens of the Republic made up the *hastati*, *principes* and *triarii*, who formed the legion's three lines of battle. Younger and poorer citizens served as *velites*, light troops who screened the main body of the legion. By the early Imperial period, in the first century A.D., the old three-tier structure had disappeared, and most legionaries were recruited outside Rome and central Italy. Soon legions had not only a number but also an honorific title, like Legio III *Augusta pia fidelis* and Legio IX *Hispana*.

At the height of Rome's success as an imperial power the organization of the legion bore more than a superficial resemblance to that of a modern infantry unit. The smallest brick of its construction was the eight-man *conturbernium*, equating to the modern squad or section. Next came the eighty-strong century (company), six of which made up a cohort (battalion). The legion (brigade) had ten cohorts, the first of which was extra strong, containing five double centuries. A *legatus legionis*, a man of the senatorial class destined for a political career, commanded each legion, assisted by a senior tribune and five other military tribunes. The senior tribune was usually a young senator designate, while the other tribunes were of equestrian rank – the next below senators in the Roman hierarchy.

A healthy leaven of practical experience was provided by the camp prefect, who took command of the legion in the absence of the legate and the senior tribune, and upon whose advice the wise legate might well rely. He was an ex-ranker, probably at least in his fifties, and his office represented the culmination of the professional soldier's career. Camp prefects were promoted from the ranks of the centurions, the experienced professionals who commanded the centuries. These

58

A relief from the column of Antonine shows Roman legionaries advancing; standard bearers can be seen at the top centre

officers, sixty to each legion, were of graded seniority: most senior was the *primus pilus*, commander of the first century of the first cohort.

The dress and equipment of the legionary was sturdy and practical. He wore a linen undershirt and a short-sleeved woollen tunic, with leather trousers if the climate was particularly cold. The military boot was a heavy hobnailed sandal, which could be lined with wool or fur. Over the tunic went a cuirass made up of metal strips, and a bronze helmet with cheek-pieces and a neck-guard protected the head. The legionary's leather belt supported not only his dagger but also a dangling apron made of leather strips reinforced with metal, which covered his lower stomach in battle.

The legionary carried a large oblong shield, curved to fit his body, and wore a short stabbing-sword hitched well up on his right-hand side. But his main weapon was the throwing-spear, the *pilum.* This had a wooden shaft four feet long, tipped by a three-foot iron spike. The tip was tempered but the rest of the point was left soft; it bent on impact with an enemy's shield and could not be extracted. Julius Caesar tells how the *pilum* helped him defeat the Helvetii, a Gallic tribe, in 58 B.C.

Caesar . . . drew up his four legions of veterans in triple line, half way up the hill . . . Then, after a speech to encourage his troops, he joined battle. The legionaries, from the upper ground, easily broke the mass-formation of the enemy by a volley of javelins and, when it was scattered, drew their swords and charged. The Gauls were greatly encumbered for the fight because several of their shields would be pierced and fastened together by a single javelin-cast; as the iron became bent, they could not pluck it forth, nor fight properly with the left arm encumbered. Therefore many of them preferred, after continued shaking of the arm [in an attempt to dislodge the *pilum*] to cast off the shield and so to fight bare-bodied. At length, worn out with wounds, they began to retreat.

This is a classic description of Roman infantry tactics, the volley of *pila* followed

A legionary in battle order

by the charge with the sword. Rigid discipline, constant training and long hours of drill – some of it with extra-heavy practice weapons – made the legion a finely honed fighting instrument. It could carry out a variety of manoeuvres, although the attack in a wedge-shaped formation seems to have been most usual.

The legion's effectiveness stemmed as much from its conduct off the battlefield as its performance in action. Unlike so many ancient armies, which straggled on the march and collapsed into insanitary and disorganized shanty-towns at night, the legion tramped along in good order and built its own fortified camp, always laid out on the same pattern, whenever it halted for the night. Its soldiers carried enough equipment to make them almost self-supporting. A forked stick across the legionary's shoulder suspended a wicker basket for carrying earth, containing three days' supply of wheat (for the manufacture of the hard biscuits that formed his staple diet), and an assortment of tools, while a pickaxe was stuck into his belt. Tents and other heavy equipment travelled on mules or in carts. Fully laden on the march the legionary carried a burden which weighed around sixty pounds, and in his hump-backed silhouette we see an outline familiar to generation upon generation of foot soldiers, for whom the perils of battle have sometimes come almost as a relief from day after gruelling day of marching under a back-breaking load.

The Romans made more use of cavalry than had the Greeks. A squadron of 120 horsemen, employed for scouting and dispatch-riding, formed part of each legion, while cavalry units, *alae*, normally of 500 men apiece, were recruited from amongst Rome's allies. But it was the robust, hard-marching and hard-fighting legionary who played the leading role in taking and holding an empire which, at its height, ran from Scotland to Egypt and from Portugal to Syria. Other empires were won by swarms of horsemen or wide-ranging fleets, and later conquerors had burgeoning technology to aid them. The Roman empire was that unique phenomenon: an infantry empire, carried on the hobnails of legionaries' *caligae* and won by the rough iron of their *pila*.

By the third century A.D. both the Roman empire, and the infantry who had maintained it for so long, were under intolerable pressure from barbarian tribesmen along a far-flung frontier. Civil wars wasted the army's strength, and even the Emperor Constantine's division of the empire between East and West was no answer to its long-term problems. Cavalry became increasingly important: indeed, it was the cataphract, the heavily armoured horseman, who was to become the archetypal soldier of the Eastern empire. The defeat of the Emperor Valens by the Goths at Adrianople in A.D. 378 not only struck a fatal blow at Roman power: it also sounded the death-knell of the legion. Valens' infantry, tired and straggling on a hot and exhausting day, were left unsupported after his horses were driven off, and were swamped by the Gothic cavalry:

the different companies became so huddled together that a soldier could hardly draw his sword, or withdraw his hand after he had once stretched it out. And by this time such clouds of dust arose that it was scarcely possible to see the sky, which resounded with horrible cries; and in consequence the darts, which were bearing death on every side, reached their mark, and fell with deadly effect, because no one could see them beforehand so as to guard against them.

Adrianople marked the end of the era of infantry supremacy, and plunged the foot soldier into a long night which was to last for over a thousand years, and whose gloom was to be broken only by the occasional glimmer of light. For most of this period the horseman, nurtured by feudalism, rode supreme through the wrack of peasant levies or hapless burghers, and feared only his own kind.

Infantry posed two major challenges to the armoured knights whose charge was the trump card played on so many of the battlefields of the early Middle Ages. Both were the work of foot soldiers who were specialists in the use of particular weapons. It is significant that each of these weapons, and the tactics which accompanied its use, perfectly epitomized the characteristics which had defined infantry weapons from their earliest days: fire and shock.

The soldiers of the Swiss Confederation, a loose alliance of the hardy and belligerent inhabitants of the Swiss cantons, were unrivalled exponents of shock. Their main weapon was the pike, its twenty-foot shaft held at shoulder height and

The Swiss in battle: this 1530 Holbein drawing catches the ferocity of infantry combat with pike, sword and halberd

jabbed out in a downwards thrust. Inside the thicket of pikemen were halberdiers, their weapons like huge axes on six-foot shafts, and other burly Swiss who wielded two-handed swords, or spiked clubs known as Lucerne hammers. A few of the Swiss wore breastplate and helmet, but the majority marched and fought lightly clad, which contributed to the terrifying speed with which their battle formations covered the ground. Missile weapons were not totally scorned, and crossbowmen, and later musketeers, were used for skirmishing ahead of the columns of pikemen. The Swiss usually employed three of these, a vanguard, a main body and a reserve, and, thus deployed, a Swiss army advanced in echelon with a clear gap between each column.

The battle of Morgarten, fought in November 1315, was a skilful combination of good planning and murderously effective tactics. Leopold of Austria's column of men-at-arms and infantry was marching along a narrow road between mountain and lake when it was charged in the flank. The Austrians were, quite literally, cut to pieces, as a contemporary chronicler tells us:

It was not a battle, but a mere butchery of Duke Leopold's men: for the mountain folk slew them like sheep in the shambles: no one gave any quarter, but they cut down all, without distinction, till there were none left to kill. So great was the fierceness of the Confederates that scores of Austrian footmen, when they saw the bravest knights falling helplessly, threw themselves in panic into the lake, preferring to sink in its depths rather than to fall under the fearful weapons of their enemies.

If the Swiss enjoyed the advantage of the ground at Morgarten, at Laupen in 1339 they defeated a Burgundian army in open field, on terrain traditionally dominated by feudal cavalry. At Grandson and Morat in 1476 Charles the Bold of Burgundy was routed by the impenetrable Swiss hedgehogs, and at Nancy the following year the Duke, fighting desperately amongst his rearguard while the rest

62

of his defeated army fled, was killed by a mighty blow of a halberd which cleft both helmet and skull.

The supremacy of the Swiss was eroded as much by their own obstinacy as by innovations in warfare. They were reluctant to accept formal command authority, and their dogged persistence on the battlefield sometimes became costly pig-headedness. Other infantry imitated Swiss tactics and used them with effect against their originators: battles between the Swiss and the German *Landsknechte* were notably bloody. Enemy commanders increasingly sheltered their men behind fortifi-cations which the Swiss often attacked at great cost: they lost 3,000 killed trying to break into a Spanish position at La Bicocca in 1522. Finally, the improvement of cannon in the early sixteenth century sounded the death-knell of dense formations of pikemen, who provided gunners with targets which even their primitive field-pieces could scarcely miss. At Marignano in 1515 French cavalry forced the Swiss columns to halt and close up, and French cannon played upon the inert mass. But the ferocious Swiss pikemen, as reluctant to accept quarter as they were to grant it, left an enduring mark upon the history of the infantryman, and in the Pope's Swiss Guard we see the last shadow of a fighting force which shook feudal Europe to the core.

The second major threat to the armoured horseman could scarcely have been more different. Towards the end of the thirteenth century the longbow emerged as the characteristic weapon of English infantry, and at Falkirk in 1298 Edward I's archers carried off the honours of the day by riddling the thickly clumped *schiltrons* of Scottish spearmen who had succeeded in beating off the English knights. The Scots ranks, thinned by the arrow-storm, were then penetrated by the very horsemen who had earlier made no headway against the steady hedge of spears. The fact that the English archers employed a missile weapon while the Swiss had relied upon shock was not the only difference between them. The Swiss, like the Romans before them, were predominantly an infantry army, while the English archers fought as part of a combined-arms force in which mounted knights and men-at-arms also played a part.

At Crécy in 1346 Edward III divided his army into three 'battles', each consisting of dismounted men-at-arms and Welsh spearmen with archers on their flanks. The attacking French cavalry fell in aristocratic heaps under the winnowing hail of arrows. At Poitiers (1356) and Agincourt (1415) the French dismounted most of their knights in order to conduct a more methodical advance. In both cases the archers did fearful damage to the attacking troops. At Agincourt, though, their fire could not prevent the French from pressing on to fight at close quarters, and at a crucial moment in the battle, the archers threw down their bows and ran into the brawl with sword, dagger and mallet.

Growing French reluctance to launch frontal assaults upon bowmen, and the increasing importance of cannon, both helped to reduce the value of the archer. At Formigny in 1450 an English force was badly mauled by a French army which combined the fire of its two cannon with attack by disciplined infantry and cavalry, while three years later at Castillon an English attempt to storm a well-prepared fortified position produced a predictable disaster. Nevertheless, these reverses sprang as much from the weakness of the English strategic position in France as from the shortcomings of longbowmen, and as late as Flodden in 1513 it was the bow, not the new-fangled arquebus, which carried off the honours of the day.

The sixteenth and seventeenth centuries saw the drawing together of the two tactical strands represented by the English and the Swiss. Infantry formations now combined fire and shock: the Spanish *tercio*, whose measured tread made sixteenth-century Europe tremble, drew up in deep formations with pikemen in

A stylized picture from Froissart's chronicles shows English archers engaging French crossbowmen at the battle of Crécy in 1346

A contemporary engraving of Gustavus Adlophus at the battle of Leipzig; pikemen and musketeers in action

the centre and 'sleeves' of musketeers at the corners. As we have seen, Maurice of Nassau and, later, Gustavus Adolphus, improved the effectiveness of infantry by reducing the size of units and increasing the proportion of musketeers to pikemen, as well as by lightening weapons and armour. Gustavus' battalion consisted of four companies, each of seventy-two musketeers and fifty-four pikemen. Its soldiers normally drew up in six ranks, and elaborate and well-practised drills enabled the musketeers to maintain a steady fire.

At the battle of Breitenfeld, fought on 7 September 1631, some of Gustavus' infantry drove off the Imperialist horse with their fire, while others swung round to meet a flank attack which would have collapsed a less steady army. Colonel Robert Monro described how Gustavus' Scots brigade fell upon its opponents:

The enemies Battaile standing firm, looking on us at a neere distance, and seeing the other Briggads and ours wheeling about, making front unto them, they were prepared with a firm resolution to receive us . . . but our small ordinance [light cannon attached to each regiment] being twice discharged amongst them, and before we stirred, we charged them with a salve of muskets, which was repaid, and incontinent our Briggad advancing unto them with push of pike, putting one of their battailes in disorder, fell on the execution, so that they were put to route.

At the turn of the seventeenth and eighteenth centuries the pike, a major infantry weapon for over two thousand years, vanished, to the regret both of traditionalists, who believed that it still had a useful role, and of gentleman rankers, who preferred to 'trail the puissant pike' rather than soil their hands with powder and shot. Its disappearance was in part due to the improvement of firearms, as the cumbersome matchlock, which relied for ignition upon a length of smouldering cord – the match

The age of the drillmaster: British recruits at drill in the Napoleonic period

– being applied to the priming powder in the flash pan, was replaced by the more efficient flintlock, whose charge was ignited by the spark of flint against steel. The invention of the socket bayonet, in about 1687, also helped to render the pike obsolete. The earlier plug bayonet, jammed into the musket's muzzle, prevented its user from firing once the bayonet was fixed. The British reverse at Killiecrankie in 1689 was blamed by General Hugh Mackay, the defeated commander, on the fact that: 'The Highlanders are of such quick motion that if a Battalion keep up his fire till they be near to make sure of [hitting] them, they are upon it before our men can come to the second defence, which is the bayonet in the muzzle of the musket.' But with the socket bayonet, which fitted round the musket's muzzle, the soldier could load and fire with his bayonet fixed.

It was during this period that infantry drill attained a new importance. Good weapon-handling had always been essential in any closely packed formation, but with the presence of large amounts of gunpowder in the ranks, and the use of muzzle-loading muskets whose manipulation required a series of precise actions to be carried out in a set order, the consequences of errors of drill were very serious. Indeed, Marshal Gouvion Saint-Cyr was later to estimate that one-quarter of all French infantry casualties during the Napoleonic Wars were caused by men in the front rank being accidentally shot by their comrades in the rear, and hundreds of the muskets picked up on the battlefield of Gettysburg in 1863 contained several charges of powder and ball, showing just how easy it was for a man to make mistakes in the terror and confusion of a close-range firefight.

From the early part of the seventeenth century until the third quarter of the nineteenth the infantry stamped their feet, slapped wood and iron, marched and counter-marched in the age of the drillmaster. The musket had severe limitations. A late-eighteenth-century Prussian experiment, in which a battalion of infantry fired at a target one hundred feet long by six feet high, representing an enemy unit, resulted in 25% hits at 225 yards, 40% hits at 150 yards, and 60% hits at 75 yards. Under the stress of battle the proportion of hits would inevitably decline still further: at the battle of Belgrade in 1717 two Imperial battalions held their fire until their Turkish opponents were only thirty paces away, but hit only thirty-two Turks when they fired and were promptly overwhelmed. These limitations meant that a battalion was little more than a close-range firing machine, in which drill and discipline improved the volume and accuracy of fire – and also helped keep the unit's component parts together at a time of supreme personal crisis.

There were times when all the hard work on the parade-ground paid dividends. During the reign of Frederick the Great, the Prussian army took unprecedented pains over the drilling of its infantry, and Frederick's victories of Rossbach and Leuthen (1757) owed much to the manoeuvrability and reliability of his foot soldiers. But harsh discipline and formalized tactics were no guarantee of success, as European armies found to their dismay when facing the threadbare armies of Revolutionary France in the 1790s. Moreover, linear formations and methodical volleys – even if they worked as well in battle as they did on parade – were suitable only on certain sorts of terrain. In 1755 General Braddock suffered a costly defeat at the hands of the French and their Indian allies when he tried to employ the tactics of Western Europe in the forests of North America. And, although British defeat in the War of American Independence sprang primarily from strategic over-extension, inflexible tactics caused several British defeats and ensured that some victories – notably Bunker Hill, where the British suffered 1,150 casualties, nearly half the infantry engaged – were bought at too dear a price.

The eighteenth-century preoccupation with infantry drill led to the appearance of countless drillbooks and the development of a whole host of manoeuvres, many

Volontaire venant de l'Armée du Rhin. d'Ulm.
dessiné d'après nature le 20 Oct: 1796. 5me de la Rep.

of which had little application on the battlefield. But some useful ideas were emerging. The experience of North America underlined the value of light infantry, and infantry battalions throughout Europe soon acquired a light company, intended for use as skirmishers, as a counterpoint to the grenadier company, once armed with hand-grenades but, by the end of the eighteenth century, simply a little *corps d'élite* within the battalion. During the Napoleonic Wars the British obtained excellent results from specialist rifle-armed infantry: the performance of the 95th Regiment (The Rifle Brigade) in the Peninsula re-emphasized the value of individual marksmanship, initiative and inconspicuous clothing.

The foot soldier's firearm, which had undergone little change for over a century, was transformed by the technological developments of the nineteenth century. First, in the 1830s and 1840s, the flintlock was superseded by the simpler and

C·R·

more reliable percussion lock. Next, the smooth-bore musket was replaced by the rifle. The latter, as we have seen, was already a proven weapon for picked troops, but its extension across the whole of the infantry greatly increased the range and accuracy of the weapon in the hands of the humblest foot soldier.

Opposite top: The battle of Fontenoy in 1745, depicting the linear infantry formations typical of the era. A sergeant adjusts the ranks with his partisan

The American Civil War was the first major conflict in which most of the infantry on both sides carried the rifled musket, and it demonstrated, at grievous human cost, that the new weapon gave the defender the advantage over the attacker. To launch a frontal assault upon steady infantry armed with the rifled musket was to invite catastrophe. Union troops discovered this at Fredericksburg in 1862 and even more painfully at Cold Harbor in 1864, when 7,000 attacking infantry were hit in a matter of minutes. The Confederates, with their predilection for the tactical offensive, learnt the same hard lesson, nowhere more sharply than at Gettysburg, where Pickett's charge was shot to pieces by the concentrated fire of Union infantry and gunners. The defensive bonus paid out by the rifled musket could be multiplied if the men using it were sheltered in trenches or behind earthworks, and by the end of the war it was no mere cliché to say that the spade was more useful than the bayonet.

In the 1860s and '70s the muzzle-loader was replaced by the breech-loader: the soldier was now spared the wearisome ritual of tipping powder and ball into his weapon and ramming it home. What was more, he could easily load and fire lying down, and, even with the most primitive of breech-loaders, could get off three or four rounds to the muzzle-loader's one. At Königgrätz (Sadowa) in 1866 the Prussians, with breech-loading needle-guns, faced the Austrians with muzzle-loading rifled muskets. The needle-gun gave the Prussians a decisive advantage in the infantry battle. 'We have surely done whatever may be expected from brave soldiers,' said a sergeant in the Austrian 'Black and Yellow' Brigade after the battle, 'but no man can stand against that rapid fire.' Finally, towards the end of the century, metallic cartridges and smokeless powder made possible the bolt-action magazine rifle, which was to remain the major infantry weapon until the end of the Second World War.

These changes had a revolutionary effect upon tactics. In the first place, the superiority of the foot soldier over the conventional cavalryman was emphasized as it became increasingly difficult for cavalry to charge home through an ever-growing volume of fire. In the second, the tactics employed by infantrymen against their own kind were changed beyond recognition.

Two incidents in the Franco-Prussian War of 1870–1 illustrate the latter point perfectly. On 18 August 1870 the Prussian Guard Corps attacked the right flank of the French *Armée du Rhin*'s position, at the little village of Saint-Privat outside the fortress of Metz. The Guard's commander decided – either because the silence of the French guns persuaded him that the defence was weak, or because he was eager to strike a blow before the Saxon Corps outflanked the position from the north – to launch his corps in a frontal attack. The Guardsmen went forward in thick company columns up a bare slope into a blizzard of fire from the *Chassepot* breech-loaders of the French defenders. No less than 307 officers, 7,923 men and 420 horses were hit – a quarter of the Corps' strength – mainly in the first disastrous twenty minutes. Most units were brought to a standstill between five and six hundred yards from the French position.

Saint-Privat was an expensive lesson, but it was not a wasted one. When the Guard counter-attacked the village of Le Bourget, on the outskirts of Paris, only two months later, the tactics and the result alike were very different. This time the Germans worked their way forward by rushes, one company providing covering fire for the movement of the next. The defenders had few clear targets, and were

Opposite bottom: Frederick the Great at Leuthen, 1757

The attack on Saint-Privat, 18 August 1870: the guardsmen were halted by the fire rather more abruptly than the artist suggests

constantly under fire. The village, with twelve hundred prisoners, fell at a cost of only five hundred Prussian dead.

Learning the lessons of Saint-Privat and Le Bourget in the short term was one thing, but remembering them as memories of the war receded was, alas, quite another. In the Boer War of 1899–1902 the British made several costly frontal attacks on strongly held positions, and their experience encouraged a concentration upon marksmanship which was to stand them in good stead in 1914. Trained soldiers fired an annual weapon test which consisted of deliberate, snap and rapid practices at ranges up to 600 yards. In the famous 'mad minute', men fired fifteen rounds at 300 yards, and most could put every one of these shots onto a two-foot circle. But it was all too easy for the continental powers to forget what had happened in 1870, and to suspect that the events of the Boer War and the Russo-Japanese War were not really relevant to Europe. French emphasis upon the primacy of morale encouraged the survival of infantry tactics based upon the blind offensive, and there was a general disinclination to accept that the vastly increased volume of firepower produced by the magazine rifle could paralyze injudicious attacks.

By 1914 there was also the machine-gun to be reckoned with. Inventors had long tinkered with weapons designed to disgorge a stream of bullets, though the French *Mitrailleuse*, used during the Franco-Prussian War, was the first machine-gun which had real military potential. Belt-fed, water-cooled machine-guns, usually mounted on a heavy tripod, were in general use by the early years of this century. They were 'the concentrated essence of infantry', and were to play their own deadly role in bringing deadlock to the Western Front during the First World War.

The war began as one of rapid movement, punctuated by confusing and bloody battles. Yet for the soldier trudging on under the brazen sky the abiding memory was often more of sweat than of blood. Private Fred Steele of the Royal Scots remembered the British Expeditionary Force's retreat from Mons.

It was certainly a long slog back, very hot and dusty, and when we halted by the roadside, we dropped off like logs and it took a big effort to get us moving again. Some men's feet were in a terrible state and I don't know how they kept going . . .

70

At times like those you lose all idea of time and distance, but when we reached Ham on the 27th we must have covered thirty miles since the previous evening, and the march to Noyon the next day was another fifteen.

'More sweat than blood': British troops on the march, 1916

Life was every bit as exhausting for his adversaries, like Stephen Westman of the German 113th Regiment: 'So we slogged on, living, as it were, in a coma, often sleeping while we marched, and when the column came to a sudden halt we ran with our noses against the billycans of the men in front of us.'

The firepower of the magazine rifle and the machine-gun soon stiffened the war of movement into the siege warfare of trench, dugout and barbed wire. The infantryman became a troglodytic creature, at the mercy of an ever-growing arsenal of guns and mortars which might batter him to death at any moment. Ernst Junger, a German infantry officer, tells us just how deadly shellfire was to the infantry.

The sunken road now appeared as nothing but a series of enormous shell-holes filled with pieces of uniform, weapons and dead bodies. The ground all round, as far as the eye could see, was ploughed by shells . . . Among the living lay the dead. As we dug ourselves in we found them in layers stacked one upon top of the other. One company after another had been shoved into the drum-fire and steadily annihilated.

With the night came not sleep, but the peril of patrolling in no-man's-land or, more usually, the sheer drudgery of manual labour. One Australian recalled that it took eight hours to walk four miles carrying rations: 'Give it best for a moment and your will power is broken, and despair will lead you to hysteria, and then, death from exposure. Mud from the top of our heads to the bottom of our boots, drenched to the very skin, your thought must be alone for the men perishing in the front line . . . No songs are sung and no poetry written about fatigue parties.'

71

Battles emphasized the supremacy of fire over manoeuvre. For the first two years of the war both the Allies and their opponents struggled to find a way of opening the locked front by a mixture of bombardment and infantry assault. However promising the initial success, the results always seemed the same: a penetration which could be contained or counter-attacked, and a horrific toll of dead and wounded. In 1916, the year of the Somme and Verdun, the British and the French suffered some 1,200,000 casualties on the Western Front and the Germans 800,000.

It became clear that it was the gunner, not the infantryman, who held the whip hand. In 1917 a British Senior Officers' School acknowledged that: 'The assault no longer depends upon rifle fire, supported by artillery fire, but upon the artillery solely . . .' This concept could produce either ponderous grinding-matches like the Third Battle of Ypres, best remembered by the mournfully evocative name of one of its component actions, Passchendaele, or more radical lightning attacks like the German offensive of March 1918. In both cases, though, it was the gunner who prepared the way and the infantryman who followed up.

In order to move forward over the moonscape of murdered nature and to fight amongst the battered trenches, the infantry on both sides obtained new weapons and equipment. Some of these, like the hand-grenade and the steel helmet, were rediscovered from an ancient past. Others, like the light machine-gun, were altogether novel. In order to gain the maximum assistance from artillery and, in the last year or so of the war, tanks, the foot soldier recognized that he was at his most effective when he formed part of a combined-arms team. When the war ended the infantryman, in his universally drab uniform and steel helmet, not only looked unlike his ancestor of four years before, but, with his looser tactics and greater reliance upon supporting fire, fought a new sort of battle.

72

Infantry tactics had long been the subject of learned dispute, as the rivalry between the eighteenth-century drillmasters so amply demonstrates. During the inter-war years there was fierce debate over the infantry's response to mechanization. The mounted infantryman was certainly nothing new. The 1702 *Military Dictionary* defined dragoons as: 'Musketeers mounted, who serve sometimes a-foot, and sometimes a-horseback', and mounted infantry rendered useful service during the Boer War. Some authorities, like Basil Liddell Hart, military correspondent of the London *Times*, and J. F. C. Fuller, formerly the Tank Corps Chief of Staff, and Heinz Guderian in Germany, argued that infantry should be mechanized in order to keep pace with armour, forming part of a properly balanced mobile force. The Germans took mechanized infantry most seriously, and had eighty *Panzergrenadier* battalions available in 1940. As the Second World War went on, however, most armies mechanized a proportion of their infantry by putting them in armoured personnel carriers (APCs) like the purpose-built German Sdkfz 251 or the improvised British Kangaroo, a turretless Sherman tank.

No longer was the infantryman helpless against the tank: a British PIAT, 1944

The war also accelerated the changing mix of weapons within the infantry unit. The proportion of light automatics to rifles steadily increased, and small, man-portable anti-tank weapons – like the *Panzerfaust*, PIAT and Bazooka – gave the foot soldier the ability to defend himself against enemy armour. Heavier weapons were integrated into the unit: the wheeled anti-tank gun mirrored the 'regimental piece' of the seventeenth century, and the medium mortar, one of the war's major casualty-producers, gave the infantryman the ability to reach out to the other side of the hill.

Yet for the majority of infantry in even the most sophisticated armies, the war was often more ancient than modern. Men marched across North Africa, up Italy, from the Vistula to the Volga and from Normandy to the Rhine. Terrain, as ever, was a great leveller, and a US Marine assaulting a tiny Pacific island or a British infantryman hacking his way through the jungle of Burma depended as much upon courage, determination and sheer endurance as upon the West's industrial power-base. And a large part of his job remained just what it had been at Waterloo or Verdun: providing the enemy's gunners with a target. A Canadian officer described life in a trench in November 1944.

It is an open grave – and yet graves don't fill with water, they don't harbour wasps or mosquitos, and you don't feel the cold, clammy wet that gets into your marrow. At night the infantryman gets some boards, or tin, or an old door, and puts it over one end of his slit trench; then he shovels on top of it as much dirt as he can scrape up nearby. He sleeps with his head under this, not to keep out the rain, but to protect his head and chest from air bursts. In the daytime he chainsmokes, curses or prays – and all of this on his belly with his hand under his chest to lessen the pain from the blast.

The Germans led the way with mechanized infantry, but most Second World War German soldiers, like their fathers and grandfathers before them, marched

In the forty years since the end of the Second World War technology has continued to have a dramatic effect upon the infantryman. The APC, essentially a battlefield taxi, is fast being succeeded by Mechanized Infantry Combat Vehicles like the German Marder or the American Bradley, and light automatic rifles like the M-16 are replacing both the sub-machine-gun and the heavy-calibre rifle. The proportion of riflemen to support weapon specialists continues to decline as new generations of mortars, grenade-launchers, anti-armour and anti-aircraft weapons are integrated into the infantry battalion.

It would be wrong to end with the image of an infantryman ensconced in his MICV, protected by armour, peering through a periscope to find a target to engage with a sophisticated weapon system. For, while this may indeed be the form that infantry combat will take in a future war in Europe, recent history shows quite clearly that, for all the improvement of weapons and equipment, foot soldiers remain what Tom Wintringham called them in the Spanish Civil War – 'dangerous vermin, hard to brush out of the seams of the soil.'

The infantryman's war still pivots as much upon that age-old triangle of essentials – the personal weapon, the marching boot and the loaded pack – as it ever has in the past. Ed Lackman, a machine-gunner with the US 1st Division in the Second World War, painted a picture which his ancestors would instantly have recognized.

Overleaf at top: Grunts: US infantry in Vietnam

Overleaf at bottom: The essence of the infantryman's war: Royal Marines 'yomp' into Port Stanley, 1982

You didn't have facilities to take a bath, sometimes you had your clothing on for three or four weeks at a time, and in the colder weather you never took your shoes off . . . Sleeping on the ground constantly, rain or shine . . . sometimes in the middle of the night when shells were coming in and you were cold and wet you shivered so badly you never thought you would stop . . . You were very, very tired when you were moving up in the middle of the night to – you never knew where you were . . . You were hungry because you didn't have hot food. A lot of times we didn't even have a pack, they were too cumbersome, so we just stuck things in our pockets . . .

It was certainly a spectacle familiar to John Catterson, a US Marine in Vietnam. He described the 'grunt', the infantry soldier who bore the brunt of that war – like so many others – as a man who:

hasn't slept regularly, and hasn't eaten regularly, he hasn't washed or shaved regularly and he's probably wearing the same clothes for three or four days: I think the term 'grunt' evolves from the sound that you make once you sit down. If you have a pack on your back that weighs sixty or eighty pounds, bandoliers of ammunition and a cartridge belt, that's another eighty pounds, when you walk you grunt, everything becomes an effort . . . We didn't have pack horses: you were your own pack horse.

The Roman infantryman had a nickname, too: it was 'Marius' Mule'.

Corporal Hugh Knott's Royal Marine comrades, 'yomping' across East Falkland in 1982, also faced the age-old problem of marching miles across inhospitable terrain with groaning packs. 'Once it's on your back and you get moving you're all right. It's when you start to move off and lift the pack up from the ground onto your back and get moving again, that's the hardest point . . . You've just got to encourage them on, keep them going, tell them they'll be resting in ten minutes . . . Just keep them going, tell them we can't stop here, we've got to keep on going.'

Somehow the crook-backed silhouette of a man on the march in the Falklands is a sight more truly evocative of the essence of the infantryman's war than any other. Only the detail has changed with the centuries. Top the figure with a shako and give it a musket, or replace the rifle with a *pilum* and hang a bruised bronze helmet from the pack, and you have an image almost as old as time: that of the foot soldier on his way to close with his enemy in that primitive and unforgiving world that he knows so well.

75

Cavalry 4

Some four thousand years ago, when somewhere on the edge of the great sea of grass that fills the plain of Central Asia, man first tamed the horse and broke it to his will, it was the beginning of a relationship that would transform warfare, and so trade, agriculture, class and politics.

The horses that men first tamed were not the horses we know today. Short in the leg and weak in the back, they were unsuitable for riding. Nor, in the prevailing state of technology, could man easily adapt them as draught animals. Indeed, to begin with, it was the horse's cousin, the onager or wild ass, that seems to have served man better for work. But about 1800 B.C. the steppe people of Southern Central Asia succeeded in co-ordinating their skills as horsemasters, harness makers, smiths and wheelwrights, and so produced the revolutionary war chariot. This vehicle was light enough to be drawn at speed by two horses while carrying one or two passengers, stable enough to let at least one of the passengers use a bow or javelin while in motion, and strong enough to sustain the stress and strain of a cross-country charge.

The war chariot must, however, have been an inordinately expensive creation, requiring for its construction and maintenance a heavy investment of rare skills and rarer commodities, particularly finely wrought metalwork. Those who drove and fought from chariots came naturally to constitute a distinct class – though that is perhaps a social tautology – whom pre-historians call the 'chariot aristocracies'. However obscure their origins, the chariot aristocracies were rapidly to make a mark upon the world which would not be forgotten. Bursting the bounds of their Central Asian heartland, they overthrew the established order in all the regions that surrounded it. The Aryans took the chariot through Persia to India, the Hittites and Mittani to Mesopotamia and Syria, the Kassites into Babylonia, the Hyskos into Egypt, the Celts into Europe.

Homer's description, in the *Iliad*, of battles between the chariot-driving Greeks and Trojans is of a war between two such aristocracies, but, because he is reconstructing from a folk memory how the charioteers fought, the picture he draws is misrepresentative. Homer has his warriors ride to the battlefield, but then dismount to fight on foot. Practice was quite otherwise, since the value of the chariot lay in its power to carry the warrior into the very heart of the fight. An essential fourth ingredient of the horse-chariot-man combination was his bow, the deadly composite bow of the steppe lands which, a miracle of technology centuries ahead of its time, equipped the charioteer to loose deadly shots from his tiny moving platform into the enemy ranks at point-blank range.

The composite bow was deadly for two reasons. First, it was inherently of immense power. Although developed perhaps 1500 B.C. it shot further and with

greater force than the much-vaunted English longbow; which would not make its appearance until nearly three thousand years later. Indeed it is only recently that the composite bow has been outclassed as a means of projecting an arrow, and then by bows which make use of artificial materials in their construction. The composite bow was an amalgam of natural materials, assembled in such a way that their qualities worked together to multiply each other's latent power. The body of the bow was of flexible wood, its front of elastic sinew and its back or 'belly' of compressible horn, the whole held together by animal glues which took up to a year to dry completely. When the bow was bent, the sinew strove to pull and the horn to push it back to its position of rest, on release driving an arrow as far as 500 yards and with an impetus that would penetrate armour at a hundred.

Armour – or its lack – supplied the second reason for the composite bow's deadliness. The chariot archer, being at the apex of society, wore armour. The common people, have-nots in a metal-hungry society, did not. They were consequently at the mercy of the charioteers whenever coerced or foolishly impelled to fight them. The ease with which they were beaten, and the power of the chariot aristocracies sustained, is therefore easily understood.

But the high period of chariot warfare was not of long duration. It had depended upon the congruence of several technical revolutions, and about 1400 B.C. a new one superseded them in importance, when man learnt to find, mine, smelt and work iron in quantity. The charioteers were men of bronze, an alloy of tin and copper, metals that are comparatively rare, infrequently found together and require considerable refinement before they can be combined. Iron, by contrast, is plentiful, widespread and – once the principle of raising furnace temperature by draught is discovered – quite easy to smelt with charcoal. The consequent rapid diffusion of weapons among their subjects led to the overthrow of the chariot aristocracies and to a more egalitarian social order. The complex nature of agricultural society in lands that generally rested on careful irrigation or water management did not, however, fit with this more diffuse political system. And so the chariot aristocracies were soon replaced by bureaucratic monarchies that exercised power through organized armies. Chariots and infantry both had their place in such armies, notably that of Assyria, which exercised dominant power in the Middle East between the twelfth and eighth centuries B.C.

A military system that ultimately depended upon iron and the horse was not, however, susceptible to monopoly. The Central Asian steppe remained the great reservoir of horseflesh and the use of iron spread into it by natural attraction. As long as the prevailing horse type continued to be useful only as a draught animal, the steppe peoples failed to profit from the combination. But about 900 B.C., either by accident or selective breeding, a bigger horse made its appearance in South Central Asia which was strong enough in the back to be ridden by an armed man. The resulting amalgamation of warrior and mount gave birth to the cavalry principle that would permeate and at times dominate warfare for nearly two thousand years.

Curiously it may have been the standing army of Assyria, a force for stability in the civilized world, that first implemented the cavalry principle. Certainly we can see, in surviving Assyrian bas-reliefs, representations of warriors riding astride and handling weapons. But initially the Assyrians rode in pairs, one man handling a bow, while the other held the reins of both horses. It is evidence that the Assyrians remained wedded to the chariot idea and had difficulty breaking loose from it. Eventually Assyrian cavalrymen did ride and shoot as individual man-horse teams, but only comparatively late in the empire's history. By the seventh century B.C. the empire was on the point of collapse, a state of affairs brought about by the irruption

Opposite top: The Standard of Ur, third millennium B.C. Among the earliest representations of the war horse, the mosaic depicts the clumsy ancestor of the military chariot

Opposite bottom: Seti I, Pharaoh of Egypt (reigned 1317–1299 B.C.). He drives a pair of horses and holds a composite bow

into its territory of steppe nomads who knew how to exploit the cavalry principle to the full.

The steppe nomads, who appear in the civilized world under different names and guises over the space of two thousand years, often with catastrophic effect upon it, were both driven and pulled to break out of their heartland on the sea of grass into the rich lands which lie south, east and west of it. They were driven by the fluctuating conditions of climate, which at times foster but at others disfavour the nomad way of life. During cycles of high rainfall, life on the steppe was comparatively easy for tribes which lived by grazing. Their flocks increased, milk was abundant and game plentiful. When rainfall or temperature abated, life – always fairly harsh – became more difficult. It was then that they felt the pull of the cultivated lands on the periphery of their world, 'lands of first choice', so called because temperature and rainfall or irrigation always kept them fertile.

Exits from the steppe are in three directions: southwards into Asia Minor through the gap between the Caspian Sea and the Himalayan massif; eastward into China; or westward into Europe across the land bridge between the Baltic and the Black seas. The rise of the strong and centralized Persian empire about 550 B.C. effectively closed the first gap; and it would remain closed until the Turks broke the power of the empire's successor states fifteen hundred years later. The eastern exit, though topographically easy to negotiate, was also the border zone of the Chinese empire, oldest, largest and strongest in the world. China was twice conquered by nomads, the Mongols and the Manchus, in the thirteenth and seventeenth centuries, and frequently invaded by others; but the Chinese genius for assimilating interlopers assured the survival of their system of government intact. It was in the third, western, direction that the nomads found their easiest escape from the steppe and, over the two thousand years of cavalry predominance in warfare, there that they were to make their most frequent and disruptive inroads on civilization.

The West was, however, to be protected from the steppe cavalrymen, in the early period of their rise, by the strength of the political systems that had taken root there. Europe had undergone invasion by the earliest wave of horse peoples, Celts and Greeks, but they were charioteers who had taken easily to agriculture in its fertile and temperate environment. Out of their agricultural communities, two great Mediterranean empires had sprung, the first Greek, the second Roman. Far from offering a vulnerable target to the early steppe raiders like the Hsiung-Nu, who terrorized western China in the third century B.C., these European polities were themselves expansionist powers, which under Alexander and then under Augustus extended large bridgeheads into Asia Minor, while maintaining a military frontier in the Balkans that no cavalry society could penetrate.

Strangely, perhaps, given the evidence of how effective the mounted warrior could be when properly equipped and motivated, in neither the Greek nor the Roman armies did cavalry form a major element or play a significant tactical role. Alexander the Great rode to battle at the head of his mounted Companions, who provided a decisive element of shock in his battles against the Persian emperor in the fourth century B.C. But Alexander's ride to conquest was a short-lived episode in a period of over a thousand years of infantry dominance in the Mediterranean lands. The classic Greek soldier of city-state warfare was the hoplite, so called from his heavy infantryman's shield; the classic Roman soldier the legionary, who was, if anything, his even more heavily armoured equivalent. Both settled the issue in their battles by the wielding of spear and sword in close-ordered infantry ranks. Such cavalry as accompanied them was used to scout, to harass the enemy's flanks and to pursue fugitives when his ranks broke.

From 600 B.C. to 400 A.D. the disciplined, armoured infantryman, protecting

Vase painting of Greek cavalrymen (late sixth century B.C.). They are fighting with the light lance held underhand

Roman auxiliary cavalrymen from the column of the Emperor Antoninus Pius (reigned 138–161). They ride on a saddlecloth without stirrups

but also supported by an economy of intensive agriculture, was the dominant military instrument of power in Western Europe and much of the Mediterranean region. But the charge he levied, by way of money and manpower taxes on the peasantry from which he sprang, ultimately broke the cohesion of the greatest of the polities of antiquity, the western Roman empire, and exposed it to invasion from across the Rhine-Danube frontier. The early invaders, mainly Germanic, could be absorbed, or even bribed into the empire's defence. What proved fatal to its survival was the consequent dilution of its civilized character, when followed by the assault of steppe nomads who had no desire for assimilation. Such nomads, Sarmatians from the grasslands of the Ukraine, had first appeared, and been repulsed, in 172 A.D. Early in the fifth century, a far more formidable horde, the Huns, began to press on the Rhine-Danube line. Under the leadership of Attila (r.433–453), they entered Western Europe in 450 and, though defeated by the Romano-barbarian general Aetius at Châlons the following year, caused such chaos in what remained of the western empire, that its dissolution may be dated from that episode.

The Germanic kingdoms which succeeded to authority, albeit of a shaky sort, in the West were not cavalry societies. But they would become so by indirect means. Indeed the 'knight' whose image most powerfully and enduringly encapsulates the cavalry idea in Western culture, would arise from Germanic society in the ninth century. But his prototype – an armoured cavalryman riding a heavy warhorse – had his military origins much further away in time and space, in the Middle Eastern Parthian empire of the first century B.C. The Parthians succeeded in breeding, perhaps by learning to feed stored alfalfa to their brood mares in winter, a horse strong enough in the back to carry both an armoured rider and some protective armour for itself. A force of cavalry thus equipped 'could stand quietly under the harassment of galloping steppe cavalry, exchanging shot for shot, until their assailants' quivers and horses were both exhausted, when a final charge would be counted on to break their spirit and disperse their forces. Seldom could armoured cavalry overtake light steppe ponies; but (it) could forbid any locality to the steppe bowmen and make their retreat uncomfortably hasty. The net effect, therefore, of the introduction of armoured cavalry was to establish a fairly exact balance between steppe and civilized warfare.'*

The Parthian cavalry style spread first to the Roman empire in the east (Byzantium), and then to the kingdom of the Germanic Franks, which had succeeded it in the west. The Franks, whose economy rested on cultivation by deep ploughing, had eagerly adopted the heavy horse. They were expert smiths and fashioned excellent iron armour from an early date. And about 800 A.D. they were introduced to a novel and crucial piece of cavalry equipment, the stirrup. Irresoluble controversy surrounds both the stirrup's origins and importance. It seems to have begun as a toe-loop for the barefooted horsemen of India about the first century B.C., then to have found its way to China, the steppe, Byzantium and so into Europe. Its importance to horsemen varied with their skill; for the steppe people, who rode from infancy and were almost one flesh with their horses, it may have been no more than an aid, lending them an even greater freedom to bend a bow or wield a scimitar than they knew already. To a European, however, who perhaps began to ride at the age of six, and who would always be encumbered by heavy armour, it provided a vital unity with and control over his mount. European weapons, the long sword and thrusting spear, were awkward to handle from the saddle, requiring arm movements which destabilized the rider. The stirrup corrected that instability and helped to make 'knight' and warhorse one.

*W. H. McNeill, *The Rise of the West*, Chicago U.P., 1963, p.322

82

'Knight' became knight through a complicated process in which the introduction of armour and stirrup were only one factor. Another was the transformation of the social order by which the western warrior was supported. The Germanic invaders of the Roman empire had fought on foot, as members of a society where a rough equality prevailed among its fighting menfolk. But the ethos of a conquering warband was not appropriate to the government, however crude by comparison with the Roman pattern it succeeded, of a settled state. The Frankish kings had to assert their authority over the old and new populations of their conquered domains; they had to raise revenue; they had to defend their borders; to all of those functions a force of horsemen was essential. But horsemen were extremely expensive to maintain, because of the cost of the rider's livelihood, his equipment, and of forage and pasture for his horse. Early efforts, as by the Merovingian Kings of France, to meet the costs of keeping a cavalry army at court foundered, and the failure was accelerated by continuing pressure on the eastern and southern frontiers of Frankish Europe. Those pressures required that horsemen should be constantly on call and frequently in the border regions. In consequence, it proved more feasible to devolve support of the heavy cavalryman from the court on to the peasantry. The King allotted his warriors land, from which they could directly draw a living, in return for the obligation to serve with horses, weapons and followers when the King required it.

A third major factor operating to elevate the armoured horseman to military dominance in the West was the success of the Roman church in converting the Franks to Christianity. Christianity, its purely religious character apart, was at one level a deeply civilizing influence on the Germanic barbarians and at another a powerful unifying ideology. Loyalty to the cross not only provided the Franks with an ethical as well as a material reason for resisting attack on their territories by pagan invaders; ultimately it motivated the Christian warrior to convert his enemies to the true religion, if necessary by the sword. In the middle and late Middle Ages, this convergence of ideals – religious, cultural and ideological – would resolve itself into the warrior code which came to be known as 'chivalry', a word cognate with 'cavalry', and providing the standards by which the good knight lived.

The flowering of chivalry was, however, a long and slow process. In its early years, Christian Europe had to fight for its life against the Muslim conquerors of Spain and against successive waves of steppe raiders, or peoples displaced by them, which spilled into the borderlands east of the Rhine. The success of Byzantium, in part based on cavalry effort, in repelling Islam from the Balkans, relieved these pressures in the ninth century, and its revived power was matched in the West by the appearance of a centralized Christian state, Charlemagne's Holy Roman Empire, at the same time. But the Carolingian peace was short-lived. Soon new invaders were tearing at Europe's borders again, Magyars from the western steppe at the Danube frontier, Muslim pirates at the northern Mediterranean shore, and seafaring Scandinavians – Vikings – around the whole northern and western periphery. The Vikings were to present the gravest threat for, besides enjoying fighting for its own sake – the Norse heaven was a place where fallen warriors were instantly healed so that they could return to the fray – they were devotees of the horse, which they transported in their ships or took trouble to capture when they landed. Their raids therefore penetrated deep inland, where they killed, burnt and looted with terrible effect on the peace and prosperity of inner Europe.

It was through the struggle against this second wave of determined assailants on their rich homelands that the mounted warriors of the West emerged into fully fledged feudal chivalry. On the one hand it has been argued, the insecurity created by Viking, Magyar and Muslim attacks encouraged the peasantry to pool their

Mongol horsemen, c. 1300, mounted on steppe ponies with stirrups, and armed with the composite bow

ploughing efforts, creating a 'manorial' economy of large agricultural units. On the other, these units provided overlords with the sort of landholding on which they could settle their cavalry in the assurance that they, their horses and supporters would be adequately supported. In a sense the heavy horse underlay both developments, that of the vassal knight and that of his manor, which he ruled as lord under the overlordship of a greater noble.

Yet though the new feudalism did gradually lead to a stabilization of Europe's frontiers against barbarian invasion, it did not lead to greater peace within Europe. Rather the contrary; cavalry vassals tended to consolidate the grip on their landholdings during the tenth and eleventh centuries by building themselves castles. Those that could find the manpower, materials, money and right site thereby became dominant in their locality. 'He could do what he liked,' wrote a tenth-century chronicler of Hugh of Abbeville, the founder of the County of Ponthieu, 'relying on the protection of his castle, while others, if they tried anything, were easily overcome since they had no refuge.' What such castellans 'tried' was to subdue their poorer neighbours, but also to defy their overlords if they thought force and honour permitted. Hence a great deal of the cavalry warfare which became such a distinct feature of polities in feudal Europe from the tenth to the fifteenth centuries.

The armies which fought these wars were tiny by modern standards – Henry V won Agincourt with less than a thousand knights – but their organization was quite formal. Camp followers and foot soldiers provided the main body. At its core were groups of 'lances', a knight, his squire and a servant. The knight rode and fought in armour which, until the fourteenth century, was chain mail. Originally a simple mail shirt, topped by a plate helmet, it grew to include mail trousers, plate shin and arm pieces and eventually a breastplate. Ultimately, via a stage of 'banded' armour, it developed in about 1400 into a complete suit of plate, with mail only at such joints which the ingenuity of the armourer could not cover with articulated sheet. A shield and a sword were unvarying accoutrements; sometimes also a spear, which was originally used overarm, or even thrown as a javelin. By about 1000, however, the knight had begun to use it 'couched' and by 1100 that use was general. With his lance couched – held tightly under the arm and levelled – the knight, braced in his stirrups and supported front and rear by the high pommel and cantle of a rigid wooden saddle, was almost unstoppable once launched in motion, except by

84

another knight brave and adept enough to unseat him by a counter-thrust of his own lance.

The knight's all-up weight might, however, approach three hundred pounds, so that his warhorse, large though it was, rarely managed more than a trot in action. At other times, it was led at the knight's right – hence its name 'destrier' – while he hacked on a palfrey. His armour and equipment travelled on a pack horse. Squire and servant had horses of their own so that a knight's lance might count five horses altogether.

Battles between men thus armed and mounted gain much from the imagination. The mental image is of torrents of armour meeting in a vulcanic clang on the middle of a level field empty of all other combatants. That owes more to Malory and Tennyson than it does to reality. The knight, like any other warrior, was perfectly happy to frighten his opponent into retreat if he could. Much feudal warfare, therefore, was a matter of skirmishing and stand-offs, often culminating in sieges when one group of warriors beat a prudent retreat before another into the safety of a castle. At the frontiers of Europe, moreover, the light-armed horsemen

French knights at the battle of Poitiers, 1356, under attack by English longbowmen. The English knight (left) wields the heavy lance couched

85

of the steppe made it their business, very sensibly, to keep out of the way of the 'iron people', which the nimbleness of their ponies usually allowed them to do. And even when armoured army met armoured army in fair fight, it was rarely a struggle between knights only. Spearmen, axemen, swordsmen on foot – sometimes these were dismounted knights – crossbowmen and longbowmen in the later ages; these were almost always to be found in the feudal army, and in far larger numbers than the expensively equipped and socially élite mounted men-at-arms. Early or late in the Middle Ages, cavalry played only a partial role on the battlefield in deciding the outcome.

Norman mailed horsemen at Hastings, 1066. They are riding with stirrups on the heavy horse, mounted on the rigid saddle and using the light lance overhand (centre) and couched (right)

Hastings, 1066, which gave victory to the Norman invaders of England, provides a clear example of the function of cavalry during the period of the European armoured horseman's rise. The Normans had made themselves masters of the contemporary cavalry style. The Anglo-Saxons, in their island backwater, clung to the older tactics of fighting on foot. They had taken up their station on a hilltop, where Harold's housecarls formed a shield wall around the King in the centre of the line. The Normans, attacking uphill, were formed in three lines, the first of archers, the second of spearmen, the third of armoured cavalry. The bowmen's attack was ineffective. The spearmen were repulsed. So, too, was the first cavalry charge – in any case a difficult manoeuvre uphill. Two more cavalry charges, however, gained greater success, the last because a feigned flight tempted some of the Saxons into rash pursuit. But the decisive event was the wounding of Harold by a stray arrow. His men lost heart, broke and were harried to defeat by the cavalry as they fled from the position. Hastings was certainly a cavalry battle; but to describe it as a purely cavalry victory is clearly an exaggeration.

Three hundred and fifty years later William's descendant Henry V found himself at the head of an English army in France. His attempt to reconquer Normandy had failed and in the course of his retreat he was brought to battle by the French at Agincourt, in October 1415. Virtually the whole of the French feudal cavalry was arrayed against his line, which consisted of between 6–7,000 archers and footmen and under a thousand knights. An opening French cavalry assault foundered under the volleys of the English archers – just as similar charges had at the fourteenth-century battles of Crécy and Poitiers. Even when the English clothyard arrows did not penetrate the French knights' plate armour – which at close range was possible – they wounded the horses, maddening them with pain and driving them to flight. Some careered off into the surrounding woods; others turned and crashed into the body of French knights who were following the cavalrymen on foot. This 'cavalry charge in reverse' contributed materially to the disruption of the French dismounted attack on the English line, which lost impetus almost as soon as swords were crossed. The first line of French knights were felled by the unshaken English, and successive waves toppled over those who had fallen. Something like a massacre then ensued.

Agincourt ended in complete English victory; and because of the enormous losses suffered by the French, caused a sensation throughout Europe. Nevertheless its pattern confirmed a trend for real battles to diverge in a number of ways – particularly through the dismounting of the knights and the key intervention of common warriors – from what 'chivalry' – in the sense of the military nobility – thought real battle should be. 'Chivalry' therefore looked increasingly to the staging of artificial battles as a means of satisfying the standards it felt should prevail on battlefields. Such 'tournaments' had begun in the twelfth century as a means of serious training for war. By the fifteenth century they had become great theatrical events, the favourite social occasions of the cavalry élite throughout Western Europe, and quite detached from the real business of combat.

Tournaments and warfare did nevertheless connect at the indirect level, through the powerful impetus imparted to the 'code of chivalry' by jousting and tourneying. *Noblesse oblige* is nonetheless true for being a hackneyed phrase. It implies that to stand high in society is to be bound to good behaviour – in personal relations, in love and at war. *Noblesse oblige* still underlies the system by which officers are trained in Western military academies, and it defined the breeding and behaviour of those who aspired to a high military reputation in the late Middle Ages. To ride well, to stand the shock of the charge unflinchingly in the lists, to bear wounds without complaint, to acknowledge the bravery of a courageous opponent – those were the attributes admired by the military class in the fifteenth century.

This cultural rigidity was to be of the greatest importance for the future of cavalry, because 'chivalry' reached its moment of fullest flowering at precisely the time when the appearance of new weapons called the validity of mounted warfare into question. The armoured horsemen had always suffered from severe operational limitations; in the Holy Land, for example, the Crusaders – perhaps the epitome of the type – carried all before them when the enemy agreed to fight on their terms. When they did not – which was the more usual behaviour of the Saracens, originally Turks of the steppe nomad type – the Crusaders were unable to deliver their

Cavalry in action at the battle of Lützen, 1632, firing handguns from the saddle

Italian knights at the battle of San Romano, 1432. The posture of the figure (centre rear) exactly depicts how the couched lance was used

battle-clinching charges. By the beginning of the sixteenth century, however, a more serious threat than evasive tactics challenged the knight. His armour, as well as his horse, had been vulnerable for two hundred years to the crossbow, a weapon that combined the penetrative power of the composite bow with ease of manipulation. Only its low rate of discharge had limited its usefulness. The appearance of hand-held firearms, however, really did spell doom to the knight. For the arquebus (later the musket) ball could not be kept out by any armour light enough for a soldier to wear. That being so, there was no point in wearing armour at all. It did linger on in partial form as a protection against sword and lance thrusts, though chiefly with the infantry. The fully armoured mounted warrior, on the other hand, disappeared from history, like frost from a sun-warmed battlefield, in the first quarter of the sixteenth century.

And with his going the whole status of cavalry in the Western world was called into question. Indeed, cavalrymen themselves did not at first see how to adapt to the new age. An attempt was made to meet the arquebusier or musketeer on his own terms by adopting the pistol or a shortened form of the musket – the carbine – for use from the saddle. A complicated cavalry manoeuvre, called the caracole, was even worked out, which allowed successive lines of cavalry to discharge their weapons and then wheel away to reload so that a continuous fire was kept up against the front of the enemy formation. But firearms and horses, it was soon found, do not usually mix, and by the beginning of the seventeenth century that manoeuvre had been abandoned. The question remained: what should cavalry do?

Two answers presented themselves. The first was to integrate cavalry more closely with the other arms, infantry and artillery. An early, though perhaps unintended experiment in this technique took place at the battle of Marignano in 1515, when the French cavalry successfully charged the Swiss pikemen, who were formed in blocks normally impervious to mounted attack. This success was made possible by the French artillery's prolonged preliminary cannonade against the

Lady Butler's magnificent overdramatization of the Charge of the Scots Greys at Waterloo

88

Swiss formations into which the cavalry then made thirty-five separate charges. Marignano was exceptional, made so probably by the notorious reluctance of Swiss infantry to give ground. A hundred years later, however, battles like Marignano were becoming the rule, because generals like Gustavus Adolphus deliberately emphasized the need for the separate arms to support each other. Pikemen were to provide a secure base from which 'the shot' were to pepper the opposing ranks until – assisted by longer-range artillery – the cavalry could complete victory by breaking the enemy's cohesion, and forcing him to run away.

The second answer followed from this point of the action – if it could be brought about. Cavalry became the 'pursuit arm', whose function was to ride down fugitives, capture or kill them and ensure that a broken enemy army stayed broken. The aftermath of Ramillies, when Marlborough's cavalry rode through the rout of the French army for fifteen miles, putting it out of action for the rest of 1706, is an excellent example of how decisive a ruthless pursuit could be.

These two functions of cavalry in the gunpowder age were not, however, necessarily best performed by troops armed and mounted in the same fashion. A marked degree of differentiation began to appear between cavalry regiments towards the end of the seventeenth century. The simple 'horse' of Cromwell's army was joined in the Restoration army after 1660 by regiments of dragoons – a French term, from the 'dragon' musket with which they were armed. Their role was to fight as infantry but move as cavalry, in fulfilment of the trend towards mutual support between the different arms already mentioned. This differentiation did not catch on, partly because it did not work, partly because cavalry seem to have an aversion to dismounted action, and dragoons were soon assimilated into the heavy cavalry.

A distinct 'light' cavalry was, however, emerging at the same time as the dragoons were abandoning their mounted infantry role, its task being both to push the pursuit yet faster and further, but also to act more vigorously as scouts and skirmishers than could heavy cavalry. Light cavalry of various sorts and origins had appeared in the Italian Wars of the sixteenth century, often recruited in the Balkans – 'Albanian' was a term used to describe such 'stradiots' collectively – where they had learnt some steppe nomad tactics from the Turks. European armies of the Thirty Years War recruited such light cavalry wherever they could find them. By the eighteenth century, however, it had become a tenet of military opinion that the best were obtained from Hungary, whence as 'hussars' (from the Magyar word for twenty, the number of households that had to support one cavalryman) they passed into every army in Europe.

The first to recruit them in numbers was the Austrian army, which liberated Hungary from the Turks at the end of the seventeenth century. But hussars also appeared in the French army in 1704 and in the Prussian in 1721. Their distinctive and romantic garb – fur busby with plume and coloured busby bag, frogged dolman jacket, fur-lined pelisse slung over one shoulder, tight braided trousers and concertina crinkled boots – made them an object of sartorial envy to other cavalrymen whenever they appeared. So strong was their appeal that their uniform and appearance began to be imitated by cavalrymen who had never seen Hungary. In 1805–6 four regiments of British light dragoons, the 7th, 10th, 15th and 18th, were renamed Hussars, and the men ordered to grow moustaches to complete the Hungarian effect.

At almost the same time, in 1809 Napoleon brought two regiments of Polish cavalry into the French army. They also wore a dramatic native costume, the square and flat-topped Czapka hat and the short jacket with plastron front, but the distinctive feature of their equipment was the lance. Abandoned by Western

European horsemen since the end of the Middle Ages, it had lingered on in the East, where the Polish cavalry had used it to effect in their endless wars against the Turks and Russians. The effectiveness of Napoleon's 'Polish Lancers' prompted his enemies to adopt their weapon even more quickly than they had the Hungarian curved sabre fifty years earlier. The British light dragoon regiments, the 9th, 12th and 16th, were outfitted with the lance – and also, of course, with an adaptation of Polish national costume – in 1815–16, while the Prussian and Austrians followed suit.

This passion for recruiting or, when that was not possible, imitating the wild horsemen of Europe's steppe frontier did not stop there. Russia, which throughout the eighteenth century had been pushing its frontier steadily forward into the steppe, had its own supply of wild horsemen to hand. These Cossacks took their name from the Turkish word for 'adventurer'. But, far from being Turks themselves, they were Russians who had tired of serfdom and run away to lead the dangerous life of the outlaw in the unadministered borderlands on the northern shore of the Black Sea. Through close contact with Turks and Mongols they learnt their standards of horsemanship, and by 1650 they were numerous and formidable enough for the Tsar's government to have begun organizing them into military colonies intended to defend the southern frontier. Their genius, though, was as free men who, enlisted under their elected chiefs, served the Tsar for pay in regiments of light cavalry. By 1826 there were 70,000 of them in the Tsar's service and their romantic costume, first seen in the West in 1814 when Cossacks formed part of the army that occupied Paris, caught the European imagination. Cossack boots, Cossack fur hats, the long Cossack coats with cartridge loops on the chest, became items of fashion, copied as often by women as by men. A few armies, notably the Prussian, even made attempts to reorganize some of their own cavalry regiments on Cossack lines as had been done with the hussars in the eighteenth century.

But the practice did not catch on, for reasons that perhaps had to do with the progressive decline in importance of the steppe horsemen on the Eurasian land mass. Their power had reached its height in the thirteenth century, when Mongol tribes, united under a self-proclaimed 'Perfect War Emperor' or Genghis Khan, embarked on a series of conquests which took the boundaries of his empire to the coasts of the Pacific in the east, the crest of the Carpathians in the west and the banks of the Indus in the south. The empire was not to survive as a unit Genghis' death in 1227. But his successors greatly extended the limits of Mongol domination. Ogotai, Genghis' son, penetrated Central Europe; Tamerlane, who claimed descent from Genghis, briefly conquered much of the Middle East in the fourteenth century; while in the sixteenth a Mogul (Mongol) empire was established in India. The ineradicable weakness of the Mongol system, however, was that it could not transform itself from an exploitative to an administrative mode of government. As the states on the periphery of the steppe – in China, Western Europe and the Arab Middle East – consolidated their power and amplified their wealth, the steppe horsemen found their dynamic but essentially brittle strategy of decreasing effectiveness. In particular the rise of the maritime empires, based on gunpowder, ocean-going ships and bureaucratic commerce, hedged about their room for manoeuvre with colonies and trading dependencies they lacked the force to overcome. By the end of the eighteenth century, when the British stood poised to supplant the Moguls as rulers of India, the days of nomad cavalry power were clearly numbered. By 1885, when Russia conquered Merv, the last independent Muslim principality in Central Asia, it was over. Regiments of Cossacks and of Tartars, their former enemies, would continue to add glamour and dash to the ranks of the Tsar's cavalry.

But the epoch when the rumble of steppe ponies' hooves had sent shudders of fear around the civilized world was at an end.

The cavalry of the civilized world refused, nevertheless, to accept the same verdict. In the century of overseas empire building, in Africa and Asia, that followed the defeat of Napoleon, European cavalry enjoyed an Indian summer. Much of it was recruited locally – Spahis in French North Africa, Silladar horse in British India – and its white officers led it to heady victory in dozens of small campaigns against tribesmen and rebels who resisted the ineluctable onset of European expansionism. There were never better-looking cavalrymen than these – the Spahis in streaming scarlet cloaks, Bengal lancers in turbans of peacock hue, Madrassis in French grey and silver, Skinner's irregulars in canary yellow – and never soldiers whose officers esteemed them more. But the cavalry of the regular armies at home in Europe also achieved a sartorial elegance without parallel in those years. In full dress, the Prussian Garde du Corps wore helmets crowned with a winged eagle, burnished breastplates and glittering jackboots reaching to the thigh. French hussars and *chasseurs à cheval* were dressed in sky blue jackets and red trousers, Austrian dragoons in white coatees and gold lace, the Royal Scots Greys in high

Russian cavalry on patrol, First World War, mounted on light horses and armed with the carbine

bearskin caps and scarlet tunics. This magnificence was an expression of the cavalry's fixed belief that its role on the battlefield was still the decisive one.

There were military episodes in the nineteenth century that endorsed this belief. Cavalry performed with considerable effect during the Crimean War of 1854–6; the charge of the British Light Brigade at Balaclava is remembered as a legendary disaster but the charge of the Heavy Brigade in the same battle was a success of the traditional sort. At Mars-la-Tour, during the Franco-Prussian War of 1870–1, von Bredow's brigade of lancers and cuirassiers got within charging distance of the French artillery and, though suffering fifty per cent casualties in what became known as 'von Bredow's Death Ride', got among the guns and drove the artillerymen from their pieces.

It was results of this sort that encouraged the paladins of the cavalry caste to preach to their followers the message of war's unchanging nature. For them the appearance of rifled firearms, high-explosive shells, even of quick-firing artillery and the machine-gun, were irrelevancies. It was the 'cavalry spirit' that counted and because the officers of the cavalry in all important armies – German, French, Russian, Austrian, British – continued to be drawn from the landowning class, or

French cavalry, 1918. They are still equipped with the Polish lance introduced by Napoleon in 1807

Russian cavalry of the Second World War, mounted on ponies and equipped with automatic weapons

those seeking to enter it with money made in industry and commerce, the voice of the paladins prevailed. In a garbled form, it was the voice of vanished chivalry, as well as that of the surviving aristocracy, whose power over conservative institutions, among which armies stood foremost, remained unshaken by revolution and even by the rise of democracy.

But the latent truth was entirely otherwise. The American Civil War, so little remarked by European observers, was not only the largest and longest-lasting major war of the nineteenth century, but also that in which cavalry counted least. Cavalry raiders — J. E. B. Stuart's for the Confederacy, Grierson's for the Union — retained the power to sow confusion in the enemy's rear and cause a sensation in the newspapers. But, the battle of Brandy Station in June 1863 apart, the war yielded no examples whatsoever of pure cavalry action and none in which cavalry played a decisive part. Cavalry, as mounted infantry, enjoyed a misleading renaissance during the Boer War and attracted an equally misleading amount of attention from official observers during the Russo-Japanese War of 1904–5. The iron laws of industrial progress had, nevertheless, spelt its doom, which only awaited its moment to make itself evident.

That moment came in 1914. It seems probable that there was more cavalry in the world in that year than in any before. The German army mobilized eleven cavalry divisions, the French ten, the Russian thirty-six, the Austrian eleven, the Belgian one and the British two. As a cavalry division fielded about five thousand mounted men, the total put into the field amounted to some 355,000, considerably more than the number with which Genghis Khan had subdued the greatest part of Eurasia in the thirteenth century. Some of those divisions played a useful part in reconnaissance ahead of the marching armies. Others did not; Sordet's Cavalry Corps, the major mounted formation of the French army, blundered about in the forests of the Ardennes for over two weeks in August without finding hair or hide of its opponents, while the Russian cavalry that invaded East Prussia achieved no more than a little farm-burning. And as soon as regiments of cavalrymen came up against formed infantry, they were shot off their horses in droves and the survivors sent packing to the rear.

Within six weeks of the war's outbreak, the open fronts necessary to cavalry mobility had disappeared, barbed wire and trenches appearing to mark the position occupied by the infantry. Such a development should have persuaded the High Command on all sides that their investment in horseflesh was now entirely uneconomic. So dominant did the cavalry mystique remain in European armies, however, that the cavalry divisions were kept in being, awaiting what British horse soldiers called 'the Gee in Gap', until the very last year of the war. It was only then, when the massacre of manpower had reached proportions too large for the shibboleths of military custom to prevail any longer, that the decision was finally taken to unhorse the cavalry and use its troopers to serve as infantry, or as replacements in the supporting arms. Grumbling and tearfully, hussars, dragoons and lancers said goodbye to their steeds and stumbled off to the trenches, often encumbered by spurs, swords and bandoliers quite inappropriate to their new earthbound calling but which three thousand years of tradition forbade them to discard.

Cavalry was still to enjoy, in remote sectors of the world or campaigns eccentric to war-winning strategies, a few more years of existence. In the Middle East, British and Australian cavalry would charge to glory against the disintegrating Turkish armies in 1918. During the Russo-Polish War of 1919–20 the descendants of the Cossacks and the hussars of Sobieski would tussle for mastery of the plains around Warsaw, while White or Red cavalry battled out decision in the Russian Civil War until 1921. In the Second World War, the Red Army began operations with twenty

Cossack cavalry in German service, Second World War, charging with the sabre in drill-book style

94

Cossack cavalrymen of the Second World War in German service

cavalry divisions and as late as 1944, in the breakthrough at Lvov, Marshal Konev still had six cavalry divisions under command. But none of these formations could risk meeting regular infantry, let alone armoured formations on equal terms. Their role was limited to reconnaissance, skirmishing and exploitation on subsidiary sectors of the front. Red cavalry rode with the armies that entered Berlin in 1945. But they were the symbolic rearguard of a military tradition which, though at the peak of its significance it had bestrode the world, was now consigned to history. In the armies of long continuity, like the British, Indian and French, regiments of dragoons, hussars, cuirassiers and lancers would continue to be counted in the order of battle. But their soldiers, who had never known horses, would be trained as crews of the tank. It was to that machine that the principle of military mobility had now passed.

96

Gunner 5

Stalin called artillery 'the God of War'. A romantic might think that he had in mind the guns of the 1812 Overture, from which the Almighty seems to speak in tongues of fire through a cumulus of smoke and thunder. But that dreadful old drinker of blood, Generalissimo of one of the great artillery armies of the world, would have been invoking another deity, more like one of the Dutch cartoonist Raemaeker's crowned Calibans, for whom the guns of the Great War won their daily diet of quivering flesh and pulverized bone. What was divine to Stalin in artillery was its arbitrary, insensate and remorseless energy, the man-made equivalent of the volcanic eruptions before which primitives fled in terror from what they believed was the wrath of the heavens. A man with artillery on his side – and by 1945 Stalin had, as the Soviet army still does, acre upon acre of guns – might dice with the Devil and rise from the table the victor.

The victims of artillery knew all too well what Stalin meant. Jean Galtier-Boissière, a veteran of 1915, wrote: 'The courage of Achilles came from the knowledge that with his superior strength and skill, if he attacked with vigour, he would triumph always. His courage was his best shield, it protected his life. The courage of the modern soldier – alas what good is our courage? Does a man defend himself against the earthquake which is going to swallow him up? Do you shoot at a volcano when it vomits its flaming lava?'

He spoke as a survivor of the offensives in Champagne, which had left the French trenches choked with dead heroes who had never had the chance to see the enemy, let alone cross bayonets with him. Some of them had gone to war only a year before clad in the finery of the pre-artillery age, blue coats and red trousers, with bands playing at the head of the regiment and colours unfurled at the moment of attack. Such uniforms and such tactics had already begun to cost armies dear fifty years before, on the battlefields of the American Civil War and Prussia's wars with Austria and France. In the titanic opening struggles of 1914, which statesmen and generals had expected would be settled by press of numbers, as battles had been decided for three thousand years, massed infantry had been slaughtered in droves by the shrapnel of quick-firing artillery. Cavalry, symbol of an age of chivalry which continued to exist only in the imagination of epic poets, had been scattered like chaff on the winnowing floor, never to reappear. And the effects achieved by artillery in 1914–15 were but an anticipation of what was to follow in the climactic campaigns of 1916–18. In the autumn of 1918 the French artillery would fire over half a million rounds a day on some fronts – at Waterloo Napoleon's artillery had not fired 10,000 rounds – and would calculate its efficacy in numbers of *tons* discharged for each German casualty (about five tons fired for each German killed each day). War had indeed industrialized itself, and the medium of that industrialization was the gun and the shell.

Yet the origins of artillery were, by contrast, modest, and its rise to military significance slow and tentative. Artillery, in some sense, had been known to the ancients and to the mediaeval world, in the form of missile-throwing engines which worked either through the stored energy of torsion springs or the sudden release of a counterpoised weight. The counterpoise principle powered the catapult, earliest recorded of artillery pieces, which was invented by servants of the tyrant Dionysius of Syracuse in 400 B.C. Torsion springs supplied force to the bolt- and arrow-throwing machines which, developed by the Greeks, later became standard in the imperial Roman armies. But it is important not to confuse the ancients' familiarity with the artillery principle and the frequency of its use. Torsion and non-torsion weapons were superior in power to the hand-held weapons of the infantryman and cavalryman. Both, however, depended upon muscular force and its mechanized storage was subject to severe constraints. These were of two sorts, relative and absolute. Relatively, all increases in the gravity of counterweights and the torques of springs had to be matched by increases in the bulk of the wooden frames by which they were contained. The consequent weight penalties diminished mobility, requiring that large machines be either permanently emplaced, as counter-siege engines, or built *in situ* for siege work. Absolutely, there was an upper limit on the stored strains and stresses, followed by discharge shock, that wood could withstand; and a human limit on the energy which could be transmitted into the storage medium. In operational terms, these physical constraints translated into weapons which, if mobile, were of limited power and range; if static, were large, cumbersome and slow to work.

Battlefield 'artillery' was therefore an uncommon feature of combat in antiquity; and siege engines, whether in ancient or mediaeval warfare, of notably limited effect. What was required to make mechanical weapons a dominant military force was some means of *replacing* rather than transmuting muscular effort. And that was not to appear until the later Middle Ages, when the invention of gunpowder suddenly offered the promise of substituting chemical for physical energy in the discharge of projectiles against an enemy.

Who invented gunpowder is a question that still divides historians of science. The evidence seems to suggest that gunpowder was known in the Chinese empire as early as the eleventh century A.D. So, too, were guns of a very primitive sort. Chinese armies, however, were eventually converted from muscular to chemical energy only in the Manchu period (began 1636), and then through contact with traders and adventurers from Europe. It is unquestionably in that continent, where gunpowder was independently discovered during the fourteenth century, that 'the gunpowder revolution' must be placed, since it was there that guns first played a significant role in warfare and underwent progressive and purposive improvement.

The earliest depiction of a gun which survives is in an English manuscript of 1327. Guns were used at the battle of Crécy, 1346, by the English, and Petrarch described them, circa 1350, as having become 'as common and familiar as other kinds of arms'. But that was a literary exaggeration. Early guns were crude, low-pressure constructions, of little menace to man, beast or even buildings. In the fifteenth century more effective pieces appeared, constructed either by shrinking iron hoops around iron staves, on the barrel principle, or by casting tubes in bronze. But the former were structurally and the latter metallurgically unsafe, unless used, respectively, with paltry powder charges or made so large as to be immobile. Some bronze guns were cast on site, to circumvent the difficulty of moving them, a technique favoured by the Turks, who employed giant guns to batter down the walls of Constantinople in the final siege of the city in 1453.

Guns too large to move or too unsafe to fire were unlikely to revolutionize

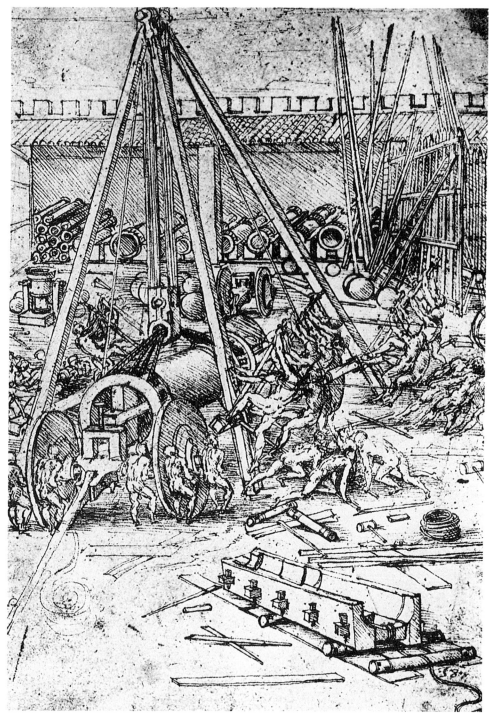

warfare. But in 1494 there appeared a force of artillery of truly revolutionary quality. It belonged to Charles VIII, King of France, consisted of cast bronze guns light enough to travel on field-carriages but strong enough to resist high-pressure propellant charges, and was dedicated to the rapid establishment of French power in Italy. Charles VIII's gunners eschewed the risk of pitting their novel artillery park on the field of battle. Instead, they committed it against a target identifiably vulnerable to artillery's power, mediaeval fortress architecture.

Sixteenth-century siege cannon at work at Parma (1515)

Since time immemorial, fortification engineers had sought to nullify attack by making defensive walls of the greatest possible height. The point was to defeat 'escalade', the attack of fortresses by men equipped with scaling ladders (hence the term) or, a later development, siege towers. Escalade was most successful when the garrison was weak – as at the capture of Jerusalem by the Crusaders in 1099. When escalade failed, or when the walls were too high or the garrison too strong for it to be attempted, attackers had been forced to resort to other methods – mining, battering or, if all else failed, starvation.

One of the Neapolitan castles approached by Charles VIII's army in 1494, Monte San Giovanni, had previously withstood a siege by traditional methods of seven years. It fell to his guns in eight hours. Three months after he set out on his path of conquest, the whole of Italy lay at his feet. The technique his gunners employed was to attack the wall at its base, swinging the gun between shots so that the heavy iron balls – themselves far more efficient than the stone balls shot by early cannon and pre-gunpowder siege engines – cut a channel in the stonework. When the channel was long and deep enough, the wall fell of its own accord. The rules of siege warfare required that once such a 'practicable breach' had been made – called 'practicable' because the hole and the pile of rubble leading to it permitted an infantry assault – the garrison should surrender or take the consequences, which included fire, sword and pillage.

Few garrisons proved resolute enough to offer resistance after a 'practicable breach' had been so rapidly made by these revolutionary weapons. As a result, there was what Christopher Duffy has called a 'Blitzkrieg' of Spanish and Habsburg fortresses by the French in Italy during the last decade of the fifteenth and first of the sixteenth centuries. And the Blitzkrieg was not only actual; it was also conceptual. For not only were ancient castles overthrown almost at the word of the new artillery's approach; the whole system of fortification on which they were designed was rendered obsolete at a stroke. Height, for which fortifications had previously striven, was now a point of weakness in fortification architecture. A new means of investing defences with strength was required if the 'offensive on the rampage' was ever to be contained.

Curiously the antidote to the new artillery had been invented seven years before Charles VIII's whirlwind campaign had begun. Called by historians of fortification the 'angle bastion', it can be first identified in the work of Giuliano da Sangallo at Poggio Imperiale in Tuscany. Its distinctive features are the glancing surface its walls present to artillery shot, their thickness and lack of height, and the broad triangular platform provided by their shape for a counter-bombardment battery. When arranged at intervals around the perimeter of a fortress, at distances calculated to be mutually supporting and with the approaches obstructed by a wet or dry ditch, a well-manned and gunned angle-bastion fortress was virtually impregnable by infantry alone and opposed a formidable obstacle to them even when they were amply supported by artillery. The reason for its great intrinsic strength was that its ground-plan left no square foot around its perimeter 'dead' to defending fire, while the bastions themselves provided counter-offensive gun positions from which to engage and subdue the attacking artillery.

So, on the defensive side, was the stage set for the great age of siege warfare that was to occupy much of the energy of armies and commanders from the beginning of the sixteenth to the middle of the nineteenth century. Naturally, the angle-bastion fortress was not perfected immediately. Certain improvisations, like the secondary earthen rampart built at Pisa to reinforce the ancient wall against French artillery attack during the siege of 1500, were successfully invoked to prolong the life of old-style fortresses – at La Rochelle as late as 1573. Conversely, sophisticated angle-bastion forts were undergoing refinement and improvement right up until the appearance of high-explosive rendered them definitely obsolete in the 1880s. But the system was, nevertheless, astonishingly rapid to take shape and to achieve acceptance – at a pace, indeed, analagous to that at which steam and iron replaced sail and wood in naval architecture *c.* 1850. Coal was to be the making of the warship revolution. Gunpowder had been the making of the fortification revolution.

Did gunpowder not also revolutionize the battlefield? In a sense, yes, but not immediately and not through artillery. Cannon were to play a notable part in two battles of the early sixteenth century, Ravenna, 1512, and Marignano, 1515. The French defeated the Spanish in the first, the Swiss in the second. But they did so because the battlefield in each case had been turned by entrenchment into a sort of artificial fortress, so denying the contesting parties, once locked in combat, the opportunity to manoeuvre. Commanders seem very quickly to have drawn the appropriate lesson that safety from artillery attack was assured by keeping to the open field. As a result, guns were to contribute little to victory in battle until the end of the eighteenth century.

Why were weapons so effective against fixed defences to prove so ineffective against men and horses for so long? To answer that it is necessary to re-examine the nature of the 'new' French guns of the late fifteenth century. Their distinctive quality was that they were cast in a particular way. The particularity had to do partly with proportions and partly with features. *Proportionally* they were thickest at the breech, where pressure of the propellant explosion was greatest, and thinnest at the muzzle, so that for a given weight of metal a gun could be made much longer than the primitive 'bombards' produced by the original bell-casting methods. Length was desirable because it imparted higher velocity and greater accuracy to the iron cannon ball. The most important *features* associated with the improved casting process were the trunnions, cylindrical projections positioned just forward of the point of balance, on which the barrel was hinged in the carriage. Previously it had been necessary to rest the barrel in a weighty wooden trough, requiring four wheels to move. Trunnions allowed the gun to travel on a much lighter two-wheeled carriage with which 'elevation' and 'depression' of the muzzle was a simple mechanical function. At a stroke the gun was made both easier to move from place to place and handier to 'lay' when it arrived there.

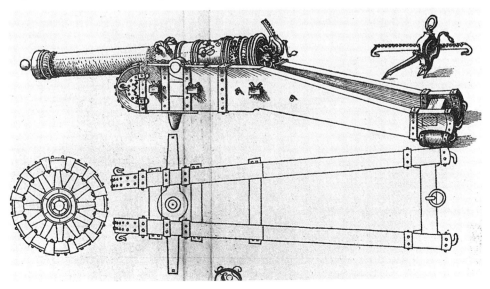

Cast bronze Renaissance cannon (Dürer, 1527). Its novel features are the trunnions, elevating gear and light, two-wheeled travelling carriage

Laying a gun on to a target entails two of four adjustments: 'elevation' and 'depression' of the muzzle upwards or downwards, to 'lengthen' or 'shorten' the range, and 'training' left or right to correct the 'bearing'. Two wheels rather than four greatly simplified training, trunnions enormously simplified elevation and depression; indeed these features, trunnions and the two-wheeled carriage, are as distinctive of modern mobile artillery as they were of the 'new' gun at the moment of its development *c.* 1490.

But the 'new' gun, though it could be brought to the battlefield much more easily than the old sort, and worked more handily when in place, resisted rapid relocation in the face of the enemy. To move the gun any distance required that its team of draught animals be brought forward and hitched to its carriage. Even when the use of the limber – a two-wheeled carriage intermediate between team and gun-carriage, which greatly simplified towing – had become general (though that was not to be until the late seventeenth century), 'limbering' and 'putting to' the team remained a time-consuming business. And manoeuvring the gun, once team and limber were hitched, was cumbersome; their combined turning circle was too large to be easily accommodated on a battlefield crowded with infantry and cavalry in close order. Guns, once in position, tended as a result to be stuck for the duration of the battle. That was what happened to the French artillery at Pavia, in 1525; after inflicting heavy casualties on Francis I's Habsburg opponents, his cannon were first masked by an ill-considered movement of French troops and then brought under attack by Habsburg arquebusiers firing from a flank. As the guns could be neither moved to return fire nor evacuated from their insecure position, they were all captured, the prelude to a complete French defeat.

Pavia is significant, in the history of military technology, because it demonstrated that the immediate future for gunpowder weapons was as handguns rather than artillery pieces. The arquebus could be accommodated in a 'battle of all arms' – the others being pikemen and cavalry – in a way that artillery could not, because the arquebusier could move on his feet with a rapidity the gun team could not match. Cannon continued to feature on battlefields of the sixteenth and seventeenth centuries. But their role was to be a secondary and circumscribed one until means were found – as they were in the eighteenth century – to enhance their tactical mobility and man-killing power.

It was chiefly as siege weapons, therefore, that the products of the gun-founder's art were to make their effect in European warfare during the sixteenth and seventeenth centuries. The angle-bastion fort had proved an effective answer to the mobile cannon of the late fifteenth century. But it was not totally cannon-proof – if cannon were handled in the right way. The 'right way' was the subject of dedicated experiment during the sixteenth century, particularly in the Low Countries, in the eighty-year religio-political conflict between the Spanish and Dutch. The pioneer of siege technique was Parma, governor of the Spanish Netherlands; his opponents and imitators, notably Maurice of Nassau, soon matched and even outdid his technique.

This technique, which was to last as long as the traditional fortress itself, rested on the principle of opposing earth-moving with earth-moving. The fortress was overcome by artillery fire; but while the artillery was being worked, it had to be protected from the fortress's counter-fire by field entrenchment. The effective range of the fortress's guns – about 600 yards – determined where the guns were emplaced for the opening duel. There a 'first parallel' was dug, a trench parallel to the particular 'face' of the fortress chosen for attack. While the guns in the 'first parallel' kept the fortress gunners busy, sappers drove forward a series of zig-zag 'saps' until the pre-determined line of the second parallel was reached. When it

104

Artillery at the siege of Münster, 1647. Heavy cannon attack the walls, and mortars fire into the city

had been dug and new battery positions constructed, the siege guns were rushed forward under cover of darkness and the duel reopened. The remaining three hundred yards were crossed as before and a third parallel opened on the lip of the ditch.

At a range so close – less than a hundred yards – this final stage of the siege was a bloody and frantic business. The besieger's aim was to pack as many heavy guns – 24-pounders were the favoured weapon – as close together as possible. Two dozen standing side by side could in a week effect a 'practicable breach', when the facing stone and earth of the rampart collapsed into the ditch, making a ramp for the assaulting infantry to climb. But to achieve that result required the discharge of eighty rounds by each gun each day. And while the gunners laboured to fire that number, the defending artillerymen strove to drive them from their pieces by a continuous return fire of gun, howitzer and mortar rounds.

This return fire was frequently effective, for the smooth-bore cannon could not be worked without much exposure by its crew. Unlike modern artillerymen who can serve their gun from seated positions behind its shield, blackpowder gunners – six or eight to each piece – had to work on their feet and keep in motion. At the start of the firing sequence, the gun was swabbed out from the muzzle by inserting a long wet mop, which doused and scoured out glowing fragments of powder from the previous round. A measure of powder was next inserted with a scoop – in the eighteenth century this charge would be inserted whole in a large paper 'cartridge' – and tamped down with the rammer. Finally the ball was lifted into the muzzle and rammed down on top of the powder. When the layer had adjusted the piece for range and direction, by working the elevating wedges under the gun's breech, and swinging the carriage left or right, the gunner would fill the touch-hole at the breech with fine powder and, standing well clear of the wheels, apply his smouldering linstock.

The resulting discharge would drive the gun an appreciable distance rearwards, though in siege work specially constructed platforms would absorb a considerable amount of this 'recoil'. But the recoil would nevertheless have put the gun out of true, and it would have to be 'run up' again before the next round could be fired, heavy work which needed muscle, sling ropes and sometimes levers to complete.

While the gunners toiled, the defenders rained down on their positions shot and shell of every description. Arquebusiers – later musketeers – tried to pick off the gun crews at their work. Mortars, the short high-angle cannon which fired explosive shells or loads of stone or scrap-iron, deluged the gun positions 'with up to two wheelbarrows' loads of stones at a time. 'The stones fly through the air in a cloud, then flog the ground with a force that can only be compared with that of pikes landing point-downwards'; so wrote Vauban, the great siege engineer, of a siege of 1672. Over a century later a British officer, describing the effects of French counter-fire at Badajoz, reported a scene which would have been familiar to siege-gunners at any date between 1550 and 1850; 'by ten in the morning, our line of batteries presented a very disorganized appearance; sandbags, gabions and fascines [siege equipment] knocked here and there; guns flung off their carriages and carriages beaten down under their guns. The boarded platforms of the batteries, damp with the blood of our artillerymen . . . bore testimony to the murderous fire opposed to us.'

In return, the besiegers would be lobbing howitzer and mortar shells into the fortress. The explosive shell, a hollow iron sphere filled with gunpowder and exploded by a burning fuse, first appeared in 1588 when used by the Spanish against the Dutch fortress of Wachtendonck. Later, explosive shells were supplemented by red-hot shot, iron cannon balls heated in ovens and fired almost as soon as they could be rolled down the gun barrel. The technique was ticklish, but the result was particularly effective if the ball lodged in the roof or floor timbers of a fortress building, where it might smoulder undiscovered until an unquenchable fire had taken hold.

To set fire to a besieged town was, however, terror tactics, to be justified only by ideological hatreds or by extreme military urgency. Besiegers, normally wishing to take possession of the town in a relatively undamaged state, concentrated their efforts on disabling the garrison. When close quarters had been reached, therefore, their gunners dedicated numbers of their pieces to 'ricochet' fire. 'Ricocher' means 'to bounce' and the object of ricochet fire was to send balls at an angle low enough just to graze the parapet of the walls or bastions. It required precise gunnery – a juggling both with the elevation of the barrel and with ounces of powder in the charge. But the effect, once achieved, was murderous. The balls swept across the gun platforms and walkways inside the fortress, decapitating and dismembering the defenders or, if they hit an obstruction, showering them with lethal splinters.

By the time the wall had been breached and its defenders slaughtered, the artillery had completed its work. The capture of the fortress – should its governor not surrender as convention required he ought – then fell to the infantry. Only if they failed in the assault would the artillery be required to recommence the preparatory bombardment. This pattern had, by the end of the seventeenth century, become unvarying; so much so that Vauban reckoned to predict the 'march' of the siege of the citadel of Lille on a precise daily time-table, forty days in all.

Sieges did not, in practice, always run as smoothly as the textbooks laid down. Equally, fortresses did not always succeed in their purpose of impeding the movement of armies about a theatre of operations. The decline in the importance of fortresses became marked in the eighteenth century. This trend was the result partly of improvements to the road and bridge network of Europe, to the drainage of flatlands and to a reduction in the area of forest; partly to the strengthening of the state apparatus, manifested in larger revenues which underpinned more efficient armies; partly in improvements in military technology that allowed battles in the open field rather than contests of strength around fortresses to be the focus of strategic effort.

The perfection of the flintlock musket, its furnishing with a handy bayonet, was one such improvement; together the two weapons permitted the conflation of the former roles of arquebusier and pikeman, with beneficial effects on the mobility and flexibility of the infantry. That arm continued to form the bulk of field armies, so that the enhancement of its efficiency was of central strategic significance. It was also important that light cavalry, able to range widely about the countryside and to forage independently, became a component of European armies in the eighteenth century. But perhaps most important was the emergence of an artillery force capable of true tactical mobility.

This new mobility was owed to the development of guns that could accompany infantry and cavalry on to the battlefield and manoeuvre while there. One ingredient of the development was technological; in 1755 a Swiss engineer, Jean Maritz, applied a new barrel-boring technique to the manufacture of French cannon. Because it gave a better fit between bore and ball, it permitted the use of weaker powder charges and so of thinner barrels. Shortly afterwards a French artillery general, Jean Gribeauval, profited from this improvement to standardize and lighten French cannon, limbers and gun-carriages. An immediate result was that gun teams, formerly often a dozen or more horses strong, could be reduced to six, which became standard until the replacement of the horse by the motor-tractor in the Second World War. The reduction in the size of teams also made it sensible to take drivers permanently on to the strength of the artillery establishment. Previously they had, like bandsmen, been civilians, often hired only for the duration of a campaign.*

This second improvement was complemented by a third, in the design of projectiles. Howitzers and mortars had long fired hollow explosive bombs. In the late eighteenth century it became common to supply field artillery with 'case shot' – a light metal canister packed with musket or heavier balls, which burst along the line of the trajectory and showered the opposing infantry with its contents. In 1784, Lieutenant Henry Shrapnel of the British Royal Artillery, invented a fused shell that produced the same effect; first used at Maida in 1803, it could be made, with accurate fusing, to burst above or directly in front of the opposing infantry with even deadlier effect.

Improved mobility and enhanced man-killing power combined to make the artillery in the late eighteenth century what it had never been hitherto, a true battlefield arm. There had been numerous anticipations of such an outcome. Gustavus Adolphus, the great Swedish soldier-king, had at the beginning of the seventeenth century provided each of his infantry battalions with two 4-pounders on carriages light enough to be drawn by two men or a single horse. Their purpose was to engage the opposing infantry at ranges slightly greater than contemporary firearms could reach. In practice they did the enemy little harm. But other generals persisted with the idea. Marlborough, during the War of the Spanish Succession, detached guns from his 'artillery park' – as the force of 'artillery of position' was usually called – to accompany his British and Dutch infantry into battle. Few were successfully brought into action; but fifty years later at Minden, Prince Ferdinand

---

* In the French army a separate Royal Regiment of Artillery was formed in 1693; in the British army the Royal Artillery was formed in 1716, but it was not until 1794 that a 'Corps of Captains, Commissaries and Drivers' was raised. In 1801 it was renamed the Corps of Gunner Drivers and in 1806 the Royal Artillery Drivers; not until 1822 were drivers directly enlisted into the R.A. The Royal Horse Artillery, in which drivers were enlisted from the start, was raised in 1793. In America, artillery units formed part of the Continental Army from the outset.

of Brunswick succeeded in bringing the British artillery into a position opposite the French from which it inflicted very heavy loss on the attacking cavalry.

The real 'father of mobile artillery', however, was Frederick the Great. That great innovator greatly enhanced the role of the 'battalion artillery' by making standard an allotment of two 6-pounder guns and a 7-pounder howitzer to each of his infantry battalions. But his truly original stroke was to create the first units which would bear the description of 'horse artillery'. They were batteries of light field guns on mobile carriages that could be moved about the battlefield as need arose to intervene where failure threatened or success promised; in short, a reserve of firepower which could be directed at short notice, with great precision and at close range wherever it was most needed.

The 'horse artillery idea' was, however, not to achieve its full realization until the Napoleonic Wars. Napoleon was, of course, an artillery officer of the French royal army, the first gunner to achieve supreme command in a modern army and, as events would prove, the first general to make artillery a decisive arm of war. The first great battle of the Revolutionary War, Valmy (20 September 1792), is usually described as an artillery contest; but the result was indecisive. Napoleon diagnosed the reason. 'Artillery,' he wrote in 1809, 'like the other arms must be collected in mass if one wishes to obtain a decisive result.' The distinctive feature of Napoleon's battle practice, therefore, became the formation of a *grande batterie* of anything up to a hundred guns, controlled and operated as a single unit, which were often progressively advanced to within point-blank range of the enemy's formations.

Friedland (14 June 1807) exemplifies his artillery methods. His enemies were the Russians, who had taken up a position in front of a sharp bend in the River Alle, outside the Prussian town of Friedland. Napoleon's plan was to drive them back into the bend by infantry assault, meanwhile using concentrated fire from ground batteries on their flanks to force them to give ground. The architect of victory was the Commander of his I Corps artillery, General Senarmont, who brought his guns successively to within 600, 300, 150 and eventually 60 paces of the enemy. Ultimately, when they were penned into the chosen river bend, he unleashed salvoes of case shot into their ranks with terrible effect. The survivors got across the river as best they could, leaving 25,000 dead and wounded – out of 46,000 who had begun the battle on the field. French casualties were only 8,000 out of an army of 80,000.

Friedland epitomized the new massed mobile artillery technique. Ironically, however, it was to be perfected and used to greatest effect by the British, who, at Waterloo, demonstrated how artillery could, in the defensive role, spoil even the most promising offensive. There, on 18 June 1815, Napoleon had assembled not only a superior force of infantry and cavalry but also a preponderating mass of artillery. His *grande batterie*, eighty guns strong, outmetalled the Anglo-Dutch army's artillery, which, overall, was one-third weaker than his. But Wellington enjoyed the advantage of controlling a force of horse artillery, established thirty years earlier, that had learnt its trade in the Peninsular War. Some of its batteries – and those of the foot artillery – were posted in fixed positions forward of the infantry squares. Some, however, were kept in reserve, ready to intervene against the French infantry and cavalry as danger threatened.

Horse artillery supported, in theory, the cavalry; in ideal tactical circumstances, it galloped with the cavalry to 'unlimbering distance', from which it fired at the enemy until the cavalry commander judged they could be broken by a charge. Such perfectly co-ordinated circumstances were, however, difficult to arrange. At Waterloo neither the French nor British were able to use their guns in this way. The French, as we have seen, largely contented themselves with bombarding

Butler's Final Crossing of the Tugela. *British horse artillery of the Boer War, manoeuvring under fire*

Wellington's line from a distance. For his part he stationed most of his guns forward of his infantry, their gunners serving their pieces until the French cavalry lapped over their positions in the series of fruitless charges that filled the afternoon. But the six horse troops of Wellington's artillery filled a different role. They were committed as crisis threatened throughout the day; but the most important interventions were by Mercer's and Bull's troops against the French cavalry attacks in late afternoon. Galloping up, they unlimbered at close range and fired into the serried ranks of French horsemen with devastating effect. Mercer, directing fire at sixty yards, first brought down the Horse Grenadiers from a charge to a walk, and then 'piled up such heaps of carcasses' that the survivors escaped as best they could. No wonder that Frazer, the artillery commander, described Mercer's and Bull's troops as moving 'with an alacrity and rapidity that was most admirable' or that Wellington exclaimed 'That is how I like to see horse artillery move.'

The victory of Waterloo was, in great part, certainly an artillery victory; the gunners were singled out for note in Wellington's despatch. But the battle was to be almost the last in which artillery was to perform in its classical role. For another technical revolution impended as the Napoleonic Wars drew to a close. Smooth-bore, iron and bronze guns were about to be replaced by material far more deadly that would allow gunners to ply their trade over distances far greater than those which field artillerymen had covered ever before.

Iron was a metal gunfounders had never quite mastered. Cast too thin, it burst under the pressure of discharge; cast too thick, it became immoveable – except by sending it to sea; ships' cannon were the only really successful iron guns. And even at sea, where weight counted for less, thick and heavy iron guns could contain casting flaws which might make themselves apparent at the most disastrous moments – in the heat of action, for example. Wrought-iron which was hammered rather than poured into shape, was not subject to that weakness; and some very successful wrought-iron artillery was produced before and during the American Civil War. But the method used was essentially a craft, not an industrial process. Armstrong, who pioneered it in England, brought it to a high standard; he was the first

109

gunfounder to calculate pressure points along the barrel scientifically and strengthen them accordingly. The real future lay, however, not with wrought-iron but with steel.

Steel guns, first exhibited by the German manufacturer Krupp at the Great Exhibition of 1851, were originally made by building up the barrel out of separate components. By the 1870s he was machining them from single billets of flawless steel. The barrels, moreover, were now rifled, giving far greater accuracy, and, since rifling also allowed the projectile to fit the bore snugly and so contain more completely the propulsive gases of the charge, of far greater range. Propellants had also, by developments in chemistry contemporaneous with those in metallurgy, also greatly improved: gunpowder was replaced in the 1880s by nitrocellulose compounds in scientifically shaped hollow grains, which burnt steadily, while detonating arrangements made it possible to burn the charge from the front first,

110

WHERE GERMANY'S GREAT "COAL-BOX" SIEGE-GUNS ARE MADE : ONE OF THE CHIEF GUN-FINISHING SHOPS AT KRUPP'S.

Nine immense workshops, each a factory in itself and covering a wide area, are set apart at the Krupp Works, Essen, for the construction of cannon only. Guns of every size are turned out there, from giant 16 or 17 inch siege-howitzers, the dreaded weapons of so much mystery in the war, and 15-inch naval guns for the German super-Dreadnought due to appear at sea next spring, down to field artillery guns, and the new type of light anti-aeroplane motor-car quickfirers, in such evidence now in Northern France. Our illustration shows the interior of "Cannon-Workshop No. 5," where artillery, of every kind is finished off. It is stated that upwards of sixty thousand cannon of all kinds have been turned out at Krupp's—mostly for Germany.—[Photograph by Courtesy of "The World's Work."]

giving a stronger and longer propulsive effort. Most important of all, artillery engineers were now having success in solving the problem of breech-loading.

Some of the earliest guns had been breech-loaders. But gunfounders had always been dogged by the problem that a bronze or iron breech could either be made gas-tight, or easy to open, but not both. By working in steel to fine tolerances, gas leaks could be eliminated; easy opening then became an engineering problem. By 1885 a solution based on an 'interrupted thread' – a cylindrical plug with gaps cut in it to coincide with others in the end of the barrel – had been found the best answer; it was the invention of a French engineer, de Bange.

These elements combined to produce the modern gun. But late Victorian guns incorporating all these features suffered from the disadvantage of remaining comparatively large and heavy; carriages had grown in weight proportionate to the increased recoil shock of the more efficient breech-loader, which in consequence made awkward equipment for field artillery. Finally, in 1897, the French unveiled a piece – to become famous as the *soixante-quinze* or '75' – in which the recoil problem was brilliantly solved.

The solution took the form of mounting the barrel on a piston which worked inside a hydraulic cylinder. When the gun fired the piece merely recoiled against the cylinder, the hydraulic fluid in it returning the barrel to its original position at the end of the stroke. As a result, the slow and heavy work of 'running up' the gun after discharge was eliminated while the carriage, needing to be strong enough only to sustain the weight of barrel and hydraulic 'buffer', not the recoil shock, could be made light almost to the point of flimsiness. It was an added advantage with the

The interior of the Krupp artillery factory at Essen, showing field and medium artillery of the First World War under construction

111

French 75 mm field gun (Model 1897), the first successful quick-firer. The open limber (left) contains the ready-use ammunition

'75' that it was provided with 'fixed' ammunition, in which charge was joined to projectile in a brass case; the consequently accelerated speed of loading, combined with the elimination of 'running up', permitted rates of fire of as much as twenty rounds a minute.

The growth in power of artillery, as it was modernized in these steps, was demonstrated in the Austro-Prussian and Franco-Prussian wars of 1866 and 1870. But it was the Boer and Russo-Japanese wars, in the years 1899 to 1905, that revealed how decisive an arm artillery had by then become on the battlefield. In Manchuria giant Japanese howitzers, of 280 mm calibre, destroyed at its moorings the Russian fleet blockaded in Port Arthur by 'indirect fire' – when the fall of shot is corrected by detached observers on to targets out of sight of the gunners, a novel technique necessitated by increasing artillery ranges. In the South African and Manchurian battles, field artillery, firing shrapnel fused to burst overhead the enemy, inflicted losses on the infantry that stopped attacks, drove them to cover and still continued to inflict casualties.

The infantry's response was to dig trenches, a tactical development to which the great European armies ought to have paid close attention. Military theorists in Germany, and even more so in France, clung, however, to the view that increments in firepower added to the force of the offensive, rather than strengthening the defence. Both the French and German armies therefore both expanded and re-equipped their field artillery for the mobile role, so that in August 1914 each could deploy over 4,000 quick-firing guns of 75 mm or 77 mm calibre, capable of moving at speeds equal to or better than that of marching infantry. Brought rapidly into action when the opposing infantry made contact, such forces of artillery – sixty guns in a French infantry division, seventy-two in a German – could put down concentrations of fire that made mass attacks impossible to push forward. Since mass attacks, in columns not much less dense than those commanded by Napoleon, remained the chosen means of defeating the enemy in battle, the casualties suffered by both sides were catastrophic. By the end of the battle of the Marne, on 15

112

September 1914, each side had lost over a quarter of a million men after only three weeks of fighting, the majority to artillery fire.

The infantry, exposed to such 'storms of steel', took to the earth. By late September extensive lines of trenches had appeared along much of what was coming to be called the Western Front, and by the end of October the lines touched neutral Switzerland at one extremity and the North Sea at the other. Recognize it or not, the two sides had created the conditions for a sort of mutual siege warfare on the Western Front, and it was as a siege that the First World War would be fought in the West for the next four years.

At the outset, the Germans were much better equipped to conduct siege operations than the French or British. The British, with a tiny regular army, had comparatively little artillery of any sort to deploy. The French, who had been of all armies most strongly committed to the doctrine of the mobile offensive, had large numbers of 75s but almost no mobile heavy artillery. The Germans, on the other hand, having taken the lessons of the Russo-Japanese War more to heart, had equipped a quarter of the field batteries in each infantry division with light howitzers – a cannon firing an explosive shell at a high angle – and allotted each corps, of two or three divisions, a battalion of medium howitzers and guns; the favoured calibre was 150 mm. Other artillery units, under higher command, were equipped with howitzers of 210 mm calibre, while both the German and Austrian armies had small but immensely powerful units of super-heavy artillery, Krupp 420 mm and Skoda 305 mm howitzers. In 1914 these were used like the 'breaching trains' of an eighteenth-century army, to break open the frontier fortresses on the Western and Eastern fronts. Once the trench lines were established, however, it was the medium guns and howitzers that came into their own. The guns could reach out to 'interdict' movement on the lines of communication with the trenches; the howitzers, dropping shells from high angles, could kill infantry sheltering in the earthworks.

The French and British, who had the initiative in the West, persisted for some time in using their light field artillery both to 'prepare' and 'support' their infantry attacks across no-man's-land, even after it was found that shrapnel shell could not cut barbed wire and did little damage to trenches. Eventually, however, the appalling casualties suffered in such attacks – in Artois in the spring and in Artois and Champagne in the autumn of 1915, which cost them over 100,000 troops on each occasion – persuaded them to accept that new methods and new equipment were necessary. New equipment was on the way; new methods took longer to develop. While they were in preparation, the Germans, who had been drawing their own lessons from the fighting, unleashed the first artillery offensive in history against the French at Verdun.

There, in great secrecy, they had stockpiled two and a half million shells and assembled 1,700 guns, from which on 21 February 1916 they opened a whirlwind bombardment of the isolated French garrison in the bend of the Meuse around the old fortress city. Within four days the Germans had overrun the French second line, seized one of the key forts and stood poised to complete their success. At the critical moment a new French commander, Pétain, appeared to save the situation. He overcame German 'interdiction' of the approach routes to the isolated city by organizing continuous convoys of trucks along its only main road. He also assembled a great 'counter-battery' force of French guns, using weapons of heavy calibre withdrawn from other French fortresses, and began to engage the Germans in a great artillery duel. Thus a battle of gunners against gunners developed, in which their infantry comrades came to play the role of mere 'cannon fodder'. By June the French had assembled an ascendancy; by the autumn the Germans had given up

113

the struggle. But the cost to both sides was unimaginable by previous standards of loss. About 300,000 casualties had been incurred by each side, most to artillery fire. The Germans had fired about twenty-two million shells into Verdun, the French about fifteen million back. The landscape around the city bears the marks to this day.

'Counter-battery' duels, which had been a regular feature of siege warfare in the heyday of the fortress from 1550 to 1850, impose severe demands of courage and endurance on gunners. So it was at Verdun, and at any other battle of the First World War in which one artillery sought directly to overcome another. In 'counter-battery', it is battery positions which are the targets and though it is sometimes possible to move them, new locations soon become known to the other side – by direct observation or during the First World War also by 'flash spotting', 'sound ranging' (on the report of the guns as they fire) and visual or photographic reconnaissance from the air. (Today gunners can fix their opponents' locations with complete accuracy by tracking with radar the starting-point of a shell back along its flight path.) Once battery positions are mutually identified, victory in the gunnery duel goes to the gunners who can fire fastest and most accurately. A vignette from an early counter-battery duel of the war, that of the 122nd Battery, Royal Field Artillery at Le Cateau on 26 August 1914 depicts what happens to the losers. 'It was an extraordinary sight; a short wild scene of galloping and falling horses, and then four guns standing derelict, a few limbers lying about, one with its pole vertical, and dead men and horses everywhere.'

The purpose of 'counter-battery' throughout the years of trench warfare remained the same as that in traditional fortress warfare: to make possible a successful infantry assault. But, because of the strength that barbed wire and machine-guns lent to the defence of simple earthworks, artillery had also to be used directly against the trenches before and during an infantry assault. Three main artillery techniques can be distinguished during these years, one succeeding another as each in turn proved ineffective.

The first consisted in a simple *rafale*, as the French called it: a drenching of the enemy positions with shrapnel fire at the moment of assault. Since shrapnel did not cut barbed wire or damage trenches this technique gave way, as soon as high-explosive ammunition became available in quantity at the end of 1915, to a much heavier and longer preparation, followed by the firing of a 'barrage' during the infantry attack. The first of these great preparations was in the twin offensives of Champagne and Artois, the latter called the battle of Loos by the British, who made their effort alongside the French at that spot. In all the Allies had assembled 2,000 heavy and 3,000 field guns for the offensive, which, after several days preliminary bombardment, unleashed heavy 'barrage' fire on the enemy's trenches. *Barrage* is the French for 'dam'; the idea was to create a barrier of exploding shells that would prevent the enemy manning their trench parapets while, further back, other 'barrages' prevented reinforcements from advancing.

Barrage firing required skilled gunnery. But as gunners perfected the skills required, they learnt to make barrages perform tricks; to 'creep' forward just in front of the infantry at marching speed; to leap forward on to positions not yet attacked; then to leap back on defending infantry emerging from their dugouts in the belief danger had passed; to fall alongside as well as ahead of the attackers so as to prevent counter-assaults on their flank. 'Creeping' barrages were first mentioned in the artillery plan for the battle of the Somme, 1 July 1916; but the main artillery effort made there was the week-long preparatory bombardment, during which one and a half million shells were fired into the German positions. That bombardment inflicted little real damage on the defenders, who were safe below ground in dugouts thirty feet deep; the barrage did equally little good, for the attacking infantry were prevented from following it by the Germans, who emerged unscathed from their shelters. During 1917, in battles at Arras, the Chemin des Dames and Passchendaele, refined barrage technique won greater success for the infantry. 'Artillery conquers, infantry occupies' had become the catchphrase of trench warfare, and artillery could indeed ensure that infantry occupied chosen patches of ground. But, so deep were trench systems becoming – up to three or four miles deep at their most elaborate – that such patches never extended over the whole depth of an attacked position. The result was that, while artillery achieved 'break-in', it never secured 'breakthrough'.

The Germans, who were on the receiving end of this artillery effort in the West, had drawn their own conclusions from the consistent failure of the Allied gunners, for all their feats of adaptation, to blast a way through a defended trench system. The chief one was that the striving after purely *material* effort was misplaced; rather, their gunners believed, artillery should seek to cause *moral* dislocation among the enemy. A senior German artillery commander on the Eastern Front, General Bruchmüller, first applied the new concept in September 1917 at Riga against the Russian army, already far advanced, by losses and revolution, in disintegration. It achieved such success that the High Command had no hesitation in making it the basis for their offensives in the West in the following year.

The final collapse of the Russian army, which the Riga victory had helped to accelerate, allowed the Germans to transfer troops westward in sufficient numbers to give them, for the first time since 1914, a preponderance in the West both of men and guns. On 21 March 1918, having assembled 3,500 field and 2,500 heavy guns against the British Fifth Army on the Somme, Ludendorff unleashed his *Kaiserschlacht* (Emperor's Battle), which he believed would end the war.

His belief was founded on the new technique of 'neutralization', the third and last artillery technique First World War gunners were to introduce. Unlike the *rafale* and *barrage* methods tried earlier, its purpose was not to kill or to destroy, but to inflict shock so sudden and intense that the defenders would be paralyzed into inactivity. No preliminary bombardment was permitted; nothing, not even ranging shots, that would reveal the presence of artillery reinforcements. All ranging was concealed within normal artillery exchanges. But enormous quantities of shells, including many with gas filling, were stockpiled; and then, five hours before the moment of assault, the 6,000 assembled guns deluged the British positions with an avalanche of shells. Surprise was complete. The defending British infantry was stunned by the shock and, when at dawn the Germans began their advance, many surrendered without resistance. By the third day the Germans had passed through the whole British position and were passing forward into their rear area.

Logistic failure eventually brought the German breakthrough to a halt. But the feasibility of 'neutralization', as the Bruchmüller method was called, was proved. The Germans employed it on four more occasions in 1918, always with success, and in April so effectively that their breakthrough was halted only forty miles from Paris. At that moment it seemed that Germany was about to win the war. When the tide was as suddenly and surprisingly reversed against them in July, the fault was certainly not the artillery's; overwhelming numbers, supplied in part by the newly arrived Americans, was the key to the Allies' survival.

The artillery arm emerged from the First World War as the dominant branch in all the armies that had fought. The Royal Artillery of the British army ended hostilities as the largest single regiment with over half a million officers and men on its roll, more than twice as many soldiers as the whole British army had fielded in 1914. Its equipment ranged in size from the 13-pounder of the horse artillery

115

Canadian Artillery in Action. *Canadian gunners on the Western Front, First World War, serving an eight-inch howitzer*

and 2.75-inch gun of the mountain batteries to 14-inch howitzers that could crush the roof of an armoured fortress's turret in a single blow. Artillery power had ultimately, at a cost as enormous to its own gun crews as to the infantry which were its principal targets, won the war. The only question, in the minds of professional gunners, was how artillery would maximize its power in the future.

It would do so in part by diversification. Artillery had, during the First World War, conformed very closely to a single role, that of preparing the battlefield for the infantry to occupy and assisting them to do so by the firing of protective barrages. Its equipment had, in consequence, continued to conform closely to its historic stereotype. Two military innovations evolved by the war, the tank and the military aeroplane, were now to require the development of novel and different equipments, the anti-tank and the anti-aircraft gun. Each was to play a major role in the second of the world wars that would convulse the twentieth century, and was to multiply in numbers far beyond the reckoning of any Great War gunner.

Anti-aircraft gunnery, in strict accuracy, had had a premature birth in the Great War, when numbers of field and light naval guns had been pressed into service on high-angle mountings, largely for the defence of observation balloons. As the bomber menace grew between the wars, however, specialized equipments were designed and manufactured. Some of these were of light calibre and high rates of fire like the Swiss 20 mm Oerlikon and the Swedish 40 mm Bofors, both excellent designs whose descendants are still to be found in the inventories of armies in the 1980s. Defence against the higher-flying strategic bomber required, however, a larger and heavier gun. Foremost among these were the British 3.7 inch, the American 90 mm and the German 88 mm. All were to be built in their thousands. Originally they were aimed at their targets by a system of sound-ranging, translated into fuse-setting by hand. An American development of a British invention would, towards the end of the Second World War, enable anti-aircraft gunners to dispense

116

with the uncertainty of hand-setting by arming each shell with a radar-actuated proximity fuse. This ensured a detonation when an aircraft entered the destruction zone of a shell fired at it. Of great utility against manned aircraft, it achieved its most valuable effect in the battle with the German V-1 flying bombs launched against British cities in the summer of 1944.

The German 88 mm gun was generally acclaimed to be the most effective of the weapons designed and developed for anti-aircraft work. But it was to achieve its greatest fame in the anti-tank role, its fitness for which was discovered almost accidentally. Purpose-built anti-tank guns of the inter-war period proved, when war came, generally too light for the task. The 20 mm, even the 37 mm, high-velocity cannon, which were the standard equipment of divisional tank units in 1940, could not penetrate the tanks encountered in the opening rounds of the Blitzkrieg, as even the attacking Germans found.

Counter-attacked by the British outside Arras on 21 May 1940, Rommel himself found that 'the anti-tank guns which we quickly deployed showed themselves to be far too light to be effective against the heavily armoured British tanks, and the majority of them were put out of action by gunfire together with their crews, and then overrun.'

He hastily brought his anti-aircraft battalion, equipped with eighty-eights, 'into action at top speed against the tanks. Every gun was ordered to open rapid fire immediately and I personally gave each gun its target. We ran from gun to gun. Soon we succeeded in putting the leading enemy tanks out of action.'

The eighty-eights pressed into service by Rommel were towed pieces of little mobility, as most anti-tanks were to remain for much of the Second World War, even though they grew in calibre to 57 mm or even 75 mm. From the middle of the war onwards, however, it became the practice to mount some of these high-velocity guns on their own tracked and armoured carriages; in the German and Soviet armies that development gave birth to a new arm, called assault artillery, which took on something of the tank's as well as the anti-tank role.

Self-propelled artillery: the American 155mm howitzer, M 109 A1, on its tracked carriage

On a simpler carriage, many heavier guns also began to support the infantry as what was called 'self-propelled artillery'. Such equipments were sufficiently mobile to be able to keep pace with mechanized infantry and even tank units, delivering their firepower on to points of enemy resistance as and when they were encountered during the progress of an advance. It was guns like these that helped to make some bombardments of the Second World War as terrible as any fired during the First, like that before Alamein in October 1942, when a thousand British guns stupefied the German and Italian defenders of Rommel's furthermost advanced position in Egypt. In 1943 that bombardment was exceeded in weight and effect by the Russian artillery in the battle of Kursk, when 50,000 guns and mortars discharged forty-two million rounds in the period July to August; while in the battle of Berlin, in April 1945, the Russians packed as many as 400 guns into each mile of front outside the city. A specialized form of self-propelled artillery favoured by the Soviet army were multiple-barrelled rocket-launchers mounted on trucks, which delivered a salvo of volcanic character over short ranges. Its destructive effect was low, but its psychological impact made it feared by infantry as was almost no other weapon of the war.

Rockets had, of course, an historic place in the development of artillery; they may, indeed, have been the first means through which gunpowder was harnessed to warfare. An artillery rocket, invented by the British gunner officer Congreve, had been deployed during the Napoleonic Wars and its use by the British in the War of 1812 explains the reference to 'the rockets' red glare' in the American national anthem. But difficulties in guiding it accurately to its target had always deterred artillerists from attempts to develop it as a major weapon, despite the attractive simplicity of its propulsive system, which obviated the need to launch it from a heavy, strong metal barrel. The guidance problem had to some extent, however, been overcome in the inter-war years by rocket enthusiasts, foremost among whom was a German, Wernher von Braun. His success had attracted official support which resulted by 1944 in Germany's deployment of two long-range weapons, one a small pilotless aircraft, the other a true ballistic rocket known to the Allies as the V-2.

Had either the V-2 or the V-1 pilotless aircraft been available to the Germans in quantity before the launching of the Normandy invasion it is perfectly possible that the invasion fleet might have been prevented from leaving its harbours. Neither was available and the invading Allied armies overran the secret weapon launching sites before they could be used to reverse the balance of advantage in the war. The V-2 was, nevertheless, a signal of the direction in which the artillery principle would henceforth find its major avenue of development. Ballistic missiles were to prove adaptable to many roles, from that of the short-range battlefield weapon, carrying a ton of conventional explosive a hundred miles or less, to the inter-continental strategic rocket armed with a multiple nuclear warhead capable of devastating several cities in a single strike. Through this development artillery achieved its apotheosis, becoming indeed 'the God of War' Stalin had called it – a savage, cannibal god powerful enough to devour its inventors, its servants and its masters, and to make the 'last argument of Kings' too terrible for any statesman to contemplate its use.

Tank 6

Necessity, the proverb says, is the mother of invention, and war imposes necessity more harshly than any other human activity. Yet, though war unquestionably stimulates human ingenuity in many directions, medical, technical, industrial, fiscal, logistic, there are remarkably few weapon inventions that can be laid directly at its door. The steamship was conceived as a commercial carrier. The aeroplane was the product of humanity's impatience at its inability to fly. High-explosive was the by-product of experiments in chemical synthesis. Chlorine, from which the early form of poison gas was derived, was first used as an agent for bleaching clothes. The list might be prolonged. Perhaps only two inventions can be singled out as the direct product of military necessity: the machine-gun and the tank. The first of these, moreover, was perfected rather because of the profit its sale promised than in response to any military exigency. It is the second which more strictly obeys the law of necessity, imposed in this case largely by the extraordinary success of the first.

The tank, now over seventy years old as a concept, still conforms very closely to the specification originally written for it. It is a motor-driven vehicle, armoured sufficiently well to protect its crew and working parts against projectiles, armed with weapons appropriate to the resistance it will encounter, and moving on caterpillar tracks that allow it to negotiate the surface of any battlefield on which troops can freely manoeuvre.

The need for such a machine, or weapons system as it would be called today, was grasped in Britain, and then in France, though inexplicably not in Germany, almost immediately after the outbreak of the First World War. Some armoured vehicles already existed, armoured cars mounting machine-guns, which, on the British side, the Royal Naval Air Service had adopted to protect its airfields during the period of mobile warfare which followed the German invasion of France. When mobile warfare was brought to an end, by the German recourse first to digging trenches and then to staking barbed wire, the armoured cars immediately lost their usefulness. For they could not operate across country, while the road network, for the short period it survived the shelling, was everywhere crossed by the trench barriers.

A man who, as early as anyone, grasped the significance of this front-wide entrenchment was Lieutenant-Colonel E. D. Swinton, who had been sent to France as an official observer in September 1914. It portended, he perceived, siege warfare with all the labour and loss of life that sieges had always entailed. Siege engines, he saw, would save life and labour and, with another flash of perception he grasped that the agricultural caterpillar tractor offered the technical base for constructing them. He discussed his idea in London on his return home in October and on

119

*A Killen-Strait
agricultural tractor
undergoing military
trials in Britain, 1915*

Christmas Day Maurice Hankey, the Secretary of the Committee of Imperial Defence, wrote a paper advocating the building of a machine with 'caterpillar driving gear . . . [which would be able to] run down barbed wire by sheer weight, to give some cover to men creeping up behind, and to support the advance with machine-gun fire.'

His paper was persuasive enough for the War Office to procure and test various caterpillar tractors. But it was the enthusiasm of the First Lord of the Admiralty, Winston Churchill, which harnessed official energy and money to the scheme. Churchill, whose powerful imagination had been fertilized by H. G. Wells' prophetic short story *The Land Ironclads*, published in 1903, encountered opposition among the generals – Kitchener had dismissed Hankey's proposal with the words 'the armoured caterpillar would be shot up by guns' – and even more strongly among the admirals. The Fourth Sea Lord wrote 'Caterpillar landships are idiotic and useless. Nobody has asked for them and nobody wants them.' Churchill wanted them, and by June 1915 had succeeded in converting the Admiral committee dedicated to the experiment into a joint army-navy body. Various prototypes – a pedirail device, an articulated pair of tractors, a 'big wheel' – had by then been examined and rejected. Attention was now focussed on a purpose-built vehicle, to be designed and constructed by the engineering firm Foster's of Lincoln, in which an armoured box body – soon for deception purposes to be called a 'tank', a word chosen by Swinton – would be mounted on a caterpillar chassis. The mock-up was christened 'Little Willie' and, as a working model, first moved about the factory yard on 8 September 1915. But a sister machine, originally called the 'Wilson', after its designer, Major W. G. Wilson, then 'Centipede', then 'Big Willie' and eventually 'Mother', was simultaneously taking shape. It differed from 'Little Willie' in having a rhomboidal shape, and tracks that passed around the top of the body.

'Little Willie', tried out over mock trenches on 19 September, consistently threw its tracks. 'Big Willie', which underwent full trials on a cross-country course on 29

120

January 1916, proved more reliable and robust. The angled thrust of its prow allowed it to climb obstacles, while the all-round travel of its track averted the throwing problem. At subsequent demonstrations 'Big Willie' impressed generals, politicians, eventually King George V, with the promise of its power to break the trench deadlock, and by 11 February the War Office had agreed to order the construction of a hundred production models, later increased to 150.

It was decided (at the instigation of the staff officer detailed to oversee their construction, Albert Stern) that they should be of two types, a 'destroyer' (later called a 'male') and a 'man-killing' (later called a 'female') tank. The former would be armed with two naval 6-pounder guns, the latter with four Vickers machine-guns, the two types to work together in mutual support. They would be manned by soldiers of a specialist service, originally called the Tank Detachment, then the Armoured Car Section of the Motor Machine-Gun Service, eventually the Heavy Branch Machine-Gun Corps, an effective cover name. Not until June 1917 would it become the Tank Corps, from which the modern Royal Tank Regiment of the British army descends.

The time lapse between the trials of 'Mother' and the appearance of production models was, by modern standards of weapon procurement, almost miraculously short. The battle of the Somme, Britain's first great offensive contribution to the Allied war effort, had begun on 1 July 1916. By September, when the battle was still raging, forty-nine tanks had been delivered to the British Expeditionary Force, of which thirty-six were serviceable to take part in the attack scheduled for that day. It was to be delivered on a front of five miles by nine British infantry divisions, with 1,200 guns in support. Earlier that year, Winston Churchill had written, in a prophetic paper entitled 'Variants of the Offensive', that 'if artillery is used to cut wire, the direction and imminence of the attack is proclaimed days beforehand. But by this method the assault follows the wire-cutting almost immediately, *i.e.* before any reinforcements can be brought up by the enemy, or any special defensive measures taken.' This was an anticipation of the future. The High Command understandably lacked the confidence as yet to trust the success of the attack entirely to the new weapon. As a result, the enemy had been thoroughly alerted by the preparatory bombardment, while the already devastated ground had been further disturbed by a new rain of shells. Many tanks 'ditched' in the broken ground before crossing the start line. The crews of others lost their way in the labyrinth of shelled trenches. Eleven of the survivors, in widely separated groups, nevertheless succeeded in entering the enemy's positions and achieved a variety of successes – driving enemy artillerymen from their guns, clearing trenches with the fire of their machine-guns or reducing units of enemy infantry to stunned inactivity. One German prisoner denounced the tank attack as 'not war but butchery'; an official German account declared that their men felt powerless to withstand the tanks; while a press report of what happened at the village of Flers, where the tanks did best, simply read 'A tank is walking up the High Street with the British army cheering behind.'

Haig, the British Commander-in-Chief, was deeply impressed by what the tank had achieved, patchy as it was. On 19 September he sent a representative to the War Office to demand the building of a thousand tanks as quickly as possible. They would be constructed to a new specification, called the Mark IV, incorporating better steering, armament and propulsion; though differing scarcely at all in outward appearance from the Mark I, these new tanks would be a distinct improvement on it. While they were being built, the British Expeditionary Force would commit the tanks it had to hand in a series of abortive offensives; in the last stages of the Somme battle, at Arras in April 1917, at Messines in June and, wholly unsuitably, at Passchendaele in July. But none of these ventures won the desired success. Lack of numbers was partly to blame – though sixty tanks were used at Arras. Unsuitable terrain was almost as important an explanation of failure. Clough Williams-Ellis, who was to become a world-famous architect but in 1917 was a Tank Corps officer, describes seeing tank men at Arras 'staggering about trying to help their machines out by digging away the soil from under their bellies and by thrusting planks and brushwood under their tracks . . . it was a desperate business for those of us who knew that there were infantry assembled who had practised with us, who looked to us for a lead across the German wire and who must now do as best they might without us.' At Passchendaele, where heavy autumn rains turned a shell-churned battlefield into a quagmire, conditions further impeded tank attacks. On 20 September only one tank out of the twenty-six that had started out arrived on the position.

More important even than bad going or lack of numbers in explaining the tanks' consistent failure, however, was the issue raised by Winston Churchill – that through the use of long artillery preparations 'the direction and imminence of the

Hyacinth, *a British Male Mark IV tank, ditched during the battle of Arras, April 1917*

attack is proclaimed days beforehand'. Here the future war leader had put his finger on the central tactical problem of the First World War. Long artillery bombardments allowed the enemy to assemble reinforcements, and so to prevent a breakthrough, even if a break-in occurred. Short artillery preparation, on the other hand, left wire uncut and trenches intact. The conclusion drawn from this impasse by the High Command was that artillery bombardments must be lengthened to the point where nothing of the enemy's defences remained. But, as Passchendaele demonstrated, this philosophy did not work either. Volcanic artillery bombardments caused such devastation that the attacking infantry were themselves unable to negotiate the battlefield while the enemy somehow always succeeded in sealing off the breach along its rearward margin.

Towards the end of the Passchendaele battle, even so single-minded a proponent of the artillery offensive as Field-Marshal Haig conceded that something different must be tried. Moreover, he had exhausted his reserves of infantry, so could no longer hope to take ground by the expenditure of blood alone. Thus it was that a plan he had originally rejected came to look more attractive to him. Prepared by the Tank Corps Chief of Staff, Colonel J. F. C. Fuller, it envisaged using a large body of armour in a giant 'tank raid' intended 'to restore British prestige and to strike a theatrical blow against Germany before the winter'.

The place fixed upon was Cambrai and the date 20 November 1917. In all 378 tanks were assembled, organized in nine battalions, which were to support six divisions of infantry. Five cavalry divisions were held in reserve, to exploit 'the Gap', once it had been created. The ground chosen, dry rolling chalk downs, was relatively undamaged by shellfire and there was to be no preliminary bombardment, only an accompanying barrage as the troops and tanks moved forward. Both the infantry and armour had been assembled in great secrecy, which was preserved up to the moment of assault. A further advantage was that mist filled no-man's-land on the morning of the attack, further concealing from the Germans what threatened them.

The first great tank offensive in history therefore opened with much to favour its success. And there were exhilarating successes at the start of the action. Captain D. G. Browne of 'F' Battalion

had a grandstand view of all 'B' Battalion tanks, with some of 'C' and 'F' Battalions almost racing down Welsh Ridge . . . It was magnificent and it was war all right . . . The whole fleet took the wire in their stride, and the cunning little manoeuvre of each section of three tanks at the two main sections was perfectly executed . . . After crossing the first trench, we met General Elles (the Tank Corps Commander) walking briskly (forward) with his fondest theories vindicated, exultant. Behind him at a respectful distance, came several crowds of German prisoners.

In many places the German defenders surrendered in droves, so that by midday the advance had reached its objectives on both flanks, the town of Cambrai lay within the British grasp and beyond beckoned the open country of the German rear area. It seemed that 'break-in' was about to become 'breakthrough', which was even more than had been hoped for at the outcome of the operation. Only in the centre had things gone less well than expected. There the 51st Highland Division lagged behind its neighbours, held up by German artillerymen who had stuck by

The A7V, the only tank constructed by the Germans during the First World War

their guns and by infantry who clung to their trenches. The reason was quickly apparent. General Harper, commanding the 51st, had no experience of working with tanks and appeared to believe they would draw fire on to his men. He therefore ordered them to keep well behind the tanks, in flat contradiction of the agreed plan, with the result that the enemy gunners were able to engage the tanks in relative safety. Once the tanks had been knocked out, the German machine-gunners engaged the Highlanders in the normal way, stopping them, and so the whole advance, in their tracks.

Much ground had been taken by the end of the day and 10,000 prisoners; but the Germans had held their line and, by counter-attack a week later, they regained much of what they had lost. Cambrai, though celebrated today by the Tank Corps' successor, the Royal Tank Regiment, at its regimental festival, thus resolved itself as a sensation rather than a victory.

The strategic initiative had meanwhile passed to the Germans, who, having completed the destruction of the Russian army at the end of 1917, were ready by the spring of 1918 to mount offensives in the West with the divisions released from The Eastern Front. This new-found numerical advantage lent their attacks such weight that throughout the months from March to July they drove through the Allied lines wherever they chose. Twice, in March and April, they came close to breaking first British and then French resistance altogether. In such circumstances it was all the Allies could do to hang on; tanks, essentially weapons of offence rather than defence, could do little or nothing to stem the tide.

The German offensives were, however, of an essentially traditional sort, mounted

A British Mark I tank of 1916, the first operational tank

by infantry and artillery alone. True, new methods of concerting their effort had been devised. The German artillery had learnt to fire preparatory bombardments which effectively 'neutralized' the defence just at the moment of assault; the German infantry had been taught to profit from this neutralization by 'infiltrating' the defenders' position at points of weakness, rather than attacking in the vulnerable wave formation practised hitherto. This combination of neutralization and infiltration proved effective. But it entailed losses as heavy as any suffered by the British and French during their offensives, so that when the offensives ultimately failed to win the war, the German army was thrust back on to the defensive in a gravely weakened state.

It was at this stage that their failure to develop a sizeable tank force of their own, or effective anti-tank defences, told decisively against them. They had, admittedly, adapted some captured British tanks to their own use. They had also constructed a large, unwieldy vehicle, the A7V. But neither in numbers nor tactical thinking had they anything to match the formidable armoured capability now assembled by their enemies. For it was by 1918 not only the British who had entered the tank age; the French, too, had kept pace with them. Colonel J. E. Estienne was the driving force behind the construction of the French tank arm, which in August 1918 comprised several hundred vehicles, some heavy tanks, the majority a light two-man model, the FT, built by Renault.

On 8 August 1918, this revolutionary tank army delivered a decisive, war-winning stroke at the battle of Amiens. The British had assembled 604 tanks, the majority the improved Mark Vs, though some were the new Whippets, capable of moving at 8 m.p.h., a high speed for its day. The French, who had committed the available bulk of their tanks in a counter-offensive at Soissons only three weeks earlier, mustered 110. In a single day this armoured phalanx succeeded in leading its accompanying British and French infantry clean through the German salient on the Somme, to reach open country, terrify the enemy and cause Ludendorff, the Kaiser's Chief of Staff, to call 8 August 'the German Army's Black Day'.

Allied victory, which ensued three months later, cannot be ascribed to the intervention of the tanks alone, or indeed to any single cause. The First World War was too titanic a struggle to be recounted in terms of a victory for one weapon system or another. Yet there is no doubt that the tank represented, even more than the submarine or the aeroplane, the most revolutionary of the technical developments spawned by the war. The submarine and the aeroplane were to dominate in the future the elements in which each operated. But operations at sea and in the air, whatever their strategic significance, would ultimately remain ancillary to operations on land; and there it would be the tank that would prevail.

Yet in the immediate aftermath of the war the tank, and such tank formations as the war had produced, fell into eclipse. 'Thank God we can now get back to real soldiering' was how an officer of the old school put his hopes to J. F. C. Fuller on the day after the Armistice, 11 November 1918. 'Real soldiering', in this context, meant a return to the traditional order of things, in which combat functions were divided between the infantry, the artillery and the cavalry. Tanks were to have no place in that order, or at very best a subordinate one. In the United States the Tank Corps, established in 1918, was actually abolished by the National Defense Act of 1920, and such tanks as survived were assigned to the infantry. In France, tanks, originally organized as units of assault artillery, were also in 1920 assigned to the infantry, which chose to regard them as an auxiliary weapon. In Britain the Tank Corps survived, but only on a temporary basis, until 1923. Its existence was then made permanent. But little money was provided to design or purchase new tanks, while the only large tank formation organized, the Experimental Mechanized Force

126

British Whippet tanks of 3rd Battalion, Tank Corps, March 1918

of 1927, was dissolved in 1929. It was not until 1934 that a permanent Armoured Brigade was formed and not until 1938, on the eve of the Second World War, that the British army got an Armoured Division.

But in Europe, meanwhile, the development of advanced tanks and large armoured formations proceeded apace. In Russia, mechanized corps, comprising a hundred tanks each, were raised in 1932; their equipment comprised both very heavy tanks and light, fast vehicles of revolutionary design, based on models devised by the American inventor Walter Christie. By 1938 there would be seven of these mechanized corps. Italy, committed by Mussolini to a programme of rapid modernization in all spheres, had a large armoured regiment by 1927, equipped with light tanks, which the dictator believed were most appropriate to the dynamism of the Italian temperament. It was in Germany, however, that the most creative

Overleaf: The German Mark III J Panzer in action on the Eastern Front, 1942

127

approach to tank development was demonstrated. Germany had been forbidden tanks by the Versailles Treaty. Covertly the German army had nevertheless proceeded with experiments in the material and technique of armoured warfare. By 1933 the German army had a promising light tank in service, the Panzer I; when it was demonstrated to Hitler at Kummersdorf in 1933, soon after the dictator's appointment as Reichschancellor, he repeatedly exclaimed 'That's what I need! That's what I want!' The leading German tank enthusiast, Heinz Guderian, was given *carte blanche* to proceed with tank development, and by 1935 three models, Panzer I, II and IV, were in production. More important, the army was proceeding with the raising of armoured, or panzer, divisions. Guderian was given command of the 2nd Panzer Division in 1935 and by 1939 six were in existence altogether. With four 'light' divisions, which included tanks, the Germans were thus possessed of the largest specialized armoured force in the world.

Moreover, the Germans had worked out their own revolutionary philosophy of armoured warfare. Two British theorists, J. F. C. Fuller and Basil Liddell Hart, had proposed, in a stream of writings during the 1920s and 1930s, that armies should in future be reorganized around the tank, whose potentiality for brutal assault and rapid exploitation would, they believed, determine the character of combat. Neither in Britain nor in France had their theories received any welcome. In Germany, however, Guderian and other tank enthusiasts had been enthralled by their message and had trained the German panzer force to operate by its dictates.

The new philosophy of warfare would shortly earn the soubriquet Blitzkrieg. In essence, it aimed at the rapid penetration of the enemy's front by a densely concentrated mass of tanks, closely supported by aircraft operating immediately in advance. Once 'break-in' was secured, the object would be to complete breakthrough by heavy reinforcement at the point of entry; thereafter the success was to be exploited by rapid advance into the enemy rear areas, while ancillary thrusts to the flanks enlarged the breach and operated in such a way as to sow confusion, alarm and despair in the enemy's ranks.

'Blitzkrieg' was the word used by the world press to describe the German success against the Polish army in September 1939. Inappropriately; the weakness of the Polish army, which possessed tens of thousands of horses but only one tank brigade, was encircled on three sides by the German deployment and was finally attacked without warning in the rear by the Russian army, ensured its defeat in any circumstances, let alone those where its attacker fielded two thousand tanks. The Blitzkrieg of 1940 in the West was, however, a different matter. There the German army faced equal odds, and strong defences which it could not outflank but had to penetrate by frontal assault. The strategic task, in short, was even more difficult than in 1914, when it had been able to use the route through neutral Belgium as a way round the French frontier defences. In 1914 the German offensive failed. In 1940 it succeeded. The difference was made by its panzer force and the philosophy that animated it.

'Lightning victory' might all the same have eluded the German army had the traditionalist thinking that prevailed in the general staff determined its war plan. Hitler himself, however, doubted that a traditional offensive would achieve the rapid result he desired. And when word came to him that General Manstein, likeminded contemporary of Guderian, was advocating that the armour be concentrated for a breakthrough at a single point, rather than dispersed across the front of attack as the High Command wanted, he ordered that it be adopted. The result, loosely known as the 'Manstein Plan', was brilliantly successful. It worked as follows.

The Anglo-French front was divided into three sectors. In the south the Maginot Line, an enormously strong belt of fortifications completed in 1936, covered the

130

Franco-German frontier as far as the Belgian Ardennes. The Ardennes sector, hilly and wooded, was judged by the French High Command to be impenetrable by tanks, and so was defended by reserve troops of low fighting quality. The third section of the front ran across the Flemish plain, excellent tank country. There the Anglo-French staff had positioned the best of the French and the British Expeditionary Force, also highly mobile, and many of the 3,600 tanks available to them. Unlike the Germans, however, the French had few purely armoured formations – only three fully formed – the rest of their tanks being dispersed among the infantry as close support weapons. It was against such dispersion that the British tank officers had struggled during the First World War, arguing that it negated the essential fighting quality of the armoured army. The sense of their objections was to be borne out again in 1940, with truly catastrophic consequences for the Western alliance.

On the morning of 10 May 1940, two low-grade French divisions defending the Ardennes sector found themselves under attack by strong German forces of tanks and aircraft. The armies of Belgium and Holland, both neutral countries, were simultaneously assaulted by other German concentrations and the mobile French and British divisions on the northern front immediately advanced to their assistance. That advance proceeded smoothly. But while the Anglo-French concentration was deploying eastward, the German tank mass in the Ardennes began crashing westward. It comprised at the outset five panzer divisions of the Kleist group, later joined by four others drawn in from the northern sector. By 12 May, the Germans had reached the River Meuse, the only great natural obstacle in their path. It was crossed the following day, and on 14 May the French forces hastily assembled to

An early version of the German Mark IV Panzer of the Second World War; when upgunned, it would prove a most successful weapon

stem the German onset were defeated in open country. On 17 May the newly raised French 4th Armoured Division (commanded by General de Gaulle) counter-attacked the German panzer wedge at Laon, but was defeated. On 21 May the British launched a similar counter-attack against the 7th Panzer Division, commanded by Erwin Rommel, at Arras, which, after an initial success, was also defeated. That day the German advanced guard reached Abbeville on the estuary of the River Somme, and shortly afterwards the Channel coast itself. The panzers had covered 240 miles in eleven days, cut the Allied armies in half and effectively won the battle of France. It was, and remains, the greatest tank victory in history.

Its consolidation, entailing the expulsion of the British army from the continent via Dunkirk and the destruction of the surviving elements of the French army, was to take another month. But at the end of those 'sixty days that shook the West', Germany appeared to have reversed the outcome of the First World War – the purpose for which she had embarked on the Second. Two obstacles alone imposed themselves between Hitler and a clean sweep of his strategic difficulties. The first was the obstinate refusal of the British, under the leadership of Winston Churchill, to concede defeat. The second was the menace to German domination of Europe that the intact power of the Soviet Union presented.

Britain, weak and isolated, could be contained, even if its army was able to sustain an active defence in the Western Desert against the efforts of Hitler's ally, Fascist Italy, to attack British bases in Egypt. Soviet Russia represented a far greater problem. Though in many ways an underdeveloped country its investment in heavy industry had provided it with a tank force greatly superior to that which Germany could put into the field. By 1941 German tank production had equipped the army with about 5,000 vehicles. Russia's tank factories had accumulated between 21,000 and 24,000 operational tanks and were continuing to produce vehicles at some four times the German rate. Moreover, the best Russian tank, the T-34, was superior to its German equivalent. By 1941 the Panzer I and II were obsolete. The Panzer III, though reliable and manoeuvrable, was undergunned. The Panzer IV's gun was heavy but lacked the velocity to penetrate armour. The Russian T-34, on the other hand, represented a remarkably successful compromise between the three elements of tank design: armour, armament and mobility. Its armour was 45 mm thick, when most German models had only 30 mm; its gun, 76.2 mm in calibre and 30.5 calibres long, could penetrate most other tanks; its high power-to-height ratio and wide tracks gave it excellent cross-country performance, and the high speed of 32 m.p.h.

In 1940 the Red Army fielded only a thousand T-34s. But the menace they represented was one of the factors which decided Hitler to abrogate the non-aggression treaty between Germany and the Soviet Union and to strike for a victory in the East as complete as that he had just won in the West. On 22 June 1941, after a delay caused by the need to subjugate Yugoslavia and Greece, his armies broke without warning into the Soviet Union and began driving eastward on three divergent axes, aimed at Leningrad in the north, Moscow in the centre and Kiev in the south.

Their initial success was spectacular, particularly in the centre. There the two panzer groups attached to Army Group Centre bit deep into the Soviet defences and then arched inwards to complete the encirclement of the Red Army's positions around Minsk and Smolensk by the end of July. Three hundred thousand Russians were made prisoner. The initiative next passed to Army Group North, which reached the outskirts of Leningrad at the end of August. Meanwhile some of Centre's tanks had been transferred to accelerate Army Group South's drive on Kiev. On 16 September its advance culminated in the largest encirclement in history, when 665,000 Russian prisoners passed into German hands.

All this had been achieved by a German panzer force of some 5,000 tanks, which remained largely intact at the end of the 1941 campaigning season. The Red Army, by contrast, lost some 17,000 tanks, through abandonment or capture as often as destruction. Reinforcements brought from Siberia during November allowed the Russians to stage a successful counter-attack at Moscow as the heavy snows of winter fell, forcing the Germans back nearly a hundred miles. But the coming of better weather and of fresh supplies of tanks and men in the spring gave the Germans the means to renew their offensive in 1942. Moscow and Leningrad proved impregnable; but on the great open expanses of the southern steppe the panzers drove onwards through the summer, to cross the Don and in August to reach the Volga at Stalingrad.

The desperate battle which took its focus around the city would culminate in the

A Russian T-34, the best all-round tank of the Second World War; infantry commonly rode on the hull

A German Mark VI 'King Tiger', the most powerful operational tank of the Second World War

first major reversal of the panzers' tide of conquest, unbroken since September 1939. The defeat, however, was largely of Hitler's infantry. Even after Field-Marshal Paulus' surrender on 31 January 1943, a sufficient German armoured reserve remained to permit a major counter-attack west of Stalingrad in mid-February, which regained Kharkov, established the reputation of Manstein, its instigator, as the leading tank general in the German army, and gave it possession of an offensive salient at the southern end of the Russian front.

The crisis of the war in the East, and of the style of armoured attack on which Germany's long run of victory rested, was now at hand. The entry of the United States into the war, together with the total mobilization of the British economy for war, had decisively altered the industrial balance which had prevailed at the outset. Russian industry, transferred factory by factory beyond the Ural mountains since 1941, had also revived. The alliance as a result outproduced Germany in all categories of arms; in tanks, it outproduced her nine to one. In 1943, when Germany produced 5,966 tanks, only double the 1941 total, the United States produced 21,000, the British nearly 8,000 and the Soviet Union over 15,000. Allied tanks, moreover, now matched German in quality. Two new German tanks, the Mark V Panther and Mark VI Tiger, were outstanding machines. But the Panther was unreliable and no better than the equal of the improved T-34/85, while the Tiger, though more heavily armoured and gunned than any counterpart, was slow and lacked endurance. By contrast the American Sherman, which would in future also largely equip the British armoured divisions, was fast and manoeuvrable, simple to maintain and available in profusion.

The Allied tank soldiers were also becoming masters of their trade, a development reflected in the organization of their armoured formations. The Germans had early learnt the lesson that successful panzer offensives required tanks and infantry to be mixed in armoured divisions in equal quantities. The British and Americans had begun by making the mistake of forming armoured divisions almost exclusively of tank regiments. By 1943 they were altering the balance, as also were the Russians. All three armies had also observed the results the Germans had obtained by combining the properties of tanks and anti-tank guns in a single tactical scheme. It had been a notable element of Rommel's success against the British in the Western Desert during 1941-2 that tanks were used to tempt British tanks down on to his lines, out of range of their own artillery, where they were then destroyed by anti-tank guns firing from concealed and protected positions. The German 88 mm gun had achieved its formidable reputation in engagements such as these. The Allies were now ready to play the same game.

This altered balance of force and advantage was to be put to the test in the great Russo-German tank battle of Kursk in July 1943. And it was to be profoundly ironic that the German defeat which was its outcome was to be decided by the Red Army's practice of precisely those tactics which the German had hitherto made its own. Operation Citadel, as they called the battle, had been conceived by the High Command as a means of retrieving the initiative lost at Stalingrad. Its object was to pinch out the giant Russian salient formed in the centre of the front between the German positions south of Moscow and those seized in the Kharkov counter-offensive. Two thousand tanks were concentrated for the attack; against them the Russians had assembled 6,000 tanks and assault guns, supported by 6,000 anti-tank guns behind minefields of a density of 5,000 to the mile.

What followed replicated on a gigantic scale and with catastrophic consequences the results of the defensive battles fought so successfully by the Germans against the British in Egypt and Libya. The Russian minefields and artillery barrages early separated the German infantry from their tanks, which, pressing onward into

134

Russian lines, were engaged by anti-tank guns firing in salvo. Damaged or forced to stop by the weight of Russian fire, the panzers were scattered and isolated. When at their most vulnerable, they were counter-attacked by T-34s which had been held in reserve. The Germans persisted with their attacks against mounting losses from 5 to 14 July, when they had penetrated at most twenty-five miles into defences twice as deep. They were then forced to give up the effort. On 3 August a Russian counter-offensive began that regained all the ground lost, broke a gap thirty-five

An early model Sherman; the casting of its turret and hull as single pieces was advanced engineering in 1942

The amphibious Duplex Drive (DD) version of the Sherman, which spearheaded the Allied invasion of Normandy in 1944

miles wide in the German lines and by 23 August had regained Kharkov. About nine hundred of Hitler's two thousand tanks had been destroyed. His capacity to take the war to the enemy was gone for good.

It was then all the worse that the war was now to be brought to him. Russia's strength in all categories of equipment was now surging ahead. Soon they would begin the great advances which, by the summer of 1944, would bring them within striking distance of the frontiers of Germany itself. The Allies' gathering of their forces was even more menacing. During 1942–3 they had mounted three major amphibious operations in the Mediterranean, in the course of which much had been learnt about the beach-landing of tanks. A great amphibious army was now assembling in southern England, which in 1944 would cross the Channel and begin the invasion of Fortress Europe from the West. Its cutting edge would be formed by an armada of amphibious and shipborne tanks.

The landing of tanks from purpose-built ships, though requiring skill, was not technically difficult. To make tanks swim, the complementary Allied achievement, approached the technically miraculous. What the Allies did was to equip their standard tank, the Sherman, with a collapsible canvas screen and a pair of propellors driven off the track transmission. The screen, which enveloped the hull of the tank, gave it just sufficient buoyancy to float. The propellors drove it through the water at about five knots.

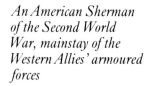

An American Sherman of the Second World War, mainstay of the Western Allies' armoured forces

This DD (Duplex Drive) tank was the invention of a Hungarian-American, Nicholas Straussler. Other vital specialist machines were the product of team effort. Among them were the flail tank, which exploded mines, the bridging tank, the flamethrower tank, the bulldozer tank and the British AVRE (Armoured Vehicle

Royal Engineers), equipped to destroy bunkers with a heavy explosive charge. All were designed to attack obstacles and defences on the beach, so permitting infantry and conventional armour to break out inland.

But among all these inventions the DD tank was to prove the key weapon. When the moment for the Allied invasion of Normandy arrived on 6 June 1944, it was the appearance of the 'swimming tanks' on the beaches, arriving simultaneously with the infantry, that worked principally to unman the German defenders. Allied bombing and naval shelling had driven them to shelter; but the direct fire of DD Shermans, concentrated on their bunkers and weapon pits, had an even more telling psychological effect than weight of fire had materially. It put heart into the assaulting British, American and Canadian infantry. It demoralized their German counterparts and opened the way from the beaches to the open country of the interior.

By July 1944 the Allies' consolidation of their Normandy bridgehead was complete enough for them to contemplate a major break-out. The Americans had two armoured divisions ashore, the British three – Guards, 7th and 11th. It was with the latter that General Montgomery planned to punch a hole in the German defence west of Caen, their linchpin, and find the road to Paris. On the morning of 18 July, after a preparatory aerial bombardment which approached in effect that of a modern tactical nuclear weapon strike, a thousand British tanks launched themselves down a narrow corridor between the River Orne and the German-held heights which closed the bridgehead's western flank. Their objective was the ridge at the bottom of the corridor beyond which lay the plains of northern France.

It was the largest tank attack yet launched by the Western allies against the Germans on any front, and everything spoke for its success. The Germans, who had learnt so much about offensive operations in the first three years of the war, had, however, also been taught much about the defensive in the period since the strategic initiative had been wrested from them. They had been taught, in particular, how to survive hostile firepower and how to improvise in adversity. These skills now came to their rescue. The German anti-tank gunners on whom the aerial bombardment had fallen emerged from their shelters to man their pieces as soon as the British tanks appeared, taking a heavy toll. When the surviving tanks reached the foot of the ridge which was their objective, they found it defended by combat engineers fighting as infantry, supported by panzer units hastily summoned from another sector of the front. By the evening of 18 July an offensive which should have resulted in glittering success had been stopped in its tracks.

A week later the American forces at the other end of the bridgehead, profiting from the dislocation and exhaustion the British attack had inflicted on the Germans, broke out into open country. By mid-August the German army in Normandy was defeated and encircled, its survivors struggling to find a way through the Allied cordon and beat a retreat to the German frontier. Far away on the Eastern Front, the Germans had just suffered an equivalent defeat with similar results. Between 23 June and mid-August, Army Group Centre had been encircled and devastated, losing twenty-five of its thirty-eight divisions. Through the gap opened by its destruction the Red Army had poured westward, to reach the River Vistula and the outskirts of Warsaw, where, four years earlier, the first German offensive of the war had been so brilliantly concluded.

The Germans, the inventors of Blitzkrieg, had thus been blitzkrieged themselves. But with this dramatic reversal of circumstances in the summer of 1944, the era of lightning victory reached its end. The collapse of Hitler's Balkan allies in the autumn allowed the Russians to subjugate most of southern Europe in a single bold advance. A winter offensive in Poland carried them to the frontiers of Germany

A British Centurion tank manned by soldiers of the Israel Defence Forces

itself. And in December, Hitler launched his last large-scale tank counter-offensive into the Ardennes, scene of his 1940 triumph, in a final desperate effort to recover the initiative in the West. It failed. And it did for reasons which were becoming apparent to the clear-eyed observer of the nature of contemporary war.

Attrition, which the tank had been invented to overcome, had reimposed its iron logic on the armies of the industrial world. Where men and firepower are accumulated in vast quantities, contention between them can only be resolved through the giving and suffering of tragic loss of life. The introduction of an apparently revolutionary weapon may temporarily interrupt the operation of this military logic. But, over time, brute material forces will reassert themselves. That is what, during the period from 1916 to 1944, had happened with the tank. Its appearance had seemed to promise hopes of waging war on land as war had been waged at sea in the Nelsonian epoch; by the infliction of dramatic and clear-cut victory through the calculated manipulation of pure force, embodied in the ship of the line. Victory at sea – as at Trafalgar – appeared to bring in its wake victory on land, with few of the distressing consequences that great land campaigns entailed. The tank had commonly been spoken of in naval terms, as a 'land ironclad', and its supporting infantry were sometimes called 'tank marines'. But the analogy, and the belief which underlay it, equally failed to square with reality. Politics, Bismarck had said, 'are made with blood and iron.' War, 'the continuation of politics', had proved itself by 1944 to be a business of blood and iron – with a vengeance. The

138

tank, though a thing of iron, was but grist to the mills of the violence that the politics of the modern world had unleashed.

That was not to say that the day of the tank was over. In many respects it had achieved its perfected form by 1945. Machines like the improved German Panther, the Russian T-34/85, the British Centurion, the American Pershing, represented a balance between the qualities of armour, armament and mobility as satisfactory as could be achieved. Subsequent improvements in engine power, suspension, hardness of armour and firepower resulted in a breed of tanks – the Leopard, the T-62, the Chieftain, the M-60 – that were larger than their wartime ancestors but, size for size, not really different from them in kind. As long as the tanks fielded by adversaries continued to match each other in quantity and – a point of the greatest significance – while the anti-tank weapons issued to the infantry failed to present armour with a threat equal to that it represented, they would retain their status as the crucial battlefield weapon. Such conventional wars as have been fought since 1945 – between the Israelis and their Arab neighbours, between India and Pakistan, between the Iranians and the Iraqis – have been dominated by the factor of tank numbers and quality. Efforts to reduce the primacy of the tank, by the development of armour-piercing guided missiles, hand-held and vehicle- or helicopter-mounted, have reduced the limits of its effectiveness without abolishing its battle-winning capacity.

But, as the nature of all conventional land battles has shown since 1945, tanks

The British Chieftain tank; its 120 mm gun was for a time the heaviest tank gun in the world

139

An American anti-tank helicopter (AH 64 Apache) firing an air-to-ground armour-piercing missile

are now but one, if the most important, of several high-technology weapons systems competing for mastery of the battlefield. During the Arab-Israeli War of 1973, anti-tank missile men scored a remarkable run of success against attacking armour. Though the basis of their success was subsequently negated, by improvements to tank armour, that distinct interruption in the tank's record of invulnerability was noted by military observers throughout the world. The anti-tank helicopter has still to prove its survivability in combat. But its very great mobility, and its ever-increasing firepower, clearly also work to threaten the tank's tactical role. So, too, do passive defences – mines and rocket firing devices – as well as the cluster and fragmentation warheads now dispensed by aerial bomb, missile and artillery shell. The instruments of defence are, as it were, massing against the principle of offence that the tank represents. Its strategic role had, as we have seen, been swingeingly reduced by the last year of the Second World War. Perhaps its tactical viability is now under threat. Unsurprisingly so; for all its adaptability, the tank as a weapon system is now seventy years old – older than the ironclad warship was when its usefulness passed – and though, like an old soldier, the tank may never die, its importance may already have begun to fade away.

140

Casualty 7

For many a soldier – be he lancer or legionary, *Panzergrenadier* or parachutist, hoplite or horse-archer – there comes a moment when luck runs out, and he fails to dodge the *pilum*, walks into the machine-gun's beaten zone, or is framed by the sniper's sight like a fly in a spider's web. Suddenly he is defined by that most bland of collective euphemisms: he is a casualty.

Wounds and death are the currency of war, and, though blunt statistics dull war's individual agony, they do give a numbing view of its human cost. At the very least half a million men were killed or wounded in the battle for Verdun in 1916, and in the Third Battle of Ypres, a year later, over half a million more were obliterated by shellfire, caught by machine-guns, choked by gas or simply lost in the mud. Even today the exact figures remain a matter of academic dispute, and the visitor to the wooded ravines around Douaumont or the lush fields below the Passchendaele Ridge can still stumble across some chalk-white relic of mortality. The First World War cost France alone 1,335,000 military dead and 4,266,000 wounded: comparable German figures were 1,773,000 and 4,215,000.

By contrast, during the Second World War the greatest blood-lettings were on the Eastern Front. The Germans suffered over half a million casualties in the battle for Stalingrad, and some 900,000 in the fighting around Kursk in the summer of 1943: in all, they lost two million dead or missing on the Eastern Front. The sheer scale of Russian losses is almost beyond comprehension. A million Russians were killed, wounded or captured in the Kiev pocket in September 1941, and at least as many again were engulfed at Vyazma and Bryansk a month later. Russian military dead and missing totalled over thirteen million – with another eleven million civilian dead.

The toll of the Pacific war was less exorbitant. However, dogged Japanese defence ensured that small islands were bought at a price in blood that bears comparison with Verdun or Passchendaele, Kiev or Stalingrad. Over 38,000 men were killed or wounded in the battle for Saipan. Iwo Jima may be a mere four and a half miles long by two and a half miles wide, but 27,000 Japanese and Americans died fighting for it, and no less than 47,000 Americans became casualties in the capture of Okinawa, where total Japanese losses exceeded 250,000.

The losses suffered in the world wars dwarf those of many battles in the past. Nevertheless, the cataclysmic defeat of Cannae cost the Romans, according to the historian Polybius, 70,000 men: even if one reduces this figure, to allow for hyperbole, to a more reasonable 50,000, the prospect of tens of thousands of men butchered by sword, spear or arrow within the compass of a few thousand square yards almost defeats the imagination.

On 17 September 1862, the bloodiest single day in American history, over 26,000

Relics of mortality:
Verdun 1916

Death in the snow,
1944–5

Union and Confederate soldiers were killed, wounded or reported missing at the battle of Antietam. Pictures of the battle's victims bring the reality of their suffering closer to us: as the *New York Times* suggested at the time, Mathew Brady's photographs of the dead of Antietam were 'like a funeral next door'. Stiffly posed portraits of the soldiers who fought there put flesh onto dry statistics, and underscore the fact that these men – just like every casualty in every war – were sons, husbands, friends, individuals whose death or injury brought with it not only suffering for the victim himself but grief for all those touched by the 'rings of sorrow' which ripple out from every single death.

The bearded John Gay received the first of his three wounds at Antietam, and died nineteen days after Lee's surrender at Appomattox. George Miller was hit in the stomach, and lived – surprisingly, for it was a time when belly wounds were almost invariably fatal – until 1919, in constant pain from his wound. Thirteen year old Charles King was his company's drummer-boy, but all the protestations that he would be kept out of harm's way came to nought when a shell splinter hit him. Alvin Flint was killed near Burnside Bridge. Both his father, aged fifty-three, and his younger brother, aged thirteen, died of typhoid within four months while serving with the 21st Connecticut.

The catastrophe which overwhelmed the Flint family makes another telling point. It was not until this century that the majority of casualties in war were caused by enemy action. During the Civil War the Union army had 96,000 men killed in battle, while almost twice as many – 183,287 – died of disease. In the Crimean War, a conflict infamous for the ravages of disease, 4,285 British soldiers were killed or died of wounds, and 16,422 perished from cholera, typhoid, dysentery, or simply from exposure. The Crimea's grim statistics are dwarfed by those of the

Seven Years War (1756–63): no less than 135,000 of the 185,000 men recruited into the Royal Navy died of disease.

Even in the First World War, when battlefield technology had increased the killing power of weapons and medical science had made inroads into sickness, 167,000 British officers and men were killed or died of wounds received in France and Belgium, and 113,000 died there of disease or accidental injury. The ratio of battle to non-battle casualties in general was, at 1:1.3, highest on the Western Front. In the notoriously unhealthy East Africa no less than thirty-one non-battle casualties were incurred for a single man killed or wounded in action.

Until the seventeenth century most battle casualties were inflicted by sword, spear and arrow. A chronicler's description of Hastings gives some idea of the wounds which edged weapons could inflict.

An English knight . . . rushed straight upon a Norman who was armed and riding on a war-horse, and tried with his hatchet of steel to cleave his helmet; but the blow miscarried, and the sharp blade glanced down before the saddle bow, driving through the horse's neck down to the ground, so that both horse and master fell together to the earth . . . There was a French soldier of noble mien, who sat his horse gallantly. He spied two Englishmen who were also carrying themselves boldly . . . he raised his shield, and struck one of the Englishmen with his lance on the breast, so that the iron passed out of his back. At the moment that he fell, the lance broke, and the Frenchman seized the mace that hung on his right side, and struck the other Englishman a blow that completely broke his skull . . .

Sir Charles Bell's watercolours record the injuries of Waterloo casualties with a surgeon's professional detachment

Most of the components of an ancient or mediaeval casualty-return are here: the traumatic amputation of limbs, and the resultant haemorrhage; the penetrating wounds of the abdomen; the depression fractures of the skull. Add the contusions and fractures that came when mail shirt or leather jerkin turned a weapon's edge

but did little to dull the force of the blow, and the slashes and hacks that nose-guards, cheek-pieces and gauntlets could never quite prevent, and one begins to grasp the dimensions of the problem faced by the surgeon in an era when medical science was still in its infancy.

Yet the military surgeons of antiquity were by no means helpless. Trepanning – removing part of the skull to relieve pressure on the brain – was used by Egyptian army surgeons, and both the Greek and Roman armies had doctors who knew of the value of diet and exercise, carried out simple operations and administered drugs. The Byzantine army included a medical corps of bearers and surgeons, with one surgeon and six to eight bearers attached to each unit, and the bearers received a special bonus for carrying off wounded when the army was in retreat.

The Byzantines were unusually advanced, and for most of the ancient and mediaeval period the plight of the wounded was unenviable. Infection made even the most trivial injuries dangerous, and if some early remedies were remarkably effective, others were quasi-magical fumblings with a human physiology which was at best half-understood. A few far-sighted doctors could undoubtedly be found. Edward I's surgeon saved his life, by what we would now term radical debridement, in 1272, and Henri de Mondeville, surgeon to Philip the Fair of France, dealt successfully with abdominal wounds. But in spite of attempts to ensure that doctors were properly trained – it was St Louis' own experience of war that induced him to found a college of surgeons at Paris in 1268, an early example of the way in which military medicine has advanced medical practice in general – many mediaeval physicians and surgeons lacked both skill and knowledge. And, while royal doctors enjoyed good pay and high status – Edward II's physician and surgeon both received knight's pay – the ordinary 'chirurgeon' eked out his income by barbering. As late as 1544 the leading English surgeon Thomas Gale complained that many of his

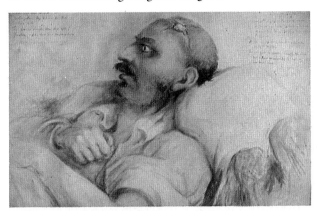

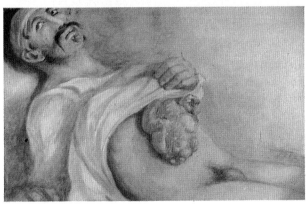

colleagues at the siege of Montreuil were tinkers, cobblers and sow-gelders, using tools more appropriate to their original trades than to surgery.

On the day of battle the numbers of wounded swamped the slender medical services available. Men of high rank might be brought off the field by their squires, and treated rapidly by their own surgeons. The overwhelming majority of wounded were likely to lie where they had fallen for hours or even days, at the mercy of their wounds, the weather and, not least, the sinister swarm of pillagers who descended upon battlefields until comparatively recent times, stealing money, jewellery and clothing, silencing a wounded man's pleas or protests with a knife-thrust. Many a brave man survived battle with a wound from which he might have recovered, only to be murdered in the dark for the few pence in his purse or the gold lace on his coat. In due course the wounded, or at least those of the victorious army, would be collected up in carts and taken to monasteries to be cared for by the monks, or to improvised field hospitals. For those whose wounds were serious the long wait or the jolting journey would prove fatal, and often fellow soldiers bowed to the inevitable and quietly finished off the hopelessly injured. Not for nothing was the slim knightly dagger called the misericord – the weapon of mercy.

It was the sight of this rough mercy being meted out that horrified Ambroise Paré, one of the fathers of modern military medicine. When he entered Milan with the French army in 1536 he saw three men hideously burned by gunpowder.

Beholding them with pity there came an old soldier who asked me if there was any means of curing them. I told him no. At once he approached them and cut their throats gently and, seeing this great cruelty, I shouted at him that he was a villain. He answered me that he prayed to God that when he should be in such a state he might find someone who would do the same for him, to the end that he might not languish miserably.

Paré disagreed with the conventional treatment of gun-shot wounds, cauterization by boiling oil. He obtained better results with a mixture of egg yolk, rose oil and turpentine. He also recognized that shattered limbs – a consequence of the growing use of firearms – should be amputated swiftly, with the incision being made high, in the sound flesh of the shoulder or thigh. Rather than apply a red-hot iron to the stump, which not only often failed to arrest the bleeding but also risked killing the patient with the shock, Paré tied off the ends of the severed arteries with cord.

Compassionate and clear-thinking men like Paré and his English contemporaries Thomas Gale and William Clowes were struggling against ignorance in their own profession and prejudice outside it. The low status of military doctors did not encourage the best medical men to join the army. Although surgeons were generally recognized as being commissioned officers by the end of the seventeenth century, for the next two hundred years they enjoyed a decidedly inferior position *vis-à-vis* combatant officers. In the nineteenth-century French army, for example, medical officers were controlled by the army's logistic corps, the *Intendance*. They exercised no command authority, so administrative officers commanded their medical order-lies and supervised hospital accounts, while officers of the transport corps ran the ambulance wagons. It is small wonder that, when the French army prepared for the 1859 Italian campaign, it was 300 doctors under strength. The demands of war forced armies to lower already depressed entry standards: during the Seven Years War Frederick the Great took on barbers' assistants, 'raw young lads who could scarcely shave a beard tolerably well, and were not even up to applying a plaster.'

In view of these disadvantages it is perhaps surprising that military medicine attracted some of the capable men that it did. James McGrigor, senior medical officer of Wellington's army in the Peninsula, was a highly effective medical quartermaster. He reorganized the filthy and ramshackle hospitals to which the

146

wounded were consigned, set up a proper base hospital near Lisbon, and established a system of medical boards which reviewed individual cases in order to ensure that malingerers were not evacuated and that the sick and wounded men were not returned to duty until they were fit for it.

McGrigor's major problem remained the transport of the wounded. His French counterparts were more successful in solving it. Baron Percy, French surgeon-in-chief in Spain, recognized that 'the assistance of first importance to a wounded man is for him to be carried promptly and properly away from the scene of conflict.' Not only did soldiers die while waiting for transport, but often sound men left the ranks to escort their wounded comrades, with damaging effects upon the army's fighting efficiency. Percy founded a corps of stretcher bearers, thoroughly trained and fully equipped, its members selected from soldiers of proven valour.

Percy had earlier experimented with a light surgeon's carriage, and Baron Dominique Larrey, Napoleon's surgeon-general, went further. He too saw that men often died before they could be treated, and organized mobile field ambulances which could move swiftly to the battlefield to succour the wounded. The ambulance consisted of two sections, one of which treated the wounded while the other carried them back to a larger field hospital. Larrey designed light ambulance carriages which were sprung in order to ease the journey, and from 1809 ambulance companies were attached to each division.

For all the efforts of men like McGrigor, Percy and Larrey, the military medicine of the Napoleonic period barely coped with either the ravages of disease or the fearful mauling of battle. On the Walcheren expedition of 1809, 23,000 British troops perished from disease while only 217 were killed by the French, and in Spain in 1812 a single battalion lost 500 men from sickness in a matter of weeks.

Large battles overloaded the medical services just as they always had. At Borodino in 1812 the French lost at least 30,000 killed and wounded and the Russians more than 44,000: almost one-third of the soldiers who fought there were hit. Captain Eugène Labaume described: 'the interior of the ravines; almost all the wounded, by a natural instinct, had dragged themselves there to avoid new blows; these unfortunates, piled up one on the other, denied aid and swimming in blood, gave horrible groans ... they asked us to put an end to their horrible agony. In the space of a square league almost every spot was covered with the killed and wounded.' Larrey carried out 200 limb amputations on the day of the battle, and even he was astonished at the severity of the wounds, which he blamed on the intensity of the close-range artillery fire.

Even those of the wounded lucky enough to survive scalpel and bone-saw still had the odds stacked heavily against them. The French army was already short of food and transport, and many of the wounded were simply packed into improvised hospitals, like that in the Kolotskoi monastery on the Smolensk road, where hundreds simply starved. Captain C. F. François was shocked to discover the corpse of one officer who had gnawed his own arm to the bone before he perished. Alexandre Bellot de Kergorre, a commissariat official, did his best to feed the wounded from pitifully inadequate stores. 'Our poor unfortunate wounded were dying of hunger and thirst,' he wrote.

They were bandaged with hay for lack of lint and linen, and they groaned dreadfully. For the first few days they lived on the few grains they could find in the straw they lay on, and on the little flour I was able to give them ... A shocking thing was the impossibility of removing the dead from the living. I had neither medical orderlies nor stretchers. Not only was the hospital full of corpses, but so were the streets and a number of the houses ... On my own I took away 128, which had been serving as pillows to the sick and were several days old.

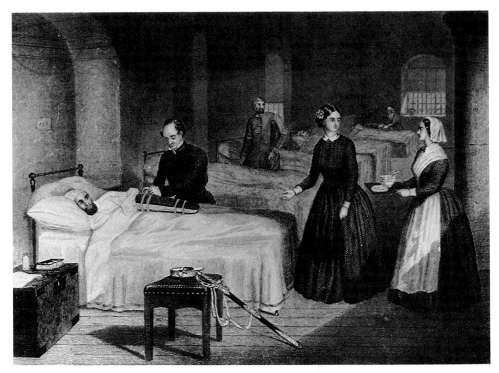

The remarkable fact is not that a high proportion of the wounded died during this period, but that any survived at all. The fortunate few owed their recovery to physical strength and endurance, and to a stoical disregard for suffering, which was an important attribute in an age when even the pain of a simple headache had to be endured. Lieutenant Harry Smith of the 95th Regiment soldiered on for five months with a ball lodged in his Achilles tendon. The members of a medical board reluctantly agreed to cut it out. 'It was,' admitted Smith 'five minutes, most painful indeed, before it was extracted. The ball was jagged and the tendonous fibres had grown into it. It was half dissected and half torn out, with the most excruciating torture for a moment, the forceps breaking which had hold of the ball.' Even more serious was Lord Fitzroy Somerset's smashed arm, amputated on the night of Waterloo. 'Here, bring that arm back,' he shouted to an orderly. 'There is a ring my wife gave me on the finger.' Equally typical of the dour toughness of the period was a British soldier's response to the cries of a wounded Frenchman, undergoing treatment alongside him. The latter's screams: 'seemed to annoy the Englishman more than anything else, and so much so, that as soon as his arm was amputated he struck the Frenchman a sharp blow across the breech with the severed limb, holding it by the wrist, saying, "Here, take that, and stuff it down your throat, and stop your damned bellowing."'

There were indeed times when the pain of a wound, or of the surgery which followed it, produced anguish which even the greatest courage could not mask. Rifleman John Harris was in action at the battle of Rolica when he heard a shriek, and looked round to see his comrade Sergeant Frazer sitting doubled up, swaying backwards and forwards as if racked with the most intense stomach-ache.

'Oh! Harris!' said he, as I took him in my arms, 'I shall die! I shall die! The agony is so great that I cannot bear it.'

It was, indeed, dreadful to look upon him: the froth came from his mouth, and the perspiration poured from his face . . . Poor fellow! he suffered more for the short time that he was dying than any man I think I ever saw in the same circumstances. I had the curiosity

148

to return to look at him after the battle. A musket-ball, I found, had taken him sideways, and gone through both groins.

Later a surgeon called Harris over to hold a patient still while a ball was extracted from his shoulder, but: 'he writhed and twisted so much during the operation that it was with difficulty Dr Ridgeway could perform it. He found it necessary to cut very deep, and Doubter made a terrible outcry at every fresh incision.' The man survived the operation but, like so many others, died shortly after it.

The second half of the nineteenth century witnessed twin developments which were to make scenes like these rarer. On the one hand, advances in medical science improved the treatment of both wounds and disease, and on the other, far-reaching changes in the organization of military hospitals provided an increasingly healthy environment for the care of the sick and wounded.

The appalling state of British military hospitals was highlighted by the Crimean War. The base hospital at Scutari had sick and wounded men strewn about the wards and corridors. The privies were all blocked, and a scum of filth floated on the floor. Two hundred camp followers lived in the cellars below, drinking, whoring and dying of cholera. By November 1854 almost half the patients admitted to this noisome warren died. On 5 November Florence Nightingale arrived with thirty-eight nurses recruited in England. They set about the daunting task of cleaning the floors, providing fresh bed-linen and cooking nourishing food. The efforts of Miss Nightingale and her devoted band – tackling the sort of task so often shunned by 'decent women' in the past – helped reduce the death-rate to a mere 2.2% within six months.

The example of the Crimea was not lost upon the Union during the American Civil War. The United States Sanitary Commission, set up in June 1861, helped press the army's Medical Department into setting up hospitals and organizing field ambulances. Yet pitched battles proved too much for even the Union's steadily improving facilities. Some 22,000 men, Union and Confederate, were wounded at Gettysburg in July 1863. They were treated in a variety of improvised field hospitals, like one in Gettysburg church, where boards were laid across the backs of pews to form a huge platform on which the wounded were packed like sardines. One nurse described how, on entering the building, she seemed to stand 'breast-high in a sea of anguish'. Volunteer nurses did sterling work amongst the human jetsam of the battle, and their fortitude and compassion went a long way towards changing the image of the nurse in the American army, just as Florence Nightingale and her colleagues had in the British. But hundreds of other wounded lay in the fields, woods and gardens round Gettysburg: five days after the battle ambulances were still bringing them in. Some of those retrieved were recognized by the overworked surgeons as being beyond medical aid: in a little wood lay a long row of men with head-wounds, left alone to twitch and grunt their lives away.

Most of the men who underwent surgery at Gettysburg enjoyed a benefit unknown to soldiers of an earlier generation: they were given an anaesthetic before they felt the knife. For hundreds of years doctors had attempted to relieve pain by administering sedative drugs like opium or mandragora. The agony of surgery could, at least in part, be dulled by opiates, alcohol, partial strangulation or the numbing of a limb by the use of a tight tourniquet. None of these methods was ideal, and surgery was usually painful for the patient and profoundly distressing for the surgeon: the great John Hunter turned 'pale as death' when he operated. In the 1840s various American doctors experimented with the use of anaesthetic gases, and in 1846 Dr Morton of Boston, Massachusetts, made medical history by removing a tumour under general anaesthetic. In the following year an Edinburgh

*A British Regimental
Aid Post on the Western
Front: both British and
German wounded are
being treated*

gynaecologist discovered the anaesthetic properties of chloroform, and by the time of the American Civil War anaesthetics were widely used.

Despite improved hospitals, increasingly efficient army medical services and the new anaesthetics, the wounded still died like flies. In the Franco-Prussian War of 1870–1 almost half the amputations carried out resulted in death – not from the surgeon's maladroitness or the nurse's carelessness, but from post-operative infection. Battlefield surgery was a dirty business. The patient, often with fragments of clothing and unburned powder in his wound, was placed on a table-top already slick with the blood of others. The surgeon clamped his knife between his teeth as he helped lift the patient, and then, giving the blade a wipe across his bloody apron, he fell to. The wound was eventually dressed with lint plucked from discarded linen: neither it nor the surgeon's instruments were sterilized.

Such scenes, terrible though they were, differed from those in a civilian operating theatre in terms of the number of operations performed rather than in the cleanliness of the surroundings. It was not until Joseph Lister's work on antisepsis in the 1860s and 1870s that it dawned on surgeons that the maintenance of the strictest antiseptic conditions could prevent post-operative infection. The effect upon military medicine was profound: the Boer War of 1899–1902 was the first conflict in which the soldier who underwent amputation was more likely to survive the operation and its effects than to die of gangrene. The infection of bullet wounds was also minimized by the use of the first field dressing, a packet containing sterile pads which a soldier could apply to a comrade's wound.

The science which removed pain from the operating table and so greatly reduced post-operative infection also helped to combat disease. The discoveries of Louis Pasteur and his successors made possible immunization against many of the infections which had decimated armies over the centuries. Typhoid was a major killer in the Boer War but, thanks to Sir Almroth Wright's development of an effective vaccine with which soldiers could be innoculated, it was of little account in either of the world wars.

The First World War posed a formidable challenge to military medicine despite

150

all the advances of the previous half-century. Science had aided the doctor, but it had also helped the gunner. During the First World War shells, bombs and grenades caused the overwhelming majority of casualties – 60.7% – in the British army. Doctors had to contend with complex multiple wounds, as well as with the casualties caused by gas, first used by the Germans in the spring of 1915 but thereafter liberally employed by both sides. Moreover, although motor ambulances and ambulance trains could speed wounded down the chain of evacuation quicker than ever before, major battles could still swamp medical facilities.

The wounded man's first problem was getting back to the Regimental Aid Post, within a thousand yards or so of the front line. He might walk, be helped back by his mates, or be carried by stretcher bearers. But he might equally well lie out in no-man's-land for days until death or chance discovery brought relief. At the RAP the regimental medical officer and his assistants tended the wounded in circumstances which were usually far from ideal, as Captain Harold Dearden remembered. 'The aid post was very crowded, however, and was a perfect shambles of mud, rain and blood. It was quite impossible to get any cover for anyone . . . We were heavily shelled all night; in the early morning a flight of Boche planes bombed us from very low down, and I had several of my wounded killed in that way.' Medical officers and their devoted stretcher bearers earned the respect and affection of the men they served. Only three British soldiers have ever won the Victoria Cross twice, and two of these, Lieutenant Arthur Martin-Leake and Captain Noel Chavasse, were medical officers.

When a man reached the RAP, the doctor made a quick decision on his chances. Walking wounded would wait their turn for patching up, hopeless cases might be given morphine and quietly put to one side, while others received quick life-preserving treatment before being sent back to the Advanced Dressing Station, and

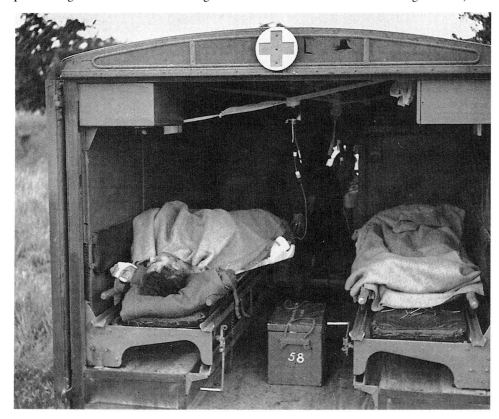

Second World War casualties receive blood transfusions in an ambulance

thence to the Casualty Clearing Station and, finally, on to hospital. The war correspondent Philip Gibbs watched the injured arriving at the CCS in Lillers town hall, behind the Loos battlefield. There were: 'men with chunks of steel in their lungs and bowels vomiting great gobs of blood, men with legs and arms torn from their trunks, men without noses, and their brains throbbing through open scalps, men without faces . . .'

Notwithstanding the frightful state in which so many of them reached the CCS, the great majority of the wounded who received treatment subsequently recovered. In the American army only 7% of them died compared with 7.61% in the British. This difference may be accounted for by the fact that blood transfusions on a large scale were impossible until 1917, the year America entered the war, when the problem of clotting was overcome. Indeed, the war gave particular impetus to research into blood transfusion, yet more reason for the Austrian Dr Zinsser to remark that: 'Nobody won the last war but the medical services. The increase in knowledge was the sole determinable gain for mankind in a devastating catastrophe.'

Nevertheless, doctors and nurses needed all their professional armour to withstand the pressures of hospital life. 'Another very busy day,' recorded Dearden.

A good many cases came in this morning, several pretty bad. Amputated one boy's leg; he's only just eighteen and looks so bad that I doubt if he will live the night through . . . We had a curious case in just now. A soldier was told to chop a tree down; and while he was doing so he missed the tree and his axe hit the ground, exploding a Mill's bomb buried there, blowing the front of his abdominal wall away . . . so that dressing him is largely a matter of keeping his intestines out of the bed. He is dying fast. He just lies and vomits with that easy grace that all peritonitis cases get; and his face with his pain, the shock and the morphia he has had is just a writhing, twisting sheet of grey linen.

Developments in the years between the wars increased the survival rate for Second World War wounded. Penicillin and the sulphonamides greatly reduced

A US Marine wounded in Vietnam in 1968 is rushed to a medical evacuation helicopter by stretcher bearers

the danger of infected wounds, and dramatic improvements in the technique of blood transfusion – notably the use of frozen blood and powdered plasma – also helped badly wounded men recover from injuries that would once have killed them.

Equally remarkable was the continuing assault upon disease. Although non-battle casualties of various sorts continued to outnumber those killed and wounded in battle – in the Middle East sickness caused almost twenty times the losses of combat – the war was fought across harsh terrain and in unhealthy climates where losses like this might be expected. Medicine had a dramatic effect upon many diseases. The use of anti-malaria drugs helped reduce hospital admissions from malaria in Burma from 628 per 1,000 men in 1942 to forty-five per 1,000 in 1945. Without such contributions the 14th Army would simply have dwindled away: in April 1942, for example, the 26th Indian Division was losing men at the rate of 18 per 1,000 soldiers each day, and would have ceased to exist in only two months.

One of the most striking life-saving developments was not connected with medical research at all. Baron Percy had observed, a century and a half before, that delay in treatment killed many wounded. The static nature of First World War operations had helped the chain of evacuation to function relatively smoothly, so that once a man reached the RAP he could expect to complete the rest of his journey within hours. The Second World War was more mobile, and its soldiers often fought in terrain almost guaranteed to make the journey to the rear painful and protracted. But the aircraft intervened to save thousands of lives. As air evacuation became the norm in the Allied armies in 1943–4 men could be whisked back from forward airstrips to hospitals deep in the rear: in the campaign in north-west Europe in 1944–5 over 100,000 of the wounded were evacuated by air.

Air evacuation has remained crucially important in post-1945 conflicts, and the increasing use of helicopters has enabled wounded to be lifted from battle to operating theatre faster than ever before. During the Vietnam War the Bell UH-1H 'Dust-Off' helicopter was a vital link in the chain of evacuation: between 1965 and

Vietnam wounded are loaded onto a UH-1D helicopter

1969 nearly 373,000 casualties were evacuated by helicopter. Devoted pilots brought their machines down into the very teeth of a firefight to pick up wounded. Often, though, the wounded man made the first stage of his journey as he always had: on foot, across a comrade's shoulders, or in a vehicle, like Marine sergeant Ron Kovic in the back of an Amtrack: 'Men are screaming all around me. "Oh God get me out of here!" "Please help," they scream. Oh Jesus, like little children now, not like marines, not like the posters . . . "Mother!" screams a man without a face. "Oh I don't want to die!" screams a young boy, cupping his intestines with his hands. "Oh please, oh no, oh God, oh help! Mother!" he screams again.' Nevertheless, a wounded man's chances were better than ever before: only 1% of the wounded reaching a medical facility died, a figure which compares favourably with the 2.2% in Korea and 4.5% in the Second World War.

Even if many modern techniques have been available to surgeons treating the wounded in recent wars, the demands of battle give their work a curiously ageless character. John Parrish, a US Navy doctor in Vietnam, found his field hospital

Even in Vietnam, some wounded came out of action as they always had, on the backs of their comrades

overwhelmed by wounded as surely as had his ancestors at Gettysburg or Antietam. 'The triage officer system broke down completely,' he wrote. 'Each doctor picked and stepped among the prone bodies choosing who to work on, who could be saved, who could wait, and who would be a waste of precious time.' Major Paul Grauwin struggled to rescue men from his shelled hospital dugout at Dien Bien Phu in 1954 in a scene not out of place at Verdun thirty-eight years before. 'Earth and rubble of every kind have covered up the three wounded men I had just been looking at. We try to get them out with our hands, tearing our nails, tugging at the thick planks . . . One is still breathing; the second has had his forehead smashed down into his jaw – he is dead; the third has had his leg broken . . .' Surgeon-Commander Rick Jolly, operating in the improvised theatre at Ajax Bay in the Falklands, saw his surgeons: 'lay the wound open to the air and remove the dark purple pieces of dead tissue. The work is careful and thorough, demanding intense concentration and a pair of scissors . . . We are simply trying to save life and limb now, so the fancy stuff with fixation bars and operating microscopes can wait until later.' He recalled that this technique still bore the name given it by Joseph Larrey: *débridement.*

The sensation of receiving a wound has changed little over the ages. Some wounds – like that suffered by Sergeant Frazer – are immediately agonizing. Others go almost undetected in the heat of battle, just as sportsmen often fail to notice an injury during a game. Bob Sanders, wounded in Vietnam, recalled that: 'At first, when I got hit, I didn't feel anything. I was too scared and I was concentrating on Charlie. I felt a little stinging, but I didn't think nothing of it.' More common is the feeling of paralyzing numbness described by a Gordon Highlander wounded in 1914: 'I knew instantly what had happened. The blow might have come from a sledge-hammer, except that it seemed to carry with it an impression of speed. I saw for one instant in my mind's eye the battlefield at which I had been gazing through my glasses the whole day. Then the vision was hidden by a scarlet circle, and a voice said, "Mr H. has got it."' George Orwell, hit in Spain during the Civil War, felt much the same. 'Roughly speaking it was the sensation of being *at the centre* of an explosion. There seemed to be a loud bang and a blinding flash of light all round me, and I felt a tremendous shock, such as you get from an electric terminal; with it a sense of utter weakness, a feeling of being stricken and shrivelled up to nothing.'

The pain usually comes later, as Captain Robert Graves discovered when an 8-inch shell burst three paces behind him at Mametz Wood on the Somme in 1916. He felt 'as though I had been punched rather hard between the shoulder-blades, but without any pain.' Put aside to die in a dressing-station, he was evacuated after lying unconscious for more than 24 hours. Then: 'The pain of being jolted down Happy Valley, with a shell hole every three or four yards of the road, woke me up. I remember screaming.' He was later evacuated to Rouen on a hospital train.

I remember the journey as a nightmare. My back was sagging, and I could not raise my knees to relieve the cramp, the bunk above me being only a few inches away. A German flying-officer, on the other side of the carriage, with a compound fracture of the leg from an aeroplane crash, groaned and wept without pause. Though the other wounded men cursed him, telling him to stow it and be a man, he continued pitiably, keeping everyone awake. He was not delirious – just frightened and in great pain.

War harms the mind as well as the body. During the American Civil War the Union Surgeon-General identified a disabling psychiatric condition which he termed 'nostalgia', which affected 2.34 per 1,000 troops in the first year of the war and 3.3 in the second. In the First World War doctors initially believed that men's brains were concussed by the close explosion of a shell, and subsequent emotional

Stretcher bearers in the Falklands, 1982

breakdown was called 'shell shock'. By the end of the war psychiatric casualties were more accurately diagnosed although, as Dr R. H. Ahrenfeldt observed, it was sometimes almost a matter of chance whether a man suffering from psychiatric breakdown was considered to be ill, to be a malingerer or even a deserter. Nevertheless, in March 1939 there were 120,000 British ex-soldiers alive who were still receiving or who had received pensions for primary psychiatric disability.

In the Second World War psychiatric casualties ran at twenty to thirty for every 100 battle casualties in general, though there were times, as with the US 1st Armoured Division in Italy in 1944, when they exceeded fifty. American psychiatric casualties in Korea initially approached those of the Second World War, but soon dropped to 6% of medical evacuations once proper first-line treatment centres had been set up, and in Vietnam evacuations for psychiatric reasons fell to a mere 2–3% of all evacuations in 1967–8. In the Arab-Israeli War of 1973 the Israelis sustained over forty psychiatric casualties for every 100 battle casualties, a very high ratio, largely explained by the speed and surprise of the Arab attack. Their experience encouraged them to take more care over the prevention and treatment of such casualties, and they succeeded in reducing the figure to 23% during the fighting in Lebanon in 1982.

Two striking facts emerge. The first is that almost all soldiers will eventually break under the stress of battle. The time they last will vary according to circumstances: it might be a matter of hours for the individual who has low morale, is poorly led and is subjected to shocks for which he is ill-prepared, or hundreds of days for a well-motivated soldier in a good unit. A Second World War American study suggested that the average man could tolerate only 200 to 240 combat days, while the British, who rotated units more frequently, reckoned on 400 days. It is also

156

clear that breakdown can be delayed or prevented by training and preparation, and that most soldiers who do become psychiatric casualties can be cured quickly and completely. Proven treatment consists of removing the victim from the worst of the battle. He is then rested, while being treated as a soldier, not a patient, and is encouraged to discuss his feelings with those who have had similar experiences. He is rehabilitated into useful work, and returned to his unit. In 1982, 75% of Israeli psychiatric casualties were returned within seventy-two hours. Only 10% needed treatment for longer than two or three weeks, and none required long-term institutional care.

The care of men wounded in body or mind, and the treatment of prisoners of war, have been aided by a growing measure of international co-operation. There had been attempts to regulate war even before the Dutch jurist Grotius called for a 'moderation of warfare' in the seventeenth century, but it was not until the nineteenth century that there was a systematic attempt to codify the laws of war. The young Swiss Henri Dunant was shocked by what he saw on the battlefield of Solferino in 1859, and his experiences led to the first Geneva conference of 1864 and the founding of the International Red Cross. Rules were drawn up for the protection of wounded soldiers, regardless of which side they fought on, and subsequent conferences at Geneva, Brussels and the Hague defined the rights and duties of belligerents.

These arrangements have sometimes worked well. In November 1941 a New Zealand field ambulance was overrun in the Western Desert. It continued to treat the wounded of both sides without interruption until the tide of battle swept the Germans away again. In Tunisia two years later, when a German brigade commander found that his casualty clearing station was being accidentally shelled, he sent a patrol through British lines to post a letter to his opposite number, telling him what was happening. Similarly, when the Germans accepted the surrender of British or Americans, or *vice versa*, the prisoners were usually well treated.

Where there were radical racial or cultural differences between combatants, both prisoners and wounded suffered. When the Japanese overran the Alexandra Hospital in Singapore on 13 February 1942, they bayoneted many of the wounded in their beds, and burst into an operating theatre to kill both surgical team and patient. Men captured at Singapore fared badly, and thousands died as a result of brutality, disease or simple neglect working on the Burma railway. It has been estimated that between six and ten million prisoners of war died while in captivity during the Second World War. The plight of the prisoner was particularly cruel on the Eastern Front, where atrocity and counter-atrocity fuelled bitterness. About 45% of the Germans captured by the Russians never returned home, while 60% of the Russians imprisoned in Germany perished.

Many of the misfortunes of prisoners of war stem from the deliberate policy of their captors. Everett Alvarez, a US Navy pilot, was shot down over North Vietnam, and spent eight and a half years in captivity. He endured savage treatment designed to break his will:

they would cut my rations down, expose me to cold, then after a while, if you still resisted, they would put you in a room and sit you there, and cut your rations and water back and not let you sleep, then . . . they'd come in and use very painful methods of physical torture: a trick was to tie your arms behind your back and pull them over your head almost, very very painful . . . they'd use these manacles, these big manacles that would cut into your arms, and many of the fellas still have the scars from those things . . .

Corporal punishment was commonplace in the Japanese army of the Second World War, and prisoners of the Japanese discovered that their guards vigorously

applied a discipline with which they themselves were painfully familiar. Australian Sergeant Ken Harrison worked on a railway cutting in Thailand, at the mercy of brutal guards.

Orders had been received that the cutting *must* be completed by September at all costs, and their latent cruelty and sadism were given free licence. Beatings and slappings were commonplace, but now each guard tried to outdo his fellows in ingenuity.

Ichinoi, to give him his due, had no special weapon and would democratically hit with the nearest object – shovel, bamboo rod, or crowbar. Others, entirely lacking the high principles of Ichinoi, started to distinguish themselves with individual 'trade marks'. One carried a pick-handle; another a length of knotted atap that cut and scratched where it hit; another found a length of fencing wire most effective in encouraging maximum efforts; inevitably his fellow guard went one better and nailed a length of barbed wire to a metre stick.

An officer estimated that sixty-eight men were beaten to death in that cutting.

Other perils are the consequence of the hard facts of war rather than deliberate sadism. Large numbers of prisoners may swamp the resources of captors who are themselves short of food, and who lack the resources to feed, transport and house thousands of extra men. By August 1864 there were 32,899 Union soldiers imprisoned in the notorious Andersonville camp: each man had an average of thirty-six square feet in which to eat, sleep and relieve himself. Although the commandant, Captain Henry Wirz, was undoubtedly brutal, his temper frayed by the constant agony of a badly amputated arm, the sufferings of the inmates stemmed as much from mismanagement, and from food shortages in the Confederacy as a whole, as from deliberate malice. Rober H. Kellogg gives a graphic description of the state to which hunger had reduced the inmates.

As we entered the place a spectacle met our eyes that almost froze our blood with horror, and made our hearts fail within us. Before us were forms that had once been active and alert, *stalwart men,* now nothing but walking skeletons covered with filth and vermin. Many of our men, in the heat and intensity of their feeling, exclaimed with earnestness 'Can this be hell? God protect us.'

If the laws of war cannot guarantee protection to the soldier, they can similarly offer only limited defence to the civilian. Civilians have frequently been killed by infuriated soldiers with dead comrades to avenge. A helicopter crewman wrote home from Vietnam that, 'now more than ever I am determined to do everything possible to wipe these rotten bastards off the face of the earth. I have a long time here, and heaven help any one of them, man, woman or child, that crosses my path. Total and complete destruction is the only way to treat these animals. I never thought I could hate them as much as I do now.' On other occasions, civilian deaths result from a policy which makes targets of cities. The strategic bombing of Germany probably killed 600,000 Germans and seriously wounded another 800,000, and by August 1946 the single atomic bomb dropped on Hiroshima had caused 320,000 civilian casualties, over 118,000 of them fatal. It is not only bombs and bullets that do the damage: hunger and disease also play their part. When the Protestant city of Magdeburg was stormed by a Catholic army in May 1631, 24,000 people were killed by the exasperated attackers or burnt when the city caught fire. Even this figure pales into insignificance when compared with the ordeal of Leningrad, which lost nearly a million of its citizens between August 1941 and January 1943, most of them from cold and hunger.

'Here lie the people of Leningrad' proclaims their memorial at Piskarevsky. The practice of commemorating the victims of war, and of according them an honoured burial, goes back at least two thousand years. The Athenians killed at Marathon

Opposite top: German stretcher bearers, their Red Cross brassards prominent, bring a wounded British soldier for treatment by a German medical officer

Opposite bottom: German prisoners of war are marched through the streets of Moscow

159

It is not always soldiers who suffer; dead Vietnamese civilians at My Lai, 1968

still lie beneath their burial-mound, and when archaeologists excavated a smaller mound they found the remains of the eleven men of the city-state of Plataea, killed in the same battle but preserving their city's individualism even in death. For much of history, however, the dead were tumbled unceremoniously into common graves. A particularly distinguished officer might be commemorated on a stone monument, but most of the dead lay anonymously in pits whose location was forgotten with the passage of the years. Near Kolin, a few hundred yards from the main road from Prague to Brno – the old *Kaiserstrasse* – stands a lonely column with the double-headed eagle of Austria glinting at its top. A handful of officers are commemorated on its plinth. But perhaps 15,000 other soldiers lie forgotten beneath the rich farmland, while the heavy lorries thunder by, their drivers oblivious to the fact that they are crossing the site of one of Frederick the Great's sharpest defeats.

Burying the dead after a great battle came a poor third in an army's priorities, lagging well behind the tasks of continuing the war and caring for the wounded. A traveller who crossed the field of Austerlitz six weeks after the battle in 1805 wrote that:

traces of the slaughter were still to be seen all over the field. The many freshly-turned piles of earth betrayed the sites of the graves. We repeatedly had to hasten past spots where inadequately buried bodies of horses had been worked over by the ravens and crows, and were spreading an intolerable stench. Worse still, you could see the severed limbs of dead or maimed soldiers, together with half-eaten skulls, bones and ribs.

The dead of conflicts like the Austro-Prussian and Franco-Prussian wars were usually buried in regimental groups, with their names recorded on a nearby monument. Thus the men of the Augusta Regiment still lie by Jerusalem Farm on the ridge of Saint-Privat, as if to hold in death the ground that cost them so dear. After the First World War there was a concerted attempt to ensure that the dead were properly commemorated, in individual graves where possible. In a strange way 'the war took stone', and northern France and Belgium are strewn with cemeteries – the Commonwealth War Graves Commission maintains 600 there – which range from the massive Tyne Cot with nearly 12,000 graves to tiny cemeteries

160

with a few dozen. Sometimes the fortune of war denied a man a known and honoured grave. All British dead are commemorated by name on monuments like the Menin Gate or the Thiepval Memorial, but the bones of perhaps 170,000 French soldiers lie in the massive ossuary of Douaumont above Verdun.

In the same way that care of the wounded depends upon co-operation between adversaries, the burial and commemoration of the dead is difficult where fierce hostility colours both war and its aftermath. Most of the dead of the Eastern Front have no known graves, and the French soldiers killed at Dien Bien Phu still lie shrouded in parachute silk in hasty battlefield graves, or under the debris of collapsed dugouts or filled-in trenches.

For all the poignancy of military cemeteries, there is at least a quiet finality to them, in that they are the resting-places of men whose troubles are over. There are, though, casualties of war whose problems do not end at the armistice. They live on, crippled in body or in mind, dependent for their livelihood upon the support of their family and friends and the gratitude of the state they served. It is a melancholy judgement upon human nature that governments usually show greater alacrity in calling men up for military service than in caring for them once the war has ended. Henry Spearman of Wiltshire petitioned Charles II for a pension fifteen years after he had received his wounds. He had, 'for many years faithfully served his late Majesty King Charles the First of ever blessed memory, in which wars he had received many wounds and bruises in his body, the loss of the use of one of his hands, and one of his eyes, whereby he is quite disabled to labour and both himself and his family are like to perish.'

A few of the crippled veterans of Frederick the Great's army were accommodated in the Invalid House at Berlin, but the majority were merely given licences to beg.

The Commonwealth War Graves Commission's cemetery at Tyne Cot in Belgium. This, the largest Commonwealth war cemetery, contains 11,908 graves

161

Home with honour: a disabled Vietnam veteran

Above right: First World War British amputees learn how to use their artificial legs at Roehampton Hospital

And, although some of Wellington's Peninsular veterans were admitted to the Royal Hospital in Chelsea, most were left to their own devices, and in 1814 John Harris saw:

thousands of soldiers lining the streets, and lounging about before the different public-houses, with every description of wound and casualty incident to modern warfare . . . The Irishman, shouting and brandishing his crutch; the English soldier, reeling with drink; and the Scot, with grave and melancholy visage, sitting on the steps of the public-house amongst the crowd, listening to the skirl of his comrades' pipes and thinking of the blue hills of his native land.

For all that the treatment of the war disabled has improved in the twentieth century, it has remained patchy. In the aftermath of the First World War there was little enough work available even for the fit, and the spectacle of the badly injured trying to supplement their pensions by selling matches or bootlaces, or even by outright begging, was commonplace throughout Europe. The victims of post-1945 conflicts are often justified in regarding their reception as symptomatic of the nation's attitude to the war as a whole. Philippe de Pirey wrote of 'the wall of utter indifference' that greeted French veterans of the Indo-China war. Many disabled American Vietnam veterans discovered that their country's gratitude was short-lived. Ron Kovic, his spine smashed by a bullet, found himself in a hospital where, 'Urine bags are constantly overflowing onto the floors while the aides play poker on the toilet bowls in the enema room. The sheets are never changed enough and many of the men stink from not being properly bathed.' Kovic's swift and radical transition from fighting soldier to immobile cripple epitomizes the fate of so many men for whom the dream of glory has become a nightmare: it underlines the price that soldiers pay.

Sapper   8

There is more to war than 'horse, foot and guns' – the three traditional *armes de mêlée*, as the French army calls them. Armies need transport columns to move their equipment, sometimes their men, over long distances. They need cooks to feed them in camp. They need armourers to repair and maintain their equipment and weapons. They need surgeons and nurses to bind and heal the wounds the enemy's weapons inflict. They need signallers to transmit their messages, veterinarians to care for their animals, provosts to police their ranks, paymasters to count them out their due. But of all the many ancillary arms of service they need none more than they do sappers – as the British Army entitles those soldiers called combat engineers by the Americans, *Pioniere* by the Germans, *Génie* by the French.

Indeed, for the British, sappers *do* belong with the élite of the *armes de mêlée*. The Corps of Royal Engineers stands in the army's order of precedence after the cavalry and artillery but before the foot guards and infantry of the line. In the US Army the Corps of Engineers stands second in order, before Artillery and Armour. Nor, when it is considered what role sappers play, is that surprising. Sappers build bridges and roads under enemy bombardment and lift mines under direct enemy fire. They demolish obstacles in advance of their own assaulting infantry, construct defensive positions in the face of enemy attack, remain with the rearguard to impede the enemy's pursuit. Sappers are the soldiers who make battle possible, the stagehands of the theatre of operations, without whose brave and laborious efforts armies could scarcely find the means to come to grips with each other.

Nothing in recent warfare better exemplifies the role and achievements of the combat engineer, or the risks he runs, than the opening of the Egyptian attack against the Israeli defenders of the Suez Canal in October 1973. Israel had seized the east bank of the canal at the triumphant conclusion of its campaign in June 1967. To hold what it had taken, its engineers constructed a fortification system, known as the Bar Lev line, consisting of twenty-six separate forts, and an enormous continuous earthwork. This 'sand rampart' was bulldozed to a height of 75 feet in places, its purpose being to prevent the Egyptians, even should they cross the waterway, finding a foothold on the Israeli side.

The Egyptians pondered how the rampart might be overcome long and hard since, unless it could, they would not be able to send armour to support their infantry when the moment for a counter-offensive came. The answer was eventually discovered by a young Egyptian engineer officer. Since the earthwork obstacles were adjacent along their whole length to water, he proposed that gaps should be opened in them by high-pressure hoses. Experiments conducted in the remoteness of the Western Desert proved that the idea worked. The Egyptian High Command was converted to its practicality. During September 1973 the army was mobilized

163

The breach in the Israeli sand ramparts of the Suez Canal blasted by Egyptian sappers with water cannon, 7 October 1973

for war and the assault units brought to their jumping-off points. Ramparts on the Egyptian side were heightened by the engineers, to provide firing platforms for their tanks into the Israeli positions beyond the sand ramparts, opposite the points selected for crossing. The five assault divisions massed for the attack started across the canal at 0400 on 6 October 1973. Under a heavy artillery bombardment, commando units moved ahead of them to secure footholds on the other side. As soon as those had been seized, pontoons mounting water cannon were floated by the Egyptian engineers into the canal and the work of opening the breaches begun. At the southern end of the front, the ramparts disintegrated into mud, which impeded the debouchment of armour into the desert beyond. Elsewhere the water cannon performed perfectly. Gaps were washed into the ramparts large and shallow enough for armour to negotiate with ease. Ten floating bridges were laid by the Egyptian sappers opposite and by 1400 hours tanks had traversed the waterway to join the commandos and assault infantry who were moving inland into Sinai. The Egyptian General Staff had been prepared to accept 10,000 fatal casualties to secure this result; in the event, only 208 Egyptian soldiers were killed on the first day of the 1973 campaign, a figure which in itself testifies to the importance of the Egyptian engineers' achievement.

That the latest notable achievement of military engineers should have taken place in the Middle East is appropriate. For it is in the Middle East that we find our first evidence of the place of military engineering in human affairs. The earliest traces of man indicate that he has always sought a refuge from his enemies, animal and human. Jericho in Palestine, the oldest human settlement to which we accord the status of 'city', reveals by its construction how central is military engineering to civilized life. The city, recently excavated by Israeli archaeologists, has been dated to 4000 B.C. Its foundation is explained by its proximity to a perpetual spring of pure water, a supply valued so highly by the settlers of Jericho that, to protect their access to it, they surrounded it with a wall, a system of defence supplemented by a tower. Wall and tower – the first providing continuous security, the second a point of dominance over an attacker – constitute the essential elements of fixed defences and, in one form or another, are found in all subsequent defensive systems.

164

Jericho's walls eventually fell to the blast of trumpets. Elsewhere in the Middle East more scientific methods of siegecraft were under development in Biblical times. The army of the Assyrian empire, which began its rise to regional power in the second millennium B.C., was notable for its early adoption of the principle of division of labour. It was an army of charioteers and foot-soldiers, many specialists in the use of particular weapons. But among its other specialist units were bodies of engineers, who made a science of both the construction and defence of strong places. When on the march the Assyrian army included siege trains containing battering rams and materials for the building of siege towers. Assyrian bas-reliefs also show that their engineers were experts in mining, by which walls and towers could be brought crashing down; some of their engineers were even taught to begin the attack on enemy strongpoints by crossing the protective moat on inflated animal skins.

Siegecraft and fortification reached a yet more advanced stage in the classical world. The catapult, originally designed as a defensive weapon, appeared at the Greek city of Syracuse in Sicily in 400 B.C. Soon adopted for attack, it became

165

and remained the siege engineer's principal weapon until the invention of firearms. But the catapult was only one of many devices and techniques of which the Roman siege engineer made use. Indeed, in the Roman army, every soldier was an engineer, expected to wield a spade as often as a sword and content to dig rather than hack his way to victory should the campaign demand it.

The Roman legion practised its engineering skills at each night's stop on the road. Unless the stage of the march brought it to a permanent camp, it would always construct a temporary one of its own. The six thousand legionaries, moving to an unvarying rhythm, would construct a square earthen rampart, with a gateway in the middle of each side, a ditch around the circumference and a palisade of stakes, of which one each was carried by every legionary, on top. This process of 'castramentation' took only three to four hours.

Little wonder that when the legionaries undertook a siege, as under Caesar at Alesia in 52 B.C., or against the Jews at Masada, 72–3 A.D., its course proceeded so inexorably. At Alesia, where Vercingetorix, the Gallic leader, had taken refuge on a fortified hilltop, the legionaries began by digging lines of 'circumvallation' and 'contravallation', both about fourteen miles round. The former was to keep Vercingetorix and his men in, the latter to keep the Gallic army of relief out. When it arrived, it made three efforts to break through the contravallation and was decisively defeated in the last, even though it outnumbered Caesar's by 250,000, it is said, to 50,000. Starvation then did its work, and Vercingetorix capitulated. At Masada, the Roman engineers faced a different problem: not that of protecting their own army while the siege proceeded, but of getting at the enemy at all. They, rebellious Jews, had occupied a sheer mountain top, and were well-supplied with food and water. For nearly two years the legionaries toiled to construct an enormous earthen ramp against the mountain side. When its crest approached the level of the summit, so that their siege engines could directly attack the defences of the rebels, the Jews committed mass suicide.

Sieges were a staple ingredient of warfare in the classical world, where populations were small, stable and rich enough to inhabit permanently fortified cities. The Acropolis ('topmost city') of Athens is the most famous surviving fortification of Greek civilization and was strong enough to survive siege by the conquering Philip of Macedon in 339 B.C. It was a mark of the extent and degree of the 'Roman peace' that the citizens of the empire, in its heyday, lived unconstricted by walls. But the empire achieved its fullest extent only at the cost of much siege engineering, while the defence of its frontiers always depended upon the existence of major engineering works – the *limes* on the Rhine-Danube line and along the fringes of the Arabian and North Africa desert, and the two walls, Hadrian's and the Antonine, on Britain's frontier with its northern barbarians. When the empire's citizens began to surround themselves with walls again, as they did in the third century A.D., it was the signal that the military primacy of the empire was drawing to a close.

The Dark Age that engulfed the Roman empire in the West was one dominated by warrior hosts, who put their trust not in stone walls but strong sword arms. So while fortification continued to flourish as an art in centres of civilization (notably China, India and Persia), Europe became for a while, like other regions in the hand of conquering peoples, a zone of unwalled settlement. In the tenth century, however, renewed pressure, external and internal, on the emergent European polities drove its military class back towards defensive strategies. 'Castellation', the building of castles and the walling of cities, was a distinctive mark of European life throughout the period from 1000 to 1400. The high walls and stout keeps whose ruins litter the European landscape to this day have their origins in those troubled times, when sea raiders from Scandinavia, horse nomads from the great steppe and Muslim

166

TERRASSE SURPRENANTE DES ROMAINS, AU SIEGE DE MASSADA, CONTINUÉE ET POUSSÉE JUSQU'AU PIED DU MUR DE LA FORTERESSE, LA PETITE ÉLEVÉE SUR LA GRANDE ET SA TOUR DE CHARPENTE DRESSÉE DESSUS.

invaders from the southern Mediterranean resumed their effort to break into the temperate, fertile and increasingly rich lands of the West.

Mediaeval fortification rested on the twin and conjoined principles evident from the excavation of the pre-historic city of Jericho – continuous walls and dominating towers. The private castles of feudal vassals as well as the state castles of their overlords all reveal these associated features. They are present in the simple 'motte and bailey' works of the Norman conquerors of England, built in the eleventh century, in the strongholds of the Crusaders in the Holy Land, begun a century later, and in the vast border outposts erected by the English kings on their Welsh and Scottish frontiers from the thirteenth century onwards.

Castles of this sort were virtually impervious to the methods available to contemporary siege engineers, which had scarcely improved since the days of the Sumerians or Assyrians. Mining, battering and catapulting were the techniques applied to castle walls by those who sought to break them down, and they were rarely successful. Rochester, held by rebellious barons against King John in 1215, was attacked by the whole might of the royal army. The King's siege engineers managed eventually to break through the outer walls but the garrison then retired into the keep and sustained the defence. The miners who had breached the outer walls redoubled their efforts. These took various forms. The most common was to tunnel under the foundations, prop up the ceiling of the shaft as digging proceeded, and eventually, when the work was complete, set fire to the wooden timbers which held the wall overhead in place. Their collapse entailed that of the wall itself. After three months' desperate work, the King's miners succeeded in bringing down a corner of the central keep and the garrison threw themselves on his mercy. In the following year, however, when the French came to the barons' aid and besieged Dover Castle by the same method, the garrison repelled all attacks by siege engines and eventually forced the besiegers to withdraw.

Because the strength of mediaeval castles so much exceeded the power that siege engineers could deploy against them, mediaeval sieges were normally concluded, if they did not merely peter out, by treachery, starvation or the outbreak of disease

167

within the walls. Disease, however, as often ravaged the besieging army as the defending garrison, forcing it to disperse. Castles were therefore rightly regarded by mediaeval kings as a pestilential threat to their authority, when they were held by disobedient subjects, and by the same subjects as an almost wholly safe retreat from the king's disfavour.

What altered the balance between kings and their castellan subjects – indeed much also in the political and military life of the whole world – was the coming of efficient artillery.

It seemed – as it would four hundred and fifty years later when the tank hove

169

on to the battlefield – that fixed defences had suddenly been robbed of all value. High walls and towers, wherever they stood, were now vulnerable to rapid breaching. Yet, with one of those flashes of adaptiveness with which man is gifted at surprising himself, the impending devaluation of fixed defences evaporated almost as soon as it appeared. The insight which underlay this counter-revolution was a simple one, as revolutionary ideas often are. Since it was height – through the physics of weight – that made fortress walls vulnerable, in future they would be built low.

Thus was inaugurated the longest and most influential epoch of the military engineer's art. But there was far more to it merely than the decision to build walls low. Height had hitherto been held desirable because, as we have seen, it made escalade more difficult. To keep infantry outside low walls required a different prescription, drawn from the revived science of mathematical geometry. As with other sciences revived by the spirit of the Renaissance, it had its roots in Italy, from which all the first great fortress engineers – Sangallo, Savorgnano, Peruzzi, Genga – were drawn; among their number must be counted Michelangelo, who, in 1545, in the course of an argument with a rival, staked his claim to what he regarded as his real status in contemporary intellectual life. 'I do not know very much about painting and sculpture' (this from the master of the Sistine Chapel) 'but I have gained a great experience of fortifications, and I have already proved that I know more about them than do you and the whole tribe of the Sangallos.'

What he knew was that a correctly drawn 'artillery trace' would protect the core or 'enceinte' of a fortress from direct artillery attack, while preventing attacking infantry from attempting escalade. The correct trace took the following form. At regular intervals around the fortress walls were placed strong gun platforms, of angular plan, called bastions. Both walls and bastions, forming together a distinctive star shape, were constructed so that their parapets scarcely rose above ground level. Around the trace, a deep sheer-sided ditch presented an obstacle to infantry, and beyond that again a gently sloping field of fire, called a 'glacis', constituted a second obstacle to the easy passage of attacking infantry.

As the science of fortification elaborated, the ditch and the glacis would be changed in plan to accommodate 'outworks', essentially advanced artillery platforms, the existence of which further complicated the siege engineer's task. The most important of these outworks were to be called 'tenailles', which protected the curtain wall between bastions, and usually stood in the ditch; 'ravelins', which were also works free-standing in the ditch, covering the point of the bastions; and various 'hornworks' and 'crownworks' built on topographical features difficult to integrate into the main plan. All, however, belonged logically within a coherent defensive scheme, the crux of which was that any arm of attack, whether artillery or infantry, should be exposed to disabling defensive fire from at least two and preferably more directions at all times.

The effects of the rise of this new fortification system were of an importance as great politically as they were militarily. The development of the new artillery had decisively altered the balance of power between subject and sovereign, in favour of the latter, because only kings were rich enough to afford large parks of bronze guns. The rise of 'artillery fortification' had an equally critical effect. Its enormous cost – the construction of the French royal fortress at Lille between 1667 and 1670 consumed sixty million bricks – excluded all but the richest states from the competition to defend their frontiers by the new methods. As a result the small Italian cities, so independent in the fifteenth and sixteenth centuries, fell easily under the sway of their more powerful neighbours – France, Venice, the Papacy – while the power of the great states was consonantly enhanced by their ability to pay for bricks and masonry. A few smaller states, protected by strong natural defences

170

*Ravelin at the Italian
fortress of Sarzanello;
built by Genoese
engineers in 1497, it is
the earliest work of
artillery fortification still
standing*

*Defence of a bastion,
sixteenth century; the
attackers have captured
the salient angle*

or with access to the sea – notably the Netherlands, which enjoyed both advantages – proved able to outface the growing power of the great. But the pervasive effect of the new fortification was to set the rise of Europe's major polities inexorably in train.

How did siegecraft work when a seventeenth-century army on the offensive took a fortress garrison on the defensive under attack? The weight of the offensive effort was shouldered at the outset by the artillery, whose task it was to win the duel with the fort's own artillery, itself normally but one link in a chain of similar fortresses commanding a frontier. But success in the artillery duel was entirely dependent upon the efforts of the attendant engineers, henceforth properly called sappers. 'Sape', in French, describes a trench dug by engineers to advance artillery positions towards the *enceinte*. The initial stage of a siege required that sappers dig a preliminary artillery position from which the besiegers' guns would bring the defenders' on the bastions under attack. While they did so, the '*sapeurs*' or sappers embarked on the extension of the entrenchment. So dangerous was this work that

Fifteenth-century engineers attacking a fortress. The sappers are undermining the curtain wall, protected by gabions

sappers were originally all volunteers, induced to serve by extra pay, which increased progressively as their efforts brought them nearer the fortress walls.

The siege of Tournai, 1709. Infantry are making their way along one of the saps dug by the engineers

Their tools were spades, wickerwork baskets called gabions, brushwood bundles called fascines, sandbags and a wheeled screen called a mantlet. Wheeling the mantlet ahead of him, the leading sapper would start digging his sap towards the sector – 'front' – of the fortress curtain wall chosen for attack. The sap ran at an angle, to form the first leg of a zig-zag, so aligned as to avert the enemy's fire 'enfilading' (passing directly along) the trench. As the sap deepened, the sappers behind the leader filled the gabions with the earth removed, ranked them on the parapet, filled any gaps with sandbags and crowned the construction with fascines. Thus a stout breastwork, bullet – if not cannonball – proof, rose on the fortress side of the sap.

The teams of sappers were replaced hourly, so dangerous but also exhausting was the work. In that time, the team would have planted five or six gabions. In twenty-four hours, for the work was kept up day and night, the sap would have been driven forward 160 yards. Then, as we have seen, at three hundred yards from the fortress, and three hundred from the original artillery position, another was dug, so that the wall and bastion could be brought under yet more direct fire. As soon as these battery positions were complete, the sappers started on the next extension of the zig-zag, which terminated on the top of the ditch itself.

The sappers, now exposed to the garrison's musketry, were about to tackle the most dangerous stage of their attack, the process of smashing a way through the ditch, its walls and outworks, either by further sapping or by mining or by a combination of the two. Mining, for which professionals were employed, was a desperate business. The mouth of the mineshift became a target for intense enemy fire, while underground the enemy dug furiously themselves to 'counter-mine' their way into the attackers' shaft before it could be exploded under the wall. When counter-mine met mine, underground battles ensued, as at the French siege of Turin in 1706. A small explosive charge 'opened up a large hole, through which

173

the French let down one of their grenadiers at the end of a rope. He was killed by a pistol shot as soon as he appeared . . . Both sides opened fire, and this awful cave resounded with the reports of pistols, muskets and grenades. The fight would have continued for some time if the smoke, stench and darkness had not imposed a truce.' But truce rarely concluded the main siege when the work had been pushed so far. The final breaching of the walls, crossing of the ditch and assault normally followed – to be averted only if the garrison offered surrender.

Little wonder that classical siege warfare bred a tough and resourceful type of military engineer. The sappers were often rough and desperate men 'with a tendency,' the great French siege engineer, Vauban, noted, 'to get drunk while they are working at the head of a sap. They throw every precaution to the winds and have themselves killed off like brute beasts.' But their officers, too, were a distinctive type. 'They need a quite extraordinary valour,' an eighteenth-century French soldier wrote. 'Unlike the other warriors, they do not have the satisfaction of exchanging blow for blow. Not only that, but they have to remain cool in the midst of the most alarming danger . . . To sum up, the engineer must be outstandingly bold and outstandingly prudent.'

If boldness and prudence were the engineer officer's most desirable qualities, they had to be accompanied by profound professional knowledge. The acceptance of that need led in the eighteenth century to the foundation of regular military engineering academies. Military engineering had long been recognized as a valuable specialization, transmitted within engineering families, coteries or through various short-lived teaching institutions. But the eighteenth century saw the emergence of schools that would be permanent – the Royal Military Academy in England (1741), the Alma Mater Theresiana (1748) in Austria and the French school at Mézières (1749). The Paris Polytéchnique (1801) and the United States Military Academy, West Point (1803) were to become even more famous as training places for engineers. Somewhat earlier the European armies had also begun to found regular engineer corps. The French existed in 1697 and the British came into being in 1716.

Like the French and many others, the British corps was originally a body formed exclusively of officers, since their rank and file were usually drawn as needed from the ranks of the infantry. Only gradually did corps of enlisted engineers – sappers, miners, artificers, pioneers – come permanently on to the establishment. The British experience is typical. The officers became the Corps of Royal Engineers in 1787, and in the same year a Corps of Royal Military Artificers was founded, to provide the army with trained carpenters, blacksmiths and other tradesmen whose skills were necessary to siegecraft. In 1797 it absorbed a Soldier Artificer Company raised at Gibraltar in 1772 to serve the fortress there, Britain's greatest overseas stronghold. The Corps changed its title to the Royal Sappers and Miners in 1812, at a time when a short-lived Royal Staff Corps of military labourers also existed. In 1856, at the end of the Crimean War, the Royal Engineers and Royal Sappers and Miners were eventually fused into a single corps.

A principal reason for the creation and enlargement of permanent engineering corps from the eighteenth century onwards was the elaboration of the tasks military engineers were called upon to perform as armies grew in size and mobility. Bridging became a common sapper task during the Napoleonic Wars; the Grand Army had its own bridging columns, which were equipped with pontoons and roadway sections carried on trains of wagons. It was thanks to those columns that it succeeded in escaping across the River Beresina during the retreat from Moscow in 1812. Sapper demolition experts were also learning to destroy fixed bridges in an emergency, while sapper officers' skills as civil engineers were increasingly in demand. The

174

Royal Engineers had helped to pacify the Scottish Highlands after the Jacobite Rising of 1745 by building a network of military roads that carried the King's authority into remote centres of disaffection, while in the 1790s the Royal Engineers designed and oversaw the construction of the Royal Military Canal in Kent, intended both as a defence against French invasion and a means of rapidly moving reinforcements should that occur.

Imperial expansion during the nineteenth century created a voracious demand for civil engineering in lands newly colonized or annexed, and it was natural that military engineer officers should fulfil the function. The US Army Corps of Engineers, still today responsible for the administration of Federal harbour and river works, was in the forefront of the exploration, survey and mapping of the western United States, from the Lewis and Clark expedition of 1801–3 onwards. Russian military engineers carried the rule of the Tsar into the Caucasus and Central Asia along the highways and bridges they constructed. French officers secured and consolidated the long-drawn-out conquest of Algeria (1830–47) by a systematic construction of roads and forts which eventually reached the fringes of the Sahara. But the most extensive and impressive of all civil engineering endeavours to be carried through by sappers was that within the ever-expanding boundaries of the British empire in its Victorian heyday. Canals, bridges, wells, railways, public buildings, telegraph networks, irrigation schemes, hospitals, barracks, even whole towns – almost the whole infrastructure of empire, as it would be called today – were the creation of Royal Engineer officers working, often in total independence, throughout the Northern and Southern Hemispheres.

The Ordnance Survey of the United Kingdom, begun in order to facilitate the construction of the Highland roads after 1745, was a Royal Engineer enterprise. By 1787 William Roy, R.E., had completed the triangulation of the whole of Southern England and in 1801 the first set of the Survey's magnificent maps of Great Britain had been issued. Survey was to make the name of many famous Royal Engineer officers, notably Gordon, who mapped in Turkey, and Kitchener, who began the mapping of the Holy Land. Royal Engineers surveyed the line of the first great highway in India, the Grand Trunk Road, and Alexander Taylor, R.E., constructed 1,500 miles of branch road from it into the Punjab in the 1850s. The first railway in India, from Bombay to Kalyan, was laid by Sappers, while in Canada, Colonel John Bye, R.E., built the Rideau Canal linking Kingston on Lake Ontario, with Montreal. The town he founded in the course of the work, first called Bytown, is now Ottawa, the Canadian capital. Arthur Cotton, R.E., designed and built the giant Godavari, Kistna and Orissa dams, each the focal point of one of those great irrigation schemes which were to be one of Britain's most valuable legacies to the population of India. Francis Fowke, R.E., designed the Victoria and Albert Museum and the Albert Hall, and Douglas Galton advised on the laying of the first transatlantic cable and planned London's modern main drainage system.

But sappers, though so often employed during the Victorian age in the works of peace, were also frequently called upon to practise the arts of war. War, however, was changing. The progress of science and industry not only put new technologies – those of the electric telegraph, the steam engine, the balloon – the sappers' way. It now confronted them with the greater challenge of learning to entrench and besiege armies enormously expanded in size. Larger armies meant more men to hold muskets – or, as the century drew on, rifles. It also meant more hands to hold spades, dig and so construct fortifications, albeit temporary in nature, far larger than any seen before. Todleben, the Tsar's engineer commander in the Crimea during the Anglo-French war with Russia, 1854–6, revolutionized military engineering. There had long been a sapper tradition of constructing extensive earthworks to cover exposed frontiers in times of emergency. The French lines of Ne Plus Ultra, built in 1709–10 to protect Flanders from Marlborough's armies during the War of the Spanish Succession, were one example; Wellington's Lines of Torres Vedras, dug to exclude Napoleon's army from Lisbon in 1810, was another. Todleben transformed this concept. His perception was that, given the greatly enlarged armies of his age, effective fortifications – 'flying entrenchment' – could be created in a twinkling where and when needed. It was a technique he was to demonstrate and employ with great profit against the British and French outside Sebastopol in 1854–5.

Sebastopol eventually fell, despite his efforts, to the Anglo-French attack. But this technique of 'flying entrenchment' was to dominate many of the wars that engaged the combatant states of Europe and America during the latter years of the nineteenth century. The Lines of Petersburg, which held the union army away from the Confederate capital of Richmond during 1864–5; the earthworks behind which the French army denied Paris to the Prussians in 1870–1; the fortifications of Plevna, by which the Turks held the Russians at bay for five months in 1877; the trenches of Mukden, in which the Russians fought for four months to deny victory to the Japanese in Manchuria in 1904–5; the lines of Chatalja, against which Turkey's Balkan enemies beat in vain from October to December 1912 in their efforts to take Istanbul; all these were evidence of the power of mass armies to frustrate the offensive efforts of their enemies, given a will to dig and to defend the resultant earthworks against attack.

Despite the proven effectiveness of improvised earthworks, military engineers were occupied for much of the later nineteenth century in programmes of city, frontier, coastal and harbour fortification far more grandiose and costly even than those built by the great seventeenth- and eighteenth-century engineers, the Dutchman Coehoorn and the Frenchmen Pagan, Vauban and Montalembert. Concrete, the favoured material of the French engineer Mougin, reinforced and often faced with steel – which also armoured the gun positions – was the new material that made possible these enormous works, of which the Belgian 'ring fortresses' at Liège and Namur were to become the most famous. They were the creations of General Brialmont, one of the most famous sappers of the nineteenth century, whom the French also employed to advise their leading engineer, Serre de Rivière, in the construction of the Lorraine fortress chain after their defeat by the Prussians in 1870. Many city fortifications, it is true, were being demolished during the years 1850–1914, notably those of Vienna. But the purpose was usually to liberate the city from its constrictive girdle so that it could merge with its suburbs. Around Paris, besieged by the Prussians in 1870–1, a new girdle of steel and concrete forts was constructed in the 1880s, so sited as to ensure that enemy artillery could never again bring the historic centre under attack.

Concrete and steel, together the fabric of what seemed the most impenetrable fortifications sappers had yet constructed, were to prove, however, the losers in the competition between offence and defence which preceded the First World War. Another product of the technology which developed reinforced concrete and case-hardened steel was high-explosive. Compound nitroglycerine, patented by the Swede Nobel in 1875, exerted an effect on fortification structures more shattering than they could withstand. Cordite, patented by the Americans Abel and Dewar in 1889, threw high-explosive-filled shells against such structures from a distance which their own artillery could not match. The result was that in 1914, when the European armies marched out to do battle with each other across their fortified frontiers, all the strongpoints in which their governments had invested so many millions to buy security crumbled like sand under a child's spade. Liège, Namur

A 'disappearing' artillery cupola of the Belgian fortifications at Namur, after its destruction by German heavy guns in the siege of August 1914

and Antwerp in Belgium, Longwy in France, Przemyśl in Austrian Poland, each a massive complex of concrete and armour-plate, were shattered in days by the shells of super-heavy howitzers, which whistled down vertically from the apogee of their trajectories with a banshee wail that actually drove some of the doomed garrison mad with anticipation.

The frontier defences shattered, armies milled about in apparently unfettered freedom for the first few months of the Great War. Then, as one or another suffered reverses in the open field, their unprecedented earth-moving ability, noted by Todleben in the Crimea, was hurriedly brought into play. So enormous were the armies of 1914 – three million French soldiers, five million Germans, eight million Russians – that, with a spade apiece and the expenditure of some sweat, they could entrench the length of a whole frontier in a few weeks. After the battles of the Marne, Tannenberg and Limanova, in France, Prussia and Hungary respectively, that was what happened. Within four months of the outbreak of a war expected to be 'over by Christmas', a gigantic entrenched camp had sprung up in Central Europe, inside which were ranged the armies of Germany and Austria-Hungary, and against which beat the armies of France, Russia and Britain.

It would take time for the generals to see that the era of fortress warfare had returned. Indeed, so dominated was their outlook by the concepts of mobile warfare which had animated the armies of Napoleon, Lee and Grant, that they were collectively to conspire against reality for at least half of the war which stretched ahead of them. Enormous cavalry divisions remained in being, though cavalry could not manoeuvre in shell-torn ground, let alone cross barbed wire. Infantry continued to be trained for 'open warfare', while the battlefields were ever more firmly enclosed by the obstacles which another part of the collective military mind was giving the orders to construct. In France the demands of mass warfare called into being virtual military cities, while the landscape behind the battlefront was transformed, as roads, railways and bridges were improved or extended to serve the trench garrisons. The scale of engineering work exceeded all previous expectations. In the first three years of the war, the British engineers were called upon to handle 730 million sandbags, a million tons of cement, eight million tons of barbed wire, a million bundles of corrugated iron and nearly four million tons of timber. The Corps, 25,000 strong in 1914, had reached a strength of over 300,000 in 1918. In 1914, its units comprised combat engineering companies only. By the end, it carried on its establishment artisan, works, electrical and mechanical, water boring, land drainage, road construction, quarrying, signal, inland water transport, railway, special (*i.e.* gas and flamethrower) and tunnelling companies as well.

The Tunnelling Companies, recruited from professional miners, undertook, on an enormously enlarged scale, exactly the same task as that familiar to the engineers of siege warfare in its classical era. Driving galleries forward under no-man's-land, from shafts sunk well to the rear, they enlarged chambers under the enemy trenches and then, at a moment timed to coincide with the infantry assault, exploded them under his front line. Such mine attacks were a notable feature of the opening of the Somme offensive in July 1916. In the Messines Ridge offensive of June 1917 the Royal Engineers excavated and detonated nineteen mines, containing a million pounds of high-explosive, the effect of which permanently altered the topography of the feature.

The French, Russian and German sappers were meanwhile engaged on works quite as extensive and labour-intensive. The efforts of the Germans, who stood on the defensive in the West, even exceeded those of their opposite numbers, since the trench line they constructed included dugouts of a depth and concrete blockhouses of a strength that the Western allies did not attempt to match. And during the winter of 1916–17 they laid out a whole new defensive complex, known to their enemies as the Hindenburg Line, more massive than any system of earthworks yet constructed.

The engineering branches of the combatant armies meanwhile spawned subsidiary organizations which, called into being by the changed nature of twentieth-century warfare, were effectively extensions of their traditional functions. It was natural that the engineers should have given birth to the German railway regiments and to the enormously expanded signal services of all armies, since steam power and electricity were forces which military engineers were better trained to understand than any other branch. But sappers, who had pioneered the military use of balloons and airships, also generally provided the first aircraft units and, in the British army, were also behind the development of tanks. Colonel E. D. Swinton, a Sapper officer, grasped as soon as he saw the trench networks in September 1914 that artillery and infantry between them could not succeed in breaching fortifications of such strength. From an inspired paper written on his return the design of the first tank directly descended.

That a sapper should have fathered the tank was entirely appropriate given the role that armoured engineering vehicles were to play in the Second World War. But the experience and results of the Great War divided the armies of the advanced countries. The victors, particularly the French, drew from their ordeal the conclusion that traditional methods had worked and that the future lay, if anything, with the fortification principle. The result, in their case, was the Maginot Line, a reproduction in concrete and steel of the deep trench systems of the Western Front. Constructed between 1930 and 1936, it consumed 150,000 tons of steel, 1.5 million cubic feet of concrete, contained sixty-two miles of tunnels and ran the whole length of the Franco-German frontier. The Belgians and Dutch were simultaneously enlarging and strengthening their border defences in the same style. The vanquished, on the other hand, the Germans and Russians, had come to contrary conclusions. Exhausted in a fruitless defensive, they embraced with the fervour of those with nothing to lose the techniques and equipment of the internal combustion age. Tanks, aircraft, self-propelled artillery, the parachute – all were tested, adapted

A portion of the French Maginot Line, constructed between the world wars to protect the frontier with Germany

The Belgian fortress of Eben Emael, on the River Meuse, captured by German airborne sappers on 10 May 1940

to and eventually integrated within a new system of offensive strategy.

In an indirect manner, the hand of the military engineer thus everywhere marked the new warfare. But sappers were also to play a direct role in Blitzkrieg. The most arresting example of what advanced combat engineering could achieve was demonstrated at the Belgian fortress of Eben Emael on 10 May 1940. Eben Emael was reported to be the strongest fort in the world. For the German penetration of the Franco-Belgian frontier screen to succeed, it was vital that it fall by *coup de main*. The problem seemed insoluble – until the German military engineers proposed the application of the 'shaped charge' principle to its attack. The secret of the shaped charge had been discovered by the American Monroe in the 1880s, when he found that explosive moulded to form a cavity would, when detonated, reproduce the same cavity in the face of the target material. A German engineer named Neumann further discovered during the First World War that lining the cavity with metal would cause a molten jet to penetrate the target material to an even greater depth. Appropriately constructed munitions, called 'beehives' from their shape, were issued to a speedily trained force of glider troops who, on 10 May, were crash-landed on to the roof of Eben Emael, where they cracked its carapace and disabled its defenders in the course of a few minutes.

The shaped charge principle would be applied to a wide range of anti-armour and demolition munitions used throughout the Second World War, and it remains effective to this day. The eclipse of fixed fortification that it helped to bring about ensured, however, that sappers would be more generally employed in activities other than siegecraft between 1939 and 1945. The cutting edge of armies in those years would be furnished by armoured troops and among them sappers would take a foremost place. And in no army more so than the British; indeed, a whole British armoured division, the 79th, would be formed exclusively of engineering vehicles, each designed to perform a particular combat engineering task. Bridging and obstacle-crossing tanks had been built for the British Tank Corps during the First World War. In the Second, the 79th Armoured Division would also field 'bobbin' tanks, which unrolled a carpet of hessian on yielding ground for other tanks to cross upon; flail tanks that exploded mines; 'petard' and demolition tanks, which projected or laid heavy explosive charges against strongpoints: flamethrower tanks; and improved fascine-dropping and bridging tanks, some with a 'scissors' bridge, others with a bridge deck on their superstructure. So effective were these AVREs (Armoured Vehicles Royal Engineers) that several types, notably the flail, bridging and flamethrower tanks, were issued to the armoured and sapper regiment of regular armoured divisions, which, without their intervention, could not have breached the obstacles the German defences presented to them.

Most notable of those obstacles was the Atlantic Wall, constructed at Hitler's orders between 1941 and 1944 to resist an Allied amphibious invasion. If Hitler's Reich is seen as the counterpart of other empires, the Athenian, the Roman, the Byzantine, the Chinese or the Persian, his recourse to frontier fortification belongs to a familiar pattern. Unlike those empires' walls, however, which might be and were breached occasionally or often without the polity they protected suffering disaster, Hitler's Reich represented a political system so odious to its enemies that its survival depended upon maintaining the absolute integrity of its defensive perimeter. After the defeat of his strategic reserve of armour at Kursk in 1943, Hitler's eastern border lay open to armoured counter-thrust across a front too wide to be closed by defensive engineering. In the West, however, engineering offered a more hopeful outcome. The Italian peninsula was narrow enough to be secured by continuous fortification, and the succession of German lines built there resisted penetration until the last days of the war. The French coast, because of its extent, was more difficult to defend. But, had more thought been given to identifying the sectors of risk, it might nevertheless have been held successfully. As it was, an enormous engineering effort – blockhouses, beach obstacles, minefields – was dissipated through the attempt to defend all vulnerable beaches. Those selected by the Allies for the descent in Normandy were in consequence too weakly protected to resist attack, all the more so as it was pressed home by squadrons of the

180

*Above: A British
flamethrower armoured
vehicle of the Second
World War in action
against an enemy
position*

*Left: British sappers
prodding for mines on
the Thala-Kasserine
road, Tunisia, February
1943*

specialized engineering armour the Allies had developed in the years of preparation.

Even in the most technically advanced forms of warfare, sappers must, however, often fight as they did in more primitive times. Sometimes they must indeed fight, exchanging 'blow for blow' with the opposing combat troops. The German army, in particular, insisted on training and using its combat engineers as infantry in an emergency. The engineer battalion of 21st Panzer Division was found by the divisional commander on the morning of 18 July 1944 to be the only reserve available to him after the massed tanks of the British 11th Armoured Division had swamped his forward positions. The engineers were rushed to his reserve line on Bourguébus Ridge, which they held with dogged tenacity all day until tanks of the 1st SS Panzer Division at last arrived to their relief. The parachute sappers of the British 1st Airborne Division, commanded by a Sapper general, fought as infantry throughout the terrible ordeal of the battle of Arnhem in 1944, suffering casualties proportionately even heavier than those undergone by their comrades who had swept lanes while under fire through the German minefields at Alamein in 1942. French sappers, trapped within the fortified airhead of Dien Bien Phu in Indo-China in 1954, welded the steel plate of the airstrip broken by the enemy's shellings under direct fire, in daylight. When the breaks became too numerous to mend, they too joined their fellow infantrymen in the trenches and fought beside them for the fifty-five days of the siege. Outside the defences, Vietnamese sappers, with a Japanese-like disregard for their own survival, strapped explosives to their bodies and threw themselves into the barbed wire entanglements.

Other Vietnamese sappers would do the same thing in the later war against the Americans. It was a war in which the US Engineers were obliged to undertake one of the most nerve-chilling of all military engineering tasks. Confronted by the existence of enormous tunnel complexes, in which the Viet Cong hid everything from arms factories to hospitals, the Corps raised companies of 'tunnel rats', who, torch and pistol in hand, descended into the labyrinth to explore the maze of passages and place demolition charges at chosen points. Most recently, in 1982, British sappers unflinchingly suffered wounds and death in the Falklands finding and lifting Argentinian mines made of materials undetectable except by sight and touch.

The way of the sapper is hard and dangerous, and lies always across the ground between friend and foe. It calls for the best and bravest in any army. 'What is a Sapper?' asked the British Royal Engineer Connolly eighty years ago. 'He is a man of all work of the army and the public, astronomer, geologist, surveyor, draughtsman, artist, architect, traveller, explorer, antiquary, mechanic, diver, soldier and sailor; ready to do anything or go anywhere; in short he is a SAPPER.'

Air Power 9

The aircraft, like the tank, is a newcomer to the battlefield. Yet its significance has grown rapidly over the past seventy years, and it now has a number of tasks which have the most profound impact upon the soldier. Firstly, it retains what was in fact its earliest military function: reconnaissance. This remains important, even if it tends to be eclipsed by the more dramatic role of providing close air support to land forces. Today the ground-attack aircraft is a major battlefield weapon, with a range of ordnance that threatens all sorts of ground units as well as the infrastructure that supports them. Interdiction, the use of air power well behind the battle line to cut roads and railways and 'freeze off' part of the front, may not be observed by the soldier, but its effects upon him will progressively become apparent. Finally, transport aircraft not only carry supplies of food, fuel and ammunition: they also fly reinforcements in and casualties out. Fixed wing aircraft can – albeit with increasing risk – drop parachute troops over the battlefield, and assault helicopters can deliver them directly to it.

All these functions of air power influence the land battle and the soldiers who fight it, and they are our prime concern in the pages that follow. But air power has other roles. High above the battlefield air forces struggle to gain air superiority; their long-range bombers attack strategic targets deep in the enemy homeland; and their interceptors strive to catch incoming bombers before they release their deadly loads. The strategic bomber has been the focus of considerable attention. Its advocates in the inter-war years argued that it was a war-winner in itself, but its effectiveness during the Second World War is a matter of dispute. Strategic bombers remained important in the post-1945 period – the massive B-52 seemed to symbolize US global power in the 1950s and early 1960s – and they survive today, in the ageing B-52s and the newer US B-1s and Soviet Backfires. Nevertheless, in an era of inter-continental ballistic missiles, the strategic bomber has lost much of its utility. The debate over the bomber has been sharpened by moral concerns, for most of those killed by strategic bombing have been civilians rather than soldiers.

Detailed examination of strategic bombing lies outside the compass of this book. Nevertheless, it is worth remembering that many of the soldiers who fought in the Second World War were often more worried about their families in the bomb-ravaged towns of Britain, Germany and Japan, than they were about themselves. And, if humanity stumbles into a Third World War, there can be no doubt that concern for families at the mercy of nuclear attack will loom large in the minds of the men who fight it.

For centuries, military commanders have tried to find out, as the Duke of Wellington put it, what lies 'on the other side of the hill', and it was this thirst for information which inspired the first military application of air power. In 1794 the

A Union observation balloon, 1861

Revolutionary French army set up a small balloon corps, and in June that year a hydrogen-filled observation balloon performed good service at the battle of Fleurus. Napoleon disbanded the corps in 1799, but he could not kill interest in the balloon. In 1849 the Austrians unsuccessfully attempted to bomb Venice from small hot-air balloons, and when the American Civil War broke out in 1861 both the Union and Confederate armies built captive hot-air balloons from which observers could direct artillery fire. Union aeronauts scored two important firsts: they were first to use the electric telegraph for sending messages from air to ground, and first to take aerial photographs, which, suitably gridded, made the indication of targets and the control of artillery fire considerably easier.

The early aeronauts had to contend with their fair share of official scepticism. It was not until after the Franco-Prussian War of 1870–1, when balloons were used to carry mail – and a few brave passengers – out of the besieged city of Paris, that military ballooning really came of age. By the turn of the century most major armies had balloon branches, and there was increasing interest in airships powered by internal combustion engines. Following the success of the Wright brothers' flights in 1903–5 there were numerous experiments with heavier-than-air machines, and in 1911 the aeroplane made its debut as a military weapon when the Italians flew reconnaissance missions against the Turks in Tripolitania and even dropped some small bombs on them.

No sooner had the First World War broken out than aircraft – both lighter and heavier than air – made their own contributions to it. Most spectacular was

184

the German bombing of the Belgian fortress of Liège with Zeppelin airships, foreshadowing the later Zeppelin raids on England. Of much greater practical value was the work of reconnaissance aircraft. On 19 August 1914 Captain Philip Joubert de la Ferté and Lieutenant G. W. Mapplebeck carried out the Royal Flying Corps's first wartime reconnaissance, and as the British army fell back from Mons the RFC continued to provide up-to-date intelligence, flying over the grey German torrents pouring into France. The commander-in-chief of the British Expeditionary Force, Field-Marshal Sir John French, gave unstinted praise to his pilots. 'They have furnished me with the most complete and accurate information,' he wrote, 'which has been of incalculable value in the conduct of operations.'

The German plan for war with France had been drawn up by Alfred von Schlieffen, Chief of the General Staff, and modified by his successor, Helmuth von Moltke, nephew of the great Moltke who had masterminded German victory in 1866 and 1870–1. It envisaged a massive wheeling attack, pivoting on the German 6th and 7th Armies in Alsace-Lorraine. On the outer flank of the wheel, von Kluck's 1st Army was to march between Paris and the Channel coast before swinging eastwards to trap the French armies in a gigantic battle of encirclement in Champagne.

In early September air reconnaissance confirmed that this ambitious project had been abandoned, and that von Kluck had turned in front of the French capital. On the 3rd British and French aviators reported that the German columns, previously marching southwards, were now, as Lieutenant Watteau, an aviator of the Paris garrison, observed, 'gliding from west to east'. The news had an electrifying effect at the headquarters of General Joseph Gallieni, the Military Governor of Paris. As two of his senior staff officers watched the information translated into pins on the operations map, they called out together 'They offer us their flank.' The news could hardly have been more portentous. It pointed the way to the Allied counter-attack on the Marne, and, though Watteau and his comrades had no way of knowing it at the time, it showed that German prospects of an early victory had vanished forever.

In the early stages of the war aerial observation was a useful adjunct to cavalry reconnaissance. But as the rival armies dug themselves into immobility along the Western Front, air reconnaissance assumed a new importance. Trench systems were photographed from the air so that attacks could be planned and the effects of bombardment plotted. In *Sagittarius Rising*, Cecil Lewis describes photographing the German positions on the Somme as the British bombardment reached its crescendo in late June 1916.

At two thousand feet we were in the path of the gun trajectories, and as the shells passed, above or below us, the wind eddies made by their motion flung the machine up and down as if in a gale. Each bump meant that a passing shell had missed the machine by four or five feet ...

Grimly I kept the machine on its course above the trenches, waiting, tense and numb, for a shell to get us, while Sergeant Hall (who got a DCM and a commission for his work that week) worked the old camera handle, changed the plates, sighted, made his exposures. I envied him having something to do. I could only hold the machine as steady as possible and pray for it to be over.

Observers in static balloons and aircraft directed artillery fire, enabling batteries to hit targets out of sight of observation officers in forward trenches. It was natural that the balloons and aircraft used for artillery observation should, like those taking photographs, be attacked by enemy aircraft. In 1912 a British officer had warned the Committee of Imperial Defence that the efforts of each side to prevent the other from obtaining information would result in 'a war in the air, for the supremacy of the air, by armed aeroplanes against each other.' Events proved him right, and aerial combat evolved rapidly. In April 1915 the French pilot Roland Garros shot down six German planes, using a machine-gun firing straight through his propeller, whose blades were protected by steel plates. The Germans riposted with Anthony Fokker's invention, the synchronized machine-gun, which fired between the propeller blades. In 1916 the Allies developed synchronizers of their own, but air-to-air combat had already become a regular feature of the war.

Soldiers in the trenches looked up to see a remote and lethal game played out in the skies above them as fighters swooped and twisted in the giddy ritual of the dog-fight. War in the air was certainly no safer than that on the ground: parachutes were not widely available, and the pilot of a stricken plane faced the ghastly alternatives of burning with his aircraft or leaping to his death. Nevertheless, Cecil Lewis believed that the pilot escaped the worst horrors of the war: 'You did not sit in a muddy trench while some one who had no personal enmity against you loosed off a gun, five miles away, and blew you to smithereens – and did not know that he had done it! That was not fighting; it was murder. Senseless, brutal, ignoble. We were spared that.'

The post-war development of fighter aircraft on the one hand and long-range bombers on the other shifted much of the emphasis of aerial warfare away from the battlefield. However, for all its lack of glamour, air reconnaissance, which depended upon precision cameras and skilled photographic interpretation, remained crucially important. During the Second World War photo-reconnaissance aircraft, often modified versions of fighters or fighter-bombers, flew missions against strategic and tactical targets. They recorded the effects of bombing on industrial and urban centres; enabled the success of attacks on roads, railways and bridges to be assessed; and, just as they had during the First World War, provided front-line commanders with information on the enemy facing them. By the end of the war no large-scale briefing would be complete without air photographs, and there were scores of small-scale operations – like the attacks on Pegasus Bridge and the Merville Battery in Normandy – which would have been impossible without the wealth of detail provided by photo-reconnaissance.

Since 1945 it has been strategic photo-reconnaissance, carried out by aircraft like the American U-2 and SR-71 Blackbird, that has attracted the lion's share of attention. Yet technical developments in the post-war years have also increased the effectiveness of air reconnaissance of the battlefield. Devices like infra-red Line-scan, which enables night photographs to be taken without illumination, permit photo-reconnaissance to penetrate darkness and camouflage. During the Vietnam War the Americans used ASIDs (Air Delivered Seismic Intruder Devices) to monitor Viet Cong movement. Data from ASIDs was automatically transmitted, and was received by tiny QU-22 aircraft or larger EC-121 R. Photo-reconnaissance Phantoms, equipped with sideways-looking airborne radar, cameras and infra-red detectors, could be tasked to investigate reports from the sensors.

The remotely piloted vehicle (RPV) received its baptism of fire in Vietnam. The AQM-34L, capable of transmitting 'real time' television pictures as well as taking photographs, could either fly a pre-programmed mission, or be piloted by remote control. The advantages of using RPVs for reconnaissance are numerous. They are far cheaper than high-performance jet aircraft, and their destruction does not entail the loss of a pilot, whose own training will itself have been long and costly. During Operation 'Peace for Galilee' in 1982 the Israelis obtained excellent results from their 'Scout' RPV. This can stay in the air for over four hours, travelling up to sixty-two miles from its field launching site. Its camera covers an area 400 metres long by 200 metres wide, and the film it transmits enables a commander not only to know what is going on on the other side of the hill, but to watch it on his VDU exactly as it happens.

Many of the targets detected by aircraft are attacked by other aircraft. The provision of close air support to friendly troops was essentially a First World War development. The efforts of First World War aviators were frequently devoted to fighting for air superiority over the battlefield, but there was increasing emphasis on bombing or machine-gunning the enemy's trenches. By 1918 aircraft were being built specially for ground attack. The British Sopwith Salamander – named after the legendary creature which is impervious to fire – was an armoured version of the Snipe fighter. The Salamander was completed too late to see service in the war, but the German Junkers J-1 all-metal ground-attack aircraft was in production

The Sopwith Salamander ground-attack aircraft arrived too late for the First World War

*Above: The USAF's
SR-71 Blackbird*

*Right: 'Gull-winged
silhouette and banshee
scream': the Junkers 87
Stuka*

in time for the great German spring offensive of 1918. Squadrons of J-1s vigorously supported the advancing German infantry by harrying British troops with bombs and machine-guns. British fighters did their best to assist their own hard-pressed ground forces but, flying at low level with unarmoured machines, their losses were heavy.

Frank Wootton's painting shows RAF Typhoons above the debris of German armour in the Falaise pocket, August 1944

The effect of even these relatively crude aircraft on the morale of the men they attacked could be paralyzing. Norman Gladden, serving with the Royal Northumberland Fusiliers at Ypres in 1917, recalled how panic broke out when a German plane appeared as tension built up during a relief in the line: 'Never before, despite my capacity for fear, had I felt myself for so long in the grip of a terror so absolute. All around us was the continuing threat of instant death. Yet I saw no one fall . . . The company that night was in the grip of a sort of communal terror, a hundred men running like rabbits.'

Aircraft generated fear out of all proportion to the physical damage they inflicted, a fact emphasized during the Spanish Civil War, where the German Condor Legion flew in support of the Nationalists. The Spanish experience encouraged German planners to concentrate upon tactical at the expense of strategic air power, and to develop ground-attack aircraft and the radio links with which forward observers could control them. These aircraft, acting as 'flying artillery', were an essential component of Blitzkrieg.

The Junkers 87 Stuka dive-bomber typified the air element of Blitzkrieg. Ironically, it was not a particularly sophisticated aircraft, and was notoriously ungainly in air-to-air combat. But its sinister gull-winged silhouette and the banshee

189

scream of its siren helped to make it one of the war's most-feared weapons. A sample of American soldiers reckoned that the dive-bomber was the second most terrifying enemy weapon: only the 88 mm gun inspired more fear. The Stuka helped pulverize the Polish army in the brief 1939 campaign. So striking was the moral and material impact of air attack that German ground forces sometimes found that, in the words of one officer: 'There was virtually no resistance ... There was a certain amount of sporadic fighting when we got to the river barriers, but the *Luftwaffe* had already cleared the way for us. Their Stuka dive bombers were deadly accurate, and as there was no opposition they had it all their own way.'

The dive-bomber also made a telling contribution to German victory in the West in 1940. The opposing forces were equally matched in numbers of men and armoured vehicles: it was in aircraft – and in military doctrine – that the Germans were immeasurably superior to their adversaries. On 12 May, two days after the opening of the offensive, the leading elements of the German strike force reached the Meuse at Sedan. The river was wide, and the French soldiers covering it were securely ensconced in pill-boxes on its left bank. Conventional military wisdom demanded that the Germans should bring up artillery to prepare the way for an assault crossing: such an operation would take time, and its outcome would be uncertain.

The Germans had learned their tactics from a different manual. On 13 May nearly fifteen hundred aircraft – almost equivalent to the entire Allied air strength available in France and Belgium – attacked the defenders of the Meuse front in the greatest single demonstration of tactical air power that the world had ever seen. By nightfall the Germans were across the river, and the moral disintegration of the French army had begun. As the armoured spearheads raced across northern France, Stukas and Henschel Hs 123s hammered Allied units in their path, while Dornier Do 17s and Heinkel He 111s reached out to bomb roads, railways and troop concentrations. For many British and French soldiers the lasting image of the campaign was not the mailed fist of the German panzers but the swooping menace of the *Luftwaffe*.

The 1940 campaign wrote a glowing testimonial to the ground-attack aircraft, and thereafter none of the combatants could afford to ignore it. On the Eastern Front, the anti-tank version of the Stuka, armed with two 37mm cannon, wreaked havok amongst Soviet armour. Hans-Ulrich Rudel, the *Luftwaffe*'s ace tank-killer, was credited with destroying no less than 519 tanks – as well as the battleship *Oktyabrskaya Revolutsia*, an unusual achievement for a ground-attack pilot. The Russians countered with the Ilyushin Il-2 Shturmovik, a heavily armoured plane not unfairly nicknamed the flying tank. The British produced their own ground-attack aircraft, most notably the Hurricane IID with its two 40 mm cannon, and the rocket-firing Hawker Typhoon.

If victory in 1940 had been assured by German command of the air, by the summer of 1944 the wheel had come full circle. The Allies enjoyed almost undisputed air superiority over Normandy during and after D-Day, and they put it to good use. A protective umbrella kept the remnants of the overstretched *Luftwaffe* from intervening while Allied ground-attack aircraft mercilessly savaged German troops. On 7 June, D+1, Major-General Kurt Mayer led a battle-group of his 12th SS Panzer Division to counter-attack the invaders. He could manage a mere four miles an hour along routes disrupted by air attack, and all the stops, starts and diversions exhausted his fuel. When he eventually found a fuel dump, it was a smoking ruin: Allied pilots had visited it first. Fritz Bayerlein, commanding the excellent *Panzer Lehr* division, fared even worse. 'By noon on the 7th,' he admitted,

190

my men were calling the main road from Vire to. Le Bény Bocage *Jabo-Rennstrecke* – 'fighter-bomber racecourse.' Every vehicle was covered with branches of trees and moved along hedgerows and the fringes of woods ... but by the end of the day I had lost forty petrol wagons and ninety other trucks. Five of my tanks had been knocked out, as well as eighty-four half-tracks, prime-movers and SP guns. These losses were serious for a division not yet in action.

Well might Field-Marshal Rommel, the Army Group Commander, complain that: 'Our own operations are rendered extraordinarily difficult and in part impossible to carry out [owing to] the exceptionally strong, and in some respects overwhelming, superiority of the enemy air force.' Rommel was himself destined to become the most distinguished victim of Allied pilots. On the afternoon of 17 July he was on his way back from the headquarters of Panzer Group West when his car was strafed by a Hurricane. His driver was killed, and Rommel was badly hurt when he was flung into the road as the car crashed.

The achievements of ground-attack aircraft in the post-1945 era have been mixed. Between 1964 and 1973, during the American involvement in Vietnam, aircraft – both fixed and rotary-winged – lent powerful support to ground forces. However, the terrain of South Vietnam made target acquisition extremely difficult, and high-speed, high-performance jets, with little ability to loiter over the objective, were often less useful than piston-engined aircraft like the Douglas A–1 Skyraider and the North American AT-28. Their slowness made them vulnerable to anti-aircraft fire, but they could identify obscure targets and fly in weather conditions which grounded jets. Attack helicopters enjoyed similar advantages, and it was the Bell AH-1G Huey Cobra gunship which came to epitomize American close air support in Vietnam just as the Typhoon had symbolized Allied supremacy in the skies above Normandy.

Huey Cobras over the Mekong

A USAF AC-130A gunship

There were also some strange hybrids, modified specifically for applying aerial firepower to enemy ground forces – quite literally flying artillery. The AC-47 – 'Puff the Magic Dragon' – was a transport aircraft with sideways-firing Vulcan revolving cannon added. Using the 'pylon turn' technique, the pilot circled his target, pouring a stream of shells onto it. Still more formidable was the Lockheed AC-130H, bristling with a 105 mm howitzer, one 40 mm and two 20 mm cannon, two 7.62 miniguns and a variable arsenal of grenade dispensers, rockets, bombs and missiles.

Even giant B-52 strategic bombers were used in direct support of US ground forces. During the seventy-three-day siege of Khe Sanh in early 1968, American aircraft of all types dropped over 100,000 tons of bombs around Khe Sanh, which became the most heavily bombed target in the history of war. Air support enabled the Americans to hold Khe Sanh: but although it might be a battle-winner, air power was not a war-winner. Weather, terrain and the elusive targets offered by the Viet Cong and North Vietnamese regulars reduced its effectiveness, and, though the anti-aircraft guns used in South Vietnam were often primitive by the standards of the day, they took a steady toll of US aircraft: over 3,000 helicopters were lost in the course of the war.

In contrast, air power was the decisive factor in the Arab-Israeli War of 1967. On the morning of 7 June the Israelis launched a pre-emptive attack on the Egyptian air force: in the first two days of the fighting they claimed to have destroyed 333 aircraft on the ground and another ninety-five in the air. With undisputed air superiority, Israeli pilots were free to give intimate support to their comrades on the ground. The Potez Magister, built as a trainer but modified for the ground-attack role, proved especially successful. If any Israelis questioned the value of air power, photographs of the Mitla Pass, jammed with burnt-out Egyptian vehicles, soon silenced their doubts. Israeli soldiers came to depend upon their air support as no soldiers have before or since: by the time the war ended the air force had become, in the words of one senior officer, 'a sub-contractor for every platoon commander in difficulties'.

The evidence of 1967 was not ignored by the Arabs. After the war they set

192

about rearming, and received a full range of Soviet-supplied air defence systems. Long-range SAMs were installed to cover the line of the Suez Canal; the smaller, man-portable SAM-7 was issued to the infantry, and the four-barrelled radar-controlled anti-aircraft gun, the ZSU-23/4, provided mobile air defence for armoured units. In the Yom Kippur War of 1973 it was the Arabs who got their blow in first, and Israeli pilots, struggling to furnish the support which their army had come to expect, had to contend with hostile aircraft as well as with a comprehensive arsenal of air defence weapons. So heavy were Israeli aircraft losses in the early stages of the war that soldiers, seeing the damage done, stopped calling for air support. After this initial period, improved attack techniques, increasingly effective electronic counter-measures (ECM) and ground attacks across the Suez Canal, which disrupted the Egyptian SAM cover, all helped the Israeli air force to regain a measure of its former mastery.

Although the Skyhawks and Phantoms of 1973 had little in common with the biplanes of the First World War, pilots felt isolated from the battle below just as Cecil Lewis had. Rami Hapaz, an Israeli pilot, describes how:

Even if you fight in the same battle, you are up above in the sky and he's on the ground. In the aircraft you are surrounded with the cockpit, a very clean one, even if very crowded with controls, instruments and all of the means that you have to control the airplane . . . you don't hear anything from the battle itself, you don't hear the shooting . . . you don't hear the shouts, you don't see the face and you don't see the blood of the enemy . . .

The Israelis profited from the experience of 1973 just as the Arabs had from

A bolt from the blue: destroyed Egyptian equipment in Sinai, June 1967

that of 1967. In the fighting in Lebanon in 1982 they paid particular attention to the problem posed by air defence systems. Perhaps one-quarter of the aircraft on a particular mission would concentrate on ECM, and another quarter on the suppression of gun and missile sites, while the remainder attacked hostile armour or infantry. Most aircraft dispensed 'chaff' and flares – to confuse radar and heat-seeking missiles – as a matter of course. Not only was Israeli air power restored to its full glory, but very few aircraft were lost during the operation.

The fighting in Lebanon and the South Atlantic in 1982 emphasized not only the utility of close air support but also the importance of retaining the technological edge over an opponent in aircraft and air defence weapons. Limitations in British anti-aircraft missiles, allied to the lack of an effective anti-aircraft gun, permitted the Argentinians to press home their attacks, often with obsolescent Skyhawks or piston-engined Puccaras, on British land and naval units. Conversely, Argentinian gun and missile defences could prevent British Harriers neither from putting in a psychologically damaging attack during the battle for Goose Green, nor from using 'smart' bombs against targets near Stanley in the later stages of the war.

A Sidewinder-armed Harrier lifts off in the South Atlantic, 1982

Estimates of the value of close air support in a future major war vary radically. While some analysts suggest that aircraft will find it hard to operate in an environment thick with sophisticated air defence weapons, others claim that, particularly by concentrating upon ECM, it will still be possible for aircraft to provide effective support to ground forces. Some specialized ground-attack aircraft have been built to fly slowly and to absorb heavy punishment: in the Fairchild A-10 Thunderbolt II the pilot sits in what is almost an armoured dustbin, and the aircraft's controls are duplicated to enhance its survivability. The armed helicopter has improved markedly over the past twenty years. The large, well-protected Soviet Hind-D, widely used in Afghanistan, is a flying tank in the Shturmovik tradition, while the

194

US Hughes AH-64 with its fire-and-forget Hellfire anti-tank missiles is designed for taking on more conventional armoured vehicles on the Central Front.

The flying tank: a Soviet Hind helicopter gunship

Whether the advocates of close air support are right or wrong, one thing remains certain. The threat of air attack compels soldiers to adopt passive and active measures to defend themselves against it. Even if nets and branches will not defeat modern sensors, passive defence – camouflage, concealment and dispersion – makes the ground-attack pilot's task harder. Active defence against air attack is now accorded high priority, and anti-aircraft artillery units, usually with a good mix of guns, missiles and radar, are an increasingly important feature of armies. From the divisional commander pondering the deployment of guns and SAMs to cover his line of advance, to the platoon commander posting his air sentry with an automatic weapon, defence against air attack looms large in the minds of soldiers.

Close air support is visible and audible to the soldier, whether the aircraft involved are his own or the enemy's. The use of air power for interdiction is less obvious, but its results may, in the long term, be no less striking than those of attacks on front-line targets. The complex and vulnerable logistic 'tails' trailed by modern armies, coupled with the tendency for air defence weapons to be most heavily concentrated on the battlefield rather than behind it, may make interdiction an increasingly cost-effective use of scarce and expensive air resources.

Effective interdiction was impossible in the First World War. An offensive might

195

Three Fairchild A-10A Thunderbolt IIs

take the enemy by surprise, but he would soon be able, using road and rail transport, to move reserves to the threatened sector: the attacker might break in, but he would be contained before he could break through. By the end of the Second World War the range and hitting-power of aircraft had transformed the situation, as the battle for Normandy demonstrates. Allied planners intended to throttle the German army in Normandy by cutting its communications. This had to be undertaken with care, for concentration on targets just behind the invasion sector would suggest where the blow was to fall. In the event, far more attacks were launched north of the Seine than south of it, leading the Germans to suspect that the Pas de Calais, rather than Normandy, was the real invasion objective. All these attacks helped to write down the rolling stock which the Germans needed to move men and equipment: by late May 1,500 of the 2,000 locomotives in northern France were out of action.

Even more important were the raids on the Seine bridges between Paris and the sea, bridges which would be vital when the Germans sought to redeploy to meet the invasion. By D-Day, eighteen of the twenty-four bridges had been destroyed, three were under repair, and the remaining three were under such imminent threat of air attack that they could not be used for large troop movements in daylight. Allied interdiction seriously delayed German units as they tried to move up into the battle area. It took the infantry elements of 2nd SS Panzer Division nearly a

196

fortnight to cover the 450 miles from Toulouse to Saint Lô, and the armour, parched for fuel, took even longer.

The undoubted success of interdiction in Normandy fostered the belief that it could be used to choke an enemy to death under almost any circumstances. In the summer of 1952 the Americans attempted to isolate Chinese forces in Korea by hitting roads, railways, bridges and other choke-points. They could not prevent the Chinese from bringing up sufficient supplies to keep their army in the field: they failed, too, in their political objective, which was to persuade Chinese representatives to approach the armistice negotiations in a conciliatory frame of mind. The poor results achieved by interdiction in Korea reflected the fact the Chinese army was robust and primitive, and that, by use of massive quantities of manpower, it could quickly repair destroyed or damaged facilities, or merely use men as porters to by-pass severed communications.

The same points emerged, nearly twenty years later, in Vietnam. Many of the American raids on the North were aimed at classic interdiction targets. During the *Linebacker I* operation of 1972 powerful American strike groups, with escorts and supports, attacked key targets deep in North Vietnam. The strike group itself – perhaps thirty-two McDonnell Douglas F4-E Phantoms armed with a mixture of free-fall 'iron' and laser-guided 'smart' bombs – was escorted by more Phantoms for close protection. The attack was preceded by the Phantoms and F-105G Thunderchief 'Wild Weasels' of two 'Iron Hand' flights, whose prime duty was flak suppression; close behind them flew A-7 Corsairs dispensing chaff, with their own Phantom escort. At the tail end of this huge formation came two reconnaissance

A victim of technology: the Thanh Hoa Bridge, 1972

Phantoms, which photographed the target so that a damage assessment could be made.

Despite the use of massive and carefully balanced forces like this, it was difficult to cut North Vietnamese communications, and even more difficult to keep them cut. In a country where transport was primitive, good interdiction targets were hard to come by, and were inevitably hedged about with guns and missiles. It became easier to hit point targets once smart bombs – like the tele-guided 'Maverick' – were available. The road and railway bridge at Thanh Hoa, some seventy miles south of Hanoi, was the target of 700 sorties during Operation *Rolling Thunder* between March 1965 and October 1968. Eight American aircraft were lost, but the bridge remained open. On 27 April 1972, however, Phantoms badly damaged the bridge with smart bombs, and in May it was closed for several months after a similar raid. Nevertheless, the overall achievements of interdiction in the Vietnam war were disappointing. American air raids, themselves costly in aircraft – forty-four were lost during *Linebacker I* – could reduce, but not stem, the flow of men and equipment into the South. Nor could attacks on the Ho Chi Minh trail, the major supply route through Laos, by fighter-bombers, Air Force gunships, and even B-52 strategic bombers, prevent the Communist build-up in the South.

If one of the functions of air power impedes transport, another facilitates it. During the Second World War air transport gave added flexibility to the movement of men and equipment, and permitted positions which would once have fallen when their food and ammunition ran out to be resupplied by air. During a thirty day period in 1942 the *Luftwaffe* sustained German troops in the Demyansk pocket by flying in 24,000 tons of stores and 15,000 men, and evacuating as many wounded. In February 1944 part of the 7th Indian Division was encircled by the counter-attacking Japanese in the Arakan. It stood fast and, in what became known as the battle of the Admin Box, aircraft kept it supplied until relief arrived. The Japanese cut off Imphal the following month, but it too was resupplied by air, and the 5th Indian Division was flown in to reinforce its garrison.

Air transport in Burma was not only important in specific operations like these: the entire Allied campaign was made possible only by air power. As Lord Louis Mountbatten, Supreme Allied Commander, wrote:

It was not just a question of auxiliary air supply, because ninety-six per cent of our supplies to the 14th Army went by air. In the course of this campaign we lifted 615,000 tons of supplies to the armies, three quarters of it by the US Air Force and one quarter by the Royal Air Force; 315,000 reinforcements were flown in . . . 110,000 casualties were flown out . . . In our best month, March 1945, we actually lifted 94,000 tons.

Helicopters, with their ability to operate from tiny landing zones in forward areas, are particularly useful to armies fighting counter-insurgency campaigns in difficult terrain. The French never had more than ten operational helicopters in Indo-China in 1946–54. Within four years they were using nearly 100 in their struggle against the FLN in Algeria, and by the end of the campaign they deployed no fewer than 250. The British relied heavily on helicopters during 'Confrontation' with Indonesian troops in Borneo in the 1960s, and in the rough country of the Radfan during the Aden campaign. Helicopters were also indispensable for the supply of forward units in larger wars. The Americans depended upon them in Vietnam, as did the British in the South Atlantic, where the one CH-46 Chinook which had escaped destruction when the *Atlantic Conveyor* was hit rendered outstanding service.

The helicopter has done more than merely improve air transport: it has added a new dimension to military operations. In 1963, acting on the recommendations of Lieutenant-General Hamilton Howze's study into air mobility, the US Army set up the 11th Air Assault Division, which became the 1st Cavalry Division (Airmobile) two years later. Howze had originally thought primarily in terms of air mobility in conventional war in Europe, especially in the forward zone where bridges were blown and roads cratered and mined. But American involvement in the Vietnam War was steadily increasing, and Vietnam provided the ideal testing-ground for the new division. It was quite literally airmobile: everything, from the infantry in their UH-1D Hueys to the artillery, underslung beneath Chinooks, could fly into action. Helicopter gunships softened up landing zones and engaged enemy who took on

Air mobility: UH-1Ds extract troops from a firebase in South Vietnam

the transport helicopters, and, high above the landing zone, the force commander controlled the battle from a helicopter command post.

The division enjoyed a flexibility unmatched in the history of war, but paid a heavy price for it. Losses in helicopters, particularly before gunships were perfected, were often severe. On average, a helicopter was hit by ground fire every 1,000 flying hours, and became a total loss after 9,500 flying hours. Potentially more serious was the fact that every one of these hours represented some ten hours' maintenance: simply keeping helicopters airworthy required continual hard work by skilled crews. Helicopters guzzle fuel, and if they solved some logistic problems they created others: it took ninety helicopters merely to keep the division supplied.

The concept of a heliborne formation remains attractive, but its expense is a deterrent. The US Army has one air assault division, the 101st, based at Fort Campbell, Kentucky, the British are experimenting with an airmobile brigade, and the West Germans have three airmobile brigades, lavishly equipped with TOW and MILAN anti-tank missiles. 'Their task in anti-tank defence,' writes a German general, 'is mainly to reinforce other elements at the focal points of enemy attacks, to stop armour penetrations, and to retain favourable terrain even against armoured enemy fores.' They are, in essence, a highly mobile counter-penetration force.

The Soviets maintain a number of Airborne Assault Brigades, each comprising a helicopter assault regiment, a heavy lift helicopter squadron and three airborne rifle battalions. Heliborne troops have been increasingly important in Afghanistan, where they are flown in to hilltops from which they can cover movement up the valleys – 'picketing' very much in the tradition of the British army on the North-West Frontier. Most armies – even those which concede that large-scale heliborne formations are beyond their reach – recognize that the helicopter confers remarkable flexibility upon attacker and defender alike. This is particularly true in north-west Europe, where Soviet armoured thrusts might be preceded by heliborne assaults on bridges and defiles and, conversely, checked by anti-armour teams inserted by helicopter into their path.

If the transport of troops by helicopter is very much a post-1945 phenomenon, the idea of delivering soldiers to battle by air is rather older. In 1918 Colonel Billy Mitchell, subsequently one of the fathers of strategic bombing, but then commanding the United States Army Air Corps in France, suggested that the parachute – already widely used for fairground stunts and for escape from observation balloons – could enable troops to be dropped behind the German lines. During the 1930s the Russians led the way in military parachuting, dropping a whole battalion on exercise in 1933. But it was the Germans who recognized the real potential of parachute troops. In June 1938 Major-General Kurt Student was tasked with forming an airborne division. Student and his men were under command of the *Luftwaffe*, a wise decision, which avoided quarrels between parachute and air force officers over the use of transport aircraft.

The daring use of German airborne troops in 1940 illustrated just how effective parachute and air-landed units could be, and jolted the British and Americans into pressing on with the raising of their own airborne forces. In May 1941 the Germans captured the island of Crete by parachute and glider assault after a hard-fought battle which cost them 12–17,000 men and 170 troop-carrying aircraft. A German battalion commander thought that Student had been 'visibly altered' by the battle. 'The cost of victory,' he believed, 'had evidently proved too much for him.' Crete was the last major German parachute drop. Although German parachutists were to fight on many fronts – nowhere with more distinction than in the defence of Monte Cassino – they became little more than élite infantry, going into action on foot.

200

The Allies, too, found airborne operations costly. In July 1943 parachutists and glider-borne troops spearheaded the invasion of Sicily: a good deal went wrong, with gliders landing in the sea and parachutists being scattered by the drop. Much the same happened when the British 6th and the US 82nd and 101st Airborne Divisions landed in Normandy on D-Day. Nevertheless, although the airborne divisions did not secure the flanks of the Allied lodgement area exactly as had been planned, they took many of their objectives, and their somewhat haphazard arrival helped to confuse the German High Command.

The largest airborne operation of the war was *Market Garden*, mounted in September 1944 in an effort to seize the crossings over the rivers Maas, Waal and Neder Rijn, and the Wilhelmina and Zuid Willemsvaart canals, enabling the British Second Army to outflank the defences of the Siegfried Line. The first phase of the operation went well, with the Americans taking the canal crossings and the bridges over the Maas and Waal. The British 1st Airborne Division, dropped at the little Dutch town of Arnhem to secure the bridges over the Neder Rijn, ran into difficulties. It was landed too far from its objectives, and encountered unexpectedly heavy German resistance as it moved towards them. The scale of the operation meant that there were too few aircraft available to drop the whole force in one day, so only part of the division was available for the first crucial hours.

Although Lieutenant-Colonel John Frost's 2nd Parachute Battalion took one end of Arnhem Bridge, the forces advancing to link up with the division made slower progress than had been expected, and it could not be relieved in time. On the night of 25-26 September, many of its survivors withdrew across the river: of the 10,000 men landed, 1,130 were killed and 6,450 captured. It had been an ambitious plan which narrowly failed to meet with complete success. The Neder Rijn was one water obstacle too many, and the British went, in Lieutenant-General Browning's words, 'a bridge too far'.

Troops have parachuted to battle on a number of occasions since the Second World War. In 1953 the French seized their doomed position at Dien Bien Phu with airborne troops, Americans jumped in Korea, and British and French paras dropped on Suez in 1956. The Americans made one substantial airborne drop in Vietnam – carried out by the 173rd Airborne Brigade during Operation *Junction City* in early 1967 – and in October 1983 Rangers were parachuted in to capture the airfield at Point Salinas on the island of Grenada before the main US force landed.

These actions all underline the fact that large-scale airborne operations can only be undertaken safely against an enemy whose aircraft and air-defence weapons cannot interfere with the drop. The French secured Dien Bien Phu without difficulty, but the subsequent reinforcement and resupply of the garrison became increasingly perilous in the face of intense Viet Minh anti-aircraft fire. Although the air defences on Grenada were relatively light – seventeen twin-barrelled 23 mm and five quadruple 12.7 mm guns were eventually captured – they delayed the initial Ranger drop until AC-130E gunships had cleared the way, and shot down two Cobra gunships. Airborne forces have traditionally suffered from a shortage of heavy weapons which has made them vulnerable to hostile armour. The proliferation of light anti-armour weapons has reduced this vulnerability: nevertheless, it is unrealistic to expect an airborne force to hold out for long against an enemy who is able to bring the full weight of his artillery and armour to bear upon it.

The fact that large-scale airborne assaults may be a thing of the past limits, but by no means ends, the usefulness of parachute units. They are accustomed to operating with light scales of equipment, and can be quickly flown in to trouble-spots. The rigours of parachute training – rightly or wrongly – encourage élitism,

service units, and this total did not include service units organic to the division.

This tendency for the logistic tail to thicken as the fighting teeth grow sharper was shown again in Vietnam. There, the United States enjoyed a logistic superiority unmatched in the history of war. Base areas grew into small cities which housed the men and machinery needed to keep combat troops supplied with food and ammunition, to repair increasingly complex equipment and staff a ponderous military bureaucracy. They also contained a wide range of facilities to support the combat support units. A Marine officer, Lieutenant Charles Anderson, describes how:

In the PX the GI could find all the baubles and goodies to take his mind off Vietnam and its war . . . Next to the PX there was often a drive-in, just like a Dairy Queen or an A & W stand back in everybody's Hometown, USA. But in 'the Nam' no one pulled his modified Chevy or Corvette up to the curb. Instead, the vehicles were jeeps, trucks, even forty-ton tank retrievers. But all the orders were just like back home. 'Two hot dogs and Cokes, to go.' All these comforts and services made the world of the rear a warm, insulated womb-like capsule into which the sweaty, grimy, screaming, bleeding, writhing in the hot dust thing that was the war rarely intruded.

There was, inevitably, a penalty to be paid. Charles Moskos estimated that 'approximately 70 per cent of the men in Vietnam cannot be considered combat soldiers except by the loosest of definitions,' while Peter Bourne suggested that only 14% of American soldiers were actually involved in combat. American commanders were constantly bedevilled by a shortage of infantry. In mid-1966, when US strength was 276,000 men and the Koreans and Australians produced another 30,000, there were only 44,800 infantrymen, and just 30–35,000 of them were available for operations away from bases. The 'world of the rear', with its insatiable demands, soaked up American manpower.

It is easy to equate a large logistic organization with inefficiency, and to join cost-conscious politicians and fighting generals in their demands for the improvement of the teeth-to-tail ratio. Such complaints are often echoed by combat soldiers themselves, who tend to undervalue the efforts of service personnel who live more

The world of the rear: supplies coming ashore at Da Nang

change, but its utility will persist, and the soldier of the future, like his ancestors in 1940, 1944 or 1967, will continue to scan the skies above him, hoping as anxiously for close support from his own air force as for a respite from the attentions of his opponent's.

Commander 10

'I do not know who won the Battle of the Marne,' was the answer Marshal Joffre gave to a questioner long after the victory through which he had saved France in 1914 had been fought. 'But had it been lost, I know who they would say had lost it.' Joffre, man of few words that he was, had the gift of putting his finger on the point. As the Chinese proverb has it, expressing the same idea, 'Victory has a thousand fathers, defeat is an orphan.' Many, in short, are ready to claim responsibility for success, almost no one is prepared to shoulder the responsibility for failure. Yet, if there is a single test of what distinguishes the commander from the normal run of men, it is that, while hoping to celebrate victory, he accepts the risk of being branded as a loser; and a loser whose failure condemns not only himself but his army and perhaps his country to the most painful of consequences.

What can we learn from Joffre of how those responsibilities are borne, of how the commander so handles events as to avoid failure and achieve success? In Joffre's case, little that is tangible. He had become Chief of Staff of the French Army in 1911, when he had rewritten the French war plan on the assumption that the country's most pressing strategic need was to counter a German offensive across the common frontier in Alsace-Lorraine. When war came in 1914, Germany in fact chose to attack through Belgium, whose frontier with France Joffre had left almost undefended. This lapse might have broken a lesser man, all the more so since it took much time for Joffre to recognize that the Belgian operation was a main thrust and not a feint. Once he had done so, however, his command qualities were shown to the full. There was little he could do to check the invasion at the outset, since his dispositions were so awry. He was forced to acquiesce in a long retreat, the most burdensome test of an army's cohesion and general's nerves. He bore it imperturbably.

Edward Spears, the British Liaison Officer with the French Fifth Army, describes his demeanour in those terrifying days between 24 August and 5 September, when the German armies swept forward, apparently inexorably, towards Paris.

He looked placid. Placidity and calm were his dominant characteristics. He was impenetrably calm. Very often this trait baffled his subordinates. At times when expected to speak he did not utter a word. He was known to arrive at a headquarters, listen in silence to what was said, and step back into his car without opening his mouth. This is not to say that when Joffre had something to say he did not say it, merely that he remained silent if he had no positive ideas to put forward. He was always prepared to listen and curiously enough seemed to have time upon most occasions to do so . . . His anger when roused was terrific in its concentrated, quiet force and was never withstood. There were then a few short gestures of the arms, the muffled voice rose half a tone, whilst the head was thrown slightly back; and the words which came forth from under the shaggy moustache were never either

Joseph Jacques Césaire Joffre, Marshal of France, commander of the French armies, 1914–16, and victor of the battle of the Marne

disregarded or forgotten . . . He had another quality, which proved of inestimable value; a great clarity of vision built upon a powerful self-confidence. He was a man of great courage. Events were to show that he possessed a capacity for taking punishment that might have turned a prizefighter grey with envy. He obviously required no confidant, and certainly no commander was ever less under the influence of his staff.

Nevertheless his staff officers were necessary to him, as they are to any commander in modern war, in which it is impossible for a general to do everything for himself. Colonel Zopff, his intelligence officer, was a rock of rationality and coolness. General Belin, the Chief of Staff, 'vivacious, smart and soldierly', worked so hard organizing the efforts of his subordinates 'that the strain imposed on him by the retreat of the French armies nearly killed him.' It was fortunate that the operations officer, General Berthelot, was unbreakably robust. 'He was a brilliantly clever, amazingly fat man, in his own room fond of wearing a blouse and a pair of slippers . . . in his own opinion the only suitable uniform for a General Officer who, tactically handicapped by a weight of 240 pounds or so, had to wrestle with strategy in a temperature of ninety degrees in the shade. He was always at work and universally popular.'

Joffre, too, was enormously fat. Often said to resemble Father Christmas, he was known as 'Papa Joffre' to the troops. It was a major element in his hold over them that, every day of the long retreat, while the dusty sweating columns fell back along the baking roads of northern France towards the capital, he stopped work exactly at noon, took his seat at a table laid with gleaming cloth, silver and glass outside his headquarters and, in full view of passers-by, spent the next two hours fortifying the inner man.

For all his appearance of passivity, however, Joffre had ruthless incisive powers of decision.

When, on 5 September, the Germans at last faltered in their unrelenting advance, and he saw the chance to counter-attack, he seized it unhesitatingly. The result was a shattering victory – which ensured Joffre's reputation for all time. We may, nevertheless, judge that his responsibility for the victory was essentially a moral rather than an intellectual one. He had the strength of character to recover from an almost disastrous initial decision, to sustain his personal belief that the campaign would eventually go wrong for the Germans, and to communicate his confidence to his entourage, his subordinates and ultimately to the masses under his command. In that sense, Joffre had indeed won the battle of the Marne.

Yet Joffre's role would have deeply puzzled commanders of an earlier age. Those of the era of heroic leadership would have noted that he failed altogether to show himself to the enemy, and that he probably saw not a single German throughout the campaign, unless it were a prisoner. It was not thus, by the standards of Homer's warrior chiefs, or even of Alexander the Great, that a general overcame his foe. Still further back in time, in the era of what anthropologists call 'primitive warfare', it would have been the very purpose of Joffre's generalship that would have baffled comprehension.

'Primitive warfare', still to be observed in progress in certain remote regions of the world, like the highlands of New Guinea, differs fundamentally from that of modern man in the objects for which it is fought. Modern man fights for victory, the breaking of the enemy's will to resist. Through that outcome will flow the material results of war: redress of grievance, occupation or annexation of the vanquished's territory, indemnity, disarmament, even a permanently altered balance of advantage between the two contestants. Primitive man fights for no such clear-cut set of objectives. With him, war is a state of being, in which relations with neighbours

206

are always warlike, a condition of their belonging to different villages, clans or tribes. The purpose of fighting is not to 'win' in the modern sense, but to assert and emphasize their separate identities.

Since that is so, fighting in primitive warfare takes a form quite other than that known in 'advanced' societies. Much of it is of a low-level endemic quality – ambush and raiding, often with the object of kidnapping the neighbours' womenfolk. Occasionally, however, circumstances come to a head, and a battle is arranged. 'Arranged' is an exact description. The boundaries between tribal areas, though physically undefined, are well recognized and usually separated by wide no-man's-lands. Places suitable for a formal armed encounter are equally well recognized, so that all that needs to be done to bring one about is the issue of a formal challenge. The warriors and their audiences then assemble at the appropriate distance and, after a display of hostile intention and exchange of threats, action begins. Since there is no intention to win, however, the fighting is conducted at long distances, usually with missiles, and casualties are few. Tempers, of course, may get out of hand. But there is a command mechanism at work to see that, as far as possible, little real harm is done. Command is, in fact, exercised from the rear, by men of reputation and authority who restrain the young warriors if blood threatens to be shed in any quantity. A death, even a serious wounding, is normally the signal for the battle to be brought to an end and overtures of peace to be initiated.

It is over idealistic to argue that the warfare of those people, so inappropriately called 'primitive' by the bellicose societies of the industrial world, is entirely symbolic and altogether without result. Over time, anthropologists have noted, shifts of territory do tend to follow the balance of advantage in war, the weaker tribes almost imperceptibly yielding occupation of living-space to the stronger. But of outright conquest and occupation there is no trace. Why should war among the 'primitive' have results so different from that among the advanced peoples of the world? And how did the change from one form of fighting to another come about?

Any answer to the first question must accept that primitive warfare takes place in beneficent climates, where winning a living is easy and pressure of population on land is low. Primitive warfare can, in short, be apparently purposeless because the material pressures making for the urge to conquest are low. Curiously, they seem equally low in environments, like those inhabited by the Eskimos, where the sheer struggle for existence against the harshness of nature consumes all human energy. It is at some median point on the material spectrum between the need to devote very few and almost all energies to the struggle for existence that the change from 'primitive' to what we may call 'purposive' warfare occurs. The change appears to be associated with the adoption of particular economic forms of organization or, alternatively, with encounters between those which differ markedly from each other. The appearance about 3000 B.C. of the so-called 'hydraulic' societies in the Middle East, which depended upon irrigation and precise water management, required both that irrigation systems be protected from invaders and that the agriculturists who benefited from them acquiesce in the organizing power of a strong central authority. These two factors combined to produce what we may recognize as the first armies, distinguished by hierarchy, drill, tactics and a clear functional purpose, whether defensive or, if need be, offensive. War, in short, thus acquired a purpose. The wealth created by these hydraulic societies added further point to that purpose because it became a magnet for the envy and greed of those outside the borders of prosperity. The rich societies actually, though unintentionally, excited such greed by their natural tendency to trade with the undeveloped regions for commodities – often metal ores – in which they were not self-sufficient; the manufactured goods

207

they offered in exchange for raw materials fed an appetite not for more trade but for invasion, plunder, even the hope of conquest.

If challenges of this kind were to be met, or indeed levelled, an enormous premium was suddenly laid on the capacity for leadership – organizing, motivating, directing, battle-winning – in short, what the modern world calls generalship. Some of the 'hydraulic' kings of whom we have knowledge, Thutmose III of Egypt, victor of Megiddo, 1469 B.C., the first recorded battle of history, and Tiglath-pileser III of Assyria (reigned 745–727 B.C.) were clearly generals as well as kings. They may indeed have reigned because of their military qualities, rather than through their enjoyment of traditional divine or demi-god status. It is as we more nearly approach our own times, however, that the nature of such leadership becomes more apparent. The conquering dynasty of Macedon in the persons of Philip II and even more notably his son Alexander II the Great, provide us with graphic examples of how such royal generals functioned.

Mummified head of the Pharaoh Rameses II, victor of the battle of Kadesh, 1294 B.C.

Macedon was a small, poor, semi-civilized highland kingdom on the northern border of Greece. Unified by Philip, who also established hegemony over the Greeks, it was led by Alexander in a campaign of extraordinary boldness against the great empire of Persia in 334 B.C. Persia was at least twenty times as populous as Macedon, fifteen times as rich and a hundred times as large. This disparity threatened Alexander with disaster from the outset. How, in practice, did he overcome his disadvantages, so that within four years of crossing from Europe to Asia he had made himself master of his enemy's empire?

His first achievement was to impose his leadership on the Macedonian army, the core of which was a cavalry force composed of the national aristocracy. Called the Companions, they expected to be led by a warrior of their own kind, who excelled them in warriordom. That Alexander certainly did. He had proved his bravery in Philip's decisive battle for Greek hegemony, Chaeronea, and he had established his generalship in a series of preliminary campaigns against Macedon's Balkan enemies between 336 and 334 B.C. But he was rightly not content to rest his leadership on reputation alone. He was a brilliant organizer and provisioner, who took immense trouble to see that his army was fed, housed, clothed and paid. His wounded were cared for as well as contemporary medicine would allow, the families of the dead supported and the dead themselves honoured and commemorated. Direct as well as indirect appeal to the interests and loyalty of his followers was also one of his principal leadership techniques. In his famous speech to the army at Opis, he reminded his soldiers that the royal house to which he belonged had raised them from poverty to wealth and from obscurity to greatness. And before each of his battles, the Granicus, Issus and Gaugamela, he appeared before the assembled ranks, clad in magnificent fighting apparel, appealed to their pride, ridiculed their fears and declaimed promises of victory and the spoils it would bring.

Alexander's leadership was thus highly political in its quality and rhetoric; his army was in a sense also his constituency. But he was not merely a politician. In the last resort, he led by example. Always hugely outnumbered by his enemies, he won by taking risks – risks for the army but above all for himself. Boldness was his creed, demonstrated by his practice of choosing the point where the enemy appeared strongest, rather than weakest, and making that the focus of an all-or-nothing cavalry charge which he led himself. At Gaugamela, the decisive battle of the conquest, he waited until a gap opened in the Persian lines and then 'led the Companions on at the double and, with a loud battle cry, straight at Darius.' The Great King turned and fled, and Alexander pursued him to his death.

What Alexander practised, we may call 'heroic leadership'. It was in the style of

Homer's heroes, Ajax and Achilles, and deliberately so, for we know that Homer's epics were a major influence upon his kingship. It was also the style which would persist into the last days of Greek greatness. Xenophon, writing at the beginning of the fourth century B.C. when Homer's age was long past, set himself to enquire whether, in a more sophisticated world, the general still ought to make his own person the exemplar of his army's courage or whether he ought not hold himself out of danger so that by observation and cool decision he could direct his army's efforts to best effect. After some discussion, he comes to the conclusion that it is still best for the general to show bravery, because of the example that gives. Even to Greeks living in the age of Plato and Aristotle, therefore, it was deeds rather than thought which counted in war.

*Alexander the Great (*left*) at the battle of Issus, 333 B.C., his second victory over Darius (*right*), Great King of Persia*

But that age was nearly over. Philo of Byzantium, writing only two hundred years later, advances an entirely different theory of generalship. 'It is your duty not to take part in the battle,' is his advice to generals of his own time, 'for whatever you may accomplish by spilling your own blood could not compare with the harm you would do to your interests as a whole if anything happened to you ... Keeping yourself out of range of missiles, or moving along the line without exposing yourself, exhort the soldiers, distribute praise and honours to those who prove their courage and berate and punish the cowards.' Here is a new military world, in which the general seeks to make his soldiers act heroically without behaving as a hero himself.

The heroic ideal was not, of course, to wither away. Even within the classical world military leaders would continue to act the hero when emergency required it. And outside the classical world, where the war bands from which the aristocracies of Greece and Rome descended continued to flourish, the heroic manner remained the dominant principle of leadership. The Germanic tribes which eventually destroyed the Roman empire by their overeagerness to enjoy the advantages of living within its borders, the seafarers who, as Anglo-Saxons and later Vikings, came to invade Britain, the other Norsemen who founded states in Normandy and

209

Genghis Khan, Mongol terror of the civilized world, 1190–1227

Julius Caesar, conqueror of Gaul, 58–51 B.C.

Gustavus Adolphus, King of Sweden, the outstanding Protestant leader of the Thirty Years War

Russia, the monarchs of the feudal kingdoms which warred between each other and against the nomad and Muslim invaders of mediaeval Europe, were all led by overlords whose style of leadership would have been immediately recognizable to Homer's heroes and who were, indeed, lauded and commemorated in saga poetry and chronicles composed in Homeric vein. The Crusader kings, from Richard the Lionheart of England to Louis IX of France, all conceived it their duty to take their place in the forefront of the battleline and, if necessary, to die under the handstrokes of their enemies as an encouragement to their followers.

In a sense, too, the leadership of Christendom's most deadly enemies, the nomad horsemen of the steppe who beat against its frontiers in successive waves from Attila's campaigns in the fourth century to those of Genghis in the thirteenth, was also of heroic style, in that such leaders were nakedly men of war who took and shared risks with their followers. There was, however, about the generalship of the Mongol and Turkic conquerors a brutality, ruthlessness and vindictive cruelty from which Christian warriors drew back and eventually recoiled as heroic leadership acquired its distinctive style in Christendom. That process of distancing oneself from the arbitrary shedding of blood for its own sake, from the humiliation and contemptuous extinction of a loser, came to be codified in the system we call chivalry. Chivalry endorsed, positively glorified, hand-to-hand combat and martial display. But it also enjoined respect for the enemy, magnanimity in victory and courtesy to the vanquished.

The post-heroic leadership which had its antecedents in the generalship of imperial Rome and which emerged fully fledged in Renaissance Europe was not, therefore, simply an about-turn from the style practised by Alexander the Great. Caesar, a cool, rational and hard-headed military organizer and campaign strategist, had at least once in his career flung himself into the fray as if he were the young Alexander confronting Darius. In the battle on the Sambre against the Belgic tribe of the Nervii in 57 B.C., he suddenly received word that his Tenth Legion was wilting under their attack. Seizing a sword and shield, he dashed into the front rank, calling on his subordinates to stand forward and for the legionary standard to be advanced where all could see it. In a few minutes he restored the resolution of his men and reversed the tide of battle. Before the afternoon was out, the Nervii were beaten and Rome's conquest of Gaul was by that much further advanced. His desperate remedy would have its counterpart in the performance of Gustavus Adolphus at Breitenfeld in 1631, of Napoleon at Rivoli in 1797, of Wellington at Waterloo in 1815, of Stonewall Jackson at First Bull Run, even of Haig, so vilified for his disinvolvement in his men's sufferings, at Ypres in 1914. Great generals of the post-heroic age, even less great generals, clearly continued to accept that, in the last resort, victory or defeat would turn on their personal example, and would act accordingly.

For all that, the style of generalship adumbrated by Philo of Byzantium did come to dominate the warfare of the post-heroic world. Bureaucratic command came to replace personal leadership, and we may chart its onward march by the steady rise in the size of armies, which was a feature both of the heyday of imperial Rome and of the rise of the dynastic states of Europe. The Roman system was, by the time of the accession of Augustus, already well-defined. There a military apprenticeship was recognized to be the appropriate means by which young men of promise advanced in a political career. Starting as *contubernales*, or volunteer aides-de-camp, they rose, after an interval in political life, to the rank of tribune, when they might hold rotating command of a legion, and then, after another interval, to that of legate, in charge of several. Day-to-day authority within the legion was exercised by centurions, who were long-service soldiers promoted for good conduct.

210

Traces of this arrangement, though determined by usefulness rather than continuity, can be found in the armies of Renaissance Europe. Since they had evolved from the mercenary companies of the later Middle Ages, with which monarchs had supplemented the forces raised by the increasingly unsatisfactory feudal levy, their rank structures were an extension of those of the company. It had been commanded by a Captain, with a lieutenant *(locum tenens)* as his deputy, and a sergeant-major to exercise authority through the sergeants over the men. When groups of companies were combined to form a regiment and regiments to form armies, these offices were replicated as 'general' to the larger body; hence Captain-general, Lieutenant-general and Sergeant-major-general. It is from these titles that the modern grades of general, lieutenant-general and major-general descend. At the same time, functional appointments came into existence within armies, notably those of quartermaster, who was concerned with housing the troops, and adjutant, who was the commander's assistant. Rank came in time to be applied to such appointment, so that Quartermasters-general and Adjutants-general might, for example, be Major-generals also.

The consolidation of this system and the standardization of ranks was slow to happen. Cromwell, for example, was served by staff officers bearing the titles of Commissary-General for Musters, Victuals and Provision, by a Waggon-master-general and by a Scoutmaster-general in charge of intelligence. His chief of staff held the rank of Sergeant Major General. It would not be until Wellington's time that the quartermaster-general's and adjutant-general's departments would be definitively organized, with separately recognized functions, and not until the twentieth century that a separate 'general' staff, responsible for operations, would come into being.

From the sixteenth century onwards, however, the principle upon which a modern command organization works could be clearly discerned. Administrative duties had been allotted to officers who were subordinate to the commander; necessary though they were to the management of the army their performance had been recognized as different from that of directing the army in battle, for which the senior general had to be freed from routine. In the discharge of that task he might, if he deemed that duty demanded it, take his place in the fighting line. Normally, however, he chose a station to the rear, from which he could observe and issue appropriate orders.

It was thus that Cromwell, Marlborough, Wolfe (for all that he died in battle) and Wellington exercised their generalship. But Wellington was perhaps the last who could do so in this style, entailing as it did the devolution of administrative responsibilities on to specialist subordinates, while personal direction of the fighting remained with the commanding general, who might or might not choose a 'heroic' intervention if he judged that necessary. Wellington did so at Waterloo, where he lost most of his personal staff during the day to death or wounds, and was seen by almost every man, at the side of his troops, in the firing line. Fifty years later, by the time of the American Civil and Franco-Prussian wars, generalship of that style would no longer be possible. Armies had exploded in size, from the 70,000 Wellington had commanded at Waterloo, to 115,000 at Gettysburg, to 200,000 in Prussia's campaign in France in 1870. However much he might wish otherwise, a commander could no longer be seen by all his soldiers in the course of a single day within the boundaries of a battlefield. Indeed, as a function of this explosion in numbers, battles had begun to last two or three days or more and battlefields to comprehend what formerly had been counted theatres of campaign.

Staffs had increased in size to accommodate the growth of armies. And with that expansion had come the realization that staff officers could no longer be selected

on the basis of favour or acquaintanceship, but needed to be trained. The first Staff College, the Prussian *Kriegsakademie*, was founded at Berlin in 1810. One of its early directors was Carl von Clausewitz, the philosopher of war, whose posthumous book *Vom Kriege* (On War), was to influence professional soldiers into our own time. A successor, Helmuth von Moltke (the Elder), would make *Vom Kriege* the basis of the school's theoretical instruction. More important was the practical training that he saw it imparted. Moltke's belief was that the complexity of contemporary warfare and the wide extension of modern battlefields required that operations should be run by officers trained in a uniform intellectual outlook. His aim was not that they should be taught to think in a stereotyped style; rather that, confronted by analogous circumstances, they should react in the same way. To that end, a great deal of the training at the *Kriegsakademie* of his day was pragmatic rather than theoretical. War games, sand table discussions, staff rides – when officers surveyed the features of a piece of countryside under the eye of a teacher and suggested how it might be defended or attacked – these were Moltke's preferred methods. In their practicality, their emphasis on team work and achievement of a common view, they very much anticipated those of modern business schools, which may be regarded as direct descendants of staff colleges in general and the *Kriegsakademie* in particular.

Their efficacy, tested in the Austro-Prussian War of 1866, was proved beyond doubt in the Franco-Prussian War of 1870. There an army of self-styled 'practical' soldiers pitted its dash and rule-of-thumb methods – developed in forty years of small colonial and European campaigns – against the intellect and system of a true general staff. Not everything went quite right for the Prussians; but almost everything went disastrously wrong for the French. Their formation commanders fought individually instead of co-operatively, their unit commanders did not ensure that information from the battleline flowed upward to their superiors, above all the administration altogether failed to arrange that reinforcement and supplies flowed downward to the point of need. While the Prussian railways smoothly discharged floods of reservists at chosen deployment points, the French railways clogged their concentration area with wagons full of unwanted material behind empty wagons which they impeded from returning to base. Beaten as much by their own inefficiency as by the efforts of the Prussians, the French generals were forced to surrender in the open field after six weeks of war.

The results of 1870 alerted the armies of the whole industrializing world to the new military realities. Some of these had to do with organization. Since Napoleon, whose principal military achievement it was, the proper internal division of armies had been recognized as a crucial factor in effective command. He had created the *corps d'armée*, a subordinate body within an army self-sufficient in arms and services, and had exercised control by the careful selection and direction of his corps commanders. These men were to become famous as his Marshals – Soult, Ney, Davout, Bernadotte. But proper organization was not, by 1870, enough in itself to ensure success. It was necessary also, as the generals of the recently fought American Civil War had learnt, to have access to and to understand the new technology of war. Railways stood foremost among these means. Almost as important was the telegraph, by which a commander attuned to the rapid to-and-fro of communication could now manoeuvre formations across distances wider than any yet known to the strategist. Grant, Lincoln's favoured commander in the Union war against the South, had proved himself the master of war fought along rails and wires and the North owed a great deal among the reasons for its victory to his mastery.

Railway and signal management, army organization, staff training, these understandably became the matters to which modern armies bent their efforts after 1870.

All the more were they urgent as armies grew apace, fed by ever-increasing and healthier populations and by the expanded revenues of states growing rich on the fruits of industrialization and world commerce. By 1914 the peacetime armies of the industrial world exceeded in size those which states had with difficulty raised for war a hundred years before. France maintained an army of half a million, Germany of 800,000, Russia of 1,400,000. Even Britain, whose resources were chiefly devoted to supporting the largest navy in the world, had one army of two hundred thousand on the home establishment and another of equal size formed of Indian troops.

Union engineers laying telegraph wires, April 1864. The Civil War was the first to be conducted by modern communication systems

Officering armed forces of this size at all levels had become a major call upon the social and administrative resources of every state possessing them. The warrior class that had dominated feudal Europe had transformed itself progressively over the previous centuries into an officer class, but it had long resisted efforts both to open its ranks to outsiders or to undergo systematic training for its profession. Academies for artillery and engineer officers, perforce drawn from beyond the traditional military class, which refused to serve in those less glamorous arms, had existed since the eighteenth century. Only since the beginning of the nineteenth had academies for infantry and cavalry officers become established. And even so the quality of education and training offered within their walls continued to be inspired by the essentially 'heroic' ethos from which generalship had departed in antiquity two thousand years earlier. That, perhaps, was necessary. Personal leadership of men in battle requires heroism. But mere heroism is a recipe for tactical disaster, since the urge to display bravery militates against the cultivation of skill and ingenuity in the face of the enemy. Worse, it infects the outlook of those selected for training at staff and command levels. The Prussians of 1866–70, pioneers of intellectual generalship and in some sense military ingénues, had been so possessed by the force of their vision as to avoid the excesses of the heroic ethos. By 1914 it had reasserted its influence on their command thinking, while flourishing unchecked among the French, British, Russians and Austrians.

The result was to make for a European, ultimately a world catastrophe. Administratively, the generals" staffs coped triumphantly with the demands of going to war in 1914. Within two weeks of the outbreak, the French and Germans had mobilized four and five million men respectively, the latter, at the height of the mobilization, despatching a train across the Rhine bridges into the deployment area every minute and a half. Tactically, however, both sides found they incurred heavy losses – crippling to the units engaged – from the outset, because of the 'heroic' methods by which they were led against each other. Strategically, each found that, for all the 'scientific' approach to war planning practised by its general staff before 1914, it had calculated disastrously wrong. The French plan (Plan XVII) failed because of its lack of subtlety. It required the French armies, ignoring their unprotected flank along neutral Belgium's border, to plunge straight into German-occupied Alsace-Lorraine. They did so and were bloodily repulsed. The German plan (the Schlieffen Plan) failed because of its overcomplexity. It required the German armies to debouch exactly where the French did not expect them, from Belgium, and wheel on Paris. Apparently successful at the outset, it was progressively dogged by difficulties of supply and reinforcement, and eventually lost impetus altogether on the banks of the Marne.

Baffled and uncomprehending, the two antagonists milled about in what little free space there remained in the Western theatre for manoeuvre and, when that was lost, found that they occupied two complementary trench systems running without break from Switzerland to the North Sea. On the Eastern Front, where the Russians had attacked the Austrians and Germans simultaneously, beaten the first and been beaten by the second, similar entrenched lines had come into being. Infantry attacks from one to the other, across what would be called 'no-man's-land', failed bitterly. Artillery attack made scarcely more impression and soon ceased for lack of munitions. At the end of 1914, though Europe was inextricably locked in war with itself, its generals found themselves without either means or ideas to wage it.

Many had already been broken by the strain of grappling with forces as large and unfamiliar as the war had released. Von Moltke the Younger, the German Chief of Staff, had been relieved of command in November, too shaken to continue. The imperturbable Joffre had braved it out, but had relieved half the general officers of the French army before the end of September, because of their loss of resilience or lack of competence. Those who were to take their places, men like Foch and Pétain, were notable for their toughness of character and insensitivity to losses. But they also revealed mental flexibility and adaptiveness to the new warfare – a warfare of what the Germans would call *Materialschlachten* – battles of material. Foch had used the railways in an ingenious way to provide himself with reinforcements at the Marne in September 1914. Pétain would use convoys of motor trucks to keep Verdun supplied when he had to fight that battle in 1916. Both accepted, as did counterparts in other armies – Haig in the British, Ludendorff in the German – that it would be numbers that counted in trench warfare, numbers of men, of guns, of shells and that the side which could assemble the largest quantity and maintain discipline longest would win.

216

European, and American industry rose to the challenge these attrition-minded generals demanded of it, so that by mid-1915 offensive means were again becoming available to the armies. Joffre seized the opportunity in France, Falkenhayn, Moltke's successor, in the East. The war grumpled back into life. But it was a strange war, in no way more unfamiliar than in the style of generalship it encouraged – what has been called 'château generalship'. Because the armies were both enormous and at the same time invisible, there was no chance of, even had there been point in, the generals trying to show themselves to their soldiers in the old heroic way. Their function had become essentially organizational, and a station miles to the rear of the front, from which material and reinforcements could be sent forward, seemed more logical than one placed close to a narrow section of the trenches. This distancing reinforced the deliberate tempo of operations; information was slow to flow back to their headquarters, orders equally slow to flow forward. At the battle of Loos, in September 1915, Field-Marshal French, the British Commander-in-Chief, was operating within a communication delay of twelve hours.

'Château generalship' might have worked, nonetheless, had the premise on which it rested, smooth telephonic and telegraphic communication with the front, held good. In theory the telephone widely used by armies in 1914–18 to supplement the telegraph, which had served their needs since the 1850s, should have enabled a general like French to keep in touch with his subordinates as immediately as had Wellington at Waterloo, through word of mouth, or rapidly galloped message as Napoleon at Austerlitz. In practice, it worked very well as far as the front line, but there its wires were so frequently cut by shellfire that communication ceased, precisely at the place and time most needed. Many expedients were tried to overcome this failing; towards the end of the war the trench systems were underlaid at a depth of six feet by a telephone grid as dense and elaborate as might have been found in a city. But as soon as the front moved, as it did whenever an attack occurred, the disabling interruption at the crucial point automatically ensued. Every battle of the war, from First Ypres in October 1914 to the breaking of the Hindenburg Line in September 1918, was thus fought beyond rather than under the control of the responsible general's hand.

Yet, by one of those ironic irregularities in technological synchrony so familiar to historians, the means to solve the commander's communication difficulties were near perfection in 1914. Two technical means that would dominate warfare after 1918, the military aeroplane and the tank, were both products of the war. Radio, which would transform military communication, actually pre-dated it. 'Wireless' was widely installed in naval ships before 1914 and decisively influenced fleet operations. But radio sets for use on land could not be miniaturized quickly enough to exert a similar effect on military operations. Power sources remained too heavy, aerials too conspicuous, valves too large and fragile for the sets of the day to be taken into battle; the British 'trench set' required twelve men to carry its parts in separate loads. Given another ten years of development, all those defects would have been eliminated, and the character of the war thereby altogether altered.

A generation of younger officers who survived, often because they had held junior staff positions, which also gave them insight into the nature of the command problem, were quick to grasp how revolutionary a means radio promised to be. Foremost among them was Heinz Guderian, originally a *Jäger* (light infantry) officer who had unusually chosen to specialize in signals. He never lost his interest in radio. By the outbreak of the Second World War, when already a Corps Commander, he pioneered a method which came to be known as 'forward control'. Instead of remaining to the rear of his troops in a static headquarters as the generals of 1914–18 had done, he moved with his troops close to the advancing edge of an

attack, travelling in a command truck which contained a small personal staff and radio equipment. From it he obtained an up-to-the-minute picture of how operations were proceeding close at hand and issued immediate orders as he thought fit; less urgent directions were transmitted to his rear headquarters to be handled there.

'Forward control' appealed strongly to the man who was to acquire the widest and most lasting fame as a battlefield commander, Erwin Rommel. He simplified Guderian's system even further, often commanding from a tank and issuing orders over its radio through his rear headquarters by short pre-arranged code words. On the Allied side, Montgomery arrived at a command style similar to Guderian's by an independent route. He also lived forward of his main headquarters, attended by a group of young liaison officers who visited the units in touch with the enemy at daily or even hourly intervals, reported back and carried Montgomery's orders by direct word of mouth.

'Forward control' did not appeal to all commanders. Manstein, perhaps the most masterly of the German commanders, maintained an orthodox headquarters well to the rear, trusting to the excellence of his signal system to keep in touch. The Russians, fighting a battle for national survival and incurring casualties on a First World War scale as its price, clung to First World War methods. Since their leading generals, Zhukov and Konev, rose to high command principally because of their toughness of character – necessary both to enable them to deal with Stalin and to bear the weight of losses their generalship incurred – it was perhaps necessary that they should have commanded from a distance and through fear and punishment rather than by example. Distance, for a different reason, also characterized the command style of Eisenhower. Though a man of humane, even compassionate character, he estimated his chief role to be that of a diplomat between the commanders of the several national armies under his authority. As a result, he chose to deal most with Montgomery, Bradley and Patton rather than with their subordinates, who were in more direct contact with the enemy.

The evil genius of the war, Hitler, took remoteness to extremes. From the summer of 1941 until the end of 1944 he lived in a series of isolated, insulated headquarters, Vinnitsa in the Ukraine and Rastenburg in East Prussia, out of physical touch equally with his troops, his people and his own political associates. Ironically, he was for much of the time actually in closer contact with the armies he was trying to defeat than with those he was seeking to impel to victory. For, thanks to the genius of the Allied cryptographers, who in breaking the German Enigma cypher realized the inmost fantasy of every general since war began, the pattern of his daily orders to his armies was laid bare to his Western enemies from the early months of the war. It speaks mightily of his ferocious powers of compulsion that his generals and soldiers, betrayed by cypher insecurity to their enemies year after year, should have sustained their resistance as long and successfully as they did.

Thus, in Hitler, the long march away from the heroic ideal of generalship reached its apogee and term. Yet heroism, in some perverted form, was not absent from his personality; for all his ready recourse to terror, he maintained an appeal to his followers, derived from his 'time of struggle' in the wilderness of German politics, separate from the fear he equally inspired. But, by 1945, he was already becoming an anachronism as a military leader. The direct, flamboyant, risk-taking personalities of generals like Rommel, or the young American airborne commanders, Gavin or Maxwell Taylor, had proved better attuned to the demands for leadership expressed by soldiers who were also political animals, than that of titans who rode above the struggle as did Hitler, Stalin and Churchill. Churchill, the war leader, would fail in his campaign to retain the peace-time leadership of Britain for want of a majority of soldiers' votes. And the new heroes of warfare after 1945 – nationalist generals like the Israelis Dayan and Rabin, guerrilla chieftains like Giap and Castro, counter-revolutionary commanders like the Frenchmen Bigeard and Massu – were all men who ensured that they were seen to share the risks and hardships undergone by their soldiers and who could outdo them in tenacity and resolution.

Yet the central dilemma of leadership perceived by Xenophon has not been resolved. 'A general who is brave and stupid is a calamity,' says the Chinese proverb. Soldiers, in short, ask more of a general than mere bravery. They ask it all the same. But as the world moves deeper into the nuclear age, when its most powerful

Hitler with Keitel, head of his personal staff (centre), *and Jodl, his operations officer*

leaders scarcely dare show themselves in public for fear of assassination by madmen or terrorists, when at the approach of crisis they retreat to shelters as safe as military engineers know how to provide, and far safer than any available to ordinary citizens or subjects, Xenophon's question presents itself in ever more compelling form: 'Is it better to be brave or thoughtful?' Perhaps the way out of that dilemma lies not forward but backward towards the style of leadership practised among the primitives by the wise men who seek to contain rather than inflame the violence of their young warriors. Their philosophy is that discretion is the better part of valour. It is one that the world must learn to live by, or perish.

Sinews of War   11

It is the dramatic and momentous events at the sharp end of the war that jostle for our attention. But the inexorable advance of armoured columns, and the barrages of massed artillery – the stuff of so much of the film and literature of war – depend upon logistics, 'the practical art of moving armies and keeping them supplied.' The tendency for armies to become ever more technologically sophisticated has led to the growth of their logistic 'tails' at the expense of their fighting 'teeth'. The sudden acceleration of this process may be essentially a twentieth-century phenomenon: nevertheless, successful commanders have paid careful attention to logistics for centuries. Indeed, it is no exaggeration to say that tactics – the art of winning battles – is really no more than the art of the logistically possible. Moreover, though most aspects of warfare are closely related to developments in the civil sphere, the connections between logistics on the one hand and science and industry on the other are especially close.

The logistic requirements of the armies of the ancient world were relatively simple. However, although a certain amount of food for men and fodder for animals could be found on the march, it was rarely possible to mount a sustained operation without at least some pack-animals or wheeled transport. When the 'Ten Thousand' Greek mercenaries who had fought for Cyrus at Cunaxa in 401 B.C. marched back to the coast, they had every reason to travel light. Yet they took their wagons with them, and getting these creaking carts across difficult country provided Greek commanders with some of the most serious challenges to their leadership. For Xenophon, who led the rearguard on its perilous march, the episode provided valuable evidence for his military writings, in which he recommended that soldiers should live, as far as possible, off the local resources. If these were insufficient, up to twenty days' provisions could be carried in the baggage-train, with the emphasis upon condensed and concentrated food like salted meat.

Wheeled vehicles needed roads. It is significant that two of the greatest empires of the ancient world, the Persian and the Roman, left as enduring monuments the roads they made. The Persian Royal Road connected Susa, near the head of the Gulf, with Sardis, close to the Mediterranean coast of Asia Minor, sweeping across 1,500 miles of wild country. The Romans constructed a network of roads right across their empire to ease the passage of marching troops, their wagons and pack-animals. They also made good use of the sea and inland waterways to sustain far-flung garrisons, like that in northern Britain, and even armies in the field. When Caesar fought the Helvetii in 58 B.C. he tried to keep his army supplied with grain from boats on the River Saône, though this attempt failed because the tribesmen marched away from the course of the river and Caesar had to follow to keep contact with them.

A Roman baggage-train contained food, ammunition and specialist equipment. This relief from Trajan's column shows Roman soldiers constructing a fortified camp

The case of the Roman army shows just how difficult it was for even a well-disciplined force with comparatively simple needs to live off the land. Roman soldiers enjoyed a staple diet of corn, ground in portable querns and baked to form hard biscuits called *buccellati*. The supply of the all-important grain was ensured by each legionary carrying three days' rations on the march, and by stockpiling in the granaries of main supply-bases and fortresses. Each of the four granaries at Chester could probably have held 1,000 cubic yards, and the granaries in fortresses contained about two years' supply for their garrisons. On campaign, legionaries slept in ten-man leather tents. These were transported rolled up across the backs of pack-animals, which also carried spare missiles for archers, slingers and catapults. Some engineer stores were also to be found amongst the baggage: in the winter of 52 B.C. Caesar had enough shovels available to enable his army to dig its way through snowdrifts six feet deep which blocked the passes through the Cévennes.

In the baggage-train of a Roman army we see the essential components – food, ammunition and specialist equipment – of subsequent logistic tails. The Roman practices of building roads to ensure strategic communication, and of establishing major stores depots, also foreshadow the policy of later armies. The Byzantines followed the Roman lead and had a particularly well-organized military train, with a cart, containing 'a hand-mill, a bill-hook, a saw, two spades, a mallet, a large wicker basket, a scythe, and two pick axes,' for each sixteen of its infantrymen.

The structure of the Byzantine army reflected the importance accorded to logistics. For much of the Middle Ages, though, European armies were less cohesive: their discipline was uncertain and their logistic provision scanty. Campaigns were generally short, confined to the few months when roads were passable. The carts which did lumber along behind armies seldom contained enough food to satisfy the troops, and straggling and plundering resulted. When the English took Caen in the Crécy campaign of 1346, they spent four days there collecting provisions. These were soon exhausted and, as an English knight wrote after Crécy, 'since we left Caen we have lived off the countryside with great difficulty and much harm to our men . . . we are now in such a plight that part of our needs must be met with supplies.'

The fact that an English army got into difficulties in well-stocked France, with its fleet close by, emphasizes the poverty of supply and transport in mediaeval armies. The Black Prince set off on the Poitiers campaign with his ships 'loaded with provisions and jewels, hauberks, helmets, lances, shields, bows, arrows and more besides . . .' His army was soon reduced to living off the land, and the

222

expedition was, in Sir Charles Oman's words, 'merely an enormous and destructive raid.' A commander campaigning in a barren or unpopulated area like Scotland or Wales would need to take special precautions to protect his army against starvation, but, as Oman points out: 'a French or German army when it entered Flanders or Lombardy, or an English force in France, trusted, as all facts unite to demonstrate, for its maintenance to its power of plundering the invaded district.'

Sieges created awesome problems. The besiegers soon ate up their own rations and roamed ever wider into the countryside to find more. And if food could be obtained locally, albeit with increasing difficulty, ammunition and siege equipment could not. When Fawkes de Breauté held Bedford Castle against King Henry III in 1224 the siege swallowed resources at an alarming rate. Siege engines rumbled across England, fifteen thousand crossbow bolts were sent for from Corfe Castle, and the bailiffs of Northampton were instructed to have another 4,000 'made both by day and by night, by all the smiths of the town who are skilled in the art.' Just as the siege warfare of the Western Front seven centuries later provoked ammunition consumption which outstripped production and supply, so mediaeval sieges had precisely the same effect.

Many of the battles of the Middle Ages involved surprisingly small numbers of men. Hastings, which changed the course of English history, may have been fought by as few as 8,000 men – and certainly by no more than 19,000. Sir Steven Runciman suggests that Hattin, in 1187, was fought by the largest armies put into the field up to that date by either the Crusaders or their enemies: even so, '15,000 on the Christian side and 18,000 on the Moslem must be regarded as the maximum figures.' The army defeated at Bannockburn in 1314 was, at 20,000, unusually large for an English force: Edward III took 11,000 men to Crécy, and Henry V won Agincourt with less than 8,000.

Armies this size could usually cope by a judicious combination of living off the country and carrying a certain amount of food with them. But one of the characteristics of the 'military revolution' of the sixteenth and seventeenth centuries was a rapid growth in the size of armies. The Duke of Alva marched off to suppress the revolt of the Netherlands in 1567 with 10,600 men, an impressive force for its day. Just over fifty years later, at the height of the Thirty Years War, Gustavus Adolphus and Wallenstein each had more than 100,000 men at their disposal.

These new armies usually contained a high proportion of mercenaries, who relied upon the prompt arrival of their pay to buy food. All too often the financial burden proved too much for their employers, and the mercenaries were paid late or not at all. Even if the promised money did arrive on time, it was still no easy matter for a large army to find sufficient food to purchase. It was also depressingly common for men trained to the use of arms and subjected to indifferent discipline to take what they wanted at sword-point.

In the best-organized armies of the day soldiers were entitled to specific rations but, as Sir James Turner, an officer of wide experience, admitted, these could not always be provided.

The ordinary allowance for a soldier in the field is daily, two pound of bread, one pound of flesh, or in lieu of it, one pound of cheese, one pottle of wine, or in lieu of it, two pottles of beer. It is enough, cry the soldiers, we desire no more, it is enough in all conscience. But this allowance will not last very long, they must be content to march sometimes one whole week, and scarce get two pounds of bread all the while . . .

When commanders simply quartered their men upon the inhabitants, ordering the latter to supply them with food according to a fixed scale, this policy of last resort:

proves oft the destruction of a country: for though no exorbitancy be committed . . . when an army cannot be quartered but both close and near together, to prevent infalls, onslaughts and surprises, it is an easy matter to imagine what a heavy burthen these places bear . . . And withal it is very hard to get soldiers and horsemen kept within the limits of their duty in these quarters after they have endured hunger, thirst and other hardships in the field.

Nor was it just the soldiers who had to be fed. Their steeds and baggage-animals ate up tons of fodder, and the swarm of camp-followers who straggled after them all needed food, drink and shelter, and were not particular about how they obtained it. The armies of seventeenth-century Europe resembled nothing so much as huge maggots gnawing their way across the face of the land, leaving a trail of famine and destruction behind them.

Baggage-trains grew steadily in size. Maurice of Nassau was the careful commander of an experienced and well-found force, but there were 942 'official' vehicles with his army on the 1610 campaign – no less than 129 of them allocated to the general and his staff – not to mention the personal vehicles taken along by enterprising officers who had no intention of being uncomfortable if they could avoid it. Attempts to make a force self-supporting increased the number of wagons still further. In 1602 Maurice had 3,000 for 24,000 men, and four years later the Spanish general Spinola had over 2,000 for just 15,000 soldiers. Water transport, when it was available, could be remarkably helpful. One contemporary expert calculated that 224 tons of flour and 672 tons of fodder could be carried in only nine ships, while 600 wagons would be needed to hold the flour alone.

The increasing use of firearms lengthened the logistic tail. When the Royalist army's train of artillery was packed ready to move in October 1642, it was carried in three great divisions of wheeled transport containing over a thousand cannon-balls of various calibre, 1,200 musket-rests, two tons of musket shot, 500 shovels, 100 pickaxes, ten wheelbarrows, and a bewildering variety of smiths' tools and raw materials. The Parliamentarian New Model Army allowed itself few luxuries – and certainly none of the 'light ladies of pleasure' who could be found in the Royalist baggage – but in 1647 its artillery and baggage-train required 1,038 horses.

These ponderous columns moved slowly. On its advance to Edgehill in 1642 the King's army took ten days to cover less than 100 miles, rather better than the 8¾ miles a day averaged by the Earl of Essex's army on its march from Worcester to Kineton at the same time. Fairfax's advance into the West Country in June and July 1645 was lightning war by the standards of the age. It was a hot summer, and the roads were dry: the Parliamentarians marched the 113 miles from Leicester to Marlborough in a week, an average of sixteen miles a day, and followed this by averaging seventeen miles a day between Marlborough and Beaminster. This was a consistent feat of marching which few seventeenth-century armies could equal, and it speaks volumes for the efficiency of Fairfax's commissariat. And yet a word of caution is required. It is easy to blame the short marches of seventeenth- and eighteenth-century armies on the wagons trundling along behind them. However, unmetalled roads, themselves so few in number that an entire army was usually compressed along a single route, slowed down even the infantry and cavalry.

For continental powers, with the experience of the Thirty Years War behind them, the penalties for neglecting logistics were clearly apparent. Well might Cardinal Richelieu write that: 'History knows many more armies ruined by want and disorder than by the efforts of their enemies; and I have witnessed how all the enterprises which were embarked on in my day were lacking for that reason alone.' More recently, Professor G. Perjes pointed to what he called a 'crisis in strategy': the armies of the seventeenth century so often failed to achieve their aims because

they could not supply themselves effectively.

By 1700 the logistic obstacles confronting commanders were of staggering dimensions. An army of 60,000 men needed forty-five tons of bread – the baking of which required thirty-five tons of grain and 200 wagon-loads of fuel – each day. The grain needed milling, and as mills were often attacked by an enemy who was well aware of their importance, milling equipment had to be carried. Each of the army's sixty bread-ovens had to be dismantled and put on a cart when the army moved, and setting up a new bakery was the work of several days. The army's 40,000 horses – mounts for the cavalry and senior officers and draught animals for the artillery and baggage-train – devoured 500 tons of fodder a day in the summer campaigning season, and 250 tons of oats and straw every day in winter quarters.

The magazine system was at best part of the solution to this problem. Provision magazines were not a seventeenth-century invention, but in the 1640s and 1650s the French war administrator Michel Le Tellier made notable improvements by carefully calculating the quantity of provisions required, placing contracts with civilian sutlers for their supply, and setting up a wagon-train containing several days' reserves of food which could accompany the army. Much of the food thus

obtained was concentrated in magazines, and French commanders manoeuvred between these like a spider on its web. Le Tellier's son, François, Marquis de Louvois, refined the system. He ensured that the network of frontier fortresses always contained enough rations to feed their garrisons for six months. Larger *magasins généraux* were set up to meet the needs of field armies, and provision convoys of requisitioned wagons – or barges where possible – trekked out from the magazines to keep them supplied.

The limitations of the magazine system were striking. Despite Le Tellier's founding of a corps of *Intendants* whose task it was to supervise supply and expenditure, much depended upon the honesty of the contractors and upon the government's ability to pay them. Militarized transport services were still unheard of, and the performance of requisitioned wagons and their civilian drivers alike gave cause for concern. Even well-stocked magazines and efficient convoys could only meet a proportion of an army's needs, and much still had to be obtained locally. Finally, the magazine system seriously restricted strategic mobility, for an army could rarely move more than a week's march from its nearest magazine without enormous risk. It may be argued that Le Tellier and Louvois never intended their magazines to do more than permit the garrisons of French fortresses to hold out while their besiegers starved, and to enable French armies to besiege hostile fortresses without themselves starving.

Uncompromising logistic realities set out the parameters of eighteenth-century warfare. The campaigning season might last for six months in all. But even a commander who managed to bring his opponent to battle and win a convincing victory in the first two or three months found the remainder of the season so eroded by the need to forage, to make bread and to establish new magazines, that, in David Chandler's words, 'it was physically impossible for a victorious army to defeat its opponent's main force and then occupy a substantial area of hostile territory before the onset of the next season of Winter Quarters, during which the defeated foe could recover both his morale and his strength.'

Marches seldom averaged more than ten or twelve miles a day, and even the Duke of Marlborough's famous march to the Danube in 1704 covered just over 250 miles, most of them on friendly territory. Marlborough bought and requisitioned supplies as best he could, only setting up magazines when he was likely to be in an area for some time. His decision to fight at Blenheim was determined largely by the fact that his Franco-Bavarian opponents were sitting squarely across his line of advance into areas where he could obtain more food, and he could expect little help from his Imperialist allies to his rear. In short, he had to fight or starve. Simply staying put was no answer, for, in common with any other eighteenth-century commander operating well away from his base, Marlborough relied upon moving steadily across the countryside so as to bring fresh resources within range of his voracious foraging parties.

The Napoleonic period saw changes in the conduct of war every bit as profound as those of the military revolution of the seventeenth century. The size of armies exploded. In 1808 there were 520,000 French soldiers in the field and another 180,000 in depots. Four years later, Napoleon took up to 630,000 men to Russia at the same time that he maintained an army of 250,000 in Spain. Not only were there more actors in the drama: its pace accelerated from the measured formalism of the eighteenth century to breathless sprints like Napoleon's campaign in Italy in 1796 or his thrust into the heart of Austria in 1805. If the period produced no radical transformation of logistics, it did stretch the existing system to its absolute limits and, by doing so, presaged future developments.

For all their hierarchies of military administrators, commissary-generals, *intendants* and so on, armies continued to survive as they always had, partly by living off the country and partly by receiving rations brought up in convoys. The balance between them depended upon national policy and the dictates of geography. At one extreme was the French army of 1805, eating its way across half Europe much as Wallenstein's men might have done nearly two centuries before, and at the other was Wellington's British army in the Peninsula, supplied by an increasingly efficient commissariat and discouraged by the lash and the gallows from the brigandage which so often passed for logistics elsewhere.

In August 1805 Napoleon's 210,500 men and 396 guns began a march that was to take them from the Channel coast to the depths of Moravia. They moved widely dispersed, with a separate axis for each of the army's ten corps so as not to exhaust the resources of the countryside. While the army was still on French territory it

Above: Overloaded wagons moved ponderously behind most armies, as this British watercolour of 1802 shows

Right: 'How many times did we ruin the hopes of the villagers!' German soldiers with their spoils, 1812

was fed by arrangement with the local authorities, a plan which generally worked well, although months after the soldiers had left some officials were complaining that their bills had not yet been paid. Commissariat officials moved ahead of the advancing corps, organizing supplies for the next leg of the journey while the troops followed, averaging about thirty kilometres a day. But, as Corporal Jean-Pierre Blaise of the 108th Regiment of the Line declared:

we were often short of bread in spite of the efforts of our commanding general, Marshal Davout; and when we did receive some it was so bad that it was inedible . . . Fortunately, it was the height of the potato season, and they were plentiful in our area. How many times did we ruin the hopes of the villagers! We pillaged from them the fruits of an entire year's work. However we were, as you might say, forced to do so . . .

The corps commanders laid heavy impositions upon the areas they passed through. Marshal Soult of IV Corps forced the small town of Heilbronn, with only 15–16,000 inhabitants, to disgorge 127,500 pounds of bread, 24,000 pounds of salt, 3,600 bushels of hay, 6,000 sacks of oats, 5,000 pints of wine, 800 bushels of straw and 100 wagons. As the army moved on, Napoleon set up a chain of depots behind it, linked by convoys. His prime concern was to ensure the supply of munitions, and as the campaign went on there was a steady flow of artillery and infantry ammunition along one of the first proper lines of communication in modern history. Food was another matter. Some huge magazines were established – one at Augsburg held three million rations – and the main vehicle park carried reserves of bread and biscuit for use when the army had to concentrate. But the main source of supply remained the countryside, whose inhabitants had to yield to the demands of Soult and his colleagues or risk the more forceful attentions of Jean-Pierre Blaise and his.

When the French army closed up to fight the battle of Austerlitz on 2 December it was already feeling the pinch. Its Austro-Russian opponents were in infinitely more desperate straits. Kutuzov, the Russian commander, had already complained of: 'frightful deficiencies in supply, which caused an outbreak of plunder and indiscipline amongst our forces . . . Most of the regiments were composed of low-grade troops, and we learnt to call our vagabonds by the name of "marauders" – this was the first of our borrowings from the French.' The Allied commanders were pressed into launching their ill-considered attack on Napoleon – a manoeuvre which was to lay them open to a crippling counter-stroke – by their inability to keep their armies supplied where they were. Austerlitz, like Blenheim before it, was provoked as much by the demands of logistics as by the dictates of strategy.

Wellington's problems differed from those of his continental allies and opponents primarily in terms of scale. He rarely had more than 100,000 men under his direct command in Spain and Portugal, and he campaigned over distances which were small by comparison with those in Central Europe. Nevertheless, the Peninsula was notorious for its harsh terrain and bad roads. The British army had, furthermore, become used to operating near the coast with a fleet at its back, and once it had begun to fight deep inland its commissariat officials had to learn new lessons in the rough school of experience.

In the spring of 1813 the Anglo-Portuguese field army comprised 81,276 officers and men and upwards of 20,000 'official' horses and mules. Each man was entitled to his daily pound of meat and pound of biscuits (or 1½ pounds of bread), washed down by a quart of beer – or by a pint of wine or ⅓ of a pint of spirits. A horse's daily ration was ten pounds of oats, barley or maize and ten pounds of straw, while the hard-working mule was entitled to the same ration of straw but only half as much grain. The daily supply bill was for 100,000 pounds of biscuit and 200,000 pounds of grain, brought forward by 12,000 commissariat mules and hundreds of bullock wagons. A vast herd of cattle, slaughtered at the rate of 300 beasts a day, accompanied the army.

Some provisions were purchased abroad: meat in North Africa, corn in America and hay in Ireland. Many more were obtained locally, their owners paid in gold or, more frequently, in commissariat bills, which could be cashed in Lisbon or sold, at a punishing discount, to a dealer. The French were less scrupulous, but even so, a British official acknowledged that: 'as the Spanish and Portuguese ingenuously declared, in the event of a total lack of supplies, and in the face of the quantities absorbed by the armies, they could not eat our money or our receipt notes, neither could they purchase anything with them for miles around. How were they to live?'

Wellington's commissariat may not have been perfect, but it did enable the Duke to insist upon – and usually to obtain – high standards of discipline. Men convicted of robbery with violence or desertion were hanged, while looters and stragglers risked the lash. Some French commanders, like the stony-faced Marshal Davout, tried hard to prevent looting and straggling. But, as Jean Morvan observed of the French soldier: 'if the food supply fails, no punishment, no discipline, will keep him at his post . . . when food was lacking, veterans complained, conscripts groaned, guardsmen killed themselves, linesmen decamped . . .' French armies were plagued by massive short-term desertion provoked by lack of food: in mid-October 1805, half the men of Marmont's 2nd Corps were absent from the colours. Whatever deductions theorists might draw from the campaigns of Napoleon, one was clear enough: a logistic system based upon pillaging would not meet the needs of nineteenth-century war.

There were a number of crucial changes, some organizational and others technical, in the next century. Most important of the former was the militarization of supply and transport services. For centuries wagons and their drivers had been requisitioned as required, and the officials responsible for the purchase and distribution of rations had been either civilians or members of a quasi-military body like the *Intendance* or the Commissariat rather than soldiers properly speaking. Corruption and indiscipline were rife among such folk. The practice of maintaining fictitious soldiers on a regiment's books, for whom pay could be drawn and rations issued, appealed to dishonest officers and greedy officials alike: no less than 150,000 of these men of straw were removed from French muster-rolls in the first six months of the Consulate in 1799–1800. Michael Glover notes that Wellington's General Orders were 'punctuated by the record of the dismissal of commissaries for peculation', and a French general in the Crimea warned his commander-in-chief that: 'Nothing will go well here until you have two gallows set up to the left and right of your tent, one bearing an *intendant* and the other an administrative officer.'

If the men who supervised baggage-trains were sometimes more concerned with feathering their nests than with ensuring that soldiers were fed, the main preoccupation of the unfortunate drivers was with keeping themselves and their horses alive, and ensuring that their overloaded wagons did not disintegrate altogether. An eighteenth-century Prussian commentator wrote that: 'on campaign no one has to undergo such fatigue as a pack-horse leader or driver, especially in the artillery, not to mention the fact that in battle their lives stand in as much danger as any of the soldiers. If bad drivers run away, and good drivers become bad, it is only because they are poorly paid, poorly clad and poorly provided for.'

By 1870 military transport corps, with regular army personnel and regulation vehicles, had replaced the civilian personnel and equipment of yesteryear. True, under the strain of war armies would still need to lay their hands on any suitable vehicles to supplement their resources: British soldiers went up the line in London

230

buses in 1914, and the Israelis relied heavily upon requisitioned transport in 1967 and 1973. Commissariats, too, were militarized, their officers taking their recognized place within the army's hierarchy. In Britain, the Commissariat merged in 1888 with the Military Train – descendant of the Royal Wagon Train of the Napoleonic Wars and the Land Transport Corps of the Crimea — to form the Army Service Corps, and in America the Quartermaster, Pay and Subsistence Departments were merged into the Quartermaster Corps in 1912.

The technological advances of the nineteenth century influenced logistics as much as they did tactics. Preserved food, in the form of dried or salt meat, had long been available, though the fact that it was often unpalatable made it less than popular. During the Napoleonic Wars the French experimented with boiled (*bouilli*) beef in glass jars. The jar soon became a tin, and the name was anglicized into bully beef. T. E. Lawrence was later to write that 'the invention of bully-beef had modified land warfare more profoundly than the invention of gunpowder.' Although tinned food was never to replace fresh rations entirely, it was widely used from the 1860s onwards. During the American Civil War Union troops lived on a staple diet of pickled beef or pork, hardtack biscuits and canned or dessicated vegetables, and by 1914 tinned food, like the notorious British Maconochie stew, was a regular feature of life in the field. In the Second World War tinned food was even more common, especially in areas where the supply of fresh rations was difficult: the historian of the British 7th Armoured Division recorded that 'it was not unusual to have bully beef for all three meals each day – fried for breakfast, cold for lunch and stewed for supper.'

Developments in transport were nothing short of revolutionary. As early as 1840 the 20th Foot was taken from Manchester to Liverpool by railway, and six years later a Russian corps of 14,500 men, complete with horses and equipment, went 200 miles by train. In the Franco-Austrian War of 1859 the French moved no less than 604,381 men and 129,227 horses by rail, 227,649 of the men and 36,357 of the horses going straight to the theatre of war in northern Italy. The most striking benefit conferred by the railway was that on mobilization it enabled troops to be transported quickly and painlessly to their concentration areas, saving sweat and shoe-leather. Thereafter railheads could be established at which supplies of food and ammunition could be amassed for collection by the wagons of the transport corps. As fortresses fell and damage to the permanent way was repaired, railheads could themselves be moved closer to the advancing troops.

Railways proved of incalculable value to Prussia, permitting her to use a strategy of 'interior lines' to meet a threat which might materialize to the east, south or west. In the Austro-Prussian War of 1866 they enabled her to deploy nearly 200,000 men quickly and efficiently, but, the initial moves completed, the Prussians made numerous mistakes in their use of the railway, gaining experience which was to stand them in good stead in the Franco-Prussian War four years later. Even then the railway's greatest contribution lay in taking soldiers up to the borders of France in the early stages of the war, rather than in carrying supplies across them later. Most of the food and fodder consumed by German armies in France was obtained locally, and during the siege of Paris the German forces around the city were, in Martin van Creveld's terms, 'turned into a gigantic food-producing machine, the like of which had not been seen on the battlefields of Europe since the end of the eighteenth century.'

Things were rather different in the American Civil War. The sheer scale of the conflict, whose theatre of operations almost equalled the whole of Europe in size, much of it too sparsely farmed to enable armies to live off the land, thrust the railway into even greater prominence than it attained in European wars. Indeed,

The North's massive superiority in rail transport: Alexander Gardner's photograph of Manassas Junction, 1862

E. A. Pratt argued that 'such were the conditions under which the War of Secession in the United States was fought that without the help of railways it could hardly have been fought at all.'

The North's massive superiority in rail transport underscored its economic power. In 1860 there were 31,000 miles of railway in the United States, but only 9,000 of these were in the states that made up the Confederacy. Of the 470 locomotives built in the year ending 1 June 1860, the South produced a derisory nineteen. Time and again the North's solid logistics blunted the Confederate army's formidable cutting edge. A spectacular example of the impact of rail power was the movement of two Union corps from the Virginia front to Tennessee in September 1863, when 23,000 men with artillery, horses and baggage were carried 1,200 miles in twelve days: their arrival tilted the balance in the Western theatre. Less dramatic, but no less important, was the North's use of railways to supply its soldiers with food and ammunition. If it is the brilliance of Confederate commanders like Lee and Jackson that catches the eye, we should not forget that, as Peter J. Parish writes, 'the North excelled in the seven-eighths of the military iceberg which never surfaced on the field of battle itself – in supply and organization, and in the relationship of military matters to the grand strategy which embraced much else besides.'

Important though the railway's contribution to warfare was, the major wars of the second half of the nineteenth century demonstrated that there was more to logistics than making the trains run on time. Railways remained more valuable for the strategic transport of men and equipment than for operational moves close to the enemy: however efficient their railways might be, armies still needed a mass of horses, mules and wagons to carry stores from the railhead to the front. For all the excellence of its railroads, the North had half as many animals as men by 1864, and Grant's army used thirty-three wagons per 1,000 men – almost three times the scale recommended by Napoleon.

The First World War was a curious fusion of ancient and modern, in logistics

232

as in so much else. Railways were allocated a leading role in the Schlieffen Plan, the great wheeling march of the German armies into northern France. Infantry divisions had their own organic transport columns, and heavy transport companies, now using motor lorries, linked these to the railheads. In the mobile war of August–September 1914 German forward units were usually so far ahead of their railheads that the connecting links all but snapped. Rations arrived sparsely, so troops ate captured or requisitioned food. Ammunition was accorded priority throughout the lines of communication, and generally came up in time, though not without considerable waste of resources.

The quantity of fodder required – von Kluck's 5th Army, on the outer flank, had 84,000 horses consuming almost two million pounds a day – was utterly beyond the resources of German logisticians. Horses were fed off the country and, when enough fodder could not be found, they worked until they dropped from hunger and exhaustion. The Allied armies, falling back on their own lines of communication, found things easier. Even so, the men of the British Expeditionary Force sometimes went hungry on their retreat from Mons, and one regular officer wrote sadly of the 'martyrdom' of the BEF's transport animals.

As the war froze into immobility, the complexion of the logistic problem changed. Supplying armies with food became less difficult as railheads were set up close to the front line and transport companies and light railways shuttled stores forward. By 1918 the British army in France was using 900 locomotives, which travelled nine million track miles each month, carrying 800,000 tons of equipment and 260,000 of ammunition. Where the railway's iron web did not reach, the motor lorry bore the brunt. A single road was the artery of supply into Verdun in 1916. During the week beginning 28 February 25,000 tons of stores and 190,000 men passed up it. Soon there was one lorry every fourteen seconds, and each week the mileage clocked up amounted to twenty-five times the circumference of the earth. The equivalent of a division of soldiers worked on the road, and moved three-quarters of a million tons of road metal. Verdun was as much a victory for the motor lorry as anything else, and, as A. J. P. Taylor declared, 'Without the internal combustion engine, Verdun could not have been saved.' The road linking Verdun and Bar-le-

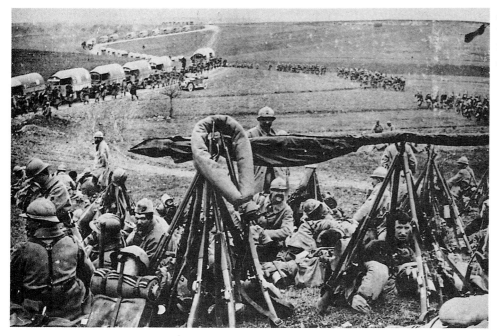

French infantry, their regimental colours cased, rest beside la Voie Sacrée, *1916*

Duc still bears the name which testifies to its lasting place in French history: *La Voie Sacrée*, the Sacred Way.

The new problem was not to feed soldiers but to keep them supplied with ammunition. Military authorities had all believed that the war would not last long, and grossly underestimated the ammunition it would require, as well as the need for replacement weapons and equipment. The supply of ammunition had rarely proved troublesome in the past, except in sieges, and both Frederick the Great and Napoleon reckoned on taking a whole campaign's supply of ammunition into the field with them. Even in 1870 the consumption of artillery ammunition was remarkably low, averaging 199 rounds per gun in the German army, scarcely more than the 157 rounds carried within each corps. The advent of the breech-loading rifle did not result in the exhaustion of infantry ammunition: the average Prussian soldier fired only fifty-six rounds, fewer than he carried, and far fewer than were available within the corps' own wagons. Local ammunition shortages did occur, but could usually be remedied by redistribution. Moreover, until the middle of the ninteenth century much ammunition was interchangeable in any case and armies could, *in extremis*, use captured stocks.

The armies of 1914 simply lost control of ammunition expenditure. In the first six months of the war the British army fired one million shells, nearly four times as many as it had in the whole of the Boer War. It began the war with 1,500 rounds in stock for each of its 18-pounder field guns, but by October these were sometimes restricted to four rounds per gun per day because of shortages. Many riflemen expended all the 300 rounds they carried in a single action: one company of 2nd Battalion, the Grenadier Guards, fired 24,000 rounds in twenty-four hours. Expenditure outran supply in all armies, and it was only by the transformation of their munitions industries – with profound social and economic implications – that they were able to cope.

A British ammunition dump, 1917

Ammunition filled an ever-increasing amount of space in railway wagons and motor lorries: by 1916 a British division in the line needed some twenty wagons of food and thirty of ammunition each day. Set-piece battles consumed prodigious quantities. British gunners fired 1,723,873 rounds in the preliminary bombardment on the Somme in 1916 – each of the 18-pounders began the battle with 1,000 rounds on the gun position. Even this was dwarfed by the 4,282,550 shells fired in the early stages of the Third Battle of Ypres the following year: this bombardment cost the (then) staggering sum of £22 million, and represented a year's production by 55,000 munitions workers.

The war also witnessed a marked rise in the number of men employed behind the lines. At the end of November 1918 the American Expeditionary Force in France had just over a million men in the forward zone, with 855,600 in the rear areas. Most of the latter were service troops, and to their number must be added 47,000 civilian workers and 35,000 prisoners of war being used as labourers. The rear of an army was now a rambling suburb of depots, workshops and transport parks, inhabited by drivers, mechanics, armourers, artificers, storemen and clerks, all servants of machinery in the age of industrialized war.

The mechanization of armies had far-reaching logistic consequences. J. F. C. Fuller pointed out that, although an army's requirements for petrol would grow as motor vehicles replaced horses, petrol was less bulky and more easily transported than fodder. He lent weight to his case by noting that though the British had shipped 5,253,538 tons of ammunition to France during the First War, the greatest single item of tonnage was oats and hay – 5,438,602 tons of it. Horses munched their way through fodder even when resting: motor transport used fuel only when running.

Nevertheless, mechanization had other implications which its authors could scarcely have guessed at. Fodder, for all its bulk, could easily be obtained in many

A British soldier leads an ammunition-mule from the mud; a light railway crosses the road behind him, and a truck approaches

theatres of war. Oil was a scarcer resource, and military demands – to say nothing of its industrial and domestic use – turned it into a strategic commodity in its own right. Ironically it was Germany, who led the way in mechanization, who found herself not only short of fuel but also out-produced in vehicles, weapons and equipment by her enemies. Fuller had described 1914–18 as 'a war between two great supply systems. A war between the Midlands and the Ruhr . . .' Major-General Brehon B. Somervell of the US Army's Service Force proclaimed in 1942 that the very fact of German mechanization guaranteed America's ultimate victory.

The road ahead is dim with the dust of battles still unfought. How long that road is, no one can know. But it is shorter than it would have been had not our enemies misjudged us and themselves. For, when Hitler put his war on wheels he ran it straight down our alley. When he hitched his chariot to an internal combustion engine, he opened up a new battle front – a front that we know well. It's called Detroit.

The statistics of United States war production underline Somervell's point. In 1943, 90,000 aircraft rolled off American production lines: even this impressive figure was exceeded by the 100,000 of 1944. 84,027 tanks were delivered to the US Army, 29,497 of them in 1943. No less than 2,166,093 trucks of various types were received by the army, with 180,417 jeeps being delivered in 1942 alone. Whatever item of war material one considers further emphasizes America's phenomenal industrial muscle. Nearly six million miles of barbed wire and 7,570 locomotives were issued to the army, while the navy totalled 78,000 vessels of all sorts by the end of the war. Some 2,500 Liberty ships were built during the war: each spent an average of fifteen days under construction, but one was built in a lightning 80½ hours. The Kaiser Yard launched its fiftieth escort carrier one year to the day after launching its first. Soviet industrial production was also awesome, particularly in view of the fact that vast industrial areas had been overrun by the advancing Germans. From 1943 onwards the Russians built around 30,000 armoured vehicles a year: German production peaked, with only 19,000 vehicles, in 1944.

In mounting her devastating Blitzkrieg operations in 1939–41, Germany fired the starting pistol for a race that she could never win. Martin van Creveld emphasizes that: 'For the Russian campaign, the Wehrmacht never had sufficient means available, and this was even more true of raw materials, reserve stocks and means of transportation than it was of combat forces.' Rommel's campaign in North Africa was hamstrung by inadequate logistics. 'For all Rommel's tactical brilliance,' concludes van Creveld, 'the problem of supplying an Axis force for an advance into the Middle East was insoluble.' The creation of panzer divisions represented a concentration of finite resources which had painful consequences for less favoured formations: as late as 1944 the infantry divisions facing the Allies in Normandy relied heavily upon horse-drawn transport.

In contrast, the Allies built up a logistic superiority which enabled them to crush the Germans in a *Materialschlacht* – a battle of equipment. Logistic considerations were a key ingredient in the plan for *Overlord*, the invasion of Europe: British and American logistic planners were overcautious before and after the invasion. Nevertheless, careful preparation paid dividends. The destruction of one of the prefabricated MULBERRY harbours and the severe damage inflicted on the other in the storm of 19–20 July did not prevent the steady build-up of stores and equipment in the Normandy beachhead. By 29 July over one million personnel, 332,654 vehicles and over 1½ million tons had been landed: it was a remarkable achievement. And, when the break-out at last came, the logistic services worked flat-out to meet the demands of the fighting troops. In the American sector, the 'Red Ball Express', with 132 truck companies – nearly 6,000 vehicles – operated

Germans on the march, summer 1941: the horse was still an essential component of war

Materialschlacht*: the Normandy beachhead, 1944*

on a one-way loop of road, moving over 12,000 tons of supplies a day at the peak of its activities.

Allied mastery of a new aspect of logistics was emphasized in another theatre of war: the Far East. In Burma, where movement on the ground was often so difficult as to be almost impossible, air transport came into its own. It enabled Wingate's Chindits to operate behind the Japanese lines. As Sir Robert Thompson, himself a veteran of the campaign, said: 'This air supply became so efficient that the troops relied on it completely. You could run yourself down to one day's rations or less, you could go a day almost without rations and know perfectly well that if you demanded a supply drop at 10.00 pm one night in a particular area of jungle or in a paddy field alongside you knew you were going to get it . . .'

Anti-aircraft gunners watch a Dakota drop supplies in Burma, 1944

Air supply also transformed more conventional operations. When the British-Indian offensive into the Arakan was sharply counter-attacked, the Japanese cut off entire formations which stood fast and fought on, supplied from the air. The great Japanese offensive on March 1944 broke against the bastions of Imphal and Kohima: once again air supply gave the Allies a decisive advantage. Well might Admiral Mountbatten, Supreme Commander of South-East Asia Command, write that: 'it was not just a question of auxiliary air supply, because ninety-six per cent of our supplies to the Fourteenth Army went by air.'

The proliferation of new equipment, motor vehicles, aircraft, tanks, artillery pieces, small arms and radio sets, brought fresh problems with it. Not only did these items have to be designed, produced and finally supplied to units in the field: they also had to be recovered and repaired when they were damaged or broke down. Even at the end of the war, when much equipment was unsophisticated by today's standards, simply keeping it in working order required large numbers of skilled men with specialist training. In 1945, 36,000 of the British soldiers in Europe – nearly 5% of the British Liberation Army's total strength – wore the cap badge of the Royal Electrical and Mechanical Engineers. The overall proportion of service troops was infinitely higher: 43% of the men of the US Army overseas were in so that airborne soldiers enjoy high morale, which makes them an asset even if they are committed to battle as conventional infantry. It was as natural for the British to employ two parachute battalions in the Falklands in 1982 as it was for the Americans to send the 82nd Airborne Division to Grenada. And, even if the dropping of major units is a high-risk venture, techniques like HALO – High-Altitude, Low-Opening – permit individuals or small groups to be inserted covertly for the purpose of reconnaissance or sabotage.

Opposite: German parachutists jump from their Junkers 52s over Crete, May 1941

The modern land battle cannot be divorced from its aerial dimension, so much so that US military theorists talk in terms of an 'AirLand Battle' in Western Europe, in which transport helicopters switch troops from position to position, anti-tank helicopters destroy advancing armour, and long-range missiles, ground- and air-launched, flay the Warsaw Pact's second attacking echelon. Critics of this doctrine suspect that it may be asking too much of both technology and the individual's ability to sustain the stress of combat. There are also claims that aircraft and their pilots alike are simply too expensive to risk in the dangerous skies over a modern battlefield. Such fears may lead to radical changes in aircraft design and employment, perhaps with the emphasis on increasing the roles of RPVs and reducing the expense of specialist ground-attack aircraft. The application of air power may

British parachutists at Arnhem, September 1944

The American way of warfare: troops of the 1st Marine Division are supplied during Operation Citrus in Vietnam, 1967

comfortably – and longer – than the men at the cutting edge of war. Logisticians are awarded their own unflattering nicknames, like the German army's First World War *Ettapenschweine* or the REMF (rear echelon mother-fuckers) of Vietnam. They sometimes fuel their detractors' resentment by absorbing more than their fair share of food, clothing and equipment: during the Second World War the American soldier-cartoonist Bill Mauldin complained that many items got 'shortstopped by some of the rear echelon soldiers who wanted to look like the combat men they saw in the magazines.'

Demands for economy, and the hostility often felt by fighting soldiers for the men who feed, equip and transport them, should not obscure the real importance of logistics. As the US Army's study of the topic emphasizes: 'What counts is the total of effective fire power that can be brought to bear against the enemy. If the greatest total of effective power can be delivered with one combat man for each service man, then that is the required ratio, but if 1,000 service troops for one combat man are needed to achieve that maximum, then that is the desired ratio.' And yet the practical problems remain immense. If technology helps to solve them by making transport, stock-keeping and bulk handling easier, as well as by creating equipment which can be quickly tested and repaired, it worsens them by increasing ammunition consumption, and by spawning high-cost, high-value weapons systems, many of which require skilled maintenance and are anything but soldier-proof. The Falklands campaign underlined that war is now more dependent upon logistics and logisticians – transport pilots, fork-lift truck drivers and missile artificers – than at any other period of history. It lent new weight to Field-Marshal Lord Wavell's judgement that: 'The more I see of war, the more I realise how it all depends upon administration and transportation.'

240

In the second half of the twentieth century warfare has been increasingly influenced by a soldier whose fighting spirit owes little to elaborate drill, externally imposed discipline or symbolic uniform, and whose sinews of war are more pliant than those of conventional armies. The irregular appears in many guises. He may be a peasant or townsman, fighting covertly against a government he despises; an intellectual visionary, striving to bring about the collapse of society in the hope that something new and worthwhile will emerge from the rubble; or even a specially trained member of a regular army, using the irregular tactics of subversion, ambush, demolitions and dirty tricks. In a sense the irregular fights war in the minor key: pitched battles are relatively rare. But it is war at its harshest, in which nice restraints are jettisoned, civilians become the targets for both irregulars and their enemies, and torture and murder assume a bitter logic of their own. Whether fighting in a revolutionary army, or in a specialist unit operating behind enemy lines in a conventional war, the irregular needs initiative, perseverance and dogged courage: for him the path of glory all too often leads to the scaffold or the firing-squad.

There are two distinct aspects to irregular warfare. Firstly, it is the classic weapon used by populations against occupying armies or oppressive rulers, and in this context it has been lent new importance by the writings and example of such figures as Mao Tse-tung, Che Guevara and Carlos Marighela. Secondly, regular armies have produced their own specialists in irregular warfare, for use against either a guerrilla opponent or a conventional enemy: the British Special Air Service or the American Green Berets both have established reputations as what might not unfairly be termed 'irregular regulars'.

The prevalence of irregular warfare in recent years can easily mislead us into thinking that it is something new. In fact, the irregular is as old as war itself: irregular tactics like the raid and the ambush stretch back into prehistory and are older than the formalized tactics of conventional war. In the fifteenth century B.C. the Hittite King Mursilius complained, in tones familiar to harassed commanders of later generations, that his irregular opponents did not dare to attack him by day, but fell upon him by night.

When the Hebrew leader Gideon attacked the Midianites at Ein Harod he employed archetypal irregular tactics. His 300 picked men, divided into three equal companies, were equipped with trumpets and torches hidden in jars. The book of Judges tells what happened when Gideon's force approached the Midianite camp.

So Gideon and the hundred men who were with him came to the outskirts of the camp at the beginning of the middle watch, when they had just set the watch; and they blew the trumpets and smashed the jars that were in their hands. And the three companies blew the trumpets and broke the jars, holding in their left hands the torches, and in their right hands the trumpets to blow; and they cried, 'A sword for the LORD and for Gideon!'

They stood every man in his place round about the camp, and all the army ran: they cried out and fled. When they blew the three hundred trumpets, the LORD set every man's sword against his fellow and against all the army; and the army fled . . .

There can be few better examples of a surprise attack by night, making good use of noise and light to confuse the enemy.

It was early-nineteenth-century Spain that brought a new word, guerrilla – literally, little war – into the military vocabulary. The countryside of Spain, with its wide expanses of rock and scrub, has long been a favourite haunt of the irregular: in the second and first centuries B.C. irregulars under their leaders Viriathus and Sartorius led the Romans an exhausting dance in this inhospitable terrain. In the Peninsular War of 1808–13 the Spanish fought what was to become regarded as a classic example of irregular war. The French had little difficulty in disposing of the Spanish regular army when they invaded in 1808. But the *juntas*, the local provincial governments, demanded continued resistance, and in April 1809 the central *junta* called for a people's war against the invader.

All the ingredients were there. Not only the countryside, but also the Spanish character, were well-suited to this type of warfare. There had been a good many smugglers and bandits in Spain before the war, and some of these *bandoleros* now took the opportunity to legitimize their activities. Other irregular bands consisted of a mixture of peasants, farmers and intellectuals, and one was led by a priest, Father Merino. Perhaps the most successful guerrilla leader was Espos y Mina, a twenty-eight-year-old farmer who took to the hills of Navarre in 1809. He began his raids a year later, and soon attracted a large number of French troops to the area. His greatest triumph came in the spring of 1812 at the pass of Salinas, when he captured a huge French convoy, killing or wounding most of its 5,000-strong escort and freeing 450 Spanish prisoners.

Yet it is doubtful if the guerrillas, effective though they were, would have accomplished anything of lasting importance had it not been for the proximity of a powerful ally. While the guerrillas operated in the French rear, falling upon isolated detachments, attacking convoys and cutting couriers' throats, Wellington's field army was the main focus of French attention. There were strong mutual interests linking Wellington and the guerrillas. Wellington supplied the guerrillas with some arms and prevented the French from concentrating against them. They, for their part, tied down French troops who would otherwise have taken the field against the British. The importance of this relationship was not lost upon subsequent theorists, some of whom were to argue that, however bold guerrillas might be, they could not win a war without regular assistance.

The Spanish experience highlighted another feature of irregular warfare, one grimly depicted in Goya's *Disasters of War*. The French often refused to regard the guerrillas as legitimate combatants, and killed them out of hand when they caught them. The guerrillas responded by butchering their own captives, sometimes in a particularly cruel way. The French in turn replied by burning villages and destroying crops, and distinctions between combatants and non-combatants became blurred. Guerrilla warfare has become synonymous with this sort of brutality, a brutality born of each side's refusal to acknowledge that the other had any right to be fighting at all. It certainly did not start in Spain: nor, alas, was it to end there.

The harsh face of the irregular's war grinned through the veneer of military protocol during the Franco-Prussian War of 1870–1 and the Boer War of 1899–1902. As the Germans invaded France in 1870, bands of irregular *francs-tireurs* sprang up to oppose them. Prince Frederick Charles of Prussia, echoing

242

Mursilius, lamented that: 'There is for a commander nothing more oppressive than a situation which is not clear, nothing more trying than bands of armed irregular troops, aided by the population and the nature of the country, and relying for support on a strong army in the neighbourhood.' The Germans denied French irregulars the status of legitimate combatants. 'We are hunting them down pitilessly,' wrote Bismarck to his wife: 'they are not soldiers: we are treating them as murderers.'

For the British, the most difficult part of the Boer War was not the period between October 1899 and June 1900, when they fought the formed armies of the Boer Republics, but the guerrilla phase which followed it and which dragged on for almost two years. At first, Boer commandos operated almost as they pleased in the country districts, ambushing convoys, cutting the railway and swooping on isolated outposts. Gradually the British tightened their grip by herding the occupants of outlying farms into 'concentration camps' (many of whose inhabitants, unused to communal living, died of disease), and by pursuing a scorched earth policy in the depopulated areas. Lines of blockhouses secured the railways, and flying columns carried out carefully coordinated 'drives' against their will-o'-the-wisp opponents. Farms were burned and sheep and cattle slaughtered: General French's Transvaal drive in early 1901 bagged 272,752 head of stock, a devastating blow to the Boer economy. Men from the Transvaal and Orange Free State were granted combatant status, but Cape Colony Boers were deemed rebels and risked hanging when captured. If some British techniques, notably anti-guerrilla drives, were to become a standard repertoire for other armies faced with a similar problem, the war's uglier side, with its gutted farms, dead civilians and executed 'rebels', boded ill for the future.

The deadlock of the Western Front gave little opportunity for the use of irregular warfare in Europe during the First World War. But there were irregular operations in East Africa, where the German Colonel von Lettow-Vorbeck fought a masterly campaign against superior British forces, and in the Middle East, where the British

supported the Arabs in their revolt against Turkish rule. The latter campaign was epitomized, at least as far as the Western public was concerned, by the enigmatic figure of T. E. Lawrence or, as he became known, Lawrence of Arabia. The publicity which Lawrence attracted can easily persuade us to overrate his importance, for ultimately it was British regular forces in Palestine, not Arab irregulars in the desert, who defeated the Turks. But Lawrence did emphasize several key aspects of irregular war in the context of a struggle against a foreign occupying power. Mobility and range were crucial, and tactics centred upon, as he put it, 'tip and run, not pushes but strokes.'

The Hejaz railway, the Turks' main artery of supply, was a prime target for Lawrence's strokes. In 1917 he exploded a mine beneath a train near Mudowara station, and his account of the action perfectly depicts the lethal, smoky confusion of an ambush.

There followed a terrific roar, and the line vanished from sight beneath a spouting column of black dust and smoke a hundred feet high and wide . . . there succeeded a deathly silence, with no cry of men or rifle-shot, as the now grey mist of the explosion drifted from the line towards us, and over our ridge until it was lost in the hills . . .

Before I had climbed to the guns the hollow was alive with shots, with the brown figures of the Beduin leaping forward to grips with the enemy. I looked round to see what was happening so quickly, and saw the train stationary and dismembered along the track, with its wagon sides jumping under the bullets which riddled them, while Turks were falling out from the far doors to gain the shelter of the railway embankment.

As I watched, our machine-guns chattered out over my head, and the long row of Turks on the carriage roofs rolled over, and were swept off the top like bales of cotton before the furious shower of bullets which stormed along the roofs and splashed yellow chips from the planking.

Central to Lawrence's philosophy of war was the conviction that: 'Our duty was to attain our end with the greatest economy of life, since life was more precious to us than money or time.' This humane belief may have been tenable in the specific

244

circumstances of the Arab revolt, but it was less useful to the population of Europe, faced, after German victories in the early stages of the Second World War, with the task of contending with a tough, self-confident occupying power. In France, the Resistance was hampered by friction between its various groups, understandable reluctance to provoke German reprisals and the fact that much of France was unsuitable for guerrilla operations.

There were, though, some areas, particularly in the south-east, where the Resistance could take to the scrub – the *maquis* – and operate almost as small-scale regular detachments. The risks of such boldness were always great. In June 1944 the Germans took the Maquis strongholds of Mont-Mouchet and the Vercors plateau, inflicting heavy casualties on their defenders. The less spectacular, but cumulatively more successful, attacks by the Resistance on road and rail transport on the eve of the Normandy landings were also costly. The SS Panzer Division *Das Reich*, delayed on its march to Normandy by air attacks as well as Resistance sabotage, destroyed the village of Oradour-sur-Glane and massacred its inhabitants. The Resistance undoubtedly made an important contribution to Allied success in the summer of 1944, but the price was always high. Perhaps its most important role was psychological: by carrying on the struggle the Resistance not only helped to keep the Germans at full stretch but helped to keep alight France's spiritual flame.

Irregular tactics were easier in Russia, where the vast area overrun by the Germans offered tremendous scope for the activities of partisans. The Russian High Command used partisans operating in the German rear as an adjunct to its regular armies, and in May 1943 the partisans came under direct army command. They claimed, in all, to have inflicted 1½ million casualties on the Germans, and to have destroyed 4,000 tanks and 16,000 locomotives. These figures are undoubtedly overoptimistic. Nevertheless, the partisans did impose a steady drain on German manpower, and at times – as during the ill-fated German offensive at Kursk in August 1943 – their activities had a palpable effect upon operations at the front. What is worth noting is that harsh German reprisals, together with the brutal treatment casually meted out to so many Russian civilians, actually helped to drive the population of occupied areas into the arms of the partisans.

In Yugoslavia things were rather different. While the Russian partisans operated in support of a regular army, in Yugoslavia the partisans *were* the army. Although their effectiveness was seriously limited by the political divisions which bedevilled Yugoslavia, and whose ferocity is demonstrated by the sad fact that more Yugoslavs were killed by other Yugoslavs than by German or Italian soldiers, they grew into a formidable fighting force. This was partly owing to the personality of their leader, Marshal Tito, to whom even Goebbels paid grudging tribute, and partly thanks to the rugged terrain of Yugoslavia and the hardiness of its inhabitants.

There was often a political element even in guerrilla struggles against an invader. The fighting in Yugoslavia was as much a contest between the Communists and royalists for the leadership of post-war Yugoslavia as a struggle against the Germans and Italians. It remains perfectly possible for a resistance or separatist movement to be motivated by little more than a desire to oust the occupying force. Nevertheless, an important change in irregular warfare has occurred over the past century, as it has taken on a crucial role in the revolutionary process in many parts of the world.

Irregular warfare did not occupy any special place in Karl Marx's world view. He evolved the concept of the class struggle, suggesting that capitalism was merely a transient phase in human history. Eventually the urban working class would rise up and seize power, creating a society in which, with neither oppressed classes nor private property, mankind would be emancipated. Marx believed that the worker's rising was historically inevitable, and would occur more or less spontaneously.

The risks of irregular war: two of Tito's partisans hanged by the Germans

Tito (centre) and his senior officials on the Island of Vis, 1943

Lenin, however, was a more practical politician, and recognized that the proletariat required organization and leadership if it were to triumph.

The Russian Revolution and Communist victory in the subsequent civil war owed a great deal to Lenin's concept of party organization. But although irregular warfare was used from time to time during the civil war, it was simply because it happened to be the most suitable tactic available, not because Lenin and his followers attached specific revolutionary significance to it. Trotsky, the Revolution's dominant military brain, called it 'a necessary and adequate weapon in the early phase of the civil war.' In the wake of Russian success, it was tempting for Communists elsewhere to study Lenin's concept of revolution and to follow the Russian example in their own countries. There were short-lived Communist successes in parts of Germany and in Hungary, but by the early 1920s it began to seem as if revolution on the Russian pattern was not easily exportable.

Karl Marx

V. I. Lenin

The Communist Party of China, founded in 1921, initially toed the Moscow line. But although there was some industry in China, the tiny industrial proletariat was outweighed by the vast mass of rural peasantry, which did not fit so easily into Marxist-Leninist logic. Attempts at urban uprisings in Nanchang and Canton failed miserably, and from 1927 the Chinese Communists concentrated on the countryside. As their future leader Mao Tse-tung wrote, slavishly following the Russian pattern was pointless: 'these laws of war and military directives in the Soviet Union embody the special characteristics of the civil war and the Red war in the Soviet Union: if we copy them and apply them mechanically and allow no change whatsoever, it will be like whittling down the feet to fit the shoes, and we shall be defeated.' It was only after the epic Long March of 1934–5, in which the main Communist force travelled, according to Mao, over six thousand miles in just over a year to reach the refuge of Shensi province in the North, that a new strategy was formally adopted.

In the wilderness of Shensi, Mao set about formulating a definitively Chinese doctrine of revolution. This took some time to evolve, and it was not until after the Japanese had invaded China in 1937 that it came to full fruition. Faced with an enemy clearly superior by any conventional index of military strength, only protracted war, in which the insurgents traded space for time and used ideology to forge an unbreakable will, could enable them to win.

There were three phases to Mao's protracted war. Firstly, in the war's early stages, when the revolutionaries were on the strategic defensive, the population had to be infiltrated and organized. Mao argued that the people were to the revolutionary what water is to the fish: without popular support the insurgents would perish. This support was to be won by kindness rather than by terror, and Mao emphasized that his soldiers should treat civilians well, respect their belongings and pay for all goods and services. Secure areas were formed to provide the revolutionaries with a firm base, and were, in effect, the nuclei of the Communist state.

Guerrilla warfare came into its own in the second phase – the strategic stalemate – when the revolutionaries sought to wear down enemy strength and to expand their secure areas. Finally, in the strategic counter-offensive, the revolutionaries would embark upon conventional warfare, taking over the countryside first and then seizing control of the towns. The process was adaptable, for if the revolutionaries suffered a setback they could simply reduce the scope of their activities while they gathered strength. Guerrillas had two functions. They operated in support of regular Communist units, and at the same time transformed themselves into regular units, ready for the third stage of the conflict. In fact, the Communists never entered this phase of war against the Japanese, for the Second World War ended

before it could be carried into effect. But they did employ it against their Nationalist rivals, exhausted and discredited by the war. In the last bout of a revolutionary contest which had begun in the 1920s, Communist armies engaged the Nationalists in pitched battles. Peking fell in January 1949, and on 1 October that year Mao stood atop the Gate of Heavenly Peace in the capital and proclaimed the Chinese People's Republic. His victory was of lasting importance: not only was there now an alternative to the Marxist-Leninist view of the revolutionary process, but it was one in which the irregular had a vital role to play.

The Chinese version of revolutionary war was exported, with only slight modifications, to Vietnam. The Vietnamese Communist leader Ho Chi Minh and his Chinese-trained military commander Vo Nguyen Giap fought a protracted war against the French between 1946 and 1954, wearing down French strength by guerrilla warfare before emerging to fight and win the decisive battle of Dien Bien Phu in the spring of 1954. After the partition of Vietnam, the same revolutionary process was used against the South Vietnamese and their American allies. The Vietnam War was not, as it sometimes appeared in the West, a guerrilla war pure and simple. It fell into the classic Maoist three-phase structure, with minor guerrilla actions taking place alongside the creation of safe areas and the mounting of large-scale conventional operations like the siege of Khe Sanh in 1968.

Time, space and will were the essential elements of Ho's strategy, just as they had been of Mao's. Despite her massive material superiority, America was unable to win a quick victory, and a long war, with its increasing demands upon conscript manpower, produced widespread opposition to the war within the United States. Once President Nixon had brought America out of the war, the shaky Republic of Vietnam crumbled under irresistible pressure as the Viet Cong and North Vietnamese unleashed the full weight of conventional warfare. Saigon fell in April 1975: the Maoist blueprint had achieved its second major success.

Yet the Chinese-inspired irregular was not invincible. Immediately after the Second World War, the Malayan Communist Party attempted to end British rule in Malaya by exploiting friction between the Chinese and Malay communities and infiltrating the trade unions. When urban riots failed to overthrow the government, the Communists took to guerrilla warfare. British-owned plantations were attacked and their labourers intimidated, and the insurgents made numerous converts amongst the squatter population living on the jungle fringes. A State of Emergency was declared in June 1948 but, after an initial drop in guerrilla activity, there was a renewed outburst in October 1949, with no less than 400 incidents, many of them raids on police posts.

In April 1950 General Sir Harold Briggs arrived as Director of Operations. With him came a package of measures designed to remove support for the guerrillas and defeat their bands in the jungle. The squatters – 423,000 of them – were rehoused in 400 'New Villages', where they could be protected and watched. Identity cards were already compulsory, and these helped the police to monitor movement. Rations were issued to villagers and, to prevent them from being passed on to the guerrillas, rice was pre-cooked and tins already pierced so that the food had to be eaten immediately. State and District War Executive Committees were established to ensure intimate co-operation between the civil, military and police authorities, and particular attention was paid to the collection and collation of intelligence. Home Guards were formed, and the strength of the police was substantially increased.

The guerrillas scored an important propaganda victory by murdering the High Commissioner, Sir Henry Gurney, in October 1951, but their plight became increasingly unenviable. Gurney's replacement, who combined the posts of High Commissioner and Supreme Commander, was General – later Field-Marshal – Sir Gerald Templer. The directive which appointed him stressed that it was Britain's policy for Malaya to become self-governing in due course, and Templer himself emphasized that there was complete integration between winning the war and running the country.

The British response to the insurgency was, therefore, based upon a fusion of military and political measures, just as the guerrillas themselves sought to combine politics and force. Templer refused to be rushed, and his careful and deliberate

The Chinese-inspired guerrilla was not invincible: British troops on patrol in Malaya

co-ordination of military pressure, propaganda and fair administration so sapped guerrilla strength that Malaya was secure enough to be granted independence on 31 August 1957. It is tempting to compare British experience in Malaya with that of the Americans in Vietnam. And, although there are many differences between the two campaigns – geography, population and external support to name but three of the most important – some authorities argue that the British campaign in Malaya was a model for counter-insurgency against a Maoist enemy. Indeed, the British counter-insurgency expert Sir Robert Thompson went so far as to say: 'I am convinced that the counter-measures developed and proved in Malaya . . . would have succeeded in the early stages in Vietnam if they had been suitably adapted and consistently and intelligently applied.' Perhaps this comment contains its own counter-argument, for the very fact that the Americans did not control the government of South Vietnam was in itself an immovable obstacle in the way of a balanced and consistent policy which combined civil and military components.

The 1950s and 1960s saw irregular warfare flare up across the globe, with wars of national liberation being fought against colonial powers in Africa and Asia, and attacks on unpopular domestic regimes in Latin America. Fidel Castro's victory in Cuba in 1958 followed an almost Maoist campaign in which the insurgents defeated President Fulgencio Batista's inefficient army in the countryside before taking control of the towns. Castro's triumph encouraged his most celebrated lieutenant, the Argentinian Ernesto 'Che' Guevara, to postulate his own thesis on revolution, arguing that popular forces with rural bases could defeat a regular army, and that a small guerrilla band could create what Régis Debray called 'revolution within the revolution' by winning victories which generated popular support and produced the climate of revolution. Guevara's theories were in part the result of overoptimistic interpretation of events in Cuba, where the Batista regime had been deeply unpopular amongst all classes of society, and his attempts to translate theory into practice failed disastrously in Bolivia in 1967. His guerrilla band, operating in an inhospitable area where strangers were mistrusted and the influence of the Catholic church was strong, was hunted down mercilessly by US-trained Bolivian troops, and Guevara himself was killed.

Perhaps the most serious of the mistakes made by Guevara was his underestimation of the importance of cities in Latin America. Throughout the 1960s families flocked from the countryside into the towns, and all too often finished up living in the cramped and squalid shanty-towns of the 'misery belts' which surround many Latin American cities. These slum dwellers, young, discontented, rootless and concentrated near all the vulnerable facilities of modern cities, were far more promising material for revolution than the conservative peasants. It was a Brazilian, Carlos Marighela, who played a key part in adapting insurgency to this new situation. Marighela, whose pamphlet *The Handbook of Urban Guerrilla Warfare* was published after its author had been killed in a bank raid in 1969, argued, like Guevara, that the revolutionary moment could be created. But where Guevara had sought without success to create the revolutionary *foco* in the countryside, Marighela looked to the towns.

Marighela hoped to foment revolution by polarizing society. Bombings and assassinations, together with strikes and demonstrations – all of them designed to gain the maximum publicity – would provoke the security forces into overreacting and at the same time increase support for the insurgents. Although Marighela's hopes that such tactics would form the catalyst of revolution were misplaced, his concentration on the cities was undoubtedly correct, and urban guerrilla movements in many Latin American states achieved impressive short-term successes. Yet usually their long-term effect was to produce a repressive regime, with a military

and police apparatus designed to combat the urban guerrilla. In Uruguay, for example, the skilful, almost puckish *Tupamaros* succeeded in bringing down a liberal government and replacing it by an authoritarian regime which promptly obliterated them. As Régis Debray observed, they had dug the grave of democracy and fallen into it themselves.

Terror has long been a weapon in the arsenal of the irregular and his enemies. Some insurgents, like Guevara, eschewed it on moral grounds: others maintained that the end justified the means, and that minor acts of terrorism were in themselves insignificant when compared with the coercive apparatus – 'state terror' – at the disposal of governments. Whatever its moral status, terrorism has several practical attractions. Firstly, terror tactics are relatively easy to employ, and therefore commend themselves to an organization which may lack sophisticated weapons or popular support. Secondly, terrorism produces a disproportionate amount of publicity, a commodity highly prized by a separatist movement or political faction which may feel that it has no other way of seizing the world's attention: a single bomb planted in a rush-hour street will attract more publicity than a pitched battle up in the hills. Lastly, spectacular atrocities illustrate that the government's ability

252

to rule is weakened, and provoke exasperated security forces into overreaction.

On Friday 21 July 1972 the Provisional IRA set nineteen bombs in central Belfast, killing nine people and injuring 130, many of them appallingly seriously. 'Bloody Friday' is typical of the attacks mounted by irregulars for whom terror is an irresistibly attractive weapon. Sometimes, as Professor Walter Laqueur observed, such terrorism came to resemble the workings of an international corporation. On 30 May 1972, for example, three members of the Japanese Red Army, acting on behalf of the Popular Front for the Liberation of Palestine, attacked airline passengers at Israel's Lod airport. They killed twenty-one and wounded many more in an outrage whose media coverage rivalled that accorded to the Munich Olympic massacre in September the same year. Skyjackings, too, brought spectacular publicity, and also provided the terrorists with hostages who could be used in bargaining with governments.

The spread of international terrorism was something which concerned the other irregulars – special forces employed by conventional armies. In 1977 the West German counter-terrorist group IG9, with assistance from the British SAS, successful stormed a skyjacked Lufthansa airliner at Mogadishu in Somalia. On 6 May 1980 the SAS pulled off its most spectacular anti-terrorist coup to date. In a mere eleven minutes, a detachment from its counter-revolutionary warfare team burst into the Iranian embassy at Prince's Gate, rescuing twenty hostages and killing or capturing all the terrorists. Although operations like Mogadishu and Prince's Gate are the most publicized role of special forces, there is a great deal more to 'the government's irregulars' than combating terrorism. Indeed, for centuries irregulars have made their own distinctive contribution to conventional operations.

The government's irregulars in action: the SAS storm the Iranian Embassy at Prince's Gate, 6 May 1980

The need for irregular troops was always acute when European powers were engaged in struggles against more primitive peoples in rough country on the fringes of their territory. Sometimes the simplest solution was to hire some of the wild men to fight the others, a scheme used by the eighteenth-century Austrians in the Balkans and by the British on the North-West Frontier of India. If genuine wild men were not available, then at least soldiers could be dressed to resemble them, but there was always the risk that such troops would adopt some of the less desirable habits of the irregulars they aped. After the battle of Mollwitz in 1741 Frederick the Great warned that: 'women, hussars and baggage drivers, if caught plundering, will be hanged without more ado.'

In the eighteenth century the British army experimented with irregulars who were better suited to operations in the forests of North America than were the stolid redcoats of line infantry regiments. Most striking of the irregular units raised during this period was Rogers' Rangers, locally recruited and characterized by practicality and self-reliance rather than conventional military discipline. Some of these units were disbanded when the need for them seemed to have passed: others, like the 60th Regiment (Royal Americans) were retained, to add an element of initiative and flexibility to campaigns in other areas. Indeed, some of the most effective Austrian troops in the Seven Years War were the Croats, recruited in what is now Yugoslavia. 'Agile, hardy and utterly loyal,' as the historian Christopher Duffy writes, 'they excelled in open-order "Indian-style" fighting, and they sought out difficult country where the close-order skills of the Prussians were at a discount.'

During the Second World War some British officers advocated taking an irregular approach to war in the desert, just as their ancestors had to fighting in North America. The result was the creation of a number of special units for operations behind enemy lines: amongst them was the Special Air Service. The principles enunciated by its founder, Colonel David Stirling, lie at the very heart of the

254

motivation and training of modern special forces, just as they mirror the robust enthusiasm of eighteenth-century irregulars. 'Hitherto,' declared Stirling,

battalion strength formations, whether Airborne formations or Commandos, had no basic sub-unit smaller than a section or a troop consisting of an NCO plus eight or ten men and it was the NCO who had to do most of the thinking for what was disrespectfully referred to as 'the thundering herd' behind him. In the SAS each of the four men was trained to a high level of proficiency in the whole range of SAS capability, and, additionally, each man was trained to have at least one special expertise according to his aptitude. In carrying out an operation – often in pitch-dark – each SAS man in each module was exercising his individual perception and judgement at full stretch.

The SAS, like their comrades in the Long-Range Desert Group and their maritime counterparts in the Special Boat Service, concentrated on long-range penetration to achieve their effort. Other special forces were used on a much larger scale. The British employed their Commandos on a wide spectrum of operations, from small raids against the coast of occupied Europe to large-scale seaborne assaults. The Commandos were named, ironically enough, after the mobile Boer forces which had so taxed the British in South Africa at the turn of the century. The US Army's Rangers harked back to the tough, independent traditions of eighteenth-century backwoods irregulars, and specialized in missions where dash, high morale and special skills were at a premium.

On D-Day, 6 June 1944, two US Ranger battalions, Lieutenant-Colonel James Rudder's 2nd and Lieutenant-Colonel Max Schneider's 5th, were tasked with securing the German battery atop the cliffs of the Pointe du Hoc, between Omaha and Utah beaches. A delay on the run-in left Rudder and three of his companies – only 225 men – with the awesome task of scaling the 100-foot-high cliffs in the face of determined resistance. Some of the Rangers climbed ropes fired to the *As SAS patrol in the desert*

cliff-top by rockets: others scrambled up using their knives to hack handholds in the chalk. The Germans above cut ropes, threw grenades and fired downwards. The surviving Rangers eventually reached the top, where they took cover in the craters left by the naval bombardment. By the end of the day less than half Rudder's men were still on their feet. It was largely wasted gallantry, for the battery's guns had not been mounted, and the bunkers on the cliff-top were empty.

The techniques developed by the Rangers, Commandos and SAS during the Second World War remain an important element of a regular army's preparations for a conventional war. During the Falklands War of 1982 the SAS made an invaluable contribution to British victory, furnishing covert patrols which supplied useful intelligence and – very much in the tradition of the SAS of the Second World War – landing a detachment which destroyed eleven parked Argentinian aircraft on Pebble Island. Nevertheless, since 1945 special forces have tended to concentrate upon spearheading governments' struggles against guerrillas. Their emphasis upon physical fitness and individual initiative makes them ideally suited for operating amongst a population which is itself subject to guerrilla attack, and for organizing and training local pro-government irregulars.

It was Sir Harold Briggs' idea of deploying a special military force into the jungle of Malaya to seek out the Communist insurgents on their own ground that led to the resuscitation of the SAS in 1951. There were some early difficulties, but by 1954 the SAS were successfully making contact with aboriginal tribesmen in the interior and turning their villages into strongpoints. Between 1962 and 1966 the SAS fought in similar circumstances during the 'confrontation' episode, when Indonesian troops crossed the border between Indonesian Borneo (Kalimantan) and Sarawak. The SAS organized Dyak villagers, and mounted damaging long-range patrols across the Indonesian border.

The French achieved some success during their war in Indo-China with what were called *Groupements de Commandos Mixtes Aéroportés* (GCMA) until December 1953, when their title was changed to *Groupements Mixtes d'Intervention* (GMI). These were guerrilla groups, each based upon a core up to 400 strong, with a handful of French officers and NCOs leading local tribesmen. Some of their achievements were remarkable: in October 1953 a commando group, reinforced by a parachute platoon, struck at a storage depot deep in Viet Minh territory, destroying it and killing 150 Viet Minh.

United States Special Forces, the Green Berets, were busy in Vietnam within a few years of the departure of the French, and long before US ground forces were committed to the war. Initially, the Green Berets advised the South Vietnamese on the organization, training and employment of the Civilian Irregular Defense Groups (CIDG). Soon the first of the Green Beret 'A' teams was deployed into an area inhabited by *Montagnard* tribesmen, who had provided the French with many hardy fighters, and set about recruiting them for the defence of villages and the provision of irregular strike forces.

'A' teams consisted of two officers and ten men, each a specialist in at least one of four major skills: light/heavy weapons, communications, demolitions/engineering and medicine. John Gallagher was 'Bush Doctor' with an 'A' team:

The *Montagnards* had never seen a doctor, and I would take care not only of my 12-man 'A' team, but of all the villagers that were in my area . . . I would treat them if they were sick, or treat them if they were wounded, or start preventive medical programmes, treat their animals, be the veterinary, and train them also in how to take care of themselves, and train the men in how to take care of combat wounds.

Although Special Forces bases were invaluable centres for patrolling against the

256

Viet Cong, they were frequently targets for attack by Viet Cong or North Vietnamese regulars. The first Congressional Medal of Honor won in Vietnam was awarded to Captain Roger Donlon, commander of the base of Nam Dong, scene of a desperate battle in July 1964. By mid-1966, 2,600 Green Berets manned over eighty camps and controlled no less than 60,000 CIDG soldiers. They also led battalion-sized 'Mike Forces', Green Beret and CIDG units which were inserted, usually by helicopter, into Viet Cong safe areas, where they employed guerrilla tactics against the guerrillas themselves. Amongst their other tasks were organizing and leading the 12-man Spike Recon Teams, used for long-range patrolling, the 'Roadrunner' trail recce units and the Search-Location-Annihilation Mission (SLAM) companies.

Members of these units fought hundreds of typical irregular actions. Tonu Palming, a former Special Forces officer, remembered being ambushed on patrol.

Ambushes in general are a very typical tactic in guerrilla and counter-guerrilla warfare . . . I was the leader of the patrol, I was the senior American on it and we had about two squads of Montagnard tribesmen with us. We were returning to camp after being out for about ten days, and the terrain . . . was terribly dense, the vegetation was just impossible to move through and because of that, for speed, we moved onto a major trail . . . where you go to gain speed, but with that you also expose yourself to danger. It was getting to be dusk, and suddenly there was a great deal of gunfire, so . . . we went into . . . a counter-ambush tactic which basically is to charge the ambush as quickly as possible without delay and force yourself through one side of it . . . We attacked the ambush, and the lesson we learnt from it was that you don't go on major trails unless it's a major emergency, that you don't make time, you never save time that way when you're engaged in guerrilla warfare.

John Gallagher glimpsed the real face of People's War when he was ambushed while patrolling from Dak To in the Central Highlands.

I took two of the men and went around the flank . . . to outflank them and take them out. Well, I got around to the side and pointed my M16 at them and this person turned around and just stared, and I froze, 'cos it was a boy, I would say between the ages of twelve and fourteen. When he turned at me and looked, all of a sudden he turned his whole body and pointed his automatic weapon at me, I just opened up, fired the whole twenty rounds right into the kid, and he just laid there. I dropped my weapon and cried . . .

The achievements of the Green Berets and their irregulars were mixed. They undoubtedly caused the Viet Cong and the North Vietnamese losses out of all proportion to the amount of US troops involved. However, the more controversial aspects of the Green Berets' activities attracted adverse publicity, and helped to bring them into dispute with senior officers who resented their independence and questioned their value. As Tonu Palming admits, detachments tended to:

use all kinds of devious methods which in the regular army would have been so irregular that they would probably have resulted in imprisonment. For example, sometimes to get transmissions for our trucks we would have to pull illicit raids on American depots by showing up with false papers and just loading up equipment . . . I once used an Australian aircraft – they were the only ones willing to pull this off – and we just flew into Cam Ranh Bay, which was a big logistics base, handed the sergeant in charge some invoices, loaded up the equipment, even took the fork lift truck, and flew back out.

On balance, though, it would be wrong if American withdrawal from Vietnam was allowed to obscure the contribution made by the 'A' teams and their *Montagnard* irregulars. As Palming observes: 'The *Montagnards* as a fighting force were probably the best investment that the United States had in terms of combat arms, because – except for rifles and uniforms – they had virtually no support from the Americans . . . They were reliable and they believed in what they were doing: not because it was Washington's war or Saigon's war, but it was a war for their tribal survival.'

The future of the irregular is disputed. Walter Laqueur argues that guerrillas succeeded where they enjoyed the support of a regular army, or where a colonial power had lost its will to govern: their successes were rare in other circumstances. 'But at present,' he concludes, 'the age of the guerrilla is drawing to a close. The retreat into urban terror, noisy but politically ineffective, is not a new departure but, on the contrary, the end of an era.' While this view is certainly a healthy counterpoint to much of the literature of the 1960s and 1970s, it may well be unduly sanguine. The Soviet invasion of Afghanistan, launched in December 1979, met with fierce, if ill-coordinated and indifferently armed, resistance from the *mujahedeen*, who employed much the same hit-and-run tactics against the Russians that their grandfathers had used against the British. In Central America both Communist guerrillas and right-wing contras apply the classic techniques of irregular warfare in conflicts marked by just as much blood and bitterness as the fighting in Spain which gave guerrillas their name.

Conflict between the armies of established governments and the irregular forces which challenge their authority is always likely to occur where change cannot be achieved by peaceful processes alone. Special forces will retain a counter-insurgency role for as long as the threat of this sort of contest looms. And, even if the irregular loses his importance as a revolutionary fighter on the one hand or a counter-revolutionary specialist on the other, the increasingly complex nature of modern conventional war will offer attractive targets to the saboteur, the long-range patrol and the airborne raider. The irregular, in one of his many guises, will be fighting his own hard and painful war for many years to come.

Experience of War   13

The experience of war is neither the prerogative nor the exclusive fate of fighting soldiers. It engulfs entire peoples. Its nature, too, is not specifically or wholly military. Warfare alters, sometimes transforms societies, and leaves no one who has been exposed to its turmoil unchanged. Children, women, the old, the non-combatant, the pacifist are all shaken from their familiar routines, sometimes by terror, by hardship, by sadness and loss, sometimes by excitement and exhilaration.

But it is still the soldier for whom the experience of war is most vivid. His sensations are complex and diverse, ranging from bitter enmity to intense affection, from paralyzing terror to serene heroism, and from stultifying boredom to frenetic activity. For some, the memory of war is one of unrelieved horror and suffering, but for the majority, war is recalled in tones of light and shade, with the warmth of comradeship and the pride of achievement and shared endeavour set alongside the anguish of anticipation, the shock of battle and the misery of privation.

'At the beginning of an undertaking,' wrote the historian Thucydides, 'the enthusiasm is always greatest. And at that time both in the Peloponnesus and in Athens there were great numbers of young men who had never been in a war and were consequently far from unwilling to join in this one.' He was describing the beginning of the Peloponnesian War between Athens and Sparta in the fourth century B.C. And, however much men recognize that war is a bloody and uncertain business, such enthusiasm is not uncommon at the start of any war, particularly one which comes at the end of a long peace.

In August 1914 young regular officers rejoiced at the prospect of exercising their profession and leading men in battle. Lieutenant Alan Hanbury-Sparrow of the Royal Berkshires went to war joyfully.

We're Regulars, Regulars mobilised, entraining and in damned good spirits at the thought of finding out – if we're Men . . . We're the lucky ones. We backed the right horse when we chose the army as a career. We're the best trained army in Europe, about to astound the world with our musketry. We'll go through the conscript army of Germany like Alexander's Macedonians through the Persian hordes . . .

Another young officer, *Leutnant* Erwin Rommel of the 124th Infantry Regiment, was equally delighted at the prospect. 'All the young faces radiated joy, animation and anticipation,' he wrote. 'Is there anything finer than marching against an enemy at the head of such soldiers?'

The wild excitement that greeted the outbreak of war in 1914 hid a sadder face. The scene at Morlaix in Brittany had little in common with the euphoria of Paris: 'In deathly silence the mayor read out the order for general mobilisation. Then petrified dumbness. Not a voice applauded. Someone sobbed once, and the crowd

stirred, and everyone went their various ways home.' A Frenchman wrote of the dull pain of the first night of the war, 'that *nuit blanche* when millions of men kissed their wives with dry lips and burned their letters.'

Those who knew what war was really like were aghast at the prospect before them. Captain James Jack of the Cameronians, a veteran of the Boer War, did not share Hanbury-Sparrow's glee. 'One can scarcely believe that five Great Powers – also styled "civilised" – are at war, and that the original spark causing the conflagration arose from the murder of one man and his wife. It is quite mad, as well as being quite dreadful . . . I personally loathe the outlook.' The French historian Marc Bloch, then an infantry NCO departing for the war from a Paris station, saw a sadly familiar sight, as 'an aged, white-haired father made heroic but unavailing attempts to hold back his tears as he embraced an artillery officer.' The father, old enough to have fought in the Franco-Prussian War, of 1870–1, had seen enough of war to realize that it was not all about blaring bands and cheering crowds.

Even in an age with few illusions about war, enlistment may seem a young man's natural response to his country's call, or perhaps presents the opportunity of escaping from a routine and humdrum existence to a new world of genuine issues and real values. 'I enlisted a couple of years after high school,' said one Vietnam veteran. 'I was young and innocent and I was under the impression that enlisting was the All-American thing to do.' Tim O'Brien considered going to Canada, but eventually decided that: 'I owed the prairie something. For twenty-one years I'd lived under its laws, accepted its education, eaten its food, wasted and guzzled its water, slept well at night, driven across its highways, dirtied and breathed its air, wallowed in its luxuries.'

Some see war as a challenge to their manhood. Shimon, an Israeli paratroop lieutenant in 1967, recalled that:

260

The first day we were called up, we all went round with big smiles, slapping each other on the back. I'd even go so far as to say that the men wanted a war at that point. I think lots of them saw it as an opportunity to prove themselves as soldiers, after they'd done everything for so many years on a sort of 'as if' basis . . . Of course, they also shared the general feeling in the country, that the political aspect of the business was justified, and that it was a just war.

An American soldier of the Vietnam era was utterly frank. 'I wanted to go to war,' he said. 'It was a test I wanted to pass. It was a manhood test, no question about it.' His words were echoed by a platoon commander in 3 Para in the Falklands. 'The only real test of a man,' he declared, 'is when the firing starts.'

Battle is the ultimate objective of soldiers in the combat arms, the consummation of their training. Most fantasize about battle when it is still distant, wondering how they will fare, often casting themselves in the role of war hero, returning home decorated and perhaps wounded – though always 'in some mentionable place.' The approach of combat concentrates the mind. 'Fear was creeping in now . . .' wrote black GI David Parks when his departure for Vietnam was imminent. 'It wouldn't be so bad, going off to war, if only we were ready.' A single question looms large, dwarfing every fear of death or wounds. 'What will battle really be like?' the soldier insistently asks himself.

As contact with the enemy draws nearer, anticipation sharpens into fear. Its physical effects are striking. The heart beats rapidly, the face shines with sweat and the mouth grows dry – so dry that men often emerge from battle with blackened mouths and chapped lips. The jaws gape or the teeth chatter, and in an effort to control himself a man may clench his jaw so tightly that it will ache for days afterwards. Many lose control of their bladder or their bowels. Nearly a quarter of the soldiers of an American division interviewed in the South Pacific admitted that they had fouled themselves, and the spectacle of soldiers urgently urinating just before they go into action is as old as battle itself.

However strong the ties of comradeship may be, in the leaden minutes before battle the soldier is on his own. 'At that time,' reflected Norman Lebrun, an American paratrooper in Korea, 'each man kind of goes into his own little private world, he's got time now to digest everything he's done and everything he is about to do . . . maybe praying to our God or thinking of our loved ones back home . . . It's a no-nonsense period.' For some, the dominant fear is of death or disabling wound. But for others the greatest terror is of failure to live up to the standards of the group, failure to comport oneself as a man at the supreme crisis. US Marine Sergeant William Rogel summed up the mixture of emotions. 'A new man . . . has two great fears. One is – it's probably an overriding fear – how am I going to do? – am I going to show the white feather? Am I going to be a coward, or am I going to be able to do my job? And of course the other is the common fear, am I going to survive or get killed or wounded?'

Similar thoughts ran through the mind of Henry Dixon, commander of a British Sherman in Normandy in 1944. He found the wait before going into action:

Nerve-racking. You obviously realise what it's like going to the dentist: you get that waiting, that fear – not fear in itself, but fear of being frightened. You are waiting for something to happen . . . You are thinking: 'Am I going to be frightened?' It goes through your mind: 'I don't want to be frightened because if anything goes wrong and I'm scared I might let my mates down.'

For leaders – officers or NCOs – this fear is heightened by the knowledge that they have status to maintain, and the realization that the lives of their subordinates hang upon their decisions. 'It's unfair that I should have twenty-seven lives so dependent on me,' thought Lieutenant Raleigh Trevelyan, commanding a platoon of the Green Howards in Italy in 1944: 'Oh, God, please don't let me disgrace myself.' Captain Charles MacDonald had not himself been in action when he took command of his US infantry company on the German border in October 1944. 'I must not appear afraid,' he wrote. 'I must give these men confidence in me despite the fact that they know I'm inexperienced.'

The first glimpse of battle is often curiously anticlimactic. Small-arms rounds crack overhead but there is no enemy in sight. 'What the hell am I shooting at?' asked an American infantryman in Vietnam. 'Yes, we are getting shot at – there are rounds snapping past your ears, if you stick your head up like an idiot – but I couldn't *see* anything.' Sometimes only the spectacle of men being killed and wounded demonstrates that the fire is real. When Staff-Sergeant Leo Jereb ordered his squad forward on Utah Beach in Normandy,

I noticed the fellow beside me didn't move, and I said . . . 'I know he's tired' – because we had gotten up at one-thirty for breakfast – 'but gee, he's sleeping already . . .' So I went over there and I tapped him on the shoulder and I said 'We're moving out . . . Come on, let's move out,' and he didn't say anything . . . So I rolled him over and I saw that he'd taken small arms fire through the head. So right then and there is when I really realized that there was a war, and I was in it.

Marine John Catterson felt the same abrupt shock in Vietnam in 1966:

I remember the first time that a bullet went zipping by my face, it literally went bzzzzz right by me like a bee, and it took me a minute to realise what was going on. The bullets were singing by us and all the people were starting to move and they don't teach you that in boot camp, you never hear that . . . A fellow to the right of me took a bullet in the chest and suddenly you face what really is going on . . . someone out there wants to kill me . . . a guy out there whose political ideologies I don't understand: and what becomes important is he has decided he wants to kill me and it is now up to me to kill him.

General George Patton argued that battle was not as alarming as people expected it to be. 'Battle is far less frightening than those of you who have not been in it are apt to think,' he declared. 'All this bull about thinking of your mother and your sweetheart, and your wives . . . is overemphasised by writers who describe battles not as they are but as writers who have never heard a hostile shot or missed a meal think they are.'

Certainly, battle administers two fear-quelling drugs. Men who have agonized about their ability to stare battle in the face suddenly discover that the sight is not intolerable. Professor R. H. Tawney, then serving as a sergeant in a New Army battalion of the Manchester Regiment, went over the top on 1 July 1916. 'I hadn't gone ten yards,' he wrote, 'before I felt a load fall from me . . . I had been worried by the thought: "Suppose one should lose one's head and get other men cut up! Suppose one's legs should take flight or else refuse to move!" Now I knew it was all right. I shouldn't be frightened and I shouldn't lose my head. Just imagine the joy of that discovery!' Simply doing something after a long period of waiting is a relief in itself: the tasks of serving a weapon, tending wounded or leading others all help to drive fear from the mind. Danny Arazi, one of the Israeli paratroopers who took Ammunition Hill in Jerusalem in 1967, did not feel frightened while he was actually fighting: 'While fighting you concentrate on what you are doing, you try to survive and you are so busy doing it that you don't have anything else in your mind, but . . . sometimes you had to wait because somebody is ahead of you . . . and so I had a few moments that were terrifying.'

Shelling is especially alarming because it brings with it not only fear, but inaction under fear: as the psychologist F. S. Bartlett wrote, the hardest thing of all is 'to

be afraid and sit still.' E. C. Vaughan, a First World War infantry officer, pointed to another of the demoralizing effects of shell fire when he wrote of its anonymous and impersonal character: 'terror and death coming from far away seemed much more ghastly than a hail of fire from people whom we could see and with whom we could come to grips.'

The shock of battle: Russians under shellfire in the First World War

Many soldiers experience battle as a half-remembered blur, a mosaic somehow fragmented and haphazardly reassembled. For Captain Wyn Griffith of the Royal Welch Fusiliers his advance into Mametz Wood in 1916 had a peculiarly dream-like quality.

It was life rather than death that faded into the distance, as I grew into a state of not thinking, not feeling, not seeing. I moved past trees, past other things; men passed by me, carrying other men, some crying, some cursing, some silent. They were all shadows, and I was no greater than they. Living or dead, all were unreal. Balanced uneasily on the knife-edge between utter oblivion and this temporary not-knowing, it seemed little matter whether I were destroyed to go forward to death or to come back to life.

A young soldier of the 71st Regiment lacked Griffith's literary powers, but he was clearly describing the same experience when he wrote of his baptism of fire at Montevideo in 1807: 'After the firing commenced, a still sensation stole over my whole frame, a firm determined torpor bordering on insensibility.'

Others retain a sharp perception of events but grow so familiar with the perils surrounding them that, like young George Hennell, who took part in the murderous storming of Badajoz in 1812, they take them in their stride.

Just as I passed the palisade ditch there came a shot from a 24 pounder ... and twelve men sank together with a groan that would have shook to the soul the nerves of the oldest

The jetsam of war: a Lewis-gun post of the British 5th Army, overwhelmed in the German March offensive, 1918

soldier that ever carried a musket. I believe that ten of them never rose again, the nearest was within a foot of me, the farthest not four yards off . . . The next four steps I took were over this heap. You read of the horrors of war, you little know what it means . . . When the balls began to whiz I expected every one would strike me. As they increased I minded them less . . . At the bottom of the hill I was accustomed to danger and would have marched up to a cannon's mouth.

For most soldiers fear is a familiar visitor who they simply learn to live with. John Catterson thought that: 'At different levels it was present all the time. Even when you were back in your so called base area there was always the possibility of a mortar attack, of a sniper in a tree shooting over the perimeter, so that you were always aware of your surroundings.'

As a man's experience of battle widens, so he becomes unpleasantly aware of the effects of weapons upon the fragile and vulnerable human body. Death grins at him with hideous faces. In 1917, Lieutenant Vaughan dug out the remains of four men killed by a direct hit on their shelter. 'The foulness of our groping in the dark,' he wrote, 'cannot be described.' The distinguished author William Manchester, a sergeant in the US Marine Corps in the Pacific, gives a graphic account of the beach at Iwo Jima. 'You tripped over strings of viscera fifteen feet long, over bodies which had been cut in half at the waist. Legs and arms, and heads bearing only necks, lay fifty feet from the closest torsos. As night fell the beachhead reeked with the stench of burning flesh.'

'War is a sad blunter of feelings,' wrote Rifleman John Harris, describing his feelings as he passed some dead French soldiers in Spain in 1808. 'The contem-

264

*'The beachead reeked
. . .' Japanese dead on
Tarawa, November
1943*

plation of three ghastly bodies in this lonely spot failed then in making the slightest
impression upon me. The sight had become, even in the short time I had been
engaged in the trade, but too familiar.' So familiar, indeed, that Harris scraped the
blood off some biscuits strewn around the corpses, and 'ate them ravenously.' Guy
Sajer, fighting in the ranks of the *Grossdeutschland* Division on the Eastern Front,
recalled how: 'Two years before I had seen a woman run over by a milk truck, and
had nearly fainted at the sight of her mangled body. Now, after two years in Russia,
visible death meant nothing at all, and the tragic element of even the best murder
novels seemed petty and frivolous.'

Even the soldier who grows accustomed to death in general will still be profoundly
moved by the killing of his comrades. 'The death of one,' believed Major Fred
Majdalany, 'always affects you more strongly that the death of many.' Henri
Barbusse, doyen of French First World War military writers, agreed that a friend's
death was shocking, because he was 'one of those who made war alongside you
and lived exactly the same life.'

Vaughan found the sundering of the close relationships forged by war supremely
sad. 'One of the most pathetic features of the war,' he wrote, 'is this continual
forming of real friendships which last for a week or two, or even months, and are
then suddenly shattered for ever by death or division.' However, the death of a
comrade is more than just depressing: it knocks away one of the props which
sustain a soldier's morale, and suggests to him that his own death may be near.
War is the business of young men, for whom death is remote. As Lord Lovat put
it, 'it was easier to believe the sky would fall than any of us might one day be killed.'

265

But the death of his friends brings home to a man the fact that he, too, is mortal. An American soldier had seen corpses laid out in funeral parlours, but the death of his comrades in Vietnam was somehow different: 'these guys were really young and peers of mine.'

The moment of impact: a French dragoon, in his curiously old-fashioned uniform, is hit by rifle fire in April 1915

Alfred de Vigny went to the heart of the military experience when he observed that the soldier is both victim and executioner. Not only does he run the risk of being killed and wounded himself, but he also kills and wounds others. For centuries the act of killing was direct and personal, accomplished at close range: it may even be so on a modern battlefield, as an Israeli paratrooper discovered when he came face to face with a huge Jordanian during the capture of the Old City of Jerusalem in 1967.

266

We looked at each other for half a second and I knew that it was up to me, personally, to kill him, there was no one else there. The whole thing must have lasted less than a second, but it's printed on my mind like a slow-motion movie. I fired from the hip and I can still see how the bullets splashed against the wall about a metre to his left. I moved the Uzi, slowly, slowly it seemed, until I hit him in the body. He slipped to his knees, then he raised his head, with his face terrible, twisted in pain and hate, yes, such hate. I fired again and somehow got him in the head. There was so much blood . . . I vomited, until the rest of the boys came up.

This consummate act of violence affects men in different ways. For some, military training creates an abstract image of an enemy whom it is their professional duty to kill. 'I didn't even think of him as another human being,' mused Norman Lebrun:

I just saw him as an enemy that had to be defeated and at the time that I sunk my bayonet into his body I didn't really give it too much thought. But when the time came to pull out my bayonet I found that it was quite difficult and so . . . I had to fire my rifle into his chest so that at the same time I could pull my bayonet out. I think I wasn't satisfied, I used the butt of my rifle and struck him somewhere on the head, I don't know exactly, to make sure it was all over . . .'

Lewis Lahorn, a Marine NCO in Vietnam, thought that his first kill was: 'just reaction . . . He was a trained soldier, and I was a trained soldier. And it was me first, or him first. And I respected him, and I'm pretty sure he respected me, you know. His job was to kill me, my job was to kill him.'

For others, killing may even be pleasurable, either because of the sheer satisfaction of hitting a difficult target or outwitting a cunning adversary, or because of hatred for an enemy whose death gratifies the desire for revenge. The future Field-Marshal Viscount Slim admitted that he was delighted when a Turk dropped to his rifle in Mesopotamia. 'I suppose it is brutal,' he wrote, 'but I had a feeling of the most intense satisfaction as that wretched Turk went spinning down.' 'It's an accomplishment, more or less stalking a person, stalking something alive, just like going hunting for deer,' said a Green Beret who had served in Vietnam. 'I enjoyed the shooting and the killing,' declared another Vietnam veteran. 'I was literally turned on when I saw a gook shot.'

When rumours of atrocities or the work of propagandists inject hatred into battle, men kill without mercy. In August 1917 an Australian soldier told how: 'In a shell hole further on I saw a wounded man and another one with him. An officer walked up and the German asked him to give his comrade a drink. "Yes," our officer said, "I'll give the . . . a drink, take this", and he emptied his revolver on the two of them. This is the only way to treat a Hun. What we enlisted for was to kill Huns, those baby killing . . .' 'I accounted for five or six Germans with bombs,' wrote another Australian, 'and we had orders to bayonet all wounded Germans and they received it hot and strong.' William Manchester saw a Marine, infuriated by the death of his popular company commander, mow down a row of Japanese prisoners. A Vietnam veteran doubted the value of taking prisoners at all. 'We didn't go through that nonsense,' he said. 'I used to shoot them.' This sort of behaviour generates counter-atrocity to produce a vicious circle of mutual brutality, and tends to be most common where opponents are divided by strongly held political views, or by racial or cultural barriers.

Even when enemies have much in common, the rough law of battle often dictates that prisoners are not taken. A man who offers to surrender during a firefight, when his opponent's blood is up, has at best a fifty-fifty chance of having his offer accepted. 'No soldier can claim a right to "quarter" if he fights to the extremity,' maintained Charles Carrington. His First World War adversary Ernst Junger agreed that: 'A man cannot change his feelings again during the last rush with a veil of blood before his eyes. He does not want to take prisoners but to kill.'

Outside these moments of supreme crisis, however, the soldier may well be reluctant to kill his enemy, recognizing him as a fellow human being who too has to run war's perilous gauntlet. As Hannah Arendt suggests in her introduction to J. Glenn Gray's remarkable book *The Warriors*, 'the first lesson to be learned on the battlefield was that the closer you were to the enemy, the less did you hate him.' Soldiers go to war focussing on an abstract image of their enemy, an image formed by training and propaganda. As they meet him in his human form, this caricature is replaced by a concrete image of the enemy as a man: hostile, perhaps, but a man nonetheless.

In the wars of the eighteenth and nineteenth centuries opposing armies tended to slip into peaceful co-existence between battles. 'Between the French and us there was no humbug, it was either peace or war,' wrote Captain John Kincaid of the Peninsula: 'The war, on both sides, was conducted on the grand scale, and, by a tacit sort of understanding, we never teased each other unnecessarily.' Union and Confederate soldiers showed no reticence about killing each other in battle, as the casualty lists for Gettysburg, Antietam and Shiloh demonstrate. On an everyday basis, though, they usually got on well enough. Pickets were reluctant to fire on one another, and often met, chatted and exchanged goods – Northern food for Confederate tobacco. In the summer heat of July 1864 opposing regiments broke off the war to plunge into the water of the Chattahoochee River at Green's Ferry. 'Hey, Yanks,' called a Confederate, 'what say we stop shootin' and go swimmin'.' The incident simply highlighted the adversaries' common humanity for, as one observer commented, 'a Yank and a Johnnie in a state of nature look very much alike.'

The combatants of the First World War were divided by language as well as nationalism, but neither prevented them from tacitly suspending hostilities on a surprisingly large number of occasions. The Christmas Truce of 1914 is the

Peaceful co-existence: British and Germans in the Christmas Truce, 1914

best-known incident. British and German officers and men met peacefully in several sectors, exchanged presents, took photographs and even played football. In some areas the truce went on until well in the New Year, despite the High Command's insistence that it should be war as usual. There were, nevertheless, isolated truces during Christmas 1915.

British soldiers help German wounded, 1917

An American medic tends a wounded German, Italy, 1943

Christmas truces came about because men felt that, in the words of Private William Tapp: 'It doesn't seem right to be killing each other at Xmas time.' There were also other reasons for truces. Sometimes there was a local suspension of hostilities to bury the dead or recover the wounded; sometimes, particularly in low-lying areas where trenches flooded easily, the outbreak of bad weather had both sides baling for their lives, hostilities forgotten. The fortune of war frequently emphasized men's similarities rather than their differences. Private A. V. Wilson and a comrade were getting water from the Ancre when they met two Germans on the same task. One German, a former Durham miner, spoke English: 'This war's no bloody good,' he said. The Englishmen made no effort to detain the Germans, even though they were armed and the Germans were not. Fred Horsenail, a First World War British cavalryman, thought that his relationship with the enemy was simple – 'either you kill him or he kills you.' He never fraternized with the Germans, but: 'Sometimes, when we got to taking prisoners down to the cage, we used to sympathise with them, because they were as bad off as what we were. They were lousy, mud covered, punch drunk and God knows what.'

In some areas the adversaries simply fell into the habit of not taking aggressive action, giving rise to the phenomenon of the 'quiet sector'. Before the summer of 1916 the rolling uplands of the Somme were remarkably peaceful, so much so that when the opening bombardment for the British attack commenced in June, a German grenadier put on his best uniform and went to see his company commander, begging that the nonsense should be stopped before somebody was killed.

There were truces during the Second World War, when the ideological rifts dividing the combatants seemed deeper than they had a generation earlier. Raleigh Trevelyan observed that aggression in one sector was discouraged by a 'keep-mum policy', and noisy activity in the British trenches was greeted with a shout of: 'Quiet there, we can't sleep.' During the bitter fighting at Cassino the Germans allowed wounded to be taken out under a flag of truce. 'You'll find the Boche are all right about it,' one CO told his relief. And, on Easter Sunday 1944, neither side fired a shot. Ed Lackman jumped into a ditch in Sicily under fire:

. . . and lo and behold there were about five Germans, and maybe four or five of us, and we didn't give any thought whatsoever to fighting at first . . . Then I realised that they had their rifles, we had ours and then shells were landing and we were cowering against the side of the ditch, the Germans were doing the same thing. And then, the next thing you know, there was a lull, we took cigarettes out and we passed 'em around, we were smoking and it's a feeling I cannot describe, but it was a feeling that this was not the time to be shooting at one another . . . They were human beings, like us, they were just as scared . . .

The fighting on the Eastern Front was characterized by brutality on both sides. Yet even so, Henry Metelmann participated in a truce on the Kerch Peninsula in 1942:

I saw two Russian soldiers coming out of their foxhole and I walked over towards them. We met half way. I spoke Russian fairly well in a pidgin way and they introduced themselves . . . They offered me a cigarette and, as a non-smoker, I thought if they offer me a cigarette I'll smoke it. But it was horrible stuff. I coughed and later on my mates said: 'You made a horrible impression, standing there with those two Russians and coughing your head off.' . . . I talked to them and said it was alright to come closer to the foxhole, because there were three dead Russian soldiers lying there, and I, to my shame, had killed them. They wanted to get the discs off them, and the paybooks . . . I kind of helped them and we were all bending down and they found some photos in one of the paybooks and they showed them to me: we all three stood up and looked at the photos . . . We shook hands again, and one patted me on my back and they walked away . . .

270

Metelmann was called away to drive a half-track back to the field hospital. When he returned to the battlefield, over an hour later, he found that the Germans had overrun the Russian position. And, although:

... there were some of my friends killed ... I enquired about the two Russians. I said, 'Those two Russians, what happened to them?' 'Oh they got killed,' they said. I said: 'How did it happen?' 'Oh, they didn't want to give in. Then we shouted at them to come out with their hands up and they did not, so one of us went over with a tank,' he said, 'and really got them, and silenced them that way.' My feeling was very sad. I had met them on a very human basis, on a comradely basis. They called me comrade and at that moment, strange as it might seem, I was more sad that they had to die in this mad confrontation than my own mates and I still think sadly about it.

Flashes of humanity lit even the darker post-war conflicts. When *Groupement Mobile 100* was ambushed in Indo-China in April 1944, French rescuers found 'one wounded Frenchman lying in the middle of the road, bandaged and fed.' The American combat analyst S. L. A. Marshall described the meeting between Captain Willis, leading his company along a stream-bed in Vietnam in 1966, and a North Vietnamese soldier:

Willis came abreast of him, his M-16 pointed at the man's chest. They stood not five feet apart. The soldier's AK 47 was pointed straight at Willis.
    The captain vigorously shook his head.
    The NVA soldier shook his head just as vigorously.
    It was a truce, cease-fire, gentleman's agreement or a deal ... The soldier sank back into the darkness and Willis stumbled on.

Such behaviour frequently reflects a fighting man's regard for his enemy's soldierly qualities. Norman Gladden heard a 'murmur of approbation' as his company advanced past the body of a German who had died making a single-handed stand in an advanced post, and a British officer described the German machine-gunners who had cut down his comrades as 'topping fellows.' In the Second World War Bill Mauldin thought that GIs had 'a deep respect for the German's ability to wage war. You may hear a doggie call a German a skunk but you'll never hear him say he's not good.' An Israeli lieutenant who fought in Lebanon in 1982 was quick to distinguish between the Syrian army and the PLO. 'The Syrian army I regarded as an enemy: I know that they're very professional, they're a good army and good soldiers. When I met them in combat I felt that too, and I respect them as people and as soldiers. The PLO, I don't think they fight too good and I don't respect them as people, because they'd shoot on any target any way they can.'

Men must contend not only with the risks of battle, but also with exhaustion, filth, vermin, lack of privacy and the unremitting pressures of terrain and climate. These too leave lasting memories. Count Philippe de Ségur wrote of the abject misery of French soldiers on the retreat from Moscow in 1812:

Everything in sight became vague, unrecognisable. Objects changed their shape; we walked without knowing where we were or what lay ahead, and anything became an obstacle ... Yet the poor wretches dragged themselves along, shivering, with chattering teeth, until the snow packed under the soles of their boots, a bit of debris, a branch, or the body of a fallen comrade tripped them and threw them down. Their moans for help went unheeded. The snow soon covered them up and only low mounds showed where they lay. Our road was strewn with these hummocks, like a cemetery.

Henry Metelmann and his comrades found 'General Winter' just as formidable an opponent over a century later. 'We had lectures on the fact that we were living in a very dangerous climate,' he recalled,

271

and we were told that when you feel very cold and then you suddenly feel warm and there is no reason for feeling warm, that is the danger point. I had one friend of mine who went out to do his business – and that was in the evening – and next morning somebody said: 'Where is Helmuth?' . . . We went out and looked for him and Helmuth was still in the position trousers down, and rolled up lying in the snow – and he had a very happy expression on his face. I saw quite a few who died from cold. They all had a very pleasant expression because feeling very cold is very very bad and suddenly you feel pleasantly warm, but that is death creeping up on you.

The bonds of affection which link men in a good unit are astonishingly powerful. Montague Cleeve remembered his battery with evident pride. 'The comradeship was marvellous because in my particular case the men of the 36th Siege Battery were all Kitchener volunteers and they were nearly all Durham miners and were absolutely marvellous . . . we became great friends and one just can't describe the affinity there was, we are all in it together and it was a question of what's mine is thine . . .'

Lieutenant Andrew Wilson had a 'terribly close relationship' with the crew of his tank. 'It was something, I suppose, that I have looked to find ever since in my life. I mean it just hasn't been there and never could be anything quite like that. It was, after all, four or five men living together within this little steel shell and sleeping together in the same bivouac. And a lot of things passed between us which had nothing to do with the war.' It was the same for Lewis Lahorn in Vietnam, where, 'I had a good squad, good fire-team. I would do anything for them, they would do anything for me. We were all grunts, infantry. And that's how we lived, and that's why we loved and respected each other. We prayed for each other.'

Prayers are not always answered. Some days after D-Day, Sergeant Leonard Lommel walked back across the battlefield his Ranger company had fought over:

They had about 75 or 80 of my closest friends, laying alongside the ditches of this road, this little dusty road . . . ready for pick-up by the Graves Registration Unit . . . You walk by them and you see their faces, and it's a sad thing, you think immediately of the many good times you've had together and the plans that young man had – he was going back to school, he was going to get married – or whatever his plans were for the future, all of that flashes through your mind, and it does upset you . . .

The shock of bereavement strikes parents, wives and children. Even now I find it hard to remain dry-eyed when I think of the headstone above Captain Cormack's grave on the Villers-Bretonneux road, with its inscription: 'The Lord God hath taken away our hero Daddy.' In Ovillers Military Cemetery, a few hundred yards north of the Roman road from Albert to Bapaume, lies Captain J. C. Lauder, son of the music-hall star Sir Harry Lauder, who heard of his son's death on 1 January 1917. 'I had looked on my boy for the last time,' he wrote sadly, 'and it was for this moment that we had all been waiting ever since we had sent John away. We had all known that it was too much to hope that he should be one of those spared. For a time I was quite numb. Then came a great pain and I whispered to myself over and over again that terrible word "dead".' The future Field-Marshal Lord Allenby was a professional soldier and no stranger to death. In July 1917 his only child, Michael, was killed in France. 'He was all that one could desire in a son,' wrote Allenby, 'and I am proud to have been his father . . . There is not a day of his life I could wish to be otherwise than as he lived it. In simplicity, gentleness, cheerfulness and honour he walked from his birth until his death. I rejoice in every remembrance of him.' The letter bore eloquent testimony to its author's anguish, for his 'strong, careful script was blotched with tears.'

It is not only living creatures that suffer. War also inflicts what modern strategists,

Opposite top: At the mercy of General Winter, French soldiers endure the misery of the retreat from Moscow, 1812

Opposite bottom: German infantrymen in the snows of Russia, 1941

273

Collateral damage: the French town of Valognes, June 1944

by a masterpiece of circumlocution, call 'collateral damage'. Captain J. E. Crombie of the Gordon Highlanders passed through the deserted town of Arras in March 1917: ' . . . the long narrow ribbon of street was utterly silent, and the walls, with nothing but ruin behind them, aslant and tottering, till it seemed a push with your hand would overset them . . . It is these ghastly, sightless, purposeless walls that catch you, and the silence.' Montague Cleeve was forward observation officer for his heavy battery on the Somme.

There is a village called Irles which was more or less intact behind the German lines, and it distressed me enormously because it was a very pretty little village with houses on both sides of the road and I only had to fire four rounds – 1 – 2 – 3 – 4 – to see the spire of the church collapse and the whole of the village flattened out. Four rounds only from our 8-inch howitzers.

The strains of war do not end with homecoming. Picking up the threads of the old life is rarely easy. The habits of war die hard: Captain Robert Graves, recovering from pneumonia in 1918, walked his favourite hill behind Harlech. 'I could not help seeing it as a prospective battlefield,' he admitted. 'I would find myself working out tactical problems, planning how best to hold the Upper Artro valley against an attack from the sea, or where to place a Lewis-gun if I were trying to rush Dolwreiddiog Farm from the brow of the hill, and what would be the best cover for my rifle-grenade section.' William Manchester found his conditioned reflexes an embarrassment in peacetime, when: 'the sudden zip of a heavy zipper made me

Opposite: A time for reflection: a veteran views the Vietnam memorial in Washington

274

jump for a year after I had discarded my uniform, and it was late in the 1940s before I could walk near New York's old Third Avenue E1 without trembling.' The return to peacetime life, so eagerly awaited, is often a shattering anticlimax. The comrades of war have gone, to be replaced by people with whom the veteran has little in common, and to whom his experiences mean nothing. 'They didn't really want to listen,' complained a Vietnam veteran. 'They didn't even wait for an answer. I could have read off the thirty-one flavours at Baskin-Robbins and it wouldn't have made any difference.'

Some men look back on their experience of war with resignation. 'I did it once,' said Lewis Lahorn, 'but I wouldn't want to do it again. I did the job the best way I know how. War may not have been right: who's to say it was wrong or right? . . . We did the best we could . . . It was my time in history, maybe. I was destined to be out there, and I guess I just made it out, maybe to tell a story . . .' Others see war as part of the process of growing up, or even as a bright patch of colour and excitement in an otherwise drab life. Still more recoil in horror from the worst of their memories, agreeing with an Israeli soldier that war is 'murder and fear, murder and fear'. Henry Metelmann retains a stark image of the burning of some peasant huts in Russia, their owners still inside them. 'We saw the children and the women with their babies and then I heard the poouff – the flame had broken through the thatched roof and there was a yellow-brown smoke column going up into the air. It didn't hit me all that much then, but when I think of it now – I slaughtered those people. I murdered them.'

These dark memories are usually thrust into the background, as Brigadier Peter Young tells us:

The veteran has compassion for the civilians hurt, the soldiers slain - even the enemy soldiers - but, having survived a hundred perils, he would not have things other than they were. He remembers the good times, the careless – almost carefree – life of disinterested comradeship amidst brave and generous friends. His senses reject the memory of the butcher's shop that was an observation post until the Japanese scored a direct hit, and the sickly sweet smell of corpses rotting in a Sicilian farmyard. He is glad that when the challenge came he achieved rather more than he thought he would. However regrettable it may be, there are still a great many men in this world who feel quite different from the common run of mortals because they have been under fire. It is as though it were some sort of hallmark.

Most veterans would agree with the Israeli Lieutenant Gilli that 'killing is the worst thing that one man can do to another man . . . it's the last thing that should happen anywhere.' But war usually retains its puzzling fascination, even for those who know it best. An American summed up the whole ambivalence of man's experience of war when he said, 'Thinking about Vietnam once in a while, in a crazy kind of way, I wish that just for an hour I could be back there. Maybe just to be there so I'd wish I was back here again.'

Conclusion

'Every man thinks meanly of himself for not having been a soldier,' wrote Dr Johnson to his biographer, James Boswell, in April 1778. The shaft was well aimed. Boswell's youthful ambition had been to serve in the Foot Guards and he had often affected an officer's scarlet coat, though quite unentitled to it, on his travels in Holland and Germany. Johnson, on the other hand, was the most unwarriorlike of men. Corpulent, slothful and unkempt, he could never have been mistaken for a man of war, and was disparaging of the military ethos. Patriotism he characterized as 'the last refuge of a scoundrel', and he summed up the way the world works in terms of 'mutual cowardice'. 'Were all brave,' he said, 'mankind would lead a very uneasy life; all would be continually fighting; but being all cowards, we go on very well.'

But these words were spoken in the third year of Britain's war against her American colonists, when brave men from both sides of the Atlantic were by no means going on very well together, and when Johnson himself was ready to give his own xenophobia full rein. 'I am ready to love all mankind, *except an American,*' he told Boswell at that time; while of Lord Mansfield, who personified the world of the law rather than of the sword, he remarked that 'if he was in the company of generals and admirals who had seen service, he'd wish to creep under the table.'

Johnson, in short, was as human as the rest of us in his attitude to soldiering. The philosopher in him deprecated mankind's violent and selfish tendencies and took comfort from the power that reason and compromise exercise over human affairs. The realist in him accepted the strength of the masculine urge to bellicosity, group loyalty and military display. What reconciliation he achieved between these two halves of his mind neither his own writings nor Boswell's biography reveal. Presumably, as in Scott Fitzgerald's definition of an intellectual, he continued to hold two mutually contradictory ideas while continuing to function as a rational man. Had it been otherwise, he would be remembered either as a noted pacifist or – to use Professor Michael Howard's useful coining – a notable bellicist. Being remembered as neither, he belongs with the majority of mankind in seeing war as both good and bad, and the soldier as a creature to be both cursed and blessed, depending upon circumstances.

The circumstances when men curse the appearance of soldiers, with the full voice of desperation or the discreet hiss of acquiescence are not difficult to recreate.

'I climb the towers' wrote Rihaku, a Chinese poet of the eighth century,

To watch out the barbarous land.
Desolate castle, the sky, the wide desert.
There is no wall left to this village.

277

Bones white with a thousand frosts,
High heaps, covered with trees and grass;
Who has brought this to pass?
Who has brought the flaming imperial anger?
Who has brought the army with drums and with kettle-drums?
Barbarous kings.
A gracious spring, turned to blood-ravenous autumn,
A turmoil of wars-men, spread to the middle kingdom,
Three hundred and sixty thousand,
And sorrow, sorrow like rain.

Rihaku's lament finds its counterpart in a thousand railings by the people of peace against the men of war. 'The beauty of Israel is slain in the high places' wails Samuel in his Second Book of the Old Testament. 'How are the mighty fallen. Tell it not to Gath, publish it not in the streets of Askelon; lest the daughters of the Philistines rejoice, lest the daughters of the uncircumcised triumph. Ye mountains of Gilboa, let there be no dew, neither let there be rain, upon you, nor fields of offerings; for there the shield of the mighty is cast away, the shield of Saul, as though he had not been anointed with oil.' The children of Israel were people of the sword as well as the Book. Milton, in whom the Book worked powerfully, appeals to the Lord of Hosts to avenge children of his, the Protestant martyrs of Piedmont, who put their trust, fruitlessly, in the word alone:

Forget not; in the book record their groans
Who were thy sheep and in their ancient fold
Slain by the bloody Piedmontese that rolled
Mother with infant down the rocks. Their moans
The vales redoubled to the hills, and they
To heaven.

No wonder that a poet of the century after Milton's, John Scott of Amwell, could write with bitter distaste of the poisonous appeal that armies make to the emotions of the young and impressionable:

I hate the drum's discordant sound,
Parading round, and round, and round;
To thoughtless youth it pleasure yields,
And lures from cities and from fields . . .
I hate that drum's discordant sound,
Parading round, and round, and round;
To me it talks of ravaged plains,
And burning towns and ruined swains,
And mangled limbs, and dying groans,
And widows' tears, and orphans' moans;
And all that Misery's hand bestows,
To fill the catalogue of human woes.

Two hundred years after Scott penned his tirade against war in the abstract, a twelve-year-old Dutch boy graphically describes his first sight of an invading army, in this case the airborne vanguard of the Wehrmacht's drive into Holland in 1940:

This afternoon we saw our first parachutist. We were pasting strips of paper across the Baron's windows and across the windows of our own house so they won't break any more when the bombs come. The parachutists came down at three o'clock. About fifty came down at once. This one was separated from the others. Mijnheer van Helst called out to the women to go inside and then ran towards the man. The man came down behind the Baron's barn. We saw Mijnheer van Helst take out his pistol and aim and fire three times. He came back a moment later looking very sad and said the German was shot. Heintje

Klaes ran forward to see the German and came back and said the German was really dead and he was glad. Mijnheer van Helst didn't look glad and his hands were trembling. He is an old and very kind man and not used to shooting people the way regular soldiers do.

The boy's father was fighting with the Dutch army. Soon Heintje Klaes, who had gloated over the German parachutist's death, went out to watch some bombing and was killed too. Later 'Uncle Pieter came back. He didn't find Mother because she is dead. I can't believe it but Uncle Pieter wouldn't lie. We aren't going to tell my baby sister yet.'

So began for the Dutch four and a half years of occupation by the German army, which would culminate in the terrible 'hunger winter' of 1944–5. For the peoples of the lands further to the east – the already beaten Poles, the Yugoslavs, the Greeks, above all the Russians of Belorussia and the Ukraine – German occupation would bring even greater suffering, so that the mere sight of German uniforms would drive farmers and villagers into flight or hiding, for fear of the consequences that might flow from propinquity to the invaders. Colonel von der Heydte, dropping with his parachutists on 20 May 1941 on the Cretan village of Alikianou, 'could see people in the streets staring up at us, others running away and disappearing into doorways. The shadow of our planes swept like ghostly hands over the sun-drenched white houses.' It was the repetition of events old in European history. Dutchmen had fled the approach of the Spanish army in the Eighty Years War, Spaniards Napoleon's army, Belgians the Germans in 1914. In the first months of 1945 the Germans of Prussia and Pomerania would flee westward in their millions before the Red Army, leaving lands their ancestors had conquered a thousand years earlier to become Slav once again.

But soldiers do not have to be hostile or even foreign to arouse civilian antipathy, as Kipling, champion of the despised underclass that filled the ranks of the Victorian army, reminds us:

> Yes, makin' mock o' uniforms that guard you while you sleep
> Is cheaper than them uniforms, an' they're starvation cheap;
> An' hustlin' drunken soldiers when they're goin' large a bit
> Is five times better business than parading in full kit.

Respectable Victorians looked down on Tommy Atkins because he was widely thought to come from the gutter and to prefer the gutter for his lodging and his pleasure. Starved of pay, forbidden to marry, he was not held respectable company for a girl of decent family, and many decent families hung their heads if a son 'went for a soldier'. The mother of the future Field-Marshal Sir William Robertson, who gave up a footman's place to enlist as a trooper in the 16th Lancers in 1877, wrote to him that she 'would rather see him dead than in a red coat', so shaming did she think the exchange. In contemporary France or Germany, where conscription gathered the sons of every family into the ranks, military service did not carry the same stigma (though the middle classes benefited by an arrangement which allowed their sons to live outside barracks as potential reserve officers). In Britain – as in America, and any other country which recruited its army by voluntary enlistment – it was 'Tommy this and Tommy that – go away, wait outside, fall be'ind,' as Kipling catalogued the slights; even though 'Tommy this an' Tommy that an' "Chuck him out, the brute!"' gave way to 'Saviour of 'is country when the guns begin to shoot'. The Chinese, though holding skill in the martial arts wholly appropriate to the land-owning gentry, shared a similar distaste for men who followed the calling of soldier as a trade; 'rapacious and licentious', Edmund Burke's verdict on the paid soldiery, accorded absolutely with the Chinese outlook.

The Islamic world tends to a similar view (though Islamic India shares the Hindu respect for those whom heredity calls to a martial way of life). Islam solved the problem of maintaining a regular army, which might be called upon to fight fellow Moslems, by recruiting its soldiers from its slave population. The result was paradoxical. Islam's slave soldiers, among whom the Janissaries of the Ottoman Sultan became the most famous, came to exercise something close to dominance in the Ottoman state, while being denied the most fundamental of human rights, like that of contracting marriage.

Civilian repugnance for the soldier may, therefore, take a variety of forms. The respectable citizen may despise and fear him as a barely tamed element of his own society, to be held in check only by social disapproval and ferocious military discipline. When he appears as marauder, invader or conqueror, he may arouse yet more violent emotions – hatred, terror, blind panic. 'From the moment the Spaniards first entered the Netherlands,' writes Geoffrey Parker, the historian of the Habsburg war against the people of that land, who were constitutionally Habsburg subjects, they acted 'as if they were in enemy territory, confiscating everything, rightly, wrongly, saying that everyone is a heretic, that they have wealth and ought to lose it.' Even in the seventeenth century, when the foreign troops were more domesticated, countless cases of rape, murder, robbery and arson were committed by the soldiers. The brutality of the Spanish troops in 'Flanders' became so legendary that it even gave rise to a proverb in Spain: 'Are we here or in the Netherlands?' meaning, 'Is that a proper way to behave?' The garrisons of the Spanish Netherlands, concentrations of bored, impoverished, but well-armed young men, inevitably formed a pool of lawlessness, of gambling and vice, crime and cruelty, lechery and licence in the centre of every community.

Such is the dark side of soldiering. But it has an obverse, which may stand in the sharpest relief, known to everyone who has ever welcomed an army of relief or of liberation. A member of the Agnelli family, the industrial paladins of Turin, recalls her sense of elation at the departure in 1944 of the overbearing but beaten Germans and the appearance at the ancestral mansion of two young British Guards officers, 'impeccably uniformed and beautifully mannered'. In more bucolic mood, 'the Belgian people were so overjoyed to see our troops,' wrote J. L. Hodson, a British war correspondent who took part in the brief British incursion into the Low Countries to stem the German invasion of 1940, 'that our car was partly filled with tulips and narcissi, our drivers were taken to lunch and loaded with cigarettes. A Lancashire lad said, "Ee, I'm havin' a terrible time" – he'd been kissed by half-a-dozen girls.'

When true deliverance came to Western Europe four years later, civilian jubilation approached the hysterical. 'We are marching twenty-four abreast down the Champs Elysées,' remembered Private Verner Odegard of the American division that symbolically liberated Paris, 'and we had a hell of a time trying to march, because the whole street was jammed with people laughing and yelling and crying and singing.' The Canadians who reached Dieppe, scene of the calamitous landing of 1942 in which so many of their comrades had died, experienced the euphoria of the liberated in a still more extreme form, as Ross Munro, a war correspondent, describes:

In ten seconds we were surrounded by laughing, extravagantly happy civilians. An old lady tottered up to my scout car with a huge bouquet of flowers. A pretty girl gave us another bouquet she had picked that morning from the town gardens. A hundred Dieppe people crushed around the car, wanting to shake our hands, to kiss us and tell us how welcome we were. It was the same with everyone who entered Dieppe that day. They were literally mobbed by the crowd, taken off to cafés and to homes to be plied with liberation wine and to be applauded like the victors they were.

Even German civilians, trapped between attackers and defenders in their own dwellings, would eventually welcome the enemy as deliverers, if only from the horror of war itself. An Allied soldier who entered Aachen in November 1944 found himself confronted by

the drabbest, filthiest inhabitants of the underworld I have ever seen, as people came stumbling out into the light, dazed, then catching a breath of fresh air, and finally starting to jabber, push, scream and curse. Where have you been so long, they shouted. Why didn't you deliver us sooner. It was a stunning sight. These were the people of the first German town occupied by the Allies. And they were weeping with hysterical joy amid the smouldering ruins of their own homes. We have been praying every day for you to come, said a woman with a pale, thin face. You can't imagine what we have had to suffer . . .

In the same mood, anticipation of civilian suffering brought the German defenders of Berlin not welcome but rejection by their own people in April 1945. A suburban housewife wrote:

We brought the boys up from the cellar to let them play in the air and light, as they were so white and heavy-eyed from living underground. We kept the shutters across the windows, and played games, and read to them quietly. Except for the distant noises of machine-gun fire there was peace round our house on a lovely spring day. But not for long. Suddenly there was the tramp of heavy boots around the house. We peeped through the curtains. German soldiers! We opened the windows to speak to them. To my horror they wanted to come into the house to use it to fight from. Hearing my conversation the boys ran into the garden. 'Oh, you have children?' said the eldest of the group. 'All right then, we'll leave you in peace.'

The truth was, the mother quickly grasped, that the soldiers were no keener on there being a battle round her house than she was. Their only thought was to get away from the Russians. When she told them that the escape routes were cut, 'to my astonishment one of the soldiers burst into tears. He pushed his steel helmet well over his face, but we could see the tears streaming down his thin cheeks. He looked not a day more than seventeen. None of the other men said a word to him. Indeed, they all looked exhausted and ready to cry too.'

Her mother's heart went out to these tired and frightened young men, a pang of emotion as universal as the curses and blessings that soldiers bring on themselves, and perhaps ultimately more valid than either. For the soldier, who makes victims, is always potentially and all too often actually a victim himself. As painted allegorically by Rubens or caricatured by Raemaekers, he shows an iron mask of pitiless cruelty in the world. Photographs more often reveal anxiety, inexperience, even a sort of innocence in those who have been suddenly confronted with the face of battle.

Before the coming of photography, even more so of television, it was natural that the predicament of the soldier should have been misconceived. Yet the imaginative, like Samuel Taylor Coleridge, could guess at the truth nonetheless:

    Boys and Girls,
And Women, that would groan to see a child
Pull off an insect's leg, all read of war,
The best amusement of our evening's meal;
As if the soldier died without a wound;
As if the fibres of this godlike frame
Were gored without a pang; as if the wretch,
Who fell in battle, doing bloody deeds,
Passed off to heaven, translated and not killed . . .

Despite his insight, Coleridge still romanticized. Few soldiers fall in battle 'doing bloody deeds'. 'What passing bells for those who die as cattle?' asked Wilfred Owen, an outstanding young infantry officer who had survived the trench battles of the Western Front to die in the period of 'open warfare' at the very end of the First World War. He preserved no illusions about how most soldiers die, as in his lines on the victim of a gas attack:

> If in some smothering dreams you too could pace
> Behind the wagon that we flung him in,
> And watch the white eyes writhing in his face
> If you could hear, at every jolt, the blood
> Come gargling from the froth-corrupted lungs,
> Obscene as cancer, bitter as the cud
> Of vile, incurable sores on innocent tongues –
> My friend, you would not tell with such high zest
> To children ardent for some desperate glory,
> The old Lie . . .

The 'old Lie' is, of course, that a soldier's death is 'dulce and decorum' – sweet and fitting. Owen, who was to find a soldier's death himself at the age of twenty-five, knew that for the majority it is neither. Even in the heroic age, Homer's warriors died with the bitter lie on their tongues. Achilles exulted when he struck Hector the fatal blow which 'drove straight through the tender neck but did not cut the windpipe', taunting his victim with the promise that 'dogs and kites will rip your body.' Hector begged him by his soul, and his parents, 'do not let the dogs feed on me . . . Let them have my body back so that our men and women may accord me decency of fire when I am dead.'

Hector died in single combat, under the eyes of spectators as keen to applaud a brave death as a cunning swordstroke, and was deprived of a hero's funeral only through Achilles' blood hatred for him. Few soldiers succeed in dying with the eyes of the world upon them. In modern war, many just disappear, disintegrated by a shell burst or amalgamated with the soil of a ruined battlefield by the feet of marching comrades or the wheels of a passing vehicle. Kipling, whose treasured only son disappeared during the battle of Loos in September 1915, managed to write a little verse epitaph for him:

> My son was killed while laughing at some jest. I would I knew
> What it was, and it might serve me in a time when jests are few.

The truth was far worse than anything at which Kipling had allowed himself to guess. John Kipling, eighteen years old and so short-sighted that it was only his father's influence that had procured him a commission in the Irish Guards, was last seen by one of his soldiers stumbling in tears from the battlefield at the pain of a wound in the mouth.

Herman Melville, another nineteenth-century devotee of the heroic who, unlike Kipling, had seen modern mass warfare before his artistic vision had found its final form, perceived a truth about the deadly attraction that vibrates between young men and the soldier's calling which, if vouchsafed to Kipling, might have spared him the agony in which he lived out the years after 1915, as well as the life of his son. The truth came to Melville as he watched a column of Union soldiers marching off to the battle of Ball's Bluff, in October 1861, where four regiments were pinned against a hundred foot cliff on the banks of the Potomac River and a thousand of them killed in a few hours of fighting:

One noonday, at my window in the town,
I saw a sight – saddest that eyes can see –
Young soldiers marching lustily
Unto the wars,
With fifes, and flags in mottoed pageantry;
While all the porches, walks, and doors
Were rich with ladies cheering royally.

They moved like Juny morning on the wave,
Their hearts were fresh as clover in its prime
(It was the breezy summer time),
Life throbbed so strong,
How should they dream that death in a rosy clime
Would come to thin their shining throng?
Youth feels immortal, like the gods sublime.

Old soldiers never die; but ninety-nine soldiers in a hundred are pitiably young, and they die in their millions, without beginning to guess why it is that life asks that of them. *Soldiers*, both the book and the television series that it accompanies, is about ten thousand years of human history in which young and old alike have felt that the way the world works offers no one any alternative to the death of its young men under arms. May the world, in its next ten thousand years, find a way of working that spares the old the need to ask the young that sacrifice.

Index

Adrianople, battle of, A.D. 378 61
Afghan *mujahedeen* 258
Agincourt, battle of, 1415 26, 63,
  86–7, 223
  archers' role 63
Air warfare
  aeroplane 14, 183, 184
    fitted with machine-guns 186
  air defence systems 193, 194,
    195
  air evacuation of wounded
    153–4, 183, 198
  airborne troops 200–1
  'AirLand Battle' theory 201, 203
  balloons 184, 186
  dive-bombers 189–90
  dog-fights 186
  German success in 1939–40
    15–16, 190
  ground attack 183, 187, 189,
    191, 192, 194
  helicopters 191, 194–5,
    198–200, 203
  importance of technological
    edge 194
  interdiction 183, 195–8
  parachute units 201
  reconnaissance 185, 186, 187
  remotely piloted vehicles (RPV)
    187, 203
  strategic bombing 183
  supply by air 183, 198, 238
  Zeppelins 185
Alamein, battle of, 1942 118, 182
Albuera, battle of, 1811 47
Alesia, siege of, 52 B.C. 166
Alexander the Great 80, 206, 210
  'heroic leadership' style 208–9
  infantry of 57
  power of 'great horse' and 12,
    80
Allenby, FM Lord
  on death of son, 1917 273
American Civil War 97, 214
  co-existence of troops during
    268
  improved firearms 14, 69
  Lines of Petersburg 176
  medical care 149
  psychiatric disablement in 155
  small role for cavalry 94

  Union casualties
    by disease 143
    in battle 143
  use of balloons 184
  use of railways 231–2
  victory for better-equipped side
    31, 232
Amiens, battle of, 1918 15, 126
Antietam, battle of, 1862 141, 143
Arab-Israeli Wars
  of 1967
    use of air power 192
  of 1973 140
    Egyptian crossing of Suez
      Canal 163–4
    psychiatric casualties 156,
      157
    use of air power 193
Ardennes, offensive of, 1944 138
Arquebus 27, 104
Arras, battle of, 1917 122
Artillery 13, 15, 27, 107
  ancient 98
  anti-aircraft 116–17
  anti-tank 117
  assault artillery 117–18
  breech-loading 111
  case shot 107
  early guns 103–4
  explosive shell developed 106
  horse artillery 108
  mobile, 18th c. 14, 27, 107
  self-propelled 118
  shrapnel 107
  siege warfare by means of 99,
    102, 104–6
  solution of recoil problem
    111–12
  steel guns 110
  unsuitability of iron for guns
    109–10
  use of red-hot shot 106
Assyrian empire
  development of cavalry 79
  use of army engineers 165
Attila the Hun 82
Austerlitz, battle of, 1805 54, 160,
  217, 229

Badajoz, storming of, 1812 53,
  106, 263

Balaclava, battle of 93
Bannockburn, battle of, 1314 223
Battle
  discipline and 23–4
  heroic age of 22–3, 209, 282
  knightly 19, 24–6, 27, 84, 85,
    86
  modern 19
  response to danger 21, 38
  soldiers' feelings
    before 261–2
    during 262–5
Bayerlein, Fritz
  on Allied air superiority, 1944
    190–1
Belgium
  German attack on Eben Emael,
    1940 179–80
  'ring fortresses' 177
  welcome for British, 1940 280
Berlin
  battle of, 1945 118
  end of SWW in, 1945 281
Beuil, Jean de 19
Bismarck, Prince Otto von 138
  on *francs-tireurs* 242
Blenheim, battle of, 1704 227
Boer War, 1899–1902 94, 112,
  150, 242
  Boer commandos 242
  costly British frontal attacks 70
Born, Bertrand de 25–6
Borneo confrontation 198, 256
Borodino, battle of, 1812 147
Bourne, Peter 49, 239
Bows 23, 27, 63, 77, 79, 88
Breitenfeld, battle of, 1631 65, 210
Briggs, Gen Sir Harold 250, 256
Bronze weapons 22, 79
Burma
  air supply in SWW 198, 238
  Wingate's Chindits in 238
Byzantine army 222
  medical care 145

Caesar, Julius 166, 221, 222
  on *aquilifer* during landing in
    Britain, 55 B.C. 46
  on battle against Nervii, 57 B.C.
    24
  on defeat of Helvetii, 58 B.C. 59

  style of leadership 210
Cambrai, battle of, 1917 15,
  123–5
Cannae, battle of, 218 B.C. 57–8,
  141
Casualties 141
  by warfare and disease 143–4,
    153
  experiences of wounded 155
  psychiatric 155–7
  soldiers' toughness 148
Catapult 165–6
Catterson, John
  on fear 264
  on infantry 'grunt' 75
  on shock of battle 262
Cavalry
  colonial 92
  conservatism 15, 93–4
  development of armour 24–5,
    84
  development of 'great horse' 12,
    79, 82
  development of stirrup 12, 24,
    82
  dress 92–3
  eclipsed by firearms 27, 88, 94
  final flourishes 95–6
  knights 19, 24–6, 27, 61, 83–8
  light cavalry 90–1
  pursuit role 90
  steppe nomads 12–13, 27, 80,
    86, 91
Châlons, battle of, 450 A.D. 82
Chamberlain, Col Joshua 39–40
Chariots and charioteers 11, 12,
  77, 79
Charles VIII, King of France 102
  artillery train 99
China
  absorption of conquerors 80
  Communist take-over 248, 249
  distaste for soldiery in 279
  early artillery 98
  early battles 23
Chivalry 83, 87, 210
Churchill, Winston 35, 120, 132
  'Variants on the Offensive' 122
Clausewitz, Carl von
  on importance of morale 39
  Vom Kriege 214

Cleeve, Montague
  on comradeship 273
  on war's destruction 274
Coleridge, Samuel Taylor 281,
  282
Commonwealth War Graves
  Commission 160
Constantinople
  siege of, 1453 98
Crécy, battle of, 1346 63, 86, 222,
  223
  archers' role in 63
  use of artillery 98
Crete
  Cretan archers 57
  German airborne invasion, 1941
    200, 279
Crimean War, 1854–6 93
  appalling state of British
    hospitals 149
  casualties in battle and by
    disease 143
  siege of Sebastopol 176
Crombie, Capt J. E.
  on destruction of Arras, FWW
    274
Crusades 12, 13, 87–8
  capture of Jerusalem, 1099 102
  heroic style of leadership 210

Davout, Marshal 214, 229, 230
Dead, the
  burial of 160
  civilian 159
  commemoration of 159–60, 161
  friends 265–6
Dearden, Capt Harold
  on difficulties at Regimental Aid
    Posts 151, 152
Debray, Régis 251, 252
Desertion 55–6
Dollard, John 49
Dragoons 73, 90
Duffy, Christopher 102
  on Croats as irregulars 254
Dunant, Henri 157
Dunkirk evacuation, 1940 132

Edward I, King 63, 145
Edward III, King 63, 223
Eisenhower, Gen Dwight D. 219
English Civil War 224

Falklands War 75, 155, 201, 240
  air operations 194, 198
  mine clearance after 182
Feudalism 12, 25, 83, 84
Fighting spirit 17–18
  'buddy system' and 18, 52–3, 56
  culture-sustained 50–1
  discipline and 55
  drill and 43–4
  effect of lack of 41–2
  esprit de corps 44, 46, 53
  examples 39–41
  importance of morale 39
  importance of regimental
    colours 46–7
  lure of reward and 53–4

oath-taking and 42
patriotism and 49
regimental system and 47–8
religion and 51–2
soldierly pride and 49
superstition and 52
sustained by drink and drugs
  53–5
First World War 70–2, 216, 217
  air power in 185–6, 187, 189,
    195–6
    reconnaissance 185, 186
  artillery in 72, 97, 112–14,
    115–16
    techniques 114–15, 126
  battle of supply systems 235
  British executions for desertion,
    etc. 55
  casualties 17, 33–4, 72, 113,
    114, 141, 144
    battle to non-battle 144
    dealing with 150–2
    'shell shock' 155–6
    'wrong' and 'right' wounds 34
  'château generalship' 217
  'Christmas Truce', 1914 268
  co-existence among combatants
    268–70
  feelings at beginning 259–60
  fodder supply 233, 235–6
  'heroic' style of leadership 216
  Hindenburg Line 178
  irregular warfare 243–4, 248
  nemesis of cavalry 94
  poor communications 217
  problem of ammunition supply
    234–5
  rum ration before battle 54
  Schlieffen Plan 185, 216
  stalemate in 15, 72
  tanks in 122–6
  tinned food in 231
  trench warfare 70–2, 113, 115,
    177
  use of railways 233
  use of road transport 233–4
  war graves 160–1
Formigny, battle of, 1450 63
Fortifications 13
  castles 13, 166–7
  consumption of resources in
    sieges 223
  disease during sieges 169
  first use of artillery against 99,
    102–3, 169
  invention of 'angle bastion'
    102
  medieval assault techniques
    167
  development of science of 170,
    172
  effect of high-explosive on
    176–7
  'flying entrenchment' concept
    176
  frontier 178, 180
  siegecraft, 17th c. 172–4
  steel and concrete, 19th c.
    176–7

trenches as, 20th c. 177–8
France
  desertions from Napoleonic
    armies 230
  French '75' gun 111–12
  lack of fighting spirit, 1940 41
  Maginot Line 178
  military engineers' work in N.
    Africa 175
  nineteenth-c. fortresses 176
  Resistance in SWW 245
  Royal Regiment of Artillery
    formed 107n
  use of balloons 184
  use of helicopters in Algerian
    War 198
Franco-Prussian War, 1870–1 97,
  211, 214
  francs-tireurs in 242–3
  German use of railways 231
  infection of wounded 150
  lessons learnt by Germans
    69–70
  'von Bredow's Death Ride' 93
Franks
  conversion to Christianity 83
  power of cavalry 82, 83
Frederick Charles, Prince, of
  Prussia
  on guerrilla warfare 242–3
Frederick the Great, King of
  Prussia 27, 42, 55, 66, 146,
  234, 254
  development of artillery under
    108
French, FM Sir John 40, 41, 185,
  243
Friedland, battle of, 1807 108
Fuller, Col J. F. C. 73, 126, 130,
  235, 236
  plan for 'tank raid', Cambrai,
    1917 123
Fussell, Paul
  on carrying of amulets in battle
    52
  *The Great War in Modern
    Memory* 52

Gale, Gen Sir Richard 49
Gale, Thomas 145, 146
Gallagher, John
  on being ambushed in Vietnam
    257
  on *Montagnards* 256
Generalship
  'château' 217
  'forward control' 217–19
  heroic 206, 207–8, 210, 215,
    216, 219
  post-heroic 209, 210, 211
Genghis Khan 12, 16, 27, 91, 94,
  210
Germany
  army oath-taking 42
  importance of *Heimat* (home) to
    soldiers 49
  in SWW
    civilian dead 159
    end of war 281

high tide of victory, 1941 35
inferiority in war production
  236
treatment of prisoners of war
  157
use of airborne troops 200
Landsknechte 63
strong morale in forces 49
tank development, inter-war
  127, 130
Gettysburg, battle of, 1863 66, 211
  dealing with casualties 149
  Pickett's charge 69
  Union defence of Little Round
    Top 39–40
Gideon
  attacks Midianites 241–2
Gladden, Norman
  on effect of air attack, 1917 189
  on soldiers' appreciation of
    enemy 271
Gloucester Regiment
  at battle of Alexandria, 1801 46
  esprit de corps 46
Grauwin, Major Paul 155
Graves, Capt Robert
  doubts about patriotism in
    trenches 49
  experience of wound in FWW
    155
  on adjusting to peace 274
Gray, J. Glenn
  on modern battle drill 44
  The Warriors 268
Greece and Greeks
  hoplite 18, 80
  'Ten Thousand' in Persia 221
  use of mercenaries 23
Grenada invasion, US 201
Griffith, Capt Wyn
  on battle 19, 263
Guderian, Heinz 73, 130
  leadership style 217–18
Guevara, Che 241
  eschews terror tactics 252
  revolutionary failure in Bolivia
    251
Guibert, Comte de 46
Gunpowder 13, 31, 98, 103
Gurney, Sir Henry
  murdered by Malayan
    Communists, 1951 250
Gustavus Adolphus, King of
  Sweden 27, 210
  military organisation 65, 90
  size of army 223
  use of artillery 107

Haig, FM Sir Douglas 39, 40, 41,
  122, 123, 210, 216
Hanbury-Sparrow, Lt Alan 260
  welcomes war in 1914 259
Hannibal 57
Hapaz, Rami 193
Harris, Rifleman John
  on brutalisation caused by war
    264–5
  on neglect of veterans, 1814 162
  on sufferings of wounded 148–9

Harrison, Sgt Ken 51, 159
Hastings, battle of, 1066 86, 144, 223
Hattin, battle of, 1187 223
Hennell, George
    on storming of Badajoz, 1812 263–4
Henry V, King 84, 223
Hiroshima 159
Hitler, Adolf 130, 132, 138, 180, 236
    remote style of leadership 219
Ho Chi Minh 249
Holy Roman Empire 83
Homer's *Iliad* 22–23, 77
    heroes in 209, 210, 282
Horse
    'great horse' 12, 79
    steppe ponies 12, 77, 82
    trained to draw chariots 11, 77
Hussars 90–1

IG9 counter-terrorist group, W. German
    storm skyjacked airliner at Mogadishu, 1977 253
Infantry
    company basis 14
    conservatism of 15, 70
    developed by Romans 57–61
    development since SWW 75
    earliest 11, 57
    era of bowmen's predominance 63
    firearms restore predominance over cavalry 63, 65, 66, 69
    increased firepower, 19th c. 69
    importance of drill from 17th c. 66
    introduction of 'regiments' 14
    invention of socket bayonet for 66, 107
    light infantry 67
    loses major role to cavalry, 4th c. A.D. 61, 82
    mechanized 73
    mounted 73
    musketeers 13, 27, 65, 66
    pikemen 13, 27, 61–3, 64–5
    power from 600 B.C. to 400 A.D. 80, 82
    primacy challenged by artillery 14, 63
    primacy challenged by improved firepower, 19th c. 14
    projectile weapons 57
    receives machine-guns 70, 72
    'regulars' introduced 14
    shock weapons 57
    strengthened by advent of gunpowder 13, 27
International Red Cross 157
Iron weapons 12
Irregular warfare 16–17, 241
    ancient 241–2
    nineteenth c. 242–3
    twentieth c. 243–58
    use of terror tactics 252–3

Israel
    army 44
        soldiers' respect for Syrian Army 271
        use of requisitioned transport 231
    Lebanon fighting, 1982 194
    See also Arab-Israeli Wars
Italy
    co-existence between combatants, SWW 270
    lines of fortification, SWW 180
    tank development, inter-war 127
Iwo Jima 51, 264
    casualties in taking of, SWW 141

Jack, Capt. James 260
Japan
    brutal behaviour of soldiers 50
    bushido precepts 50
    casualties in SWW 141
    effect of religion on morale 51
    soldiers' courage in battle 51
    treatment of prisoners of war 157, 159
    war in China, from 1937 248
Japanese Red Army 253
Jena, battle of, 1806 44
Jereb, Staff-Sgt Leo 262
Jericho 164–5, 167
Joffre, Marshal 205–6, 216
Johnson, Dr Samuel
    attitude to soldiering 277
Jolly, Surgeon-Commander Rick 155
Junger, Ernst
    on question of 'quarter' 267–8
    on shellfire 71
Junkers 87 Stuka dive-bomber 189–90

Kellogg, Robert H. 159
Kincaid, Capt John 268
Kipling, Rudyard 52
    defends Tommy Atkins 279
    verse on death of son, 1915 282
Kitchener, Lord 120, 175
Klaes, Heintje
    on German invasion of Holland, 1940 278–9
Knights, *see* Cavalry
Knott, Corporal Hugh 75
Korean War
    failure of US air interdiction 197
    psychiatric casualties 156
Kovic, Sgt Ron
    on hospital neglect 162
    on wounded in Vietnam 154
Kursk, battle of, 1943 118, 134–6, 141, 180

Lackman, Ed
    on co-existence between combatants in Sicily 270
    on infantry life 75
Lahorn, Lewis

on comradeship 273
    on killing 267
    on war experiences 276
Lake Trasimene, battle of 57
Lancers 90–1
Laqueur, Prof Walter
    on guerrillas 258
    on terrorism 253
Lauder, Sir Harry
    on death of son, 1917 273
Lawrence, T. E.
    Middle East campaign against Turks 243–4
    on bully beef 231
Le Cateau, battle of, 1914 114
Le Tellier, Michel 227
    develops French magazine system 225–6
Lebrun, Norman
    on killing 267
    on waiting before battle 261
Lenin 248
Leningrad siege, 1941–3 159
Lettow-Vorbeck, Col von 243
Lewis, Cecil
    on air photography, 1916 186
    Sagittarius Rising 186
Liddell Hart, Basil 73, 130
Lister, Joseph 150
Logistics of warfare
    ancient world's 221–2
    artillery train, 17th c. 224
    baggage-trains 224
    defined 221
    development of military transport corps, 19th c. 230–1
    development of tinned food 231
    First World War 233–6
    hostility of front-line to service troops 239–40
    limits of campaigning season and 227
    limits on length of marches 227
    magazine establishment 225–7
    medieval 222–3
        living off the land 222
        sieges 223
        smallness of armies 223
    Napoleonic supply system 227, 229
        peculation and 230
    Peninsular War supply system 229–30
    problems by 1700 225
    rations, 17th c. 223–4
    Second World War 236, 238
    transport developments, 19th c. 231–2
    Vietnam War 238–9
Lommel, Sgt Leonard 273
Loos, battle of, 1915 114, 217
Ludendorff, Gen Erich 126, 216

MacDonald, Capt Charles 262
McGrigor, James
    medical reforms in Peninsular War 146–7
Machine-guns 14, 223

Malaya
    British defeat of Communists, 1948–57 249–51, 256
Manchester, William
    describes beach at Iwo Jima, SWW 264
    on adjusting to peace 274, 276
    on killing of Japanese prisoners 267
Manstein, Gen 130, 134
    style of leadership 219
Mao Tse-tung 241, 249
    doctrine of revolution 248
Marathon, battle of 159–60
Marighela, Carlos 241
    Handbook of Urban Guerrilla Warfare, The 251
    revolutionary theory 251
Marignano, battle of, 1515 63
    use of artillery and cavalry 88, 90, 103
Marlborough, First Duke of 90, 211
    march to Danube, 1704 227
    supply system 227
    use of artillery 107
Marne, battle of the, 1914 112–13, 177, 185, 205, 206, 216
Marshall, S. L. A.
    on 'buddy system' 18, 52, 56
    on truce in Vietnam, 1966 271
Marx, Karl 246
Mauldin, Bill 53
    complains of rear echelon soldiers 240
    on GI's respect for Germans 271
    on use of drink and drugs in warfare 54
Maurice of Nassau 27, 65, 104, 224
Medical care 17
    ancient 145
    development of blood transfusion 152, 153
    effect of work on antisepsis 150
    importance of air evacuation of wounded 153–4
    inferior status of medical officers, 17th–19th c. 146
    invention of anaesthetics, 19th c. 149–50
    medical developments, SWW 152–3
    mediaeval 145–6
    primitive nature, 19th c. 148–9, 150
    problems of wounded, FWW 151–2, 155
    psychiatric care 156–7
    reforms during Napoleonic Wars 147
    'shell shock' and 155–6
    treatment of disabled 162
Megiddo, battle of, 1469 B.C. 23, 208
Melville, Herman
    on soldiers' deaths 282–3
Mercenaries 14, 223

Metelmann, Henry
  on horrors of war 276
  on Russian winter 271, 273
  on soldiers' motivation 49, 52–3
  on truce in Russia, 1942 270–1
Military organisation
  development of 211, 214
  officer training 214, 215
Milton, John
  lament for martyrs of Piedmont
  278
Minden, battle of, 1759 107–8
Mitchell, Gen Billy 200
Mongols 12–13, 27, 80, 91
Mons, British retreat from, 1914
  70
Montgomery, FM Viscount 137
  on importance of morale 39
  style of leadership 218–19
Moorehead, Alan 42
Moslems
  attacks on West 83
  heroic style of leadership 210
Mountbatten, Lord Louis
  on air supply in Burma, SWW
  198, 238
Munro, Ross
  on liberation of Dieppe, 1944
  280–1
Muskets
  flintlocks 66, 67, 107
  inaccuracy 66
  matchlocks 65–66
  replaced by rifles 69

Napoleon 27, 214, 217, 232, 234
  defeat at Waterloo 30–1
  on importance of morale 39
  supply system 227, 229
  use of artillery 108
Netherlands
  German invasion, 1940 278–9
  Spanish in, 16th c. 223, 280
Nightingale, Florence 148

Odegard, Pte Verner
  on liberation of Paris, 1944 280
Ogotai, King of the Mongols 13,
  91
Okinawa 51, 141
Oman, Sir Charles 223
Orwell, George 155
Owen, Wilfred
  on soldier's death 282

Palming, Tonu
  on being ambushed in Vietnam
  257
  on Green Berets 257
  on Montagnards 257–8
Paré, Ambroise 146
Paris
  liberation of, 1944 280
Parker, Geoffrey 280
Parks, David 42, 261
Parrish, John
  on dealing with wounded in
  Vietnam 154–5
Parthian cavalry 82

Patton, Gen George 219
  on battle 262
Pavia, battle of, 1515 104
Percy, Baron 147, 153
Persian empire 80
  reliance on 'great horse' 12
  road building 221
Pétain, Gen Philippe 113, 216
Philip II, King of Macedon 166,
  208
Philo of Byzantium
  on generalship 209, 210
Poison gas 119
Poitiers, battle of, 1356 63, 86,
  222–3
Poland
  German invasion, 1939 130
Prisoners of war 154, 157, 159
Provisional IRA 253
Prussia
  army drilling 66
  cavalry 92
    facings 46
  efficiency behind victories, 19th
  c. 31
  savage army punishments 55
  Staff College 214
Punic Wars 57–8

Queen's Regiment 47

Radio 217
Railways in warfare 231–2, 233,
  235
Ramillies, battle of, 1706 90
Ravenna, battle of, 1512 27, 103
Read, Herbert 42
Richelieu, Cardinal 224
Rifle Brigade 67
Rifles
  bolt-action magazine
  breech- replace muzzle-loader
  69
  replace muskets 69
Rihaku
  war lament 277–8
Rogel, Sgt William 261
Rogers' Rangers 254
Roman legion 18, 24, 58–61, 80
  dress 59
  engineering work 166
  importance of eagle to 46–7
  lines of battle 58
  officers 58–9, 210
  organisation 58, 60–1
  punishment for desertion 55
  supplying 222
  tactics 59–60
  use of cavalry 61, 80
  weapons 59
Rome
  ascent to power 57–8
  collapse of empire 61
  road building 221, 222
Rommel, FM Erwin 42, 117, 118,
  132, 134, 191
  injured in air attack 191
  logistical defeat in N. Africa 236
  style of leadership 218, 219
  welcomes war in 1914 259

Royal Army Service Corps 231
Royal Artillery 107n, 115
Royal Electrical and Mechanical
  Engineers 238
Royal Engineers 163, 182
  Armoured Vehicles Royal
  Engineers 180
  civil engineering work
    throughout British empire
    175
  design Royal Military Canal,
    Kent 175
  formation and development 174
  increase in strength, FWW 178
  Ordnance Survey work 175
  road building in Highlands
    174–5
  Tunnelling Companies 178
Royal Military Academy 174
Royal Tank Regiment 121, 125
Russia
  airborne and parachute troops
  200
  Civil War, 1917–21
    irregular warfare 246
    use of cavalry 94
  French retreat from Moscow,
    1812 271
  military engineers' work under
    Tsar 175
  Second World War in 132–6,
    138
    casualties 141
    partisan warfare 246
    style of leadership 219
    treatment of German POWs
    154
    use of artillery 118
    war production 236
  tank development, inter-war
    126, 132
Russo-Japanese War, 1905 31, 70,
  94, 112

Samuel, the Prophet
  war lament 278
Sangallo, Giuliano da 102, 170
Sappers 13
  bridging work 174
  civil engineering work 175
  dealing with mines 182
  development of special vehicles
    180
  earliest 164–6
  'flying entrenchment' 176
  fortification building 176, 177,
    178
  importance of 163
  infantry role 182
  mapping 175
  railway work 178
  road building 175
  schools for 174
  siege work 166, 167, 170,
    172–4
Scipio, Publius Cornelius 58
Scots
  defeated by archers at Falkirk,
    1298 63

victory at Killiecrankie, 1689 66
Scott, John, of Amwell
  tirade against war 278
Second World War 15, 16, 17,
  34–8, 73–4
  air power in 190–1, 196–7
  air supply 238
    use of airborne troops 200–1
  Allied invasion and advance,
    1944 136–8
  Allied logistic superiority 236,
    238
  Atlantic Wall 180
  Blitzkrieg tactics 15, 16, 35,
    130–2, 190
  breaking of German Enigma
    cypher 219
  casualties 141
    importance of air evacuation
    153
    psychiatric 156
  co-existence of combatants
    during 270–1
  improved medical facilities 35,
    153
  infantry role 73–4
  irregular warfare 16, 245–6,
    254–5, 255–6
  jubilation of liberation 280–1
  Overlord 236, 238
  Russian front, see Russia
  soldiers' tales of tragedy 35–8
  tinned rations in 231
Ségur, Count Philippe de 271
Seven Years War, 1756–63
  Austrian Croat irregulars in 254
  RN deaths by disease 144
Sino-Japanese War, 1894–5 31
Slim, Gen (later FM) Bill
  on fighting at Mandalay 38
  on killing a Turk, FWW 267
  on panic during Eritrean
    campaign, 1940 42
  on regimental esprit de corps,
    FWW 46
Slovik, Pte Eddie D. 56
Soldiers, BBC TV series 11, 283
Somme, battle of the, 1916 32–4,
  72, 114, 122, 178
Soult, Marshal 47, 214, 229
Spanish guerrillas 242
Spears, Edward 205
Special Air Service 16, 241, 253
  foundation 254–5
  organisation 255
  post-SWW actions 256
  storms Iranian embassy,
    London, 1977 253
Special Boat Service 255
Stalin, Josef 97, 118
Stalingrad, battle for, 1942–3,
  133–4, 141
Steele, Pte Fred 70
Steinbeck, John 52
Stirling, Col David 254–5
Student, Major-Gen Kurt 200
Sulzbach, Herbert 44
Swinton, Lt-Col E. D.
  idea for the tank 119–20, 178

Swiss Confederation 61
  military prowess 61–3

Tank Corps 121, 180
Tanks
  decisive success, 1918 126
  development 120–2, 126
  first battle success, 1917 123–5
  idea for 119–20
  inter-war development 126–7,
    130
  introduction to battle 15, 122
  post-SWW 139–40
    fading importance 140
  special 136–7
  theory of Blitzkrieg and 130–2
  use in SWW 132–8
Tawney, Prof R. H. 262
Taylor, A. J. P. 233
Templer, FM Sir Gerald 250–1
Thompson, Sir Robert
  compares Malayan emergency
    with Vietnam 251
  on air supply in Burma, SWW
    238
Thucydides 259
Thutmose III, Pharaoh, 23, 208
Tito, Marshal 246
Todleben, Gen 175, 177
  develops 'flying entrenchment'
    concept 176
Tournaments 87
Trebia, battle of River 57
Trevelyan, Lt Raleigh
  on co-existence among
    combatants 270
  worries of responsibility
    261–2
Trotsky, Leon 248

Turks 26, 27, 66, 80, 244
  use artillery against
    Constantinople, 1453 98
Turner, Sir James
  on quartering men on
    inhabitants 224
  on 17th-c. rations 223

United States of America
  AEF service troops, FWW 235
  Army Corps of Engineers 175
    'tunnel rats' in Vietnam 182
  army oath-taking 42
  Continental Army artillery 107n
  Green Berets 241
    in Vietnam 256–7
  Military Academy, West Point
    174
  Quartermaster Corps 231
  Rangers 255
    D-Day action, 1944 255–6
  war production, SWW 236
  See also Vietnam War

V1 and V2 missiles 118
Vauban, Sébastien, Seigneur de
  106, 174, 176
Vaughan, Lt E. C. 264
  carries amulets into battle 52
  on death of friends 265
  on shellfire 263
Verdun, battle for, 1916 35, 72,
  113–14, 141
  La Voie Sacrée 233–4
Vietnam War
  American drug abuse 54, 55
  French use of guerrillas 256
  killing of civilians 159

mixture of conventional and
  irregular warfare 249
Montagnard irregulars 256–7
psychiatric casualties 156
soldiers' belief in Americanism
  49
soldiers' feelings about
  enlistment 260, 261
treatment of US POWs 154
US logistical tail 238–9
use of irregulars 256–8
use of US air power 191–2
  airborne operations 201
  evacuation of wounded
    153–4
  failure of interdiction 197–8
  reconnaissance 187
  use of helicopters 198–9
Vigny, Alfred de 266
Vikings 83, 209
  pre-battle use of drugs 54

War of American Independence
  66
Warfare
  comradeship 273
  co-existence during 268–71
  destruction caused by 273–4
  experience of 259 et seq.
  humanity during 271
  primitive 206–7, 220
  problem of return to peacetime
    274, 276
  purposive 207–8
  respect for enemy 271
  shock of bereavement 273
  soldiers' feelings about killing
    266–8
Warwickshire Regiment

esprit de corps, FWW 46
Waterloo, battle of, 1815 30–1,
  46, 217
  use of artillery 97, 108–9
Wellington, First Duke of 30, 183,
  210, 211, 217, 242
  supply system 227, 229–30
  victory at Waterloo 30–1, 108–9
Westman, Stephen 42, 71
  on German drunkenness during
    March offensive, 1918 53
Wilson, Lt Andrew 273
Wintringham, Tom
  on infantry 75
  on panic during Spanish Civil
    War 42
Wolfe, Gen James 55, 211
Worcestershire Regiment
  recapture of Gheluvelt, 1914 41
Wright, Sir Almroth 150

Xenophon
  on dilemma of generalship 209,
    219, 220
  on importance of morale 39
  on supplying soldiers 221

Young, Brig Peter 276
Ypres, Third Battle of, 1917 72,
  115
  casualties 141
  cost of British bombardment
    235
  use of tanks 122, 123
Yugoslav partisan warfare, SWW
  246

Zama, battle of 58

RD1R